Turbo Prolog: Step by Step

With Turbo Prolog 2.0

Ralph Cafolla
Queens College

Daniel Albert Kauffman
Florida Atlantic University

Instruction Design by
Don Gorman
Florida Atlantic University

Merrill Publishing Company
A Bell & Howell Information Company
Columbus • Toronto • London • Melbourne

Published by Merrill Publishing Company
A Bell & Howell Information Company
Columbus, Ohio 43216

This book was set in New Century Schoolbook and Helvetica

Administrative Editor: Vernon R. Anthony

Production Coordinator: JoEllen Gohr

Cover Coordinator: Brian Deep

Library of Congress Catalog Card Number: 88-63337

International Standard Book Number: 0-675-20816-5

Printed in the United States of America
1 2 3 4 5 6 7 8 9 – 92 91 90 89

To those who were always there –
Susan, Rose, Joyce, Chari, Shannon and Florence

Preface

Artificial intelligence (AI) is a relatively new term. Until now, AI was a term known only in the research laboratories of the world's leading universities. However, after thirty years, the science of artificial intelligence has bounded upon the American scene and promises to revolutionize the way we use computers.

For the first time, microcomputers have enough memory, speed, and sophistication for the development of useful artificial intelligence products. With the advent of computer languages such as Turbo Prolog, AI products will come into the marketplace for use in all aspects of human endeavor. You will see a host of applications used in the workplace, in homes, and in schools.

For example, we wrote this book on a personal computer using a sophisticated word processor. As we typed the words, a computer program called Turbo Lightning (Borland International) checked the spelling. If a word was spelled incorrectly, Turbo Lightning beeped. Then with one keystroke, a menu appeared on the screen with a list of the most probable replacement words. The most likely word was at the top of the list. With another keystroke, Turbo Lightning replaced the misspelled word with the correctly spelled word. All this took place in a few seconds. Turbo Lightning is just one of the many exciting products that are the result of research in artificial intelligence. Other products are on the way.

What Is Turbo Prolog?

Prolog is a contraction for Programmed Logic. Professor Alain Colmerauer of the University of Marseilles developed the first version of Prolog in 1970. His version of Prolog was designed to assist in the solution of problems based in logic.

Logic uses symbols. Prolog is a computer language which is designed to manipulate symbols. Prolog can also perform mathematical operations, but its strength lies in its ability to work with symbols and logical expressions.

Turbo Prolog is a version of Prolog designed for use on MS-DOS compatible microcomputers. It is an excellent implementation of Prolog and should become a standard in the industry.

Turbo Prolog is a descriptive or propositional language. The basis of the language stems directly from the field of formal logic. Logic means valid reasoning. Most human activities require valid reasoning. For example, consider the following expression:

If I cross the street when cars are moving, then I might be injured.

This is an example of valid reasoning. If people could not understand this statement, a huge number of pedestrian-automobile collisions might occur. The preceding statement is the type of simple if-then logic that can be programmed in any computer language. Logic as carried out in Turbo Prolog, however, is much more advanced.

Turbo Prolog, provided with facts and rules about the relationships between these facts, can solve problems using deductive reasoning. In Turbo Prolog, after the facts and rules have been stated, the user poses a goal or question. Turbo Prolog uses the stated facts and rules and its inference engine to solve the problem. For example, given the following facts:

Joe likes hang gliding.
Sam likes scuba diving.

and a rule such as:

Mary likes anything Sam likes.

Turbo Prolog is able to deduce that:

Mary likes scuba diving.

Turbo Prolog has deduced a new fact from existing facts. This is the power that Turbo Prolog offers. Turbo Prolog is truly a revolutionary computer programming language. To appreciate how different it is, recall how traditional computer programming languages were developed.

Traditional Computer Languages

Machine language was the first type of computer language developed. It is the native language of the computer. It is a language of ones and zeros representing electrical circuits within the computer that are either turned on or off. To program in machine language, a person had to learn the native tongue of the specific computer. Programming computers in this manner was a painstaking activity which required extensive training and time.

The next generation of computer languages was called **assembly languages**. While assembly languages are slightly more understandable than machine language, the programmer still must do most of the work in breaking the program into a sequence of steps which the machine can understand. Additionally, each brand of computer has its own special assembly language. A machine or assembly language program written on one brand of computer will not run on another brand. Thus, the need for computer languages that were independent of brand arose.

The third generation of computer languages, classified as high-level languages, represent the predominant type of languages used today. These computer languages, which include Fortran, Cobol, BASIC, C, and Pascal, are called **procedural languages**. These languages, while using an English-like vocabulary, still require a highly skilled programmer to write a set of step-by-step procedures. The program results are predetermined and will always be the same when given the same input.

Procedural languages are much like recipes. The results can be accurately predicted prior to execution. In fact, the programmer must know the desired outcomes prior to writing a program. While these procedural languages are important in today's computing world, they are cumbersome to use as symbol manipulators. They are much better suited to the computation of mathematical operations than they are to the performing of logical operations.

The fourth generation of computer languages is called **declarative language**. These languages include Smalltalk and Prolog. Because these languages are adept at manipulating symbols, they are useful in representing human logic processes. In Turbo Prolog, the programmer does not need to specify the steps needed to solve a problem. Turbo Prolog uses its own **inference engine** to determine the solutions.

If you are an experienced computer programmer, you will find learning Turbo Prolog requires different skills from those required by traditional languages.

Compiled Languages

Turbo Prolog is a compiled language. This means that, before Turbo Prolog's inference engine executes the program, the Turbo Prolog statements must first be translated into machine language. Unlike traditional compiled languages, Turbo Prolog allows you to interactively develop a program. You can execute portions of the program as you develop it.

After you write your Turbo Prolog program, you instruct your computer to run the program. Then the program statements are compiled (translated) into machine language. During compilation, Turbo Prolog checks for syntax errors (errors in typing, grammatical mistakes, etc.). If the syntax of the program is correct, Turbo Prolog's inference engine executes the program. If the syntax of the program is incorrect, Turbo Prolog stops and points to the error. You correct the error, and Turbo Prolog continues the process. This interactive feature of Turbo Prolog will save you hours of program development time.

About This Book

We titled this book **Turbo Prolog: Step by Step**. It provides an easy guide to learning Turbo Prolog. We believe that Turbo Prolog is a language suited for everyone. The Japanese also believe this and have chosen Prolog as the high-level language for their fifth-generation supercomputers.

Turbo Prolog is an excellent implementation of the Prolog language. With its low price and its microcomputer orientation, it is a language that anyone can acquire and learn in a reasonable amount of time. Because of its ease of use and low price, we believe Turbo Prolog will become a standard of the Prolog language.

We wrote this book with both the beginning and experienced programmer in mind. Beginning programmers will find the step-by-step approach of the book easy to follow. Experienced programmers will enjoy the opportunity to learn an exciting new approach to programming.

Division of the Book

We have divided the book into thirteen chapters and one appendix. Each chapter depends upon knowledge gained in previous chapters. Thus, we recommend you start with Chapter 1 and work your way through the remaining chapters in the order given. However, if you understand a concept, feel free to skip it and move on to the next.

Acknowledgments

We would like to thank all of our students in the Artificial Intelligence classes for their patience in working through early versions of this text. We are grateful to Dave Shaw and Bill Berry for their critical analyses and suggestions.

We would also like to acknowledge the reviewers who contributed with their comments and criticisms, including Jason Chen, Gonzaga University; Takeshi Ohara, California State University, Long Beach; Steve Hanson, Johnson County Community College; and Michael O'Neill, Seattle Community College.

We would like to thank Vern Anthony, Administrative Editor and JoEllen Gohr, Production Manager, for their support in the preparation and production of this manuscript. Connie Grove's efforts in formatting the text are much appreciated. We are also grateful to Mike Moses, whose critical analysis of the text went far beyond proofreading.

Contents

Chapter 3
Variables

Chapter 4
Compound Goals and Backtracking

Chapter 5
Rules

Chapter 6
Controlling Turbo Prolog Programs............168

Chapter 7
Arithmetic in Turbo Prolog.....................208

Chapter 8
Data Structures 234

Chapter 9
Recursion: A Closer Look 262

Chapter 10
List Processing 306

Chapter 11
The Cut

Chapter 12
Files

Chapter 13
Dynamic Data Bases
and Expert Systems

Appendix A
Standard String Predicates ...467

Index ...477

Chapter 1
Getting Started

*This chapter starts you off with an introduction to the Turbo Prolog's programming environment. You will learn how to use Turbo Prolog's windows, the Main Menu, and the commands associated with each window and menu. Chapter 1 contains two tutorials. Tutorial 1-1 provides **A Guided Tour of Turbo Prolog's Programming Environment**. Tutorial 1-2, **Running the Towers of Hanoi Program**, gives you practice loading, executing, and editing a program.*

Getting Started

What Is a Programming Environment?

Learning a computer language involves learning the commands, rules, procedures, and syntax of the language. However, before you can actually write a program, you need to become familiar with the programming environment of the language. This chapter introduces you to Turbo Prolog's programming environment.

Turbo Prolog's programming environment can be thought of as a bridge between you and the language. It provides a method for entering, editing, running, and debugging your program. It provides a Trace feature that lets you see step by step how your program runs. It provides the means to save and load your program to and from disk. It also provides features relating to the maintenance of files, changing the size and colors of the windows, and other tasks designed to make your life as a programmer easier. In short, Turbo Prolog's programming makes it easy to:

> Enter a program.
> Run a program.
> Make changes in a program.
> Save a program from memory to disk.
> Load a program from disk to memory.
> Display the program results on your monitor.

Turbo Prolog is a complete programming language. It provides everything you need to create, edit, debug, compile, and link (connect) programs. You can rapidly switch between the Editor and Dialog Windows. You can use the **Trace** command to display the steps Turbo Prolog uses as it runs your program. Turbo Prolog's programming environment is versatile. As you progress through this book, you will learn how easy it is to use.

Tutorials

This book includes a number of tutorials that help you learn all about Turbo Prolog. The way the tutorials work is explained on the next page.

How the Tutorials Work

The tutorials in this book use four simple prompts that guide your learning. These prompts are shown in Figure 1-1 below.

Figure 1-1: Prompts Used in Tutorials

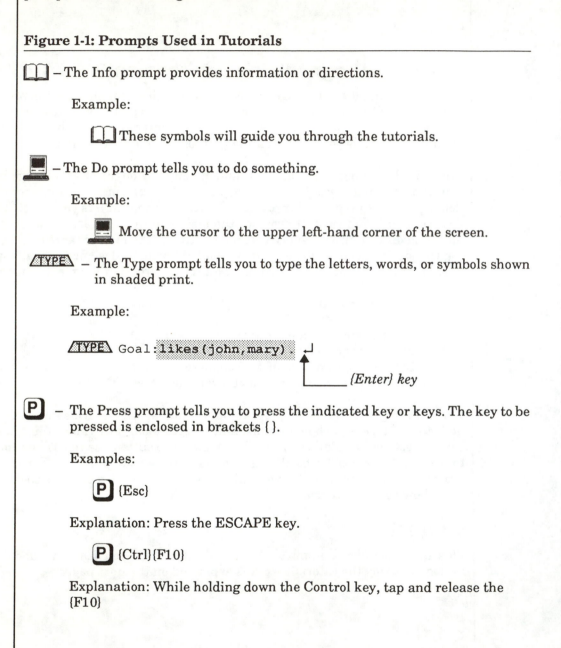

– The Info prompt provides information or directions.

Example:

These symbols will guide you through the tutorials.

– The Do prompt tells you to do something.

Example:

Move the cursor to the upper left-hand corner of the screen.

– The Type prompt tells you to type the letters, words, or symbols shown in shaded print.

Example:

Goal: likes(john, mary)   ↵

└─── *{Enter} key*

– The Press prompt tells you to press the indicated key or keys. The key to be pressed is enclosed in brackets { }.

Examples:

P {Esc}

Explanation: Press the ESCAPE key.

P {Ctrl}{F10}

Explanation: While holding down the Control key, tap and release the {F10}

This tutorial introduces the Turbo Prolog programming environment. You will learn how to use Turbo Prolog's windows and menus along with their commands. You will learn how to select various options from the Main Menu and from the pull-down menus. You will learn how to load, edit, run, and save a program. Carefully follow the prompts and compare what you see on your screen with the screens in this book. Experiment and don't be afraid to make a mistake. No one is looking. Good luck and have a good time learning Turbo Prolog.

Preparing Your Disks

If you have not already done so, you should make a backup copy of your Turbo Prolog diskettes. After making your backup copies, store the original Turbo Prolog disks in a safe place. Should your backup diskettes become unusable, you will still have the original diskettes to make a new copy. Since Turbo Prolog is not copy protected, the disks may be copied with the DOS **DISKCOPY** command.

Note: Do not use the original Turbo Prolog diskettes except to make backup copies.

Before you begin the tutorial, you must prepare a working copy of Turbo Prolog. The directions for floppy disk users and hard disk users are below. Follow the directions appropriate for your system.

Making a Working Copy of a Two-Disk Drive System

Step 1 - Format five (5) floppy disks and mark them as follows:

> Examples
> Boot Disk
> Programs
> Run Disk
> Library

Step 2 - Boot your computer. At the A> DOS prompt, place the copy you made of the Turbo Prolog disk marked "Install/Readme" into the A drive.

Step 3 - ⟨TYPE⟩   install a: b: ↵

Step 4 - After you press (Return) ({↵}), follow the instructions given on the screen.

Making a Working Copy with a Hard (Fixed) Disk System

Step 1 - Boot your computer. At the C> DOS prompt, place the Turbo Prolog disk marked "Install/Readme" in the A drive. (Note: Make sure that you are logged on the hard disk you want to use. This is usually the C drive).

Step 2 - ◢TYPE◣   `a:install a: c:\tprolog2` ↵

Of course, you may use any subdirectory name you wish. Turbo Prolog automatically creates the proper subdirectories on your hard disk.

Step 3 - After you press {Return} ({↵}), follow the instructions given on the screen.

Note: If you need help in either making backup copies or in preparing a floppy or hard disk working copy of Turbo Prolog, refer to the Turbo Prolog User's Guide.

The diagram below represents a generic MS-DOS type microcomputer. Throughout the tutorials, we will use this generic computer as our model. You may have an IBM PC or one of the many MS-DOS compatible computers. These computers are much alike, and your keyboard has similar features. Some key locations may be different, but they all perform exactly the same functions. Some computers have twelve function keys across the top of the keyboard rather than ten along the left-hand side of the keyboard. Each function key will perform the same task regardless of its location. We assume that you know and understand the layout of your keyboard. If you need help, refer to your computer manual.

Starting Turbo Prolog

If you have not already done so, boot your computer to bring up the DOS prompt. Follow the steps below.

Note: At this point, you should have made backup copies and installed Turbo Prolog according to the type of computer system you use. If you are using a floppy disk system, insert your Boot Disk into drive A and the Run Disk into drive B. Close the disk drive doors.

DOS Prompt

TYPE A>`prolog` ↵   <——*The {Enter} or {Return} key.*

Filename of the Turbo Prolog program. This command loads the Turbo Prolog programming environment into your computer's memory and brings up the Turbo Prolog copyright message.

After a few seconds, Turbo Prolog prints this message:

> Prolog Overlay Loader- Can't find file PROLOG.OVL
> Enter filename prefix (X: or path name\) or '.' to quit=>

You must tell Turbo Prolog where your Run Disk is.

TYPE `b:` ↵

Now replace the disk in drive A with the Programs disk. This disk will be used in Tutorial 1-2. If you were writing your own program, you could put a formatted data disk in drive A to store your program.

Note: If you are using a hard disk system, select the Prolog directory using the **Change Directory** command (cd\tprolog2 or whatever path you chose when you installed Turbo Prolog) and type **prolog** at the DOS prompt.

If you have successfully booted Turbo Prolog, you will see the copyright message shown below.

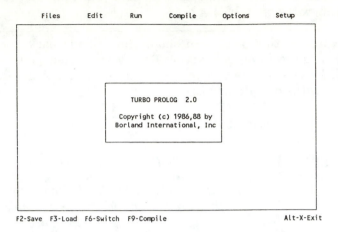

The copyright message screen shows the version of Turbo Prolog you are using. This book was prepared based on version 2.0. If you are using a different version, the screens may look different, but the examples will work.

 Press any key to continue.

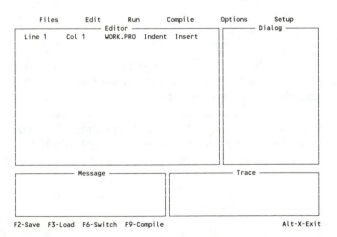

You now see the Turbo Prolog programming environment. This programming environment consists of a top line, a bottom line, and four windows. The windows allow you to see four activities at the same time. This is like having four separate monitors attached to your computer. This versatile feature allows both beginning and experienced programmers to quickly gain proficiency in using Turbo Prolog.

The Turbo Prolog Programming Windows

The Turbo Prolog programming windows make writing, running, and debugging programs simple even for new programmers. Try to get an overall understanding of the functions of these windows. You will learn more about each window as you write and develop your own programs.

Editor Window

The Editor Window is in the upper left quadrant of the screen below the Main Menu. This is where you create a new program or edit (make changes in) an existing one. When you load a program from your disk, Turbo Prolog displays the program here.

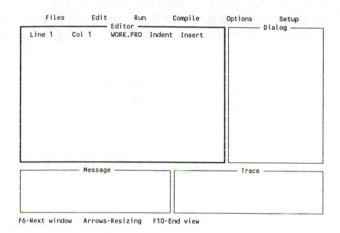

At the top of the Editor Window is the Editor Window Message Line. Below is an explanation of the Editor Window Message Line.

Line   The line number shows the line number of the cursor. Line numbering starts at the top of the file with line 1.

Col   The column number shows the horizontal position of the cursor. Column numbering starts at the left side of the Editor Window with Column 1.

WORK.PRO   This is the default name of the work file in the Editor Window. If you do not provide Turbo Prolog with a filename, it automatically uses the filename WORK.PRO. When you provide Turbo Prolog with a filename, that name appears here instead of WORK.PRO.

Indent   This On/Off switch determines the status of the automatic indent feature. You will find the indent feature useful when writing a program. This feature is controlled from the Setup pull-down menu.

Insert/
Type over
There are two modes for entering characters into the Editor Window. The Insert mode and the Typeover mode. The Insert mode inserts characters at the cursor position, moving existing characters to the right. The Type-over mode replaces the character under which the cursor is positoned. The Insert/Typeover modes are toggled by the pressing the {Ins} key.

Text Mode
Indicates whether the text mode (word wrap) is on or off. This is toggled by pressing {Ctrl}{W}. You will see this part of the message line when you learn to expand the Editor Window.

Dialog Window

To the right of the Editor Window is the Dialog Window. When you run a program, the results are shown here. As the name of the window suggests, this is the place where dialogue between you and a running program occurs.

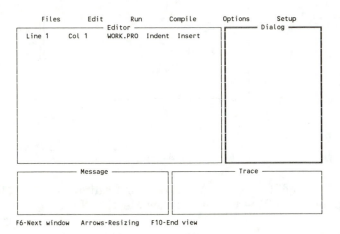

Trace Window

Directly below the Dialog Window is the Trace Window. Through this window, you can see the steps Turbo Prolog takes as it runs your program. The Trace Window is helpful when you debug (correct errors in) your program. Debugging is an important aspect of the programming process. Even the best programmers have bugs. The Trace Window will help you to get your programs to run correctly.

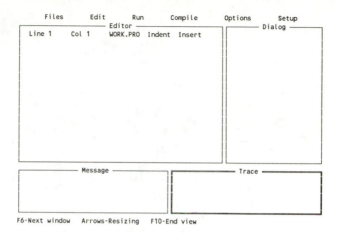

The Trace Window activates when you use the **Trace** command in a program. You will use the **Trace** command in later tutorials to help you see how Turbo Prolog works.

Message Window

In most computer languages (including other versions of Prolog), it is difficult to know what is happening as a program executes. Turbo Prolog uses the Message Window to inform you of its progress. For example, when a program compiles, Turbo Prolog displays the name of the program and information about the compilation process in this window. The Message Window also displays error messages and other information that Turbo Prolog wants you to know.

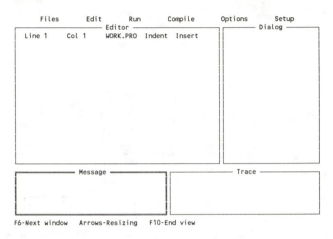

Status/Message Line

Along the bottom of the screen is the Status/Message Line. It tells you which function keys are active and what they do. The information on this line changes depending upon which window is active. When the Main Menu is active, the status line is as shown below.

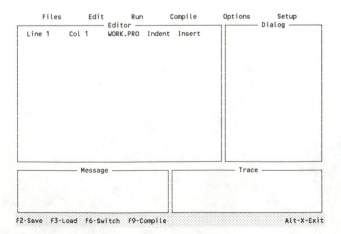

The Main Menu

The top line of the display is the Main Menu. It is the control center for Turbo Prolog. The six Main Menu commands allow you to control every action of Turbo Prolog.

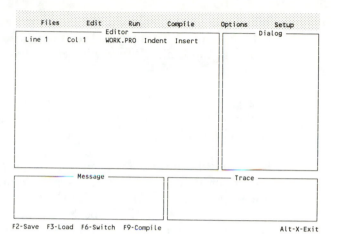

Choosing a Command

There are two methods for choosing a command.

1. You can type the first letter of the command. Turbo Prolog displays this letter in bold print.

2. You can use the arrow keys to move the highlighted cursor to the desired command. Then press the (Enter) key to activate the command.

These methods work in any menu throughout Turbo Prolog.

Four of the commands (**Files, Compile, Options,** and **Setup**) have pull-down submenus with additional commands. When you select one of these, a pull-down menu appears below the selected command. These pull-down menus have additional commands related to the selected Main Menu command and contain other commands which may or may not have additional pull-down menus. To return to the Main Menu from one of these pull-down menus, press the (Esc) key until the cursor returns to the Main Menu. Each press of the (Esc) key will return you to the previous command or window. Here is a summary of each of the six commands in the Main Menu.

The Main Menu Commands

Files   The **Files** pull-down menu contains commands that save and load your programs to and from the disk. It also provides commands for other disk related activities. The Files menu will be explained in detail later.

Edit   When you want to create a new program or edit an existing one, use the **Edit** command. This places the cursor into the Editor Window to indicate that the Editor Window is active. The Editor Window is explained later.

Run   The **Run** command executes your program. If an error occurs, Turbo Prolog returns you to the Editor Window and places the cursor at the error's location.

Each time Turbo Prolog encounters a syntax error, it stops and places the cursor at the location of the error. To proceed, correct the error and press the {F10} key. This tells Turbo Prolog to continue compiling. This process continues until Turbo Prolog has examined each line of your program for errors. Your program will not run until all errors are corrected.

Compile   Choosing this command displays a pull-down menu. The commands give options about compiling the program currently in the Editor Window. After you have debugged your program and it works properly, use the **Compile** command to translate your program into machine code. You can then save the compiled code to your disk.

Options   This command provides choices related to compiling programs.

Setup   The **Setup** command allows you to change the colors and sizes of the Windows. It also allows you to change the default settings.

A Look at the Pull-down Menus

Four of the Main Menu's commands have pull-down menus. When you select the **Files, Compile, Options,** or **Setup** choices from the Main Menu, you will see a pull-down menu. A detailed explanation of each follows.

The Files Pull-down Menu

Select the **Files** command. You can press the first letter of the command (in this case **F**), or you can move the cursor over the **Files** command and press the {Enter} key.

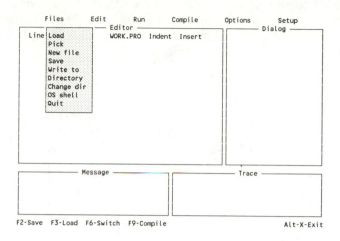

The Files pull-down menu now appears under the **Files** command of the Main Menu. These commands are concerned with the loading (retrieval), saving (storing), listing, and erasing of files. Below is a summary of these commands.

Summary of Files Pull-down Menu

Load   Reads the contents of a file from the disk and places it in the Editor Window.

Pick   Lets you choose a file from a list of the last seven files that were in the Editor Window.

New file   Erases the file in the Editor Window and creates a new file. The default name of this new file is WORK.PRO.

Save   Saves the file in the Editor Window to the disk with the default name. The old version is saved with the extension .BAK.

Write to   Writes the file in the Editor Window to disk. Prompts you for a filename.

Directory   Displays the disk directory.

Change dir Allows you to change the logged disk and/or subdirectory.

OS shell   Puts you in DOS while keeping Turbo Prolog active. To return to Prolog, type **exit**. You must have sufficient memory to use this option.

Quit   Exit Turbo Prolog. If you have not saved your work, Prolog will ask you if you want to.

The Compile Pull-down Menu

Return the cursor to the Main Menu by pressing the {Esc} key and select the **Compile** command. The commands in this pull-down menu control the compiling process. You can specify whether you want to compile in memory (the default value), to an object file, or to an exec file. It also allows you to link (connect) files or place several modules into a single project. These commands are fairly advanced and will not be covered in this book. If you wish to explore these commands, refer to the Turbo Prolog User's Guide.

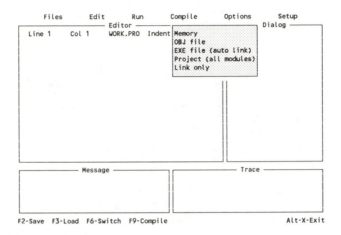

The Options Pull-down Menu

When you choose this option, you will see the screen below. These choices tell Turbo Prolog how to compile your program when you choose **Compile** from the Main Menu. These options are covered in detail in your Turbo Prolog User's Guide.

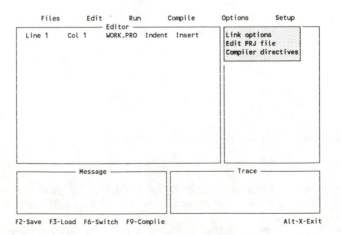

The Setup Pull-down Menu

Return the cursor to the Main Menu by pressing the {Esc} key and select the **Setup** command. The six commands in the **Setup** pull-down menu determine the physical characteristics of the programming environment and allow you to preset the environment configurations. The specific commands for this pull-down menu are not discussed here. They are described in your Turbo Prolog User's Guide.

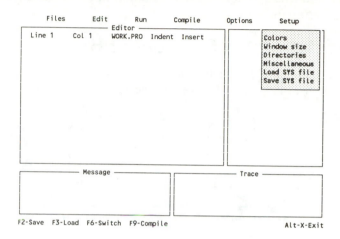

You will learn more about each of the components of the programming environment as you progress through the book. The commands and operation will be easier to understand as you learn to write programs in Turbo Prolog. You will write your first Turbo Prolog program in Chapter 2. Before going on to Chapter 2, however, you will load and run a sample program. Tutorial 1-2, Running the Towers of Hanoi Puzzle Program, will allow you to observe Turbo Prolog in action.

In this tutorial, you will start Turbo Prolog, retrieve the Towers of Hanoi Puzzle from the Prolog Programs disk, and run it. You will see a program that not only solves the Towers of Hanoi Puzzle, but also graphically displays the solution. You are not expected to understand how the program works. However, by working through this activity, you will gain familiarity with the Turbo Prolog programming environment.

Background of Towers of Hanoi Puzzle

The Towers of Hanoi Puzzle is an ancient puzzle involving three posts and any number of rings that fit over the posts.

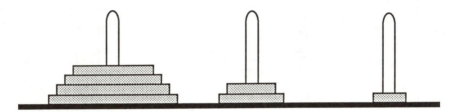

This puzzle requires the player to move the rings from the leftmost post to the rightmost post. Two rules govern the puzzle:

    1. Move only one ring at a time.

    2. Never place a larger ring on a smaller ring.

Solving this problem requires intelligence. Turbo Prolog can solve this problem. Is Turbo Prolog intelligent? We'll leave that decision to you.

Starting the Towers of Hanoi Puzzle Program

You want to select the **F**iles command from the Main Menu. If you are continuing from Tutorial 1, press the (Esc) key until the cursor is located in the Main Menu. If you are starting this tutorial from scratch, boot your computer and bring up the Main Menu of Turbo Prolog.

Choose the **F**iles command from the Main Menu by either pressing the letter **F** or moving the cursor to the **F**iles command and pressing the (Enter) key.

When you select the **Files** command, Turbo Prolog displays the Files pull-down menu.

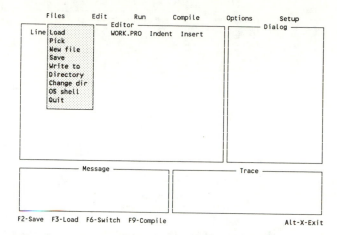

The commands in the Files pull-down menu manipulate the programs (or files) on the disk. This pull-down menu is used to load and save files. See your Turbo Prolog User's Guide or Tutorial 1-1 for an explanation of the commands in the Files pull-down menu.

The Load Command

Follow the instructions below to load the Towers of Hanoi program from the Turbo Prolog Programs diskette. If you are using a two-disk floppy drive system, you must have the Turbo Prolog Programs diskette in the A drive and the Run Disk in the B drive. If you are using a hard disk system, the Turbo Prolog Programs subdirectory is located on your hard disk (for example — c:\tprolog2\programs).

With the Files pull-down menu displayed on your screen, choose the **Load** command. You can choose this command by either pressing the letter **L** (the first letter of the command) or by moving the cursor to the **Load** command and pressing the {Enter} key.

You will see another window displayed asking for the name of the file that you want to load.

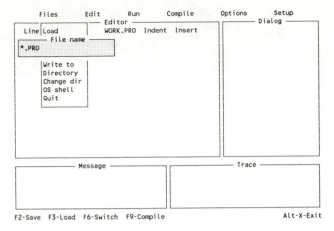

Now type in the name of the Towers of Hanoi program file as follows.

⟋TYPE⟍ HANOI.PRO ↵

> *[Hard disk users type the full pathname of the directory where the Hanoi program is located – for example, c:\tprolog2\programs\hanoi.pro]*

Note: If you press the {Enter} key without providing a filename, Turbo Prolog lists all of the program filenames located on the default drive. If you use a hard disk, the Towers of Hanoi filename will not appear in the directory listing unless you type the full pathname. You could then select the program by moving the cursor over the program name and pressing enter.

Notice that the Message Window displays a message that the program is loading.

The pull-down menu disappears, and the Towers of Hanoi program appears in the Editor Window. The filename in the Editor Window is changed to HANOI.PRO, and the cursor returns to the Main Menu.

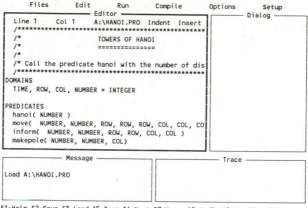

Notice that the top line in the Editor Window now displays information about the Towers of Hanoi program.

Running the Towers of Hanoi Program

Select the **Run** command from the Main Menu.

When you select the **Run** command, Turbo Prolog compiles the program, checking each line of the program for syntax errors. If any errors are found, Turbo Prolog stops and places the cursor in the Editor Window at the place in the program where the error occurred. If this happens you must correct the error. Then press the {F10} function key to continue compiling. The Towers of Hanoi Program will not have any errors.

As the program compiles, observe the lines of the program in the Message Window. The lines go by quickly, but it tells you that Turbo Prolog is working.

When the compilation is complete, the program executes. A graphics window shows the disks being moved from peg to peg.

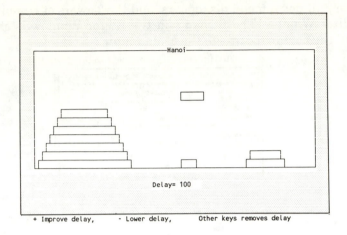

You can speed up the execution (lower the delay) by pressing the {-} key, or you can slow it down by pressing the {+} key. Try it.

When the Towers of Hanoi program completes execution, move the cursor to the Main Menu. (Press the {Esc} key.)

Editing

Now that you know how to load and execute a program, you are ready to learn some of Turbo Prolog's simple editing commands. The next steps will show you the commands that move the cursor and how to make changes to the program.

 With the cursor in the Main Menu, select the **E**dit command.

The cursor is now flashing in the upper left-hand corner of the Editor Window.

When you enter the Editor Window, the status line at the bottom of the screen changes. It now displays the use of the function keys in the Edit mode.

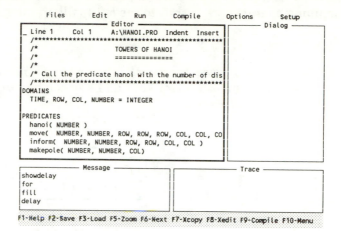

```
         Files        Edit        Run        Compile       Options      Setup
                         ┌── Editor ──────────────────────────────┐  ┌─ Dialog ──────
         _ Line 1    Col 1      A:\HANOI.PRO  Indent  Insert │  │
         /**************************************************│  │
         /*                TOWERS OF HANOI                  │  │
         /*                ===============                  │  │
         /*                                                 │  │
         /* Call the predicate hanoi with the number of dis│  │
         /**************************************************│  │
         DOMAINS                                            │  │
           TIME, ROW, COL, NUMBER = INTEGER                 │  │
                                                            │  │
         PREDICATES                                         │  │
           hanoi( NUMBER )                                  │  │
           move(  NUMBER, NUMBER, ROW, ROW, ROW, COL, COL, CO│  │
           inform(  NUMBER, NUMBER, ROW, ROW, COL, COL )    │  │
           makepole( NUMBER, NUMBER, COL)                   │  │
         └────────────────────────────────────────────────┘  └───────────────
         ┌──────────── Message ──────────┐    ┌──────────── Trace ────────────
         │showdelay                       │    │
         │for                             │    │
         │fill                            │    │
         │delay                           │    │
         └────────────────────────────────┘    └─────────────────────────────

         F1-Help F2-Save F3-Load F5-Zoom F6-Next F7-Xcopy F8-Xedit F9-Compile F10-Menu
```

Inserting and Deleting Text

Turbo Prolog makes editing easy. You can accomplish most of your editing with the arrow keys, the Insert key {Ins}, and the Delete key {Del}. As you read through this section, practice making changes to the Hanoi Puzzle program now in the Editor Window. Don't worry about changing the program. You will not save your changes at the end of this tutorial. The original HANOI.PRO file on the disk will remain unchanged.

As you type in the Editor Window, the characters appear at the cursor location. If you position the cursor under an existing letter and type a new letter, one of two things will happen. What happens depends upon the mode of the Insert key {Ins}.

Insert on: First, the computer could insert the letter at the cursor. This
                  means that all text to the right of the cursor must move over and
                  make room for the new letter.

Typeover on: The second possibility is that the new letter may replace or type-
                  over the old letter. In the Typeover mode, the letter typed re-
                  places the letter over the cursor.

The Insert key {Ins} toggles the Editor Window between the two modes. The top command line of your Editor Window displays the current mode. The Insert mode is the default mode in Turbo Prolog. If you need the Typeover mode, press the Insert key {Ins}. Try typing using both of these modes.

The Delete key {Del} is used to remove characters. It is located on the lower right-hand side of your keyboard. To delete a character, place the cursor under the character and press the Delete key {Del}. The character will disappear, and the remaining characters will shift to the left to fill up the space.

The Cursor Keys

Besides the arrow keys, there are other ways to move the cursor. Below is a summary of the cursor control keys and key combinations. Try each one to gain familiarity with their action.

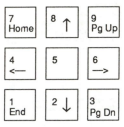

To move the cursor:	Press
One character right	{—>}
One character left	{<—}
One word to the right	{Ctrl}{ —>}
One word to the left	{Ctrl} {<—}
One line up	{↑}
One line down	{↓}
To the beginning of a line	{Home}
To the end of a line	{End}
One page up	{PgUp}
One page down	{PgDn}

A page is defined as the vertical size of the full screen in the Editor Window. The {PgUp} and {PgDn} keys will move the cursor to the top and bottom of the screen, respectively.

To a specific line	{Ctrl}{F2}

When you press the {Ctrl}{F2} keys, you are prompted to input the line number. Type the line number and press the {Ctrl}{F2} keys again. The cursor then moves to the specified line.

To the beginning of a file	{Ctrl}{PguP}
To the end of a file	{Ctrl}{PgDn}

Editing with the Function Keys

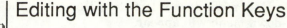

Turbo Prolog makes extensive use of the function keys to make editing easy. Below is a summary of how the function keys work when you are in the Editor Window.

{F1} Help	– Displays a help screen. This screen displays information to assist you in using the Turbo Prolog commands.
{F2} Save	– Saves the text in the Editor Window using the default name. This is the same as selecting **Save** from the Files pull-down menu.
{F3} Load a file	– Loads a file from disk into the Editor. Turbo Prolog will prompt you for the filename.
{F5} Zoom Editor	– Increases the size of the Editor Window to cover the full screen. Pressing {F5} again reduces the screen to its original size.
{F6} Goto Window	– Selects the next window in a clockwise direction. This allows you to use the cursor arrow keys to change the sizes of the windows.
{F7} XCopy	– Reads (brings in) a block of text from the external editor (below) and places it in the Editor Window. (See Turbo Prolog User's Guide for information about block commands).
{F8} Xedit	– Enters the auxiliary Editor Window. This is not covered in this text.
{F9} Compile	– Compiles the program in the Editor Window in memory and runs it.
{F10} Menu	– Goes to the Main Menu.

Exiting the Editor Window and Saving a Program

You are now familiar with the basic Turbo Prolog editing commands. This section shows you how to exit the Editor Window and save the edited program.

To exit the Editor Window, press the {Esc} key.

The cursor jumps from the Editor Window to the Main Menu. A new message line appears on the bottom of the screen.

To save the program in the Editor Window, select the **F̲iles** command from the Main Menu. The Files pull-down menu will appear.

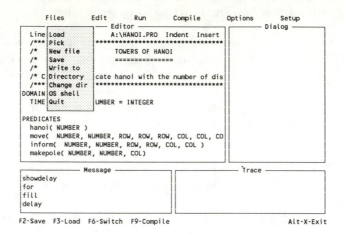

```
              Files     Edit      Run      Compile    Options    Setup
                        ── Editor ──                          ── Dialog ──
        Line │Load        A:\HANOI.PRO  Indent  Insert
        /*** │Pick        ********************************
        /*   │New file        TOWERS OF HANOI
        /*   │Save           ================
        /*   │Write to
        /*  C│Directory   cate hanoi with the number of dis
        /*** │Change dir  ********************************
        DOMAIN│OS shell
        TIME │Quit        UMBER = INTEGER

        PREDICATES
          hanoi( NUMBER )
          move(  NUMBER, NUMBER, ROW, ROW, ROW, COL, COL, CO
          inform(  NUMBER, NUMBER, ROW, ROW, COL, COL )
          makepole( NUMBER, NUMBER, COL)

                      ── Message ──                       ── Trace ──
        showdelay
        for
        fill
        delay

        F2-Save  F3-Load  F6-Switch  F9-Compile                    Alt-X-Exit
```

 Select the **W̲rite to** command from the pull-down menu.

Note: The **S̲ave** choice saves the program using the default name. If you were to choose this, the program would be saved under the name HANOI.PRO and replace the file on the disk. Since you don't want to do this, use the **W̲rite to** command which prompts you for a new name.

Another window appears, asking you to type the filename. This is a filename that you make up. When you name a file in Turbo Prolog, use the same rules for naming files under DOS. A filename consists of eight or fewer characters with no spaces. You can add a file extension of three or fewer characters to the filename if you wish. If you do not provide an extension, Turbo Prolog uses the extension .PRO. A period [.] separates the filename extension from the filename.

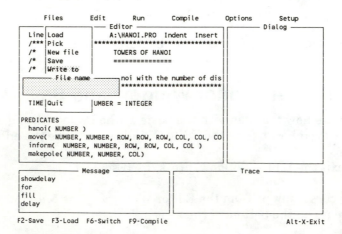

```
              Files     Edit      Run      Compile    Options    Setup
                        ── Editor ──                          ── Dialog ──
        Line │Load        A:\HANOI.PRO  Indent  Insert
        /*** │Pick        ********************************
        /*   │New file        TOWERS OF HANOI
        /*   │Save           ================
        /*   │Write to
             ── File name ──  noi with the number of dis
        │                   │ ********************************
        │                   │
        TIME │Quit        UMBER = INTEGER

        PREDICATES
          hanoi( NUMBER )
          move(  NUMBER, NUMBER, ROW, ROW, ROW, COL, COL, CO
          inform(  NUMBER, NUMBER, ROW, ROW, COL, COL )
          makepole( NUMBER, NUMBER, COL)

                      ── Message ──                       ── Trace ──
        showdelay
        for
        fill
        delay

        F2-Save  F3-Load  F6-Switch  F9-Compile                    Alt-X-Exit
```

Because of the changes you may have made while practicing the editing commands, do not save the current program under its original name HANOI.PRO. If you do use the original name, the edited program will replace the program on your disk. You don't want this to happen, so use a different name. Use JUNK.PRO for the filename.

Filename: JUNK.PRO ↵

> *(Hard disk users should use the proper pathname – for example,*
> *c:\tprolog\programs\junk)*

When you press the {Return} key, the red light on your disk drive glows briefly. This indicates that the program is being saved to the disk. When the file is saved, the filename request window disappears, and the cursor returns to the Main Menu.

Checking the Filenames

In this section, you will learn how to request to see the disk directory.

Select the Files pull-down menu, then select the **Directory** command. At the filename request, press the {Enter} key. This selects the default directory. Pressing {Enter} again selects *.PRO as the default file mask. All the files in the default directory with the extension .PRO are displayed. Find JUNK.PRO, the file that you just saved to the disk.

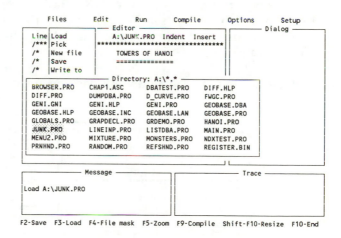

Note: The files shown on your screen may not match those shown on the above screen. This is all right as long as JUNK.PRO is displayed.

You can use the **Change dir** command to change the default disk drive that Turbo Prolog uses. To do this, select the **Change dir** command from the Files pull-down menu. A window asking for the drive specification will appear. You may then change the designated drive by typing the drive name followed by a colon (A:, B:, or C:) or by typing the full pathname.

Erasing the File in the Editor Window

You can erase the file in the Editor Window by choosing **New file** from the Files menu. Just press (Esc) enough times to return the cursor to the Main Menu line. Select the **Files** command and then the **New file** option from the pull-down menu. If you have made changes to the program, you will be asked if you want to save the changes. In this case, type **N**.

Changing the Screen Colors

Note: If you have a monochrome monitor, skip this section, and go on to Changing the Window Size.

The **Setup** command in the Main Menu lets you change the colors and sizes of the windows in Turbo Prolog environment. To change the colors and sizes of the windows, follow the instructions below.

 Make sure your cursor is on the Main Menu line and select the **Setup** command.

There are six choices in the Setup pull-down menu. You will now learn how to change the colors of the windows in the Turbo Prolog programming environment. In the next section, you will see how to change the size of the windows. An explanation of the rest of the commands of the Setup pull-down menu is presented in your Turbo Prolog User's Guide.

Select the **Colors** choice in the Setup pull-down menu.

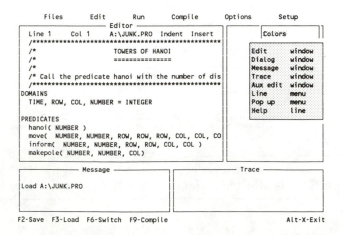

The Color pull-down menu includes commands that allow you to change the color of any window. Follow the instructions along the bottom of your screen. Choose one background color and one foreground color for each window.

You could save the new colors by using the **Save configurations** command in this pull-down menu. If you save the changes, the new color choices will be stored on your diskette under the name of PROLOG.SYS and will replace the original colors.

DO NOT SAVE THESE CHANGES UNTIL YOU ARE MORE FAMILIAR WITH TURBO PROLOG. PRESS {Esc} TO EXIT THIS MODE INSTEAD.

Changing the Window Sizes

To change the size of each of the windows, follow the instructions below.

Be sure the cursor is in the Setup pull-down menu (press the {Esc} key if you need to), and select the **Window size** command.

You will see the following display on your screen:

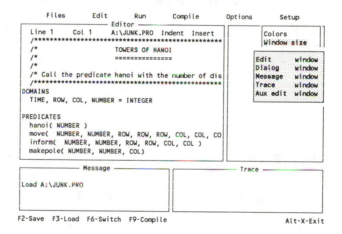

Press {↵ } to select the Editor Window for resizing.

The commands for changing the size of the Turbo Prolog windows are shown along the bottom of the screen.

Practice enlarging and reducing the Editor Window. Use the commands along the bottom of the screen to alter its size.

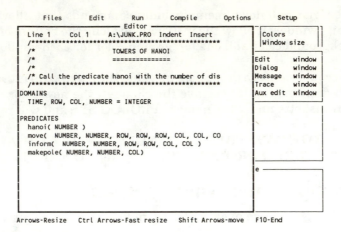

```
        Files      Edit      Run      Compile      Options      Setup
                    Editor
    Line 1     Col 1     A:\JUNK.PRO  Indent  Insert        Colors
    /**********************************************        Window size
    /*                  TOWERS OF HANOI
    /*                  ===============                 Edit      window
    /*                                                 Dialog    window
    /* Call the predicate hanoi with the number of dis Message   window
    /**********************************************    Trace     window
    DOMAINS                                            Aux edit  window
      TIME, ROW, COL, NUMBER = INTEGER

    PREDICATES
      hanoi( NUMBER )
      move( NUMBER, NUMBER, ROW, ROW, ROW, COL, COL, CO
      inform( NUMBER, NUMBER, ROW, ROW, COL, COL )
      makepole( NUMBER, NUMBER, COL)
                                                     e

    Arrows-Resize   Ctrl Arrows-Fast resize   Shift Arrows-move   F10-End
```

 Practice changing the sizes of the other windows.

AGAIN, DO NOT SAVE THESE CHANGES. WAIT UNTIL YOU ARE MORE FAMILIAR WITH TURBO PROLOG. PRESS {Esc} TO EXIT THIS MODE.

This is the end of Tutorial 1-2. Continue to Chapter 2 or exit Turbo Prolog by selecting **Quit** from the Files Menu.

Exercises

1-1. Describe the function of the four Turbo Prolog Windows.

    A. Editor Window
    B. Dialog Window
    C. Message Window
    D. Trace Window

1-2. There are six commands in the Main Menu. Name them and describe their function.

1-3. How do you move the cursor to the top menu line?

Problems

1-1. Here is a small Turbo Prolog program. Enter and run the program. Pay careful attention to upper and lower case, periods, parentheses, and quotation marks.

        predicates
                good_morning

        goal
                good_morning

        clauses
                good_morning if
                        write("I am Turbo Prolog, your servant.") and
                        nl.

1-2. Save the above program to your disk. Then check the directory to see if it has been saved. Next, use the **New file** command to clear the Editor Window. Now load the program back into the Editor Window.

1-3. Once at the top menu line, what are the key(s) you press to:

    a. Enter the Editor Window

    b. View the directory

    c. Save a program

    d. Load a program

    e. Clear the Editor

1-4. If Turbo Prolog finds an error when it compiles a program, where does it print the error message?

1-5. If Turbo Prolog requires information from the user, what window will make the request?

Chapter 2
Facts and Goals

This chapter introduces you to facts and goals as they are used in Turbo Prolog. In Turbo Prolog, a fact is a statement that is assumed to be true. A collection of facts is a data base, and a data base with rules is called a knowledge base. You will learn how to write Turbo Prolog facts and put them together in a Turbo Prolog program. You will learn how to ask questions in Turbo Prolog while learning how to write logical expressions as Turbo Prolog clauses. Tutorial 2-1 will guide you in creating your first Turbo Prolog program.

Facts and Goals

Data Base

Turbo Prolog is an object-oriented computer language. It is a computer language that is concerned with objects and the relationships of those objects with other objects. When grouped together as logical expressions, they form a data base from which information can be extracted. For example, the following logical expressions constitute a small data base that classifies animals.

A pigeon is a bird   A snake is a reptile
A cat is a mammal   Man is a mammal

If you were to somehow give this information to Turbo Prolog, it would see pigeon, cat, snake, and man as objects. It would see the relationships as is-a-bird, is-a-mammal, is-a-reptile, and is-a-mammal, respectively. If you were to ask Turbo Prolog to tell you all the known mammals in the universe, it would reply:

cat is-a-mammal
man is-a-mammal

It would relate the objects (animals) to their class (mammal). Of course, there are more mammals in the universe than cat and man. But to Turbo Prolog, its data base is the only known universe. These are the only objects and relationships it knows. It knows nothing else. If you were to inquire about dogs, you might receive a reply such as UNKNOWN or I DON'T KNOW – the computer equivalent of a blank stare.

A data base is one of the main ingredients of a Turbo Prolog program. For the animal data base above to be useful, it would have to include more about the known animals and their classifications. It would be a large data base indeed. A data base, however, does not have to be large to be useful.

If you were Sherlock Holmes trying to solve a particular murder case, the data base might include only those facts concerned about the specific case – facts such as: suspects, locations, murder weapons, motives, and so forth. It would not be a large data base at all. In fact, such a data base is shown in the Turbo Prolog User's Guide. However, to make the data base useful, Sherlock added some rules. When rules are added to a data base, it becomes a knowledge base. In this "Who Dunnit" knowledge base, facts and rules about a murder mystery are presented in Turbo Prolog format. You might want to try your hand at solving this mystery after you have learned more about Turbo Prolog Facts and Rules.

Knowledge Base

The main portion of a Turbo Prolog program consists of a set of logical expressions arranged in a grouping called a knowledge base. A knowledge base is simply a data base with rules. The animal data base did not have any rules, only facts. As you might suspect, a data base is limited in its ability to provide information. Adding rules to a data base provides a means to make inferences and generates new knowledge. Let's look at a data base with just two facts:

> Harry is the father of John
> Harry is the father of Mary

As a data base, the above two facts are quite straightforward. They tell us that Harry is the father of both John and Mary — nothing more, nothing less. Can you deduce any other information from this data base, say, the relationship between John and Mary?

Right! John and Mary are brother and sister. Observe that nowhere in the data base does it say that John and Mary are brother and sister. That information does not exist in our two-fact data base. Nevertheless, you were able deduce a relationship between John and Mary. How did you do it? You applied a rule to the existing facts and inferred a conclusion. The rule you probably applied goes something like this:

> If two people have the same parent, and the two people are not of the same sex, they are brother and sister.

Keeping in mind that the two-fact data base is the only known knowledge to the system, the deduced information is a new fact. It is new knowledge. It is knowledge that did not exist prior to the execution of the rule. This is a powerful concept— from existing facts new knowledge was inferred. Thus, we call a data base with rules a knowledge base.

Turbo Prolog Clauses

When you write a Turbo Prolog program, the first portion you prepare is the knowledge base. You write the knowledge base in the form of Turbo Prolog clauses. Clauses come in two forms: facts and rules.

A Turbo Prolog fact declares a relationship between one or more objects. A Turbo Prolog fact is always true.

A Turbo Prolog rule is a conditional fact that depends on the truth or falsity of one or more other facts. A rule can be either true or false.

The remainder of this chapter will be concerned with how to write facts as Turbo Prolog clauses, how to ask questions in Turbo Prolog, and how Turbo Prolog answers these questions. You will learn how to write and execute a Turbo Prolog program. Rules will be covered in Chapter 5.

Logic

Prolog stands for <u>Pro</u>grammed <u>Log</u>ic. Logic, a method of reasoning formalized by the ancient Greeks, characterizes a way of thinking that arrives at conclusions by following an orderly set of rules. As a formal way of manipulating facts, the rules of logic can be described in mathematical terms. Because of this, logical thought can be represented in a computer. Turbo Prolog uses logic to answer questions and to solve problems.

In logic, a **conclusion** is reached by using facts. Consider this classic example.

> All men are mortal. <—*fact*
> Socrates is a man. <—*fact*
>
> Therefore,
> Socrates is mortal. <—*conclusion*

The conclusion is the result of **valid reasoning**. Reasoning is considered valid if the facts support the conclusion. In logic, facts are presumed true, even if they are not. For example, the reasoning represented in the next example is valid, although it is not true.

> All dogs speak English. <—*fact*
> Spot is a dog. <—*fact*
>
> Therefore,
> Spot speaks English. <—*conclusion*

The conclusion, Spot speaks English, is not in conformity with what we know about dogs. However, since the conclusion derives from the facts, the logic is valid. The problem with the conclusion is that the first fact is at odds with reality.

A Logic Machine

Imagine that you have invented a logic machine. Your logic machine contains only the facts that you tell it and the rules of logic. This knowledge base, consisting of facts and rules, represents the total sum of what is known by your logic machine.

Also imagine that your logic machine speaks English and that it can answer questions about the facts in its knowledge base.

When asked a question, the logic machine attempts to answer by comparing the question to the facts and rules in the knowledge base. If it can answer by finding a matching fact in its knowledge base, it will. If no facts exist in the knowledge base to match the question, it assumes the answer is NO. This is different from the way humans think, but this logic machine isn't as sophisticated as a human brain. Humans use many problem solving strategies besides logic to answer questions.

Here is a picture of your logic machine with a listing of the facts in its knowledge base.

Photo courtesy of IBM Corporation

Logic Machine

> Fact-1: George Washington was a President.
> Fact-2: Thomas Jefferson was a President.
> Fact-3: Millard Fillmore was a President.
> Fact-4: John Kennedy was a President.

Notice that each fact is patterned according to a common form. The form is:

> X is a member of the class Y

In this form, Fact-1 is interpreted as:

> George Washington is a member of the class of Presidents.

Each succeeding fact can be expressed in this form.

Now that the logic machine has some facts stored in it, let's ask it some questions. Recall that the logic machine (LM) bases its answers only on the facts stored in it. Here are some examples:

Question: Was George Washington President?
LM Answer: Yes

Question: Was John Kennedy President?
LM Answer: Yes

Question: Was Richard Nixon President?
LM Answer: No

Why the No answer? We know that Richard Nixon was a president. Nevertheless, the logic machine says "No" because it does not contain this fact in its knowledge base.

Question: Was Elizabeth Queen of England?
LM Answer: I don't know anything about queens.

This answer is different. The Logic Machine says it doesn't know anything about queens because the machine has no information about the class of queens. It does not say "No," it says "I don't know."

This logic machine assumes that all facts are true. If we add some false statements to the knowledge base, or even some opinions, the logic machine still considers them as facts. Here is an example with new Facts 5 and 6 added:

Logic Machine

Fact-1: George Washington was a President.
Fact-2: Thomas Jefferson was a President.
Fact-3: Millard Fillmore was a President.
Fact-4: John Kennedy was a President.
Fact-5: Harvy Schmedlap was a President.
Fact-6: Millard Fillmore was a great President.

Question: Was Harvy Schmedlap a President?
LM Answer: Yes   *<— really?*

Question: Was Millard Fillmore a great President?
LM Answer: Yes   *<— in whose opinion?*

Although Fact-5 is certainly false, the logic machine had no trouble in declaring it to be true. This is because all facts in a data base are presumed to be true. Thus, Harvy Schmedlap is declared to be a president. Valid reasoning according to the data base, but invalid in the real world.

Fact-6 may or may not be true. The question whether Millard Fillmore was a great president can be argued. In reality, the greatness of Millard Fillmore is a matter of opinion. In the data base world of the logic machine, his greatness is a true fact. It is affirmed and declared to be true. Again, this is valid reasoning according to the data base, but invalid reasoning in the real world.

The point of all this is that the quality of the answers derived from a knowledge base is directly dependent upon the quality of the facts and rules it contains. Our logic machine cannot tell the difference between a true fact and an erroneous fact. Neither can Turbo Prolog.

Turbo Prolog and Logic

Turbo Prolog works almost the same way as our imaginary logic machine. It has a built-in processing device called an **inference engine**. The inference engine, the heart of Turbo Prolog, solves problems by making inferences from the knowledge base. It attempts to match the question with the facts to arrive at conclusions. Turbo Prolog's inference engine guides all of its computing actions.

Now, let's take at look at how Turbo Prolog works. First, it must have a knowledge base to which questions may be posed. Second, it must have a way to ask these questions. Turbo Prolog calls questions goals. Let's look at the Famous Greeks Knowledge Base.

> Fact-1: Socrates is a man.
> Fact-2: Aristotle is a man.
> Fact-3: Athena is a woman.
> Fact-4: Helen is a woman.
> Fact-5: Plato is a woman.

You can use these facts to answer questions. If the question was, Is Helen a woman? You could answer "Yes." Think about how you arrived at this answer. The steps you might have used could be:

1) Look at the question (Is Helen a Woman?).
2) Start at the top of the knowledge base (Fact-1).
3) Can Fact-1 answer the question?
4) If it can, give the answer Yes.
   If not, go to the next fact in the knowledge base.
5) Continue until either a match is found or the end of the knowledge base is reached.

Here are some other questions. Notice that when an answer is true, the phrase in the question matches the phrase in the knowledge base. This is called pattern matching.

Question	Knowledge Base	Answer
Is Socrates a man?	**Socrates is a man.** Aristotle is a man. Athena is a woman. Helen is a woman. Plato is a woman.	True
Is Aristotle a woman?	Socrates is a man. Aristotle is a man. Athena is a woman. Helen is a woman. Plato is a woman.	False, No match.
Is Socrates a Greek?	Socrates is a man. Aristotle is a man. Athena is a woman. Helen is a woman. Plato is a woman.	False, No match.
Is Plato a Woman?	Socrates is a man. Aristotle is a man. Athena is a woman. Helen is a woman. **Plato is a woman.**	True (Based on the knowledge base.)

Unlike the imaginary logic machine, Turbo Prolog does not speak English. Facts must expressed in a way that Turbo Prolog can understand. They are expressed as a relationship between one or more objects. This special way to express facts is called the **predicate form**. Expressing facts in the predicate form is easy. It looks like this:

termination symbol (full-stop)

relationship(object1,object2,...,objectN).

predicate

objects

The first part of the clause (relationship) is called the predicate. It represents the relationship among the objects. The objects, sometimes called arguments, are the objects of the relationship.

Look again at The Famous Greeks Knowledge Base. This time the facts are expressed as Turbo Prolog clauses.

Famous Greeks Knowledge Base

Logical Facts	Turbo Prolog Clauses
Socrates is a man.	man(socrates).
Aristotle is a man.	man(aristotle).
Athena is a woman.	woman(athena).
Helen is a woman.	woman(helen).
Plato is a woman.	woman(plato).

Notice that the translation from logical facts to Turbo Prolog clauses follows regular rules.

Rules for Turbo Prolog Clauses

1) Names of objects and predicates begin with a lowercase letter.

2) The lowercase letter can be followed by any number of characters, including letters, numbers, or the underscore character [_]. For example, we could rewrite the clause man(socrates) as man_is(socrates). We have connected man to is by the underscore character. Turbo Prolog treats this as one word.

3) Clauses must end with a period. Other terms for the ending period are full stop symbol and termination symbol.

Here are some other facts expressed as Turbo Prolog clauses:

The steak is burned.	is_burned(steak).
Sam smokes.	smokes(sam).
The airplane slides to a stop.	slides_to_stop(airplane).
The garbage has a rotten smell.	rotten_smell(garbage).
The ball was bouncing.	was_bouncing(ball).

In many cases, predicates are verbs and the objects are nouns. This is not a hard and fast rule, but it may help you to formulate facts that have some meaning to you. Not that Turbo Prolog cares about the meaning, it is only interested in pattern matching.

How to Ask Questions in Turbo Prolog

Now that you know how to express facts as Turbo Prolog clauses, you will next learn how to ask questions in Turbo Prolog. This part is easy because you already know how to ask a question. Turbo Prolog uses the same form for questions as it uses for facts. The Turbo Prolog term for question is **goal**. As you progress through the book you will begin to see the difference between facts and goals. The difference is not in how they look, but in how they work. Shown below are goals to be used in The Famous Greeks Knowledge Base.

Famous Greeks Knowledge Base

Logical Expressions	Turbo Prolog Form
Socrates is a man.	man(socrates).
Aristotle is a man.	man(aristotle).
Athena is a woman.	woman(athena).
Helen is a woman.	woman(helen).
Plato is a woman.	woman(Plato).

To ask questions of this data base, form the questions into English. Then, write them in the predicate form as Turbo Prolog goals. If these goals were to be presented to the data base, Turbo Prolog would respond as shown below.

Question	Turbo Prolog Goal	Answer
Is Socrates a man?	Goal:man(socrates).	Yes
Is Aristotle a woman?	Goal:woman(aristotle).	No
Is Socrates a Greek?	Goal:greek(socrates).	No
Is Helen a woman?	Goal:woman(helen).	Yes

Recall that Turbo Prolog answers these questions the same way you might. The question, Is Socrates a man?, translates into the Turbo Prolog clause **man(socrates)**. When you type the goal in the predicate form, Turbo Prolog's inference engine, starting at the top of the knowledge base, searches through the facts until a match is found between the predicate of the goal and the predicate of the fact. It then compares objects of the goal with the object of the fact. If they match, Turbo Prolog concludes that the goal is true and answers **Yes**. It has found a match in the knowledge base.

If Turbo Prolog's inference engine cannot find a match with the first clause, it continues the search with the next clause. This continues until a match is found or until the end of the knowledge base is reached. If it reaches the end without finding a match, Turbo Prolog replies **No** and the program stops.

Predicates with More Than One Object

A predicate clause can have more than one object. For example, you may want to express the fact that John likes Mary. This fact implies the existence of a likes relationship between John and Mary. **Likes** becomes the predicate of the clause. The objects are **John** and **Mary**. There are two ways to express this in Turbo Prolog:

> **likes(john,mary).**
>
> **likes(mary,john).**

Both clauses can mean the same thing. The interpretation depends upon you. You might interpret the first clause as John likes Mary, and the second clause as Mary is liked by John. The order of the objects is not important to Turbo Prolog as long as you are consistent. Turbo Prolog does not attach any meaning to the clauses. That is left to you, the programmer. When you write your own programs, you will learn more about the order of objects.

Here are some examples of how to write logical expressions as Turbo Prolog clauses. Look at the logical expression. Do not look at the corresponding Turbo Prolog clause until you have tried to write it yourself. Because the order of the objects is not important to Turbo Prolog, the objects in your clauses may be different.

Logical Expression	Turbo Prolog Clause
Shannon owns a car.	owns(shannon,car).
Shannon owns a blue car.	owns(shannon,blue,car).
Shannon owns a 1987 blue car.	owns(shannon,blue,1987,car).

Recall there are several ways to write each clause. All of the following are valid ways to write the logical expression that Shannon owns a 1987 blue car. Notice that the predicate remains the same. It is essential to be consistent.

> owns(shannon,blue,1987,car).
> owns(shannon,1987,blue,car).
> owns(shannon,car,1987,blue).
> owns(blue,1987,car,shannon).

Your First Turbo Prolog Program

It is time for you to write your first Turbo Prolog program. You know how to express simple logical expressions as Turbo Prolog facts, and you know how to ask questions in a form that Turbo Prolog can understand. Get ready to boot your computer. You are about to enter the exciting world of artificial intelligence programming.

The following tutorial guides you through the process of creating and executing a simple Turbo Prolog program. Carefully follow the steps. Compare what you see on your monitor with the printed screens shown in the tutorial.

Tutorial 2-1 Creating Your First Turbo Prolog Program

Starting Turbo Prolog

Boot your computer.

Start Turbo Prolog. Then at the DOS prompt,

TYPE   A:`Prolog` ↵

The Copyright Message Window will be displayed on your monitor.

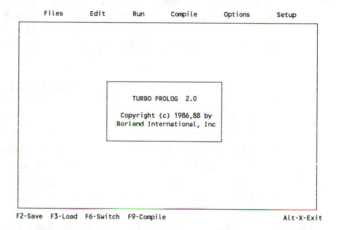

[P] {Space Bar} to move to the Turbo Prolog Programming environment.

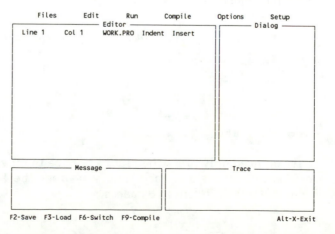

Sections of a Turbo Prolog Program

A Turbo Prolog program consists of four sections. These sections are called:

> domains
> predicates
> goals
> clauses

In writing your program, you will use three of these sections: the **domains** section, the **predicates** section, and the **clauses** section. You will not use the goals section here. You will enter the goals as the program executes.

The Clauses Section

To help you gain familiarity with the Turbo Prolog format, you will type in the Famous Greeks Knowledge Base. It is repeated here for your convenience. Follow the steps below as they guide you through this process.

Famous Greeks Knowledge Base

Logical Expressions	Turbo Prolog Facts
Socrates is a man.	man(socrates).
Aristotle is a man.	man(aristotle).
Athena is a woman.	woman(athena).
Helen is a woman.	woman(helen).
Plato is a woman.	woman(plato).

Select the **Edit** command to place the cursor in the Editor Window.

Type the following clauses as shown:

    clauses ⏎ (The ⏎ is the {Enter} or {Return} key)
<Tab> man(aristotle). ⏎
      man(socrates). ⏎
      woman(athena). ⏎
      woman(helen). ⏎
      woman(plato). ⏎

Note that you need only press the {Tab} key once to indent. The cursor returns to the previous indent position each time you press the {Enter} key. Turbo Prolog presets the automatic indent to 8 spaces.

To move the cursor back to the left margin, just press the left arrow key. Turbo Prolog does not require the program to be indented, but we recommend it. It makes the program easier to understand and debug. Also, don't forget to type the periods at the end of each clause.

Your screen should look as shown below:

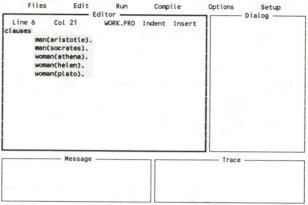

Turbo Prolog is a **compiled** version of Prolog. This means that Turbo Prolog converts the text into binary code before it actually runs. To accommodate the compiler, Turbo Prolog requires two more sections to be added to the program before you can run a program. These sections are the predicates section and the domains section.

The Predicates Section

The predicates section is where you furnish to Turbo Prolog's compiler a picture of each predicate used in the knowledge bases. It precedes the clauses section in the program.

The Famous Greeks Knowledge Base uses two predicates, **man** and **woman**. Thus, in the predicates section, the actual names of the predicates are included along with a general name for the objects of the predicates. The predicate names in the predicates section must match the predicates in the clauses section. However, the object names do not have to match. It is good practice to name the objects in the predicates section with a word that describes the object's general classification. In The Famous Greeks Knowledge Base, the objects are names of persons. Two choices would be good – **name** or **person**. We have chosen **person**. Other choices would be just as good. A general form of these predicates might look like the following:

        man(person)
        woman(person)

Again, these statements define the predicates **man** and **woman** that are used in the clauses section. Person represents the objects in the clauses section.

You might wonder why you entered the clauses section first. This is because after you have written the clauses section, the other sections are quite easy to do. Follow the steps below to enter the predicates section.

Move the cursor to the upper left-hand corner of the Editor Window.

Create a blank line at the top of the Editor by pressing the {Enter} key. Then reposition the cursor to the upper left-hand corner of the Editor Window.

Enter the predicates section as shown below:

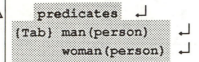

```
    predicates  ↵
{Tab} man(person)  ↵
     woman(person)  ↵
```

Notice that periods are not required in the predicates section. Your screen should now appear as shown below:

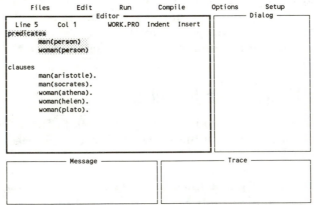

```
     Files      Edit      Run      Compile      Options      Setup
                        ── Editor ──                    ── Dialog ──
   Line 5     Col 1      WORK.PRO   Indent  Insert
 predicates
          man(person)
          woman(person)

 clauses
          man(aristotle).
          man(socrates).
          woman(athena).
          woman(helen).
          woman(plato).



                ── Message ──                  ── Trace ──



 F1-Help F2-Save F3-Load F5-Zoom F6-Next F7-Xcopy F8-Xedit F9-Compile F10-Menu
```

Chapter 2

The Domains Sections

The final section is the domains section. This section informs Turbo Prolog about data types of the objects used in the program. These data types are called domains. Turbo Prolog allows seven standard domain types. They are shown in Figure 2.1.

Figure 2.1: Seven Standard Domain Types

Symbol   A symbol is an object beginning with a lower case letter or a sequence of characters surrounded by quotation marks. The quotation marks are used when the object name does not begin with a lower case letter or when a space is part of the sequence of characters. Examples are:

> henry
> henrys_glove
> "Henry's_glove"
> a_brother_of_henry

String   A string is a group of letters, characters or words enclosed by quotation marks ("). Strings can be manipulated in ways symbols cannot. Strings can be parsed – that is, taken apart so that manipulation of the individual characters may occur. Examples of strings are:

> "henry"
> "henrys glove"
> "a brother of henry"

Symbols and strings can be used interchangeably. However, they are handled differently internally by Turbo Prolog. Symbols are kept in a look-up table, which makes the search and matching for symbols fast. The undesirable features of symbols are that the look-up tables take up computer memory and that inserting new symbols into the look-up table is time consuming. Strings do not have these problems. If memory is not a problem in a program, use symbols. If insertion speed and memory is a factor, use strings. If you need to manipulate the individual characters, use strings.

Integer   An integer is a whole number between -32,768 and +32,768. Decimal points are not displayed in an integer. Examples are:

         13   5327   4   -32544

Commas may not be part of an integer.

Real   A real number includes optional decimals. The range of the accepted real numbers is 1E-307 to 1E+308. Examples are:

         4.56
         1.36784 E+10
         8.

Commas are not allowed. Turbo Prolog represents large numbers using scientific notation.

Char   A char is a single character surrounded by single quotation marks ('). Examples are:

         'Z'   '5'   '$'

File   File is the domain type that defines a symbolic filename. Examples are:

         anyfile
         student_grades
         list_of_electronic_parts

Turbo Prolog uses the symbolic filename to send or receive information to and from the disk. Only one file domain may exist in a program. The file domain names (printer, keyboard, screen and com1) are reserved Turbo Prolog words and may not be used for any other purpose. Printer refers to the device connected to the parallel printer port, and com1 is the number one serial port. See your DOS manual for more information about these devices.

dbasedom   dbasedom refers to Turbo Prolog's special data base domain. See Chapter 11 in your Turbo Prolog User's Guide for information about using this domain type.

The Famous (or is it now infamous?) Greeks Knowledge Base uses one class of object, which we have called person. The data type of person is **symbol.** Symbols are a grouping of letters that stand for something. Symbols must begin with a lower case letter and must contain no blanks.

Enter the domains section now. Move the cursor to the upper left-hand corner of the Editor Window. Press the {Enter} key to make room for the domains section. Then enter the domains section as shown below:

 TYPE

```
domains     ↵
{Tab}    person=symbol     ↵
```

Your screen should now look like the following:

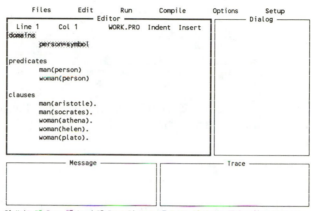

 Check to see that your program is **exactly** like the one shown above. If not, make the proper corrections. When completed move to the next section **Running the Program**.

Running the Program

 Exit the Editor Window by pressing the {Esc} key. Observe that the cursor is returned to the Main Menu.

Select the **Run** command from the Main Menu.

Turbo Prolog now compiles your program. You can watch it through the Message Window. If any errors are detected, the compiling stops, and the cursor is moved to the program line where the error occurred. If this happens, check your program for syntax errors such as misspelled words, missing parentheses, missing periods, sections in the wrong order, and so forth. Compare it with the finished program previously shown. Make corrections as necessary. To continue, press the {F10} key. Turbo Prolog will pick up where it left off and continue until it either encounters another error or it completes compiling. After Turbo Prolog successfully compiles your program, it will display a request for a goal in the Dialog Window as shown below.

Dialog Window

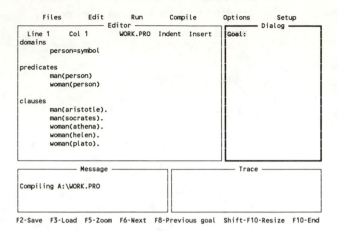

You are now going to ask Turbo Prolog to tell you whether Socrates is a man or not. The question in English is: "Is Socrates a man?" At the Goal request, type the goal as shown below:

TYPE Goal: man(socrates). ↵

Turbo Prolog answers the goal by replying Yes in the Dialog Window. The Dialog Window looks like this:

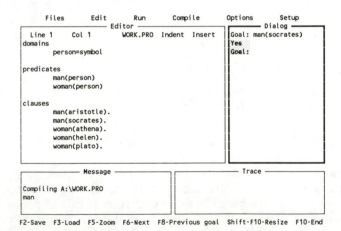

The answer to the goal statement is Yes. Turbo Prolog answers **Yes** and then displays the goals request again, waiting for a new goal to process.

Practice

Run the program again and enter the following goals in the Dialog Window. Remember, you must write the goals in a form that Turbo Prolog can understand. Complete the following exercises. Try to anticipate Turbo Prolog's answer before pressing the [Enter] key.

Pose the question, Is Aristotle a woman?

Stated in the Turbo Prolog predicate form, the question becomes:

woman(aristotle).

At the Goal request enter the new goal:

TYPE   Goal:woman(aristotle).   ↵

Your monitor should show:

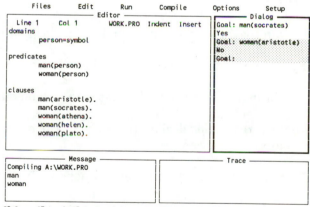

Now ask the following questions. After each goal, you will need to select the **Run** command from the Main Menu to present the Goal prompt.

Goal 1:	1) Is Athena a man?
Goal 2:	2) Is Aristotle a man?
Goal 3:	3) Is Socrates a woman?
Goal 4:	4) Is Plato a man?
Goal 5:	5) Is Helen a Greek?

This completes Chapter 2. In this chapter, you have learned how to write simple Turbo Prolog facts. You have learned to input these facts into the proper Turbo Prolog form. You learned to translate questions into Turbo Prolog goals, and, finally, you learned how to execute a Turbo Prolog program.

Exercises

2-1. Explain the difference between a knowledge base and a data base.

2-2. If your knowledge base contained the following fact:

Abraham Lincoln was the first man to land on the moon.

Would Turbo Prolog declare this to be a true or false fact?
Explain your answer.

2-3. Express the following logical expressions as Turbo Prolog facts.

a. Jimmy has a baseball bat.
b. Mary plays the piano.
c. Birds have feathers.
d. The computer is an Amiga.
e. Who is on first.
f. What is on second.

2-4. Explain the difference between a Turbo Prolog fact and a Turbo Prolog rule.

2-5. A Turbo Prolog fact is always considered to be true. Is a Turbo Prolog rule also considered to be true? Explain your answer.

2-6. Explain how Turbo Prolog searches through a data base for an answer to a question. The following questions will guide you in your answer.

2-7. What is the Turbo Prolog component that does all the "thinking"?

2-8. Write each of the following logical expressions as a Turbo Prolog fact. Each has more than one object.

        a. Sam has a 1987, green, Corvette automobile.
        b. Sam likes cheeseburgers with pickles and onions.
        c. Learning requires intelligence and memory.

2-9. Name the four sections of a Turbo Prolog program and briefly describe the function of each.

2-10. Name and describe the seven standard Turbo Prolog domain types.

2-11. Consider the following Turbo Prolog fact:

        name(last,first,middle)

The term **name** is called the _____.

The terms **last, first,** and **middle** are the _____.

2-12. A Turbo Prolog statement that is assumed true declares a relationship between several objects. What do you call these statements?

2-13. What do you call a Turbo Prolog statement that may be true or false (is conditional)?

2-14. A collection of Turbo Prolog facts is called a _____.

2-15. What do you call a collection of Turbo Prolog facts and rules?

Problems

2-1. Translate the following data base into Turbo Prolog facts.

Data Base	Turbo Prolog Facts
The sky is blue. The grass is green. Dirt is brown. Algae are green. Fungus is white. The cloud is white. Water is clear.	sky(blue).

2-2. Enter the above Turbo Prolog facts into the clauses section. Before you can run the program, you must declare the predicates in the predicates section and specify the domain of the objects in the domains section. Do this, then run the program and ask the program to answer the following questions. The first two questions have been completed to serve as a guide.

Questions	Turbo Prolog Goals	Answers
1. Is the sky blue? 2. Is the sky green? 3. Is fungus black? 4. Is fungus white? 5. Is algae green? 6. Is algae purple? 7. Is grass purple? 8. Is grass green?	sky(blue). sky(green).	Yes No

2-3. Save the program from problem 2-2. Then use the **New file** command to clear the Editor Window.

Here are the facts of another data base. Write a Turbo Prolog program that includes these facts. Ask Turbo Prolog to answer the questions presented in the following table.

Data Base
1. Einstein discovered the laws of relativity.
2. Bohr developed the model of the atom.
3. Newton discovered the laws of motion.
4. Mickey Mouse discovered money.
5. Mendel discovered the laws of genetics.
6. Beethoven wrote symphonies.
7. Watson discovered DNA.
8. Crick discovered DNA.
9. Galileo discovered the moons of Jupiter.
10. Salk discovered the cure for polio.

To help you, the first two facts are translated into Turbo Prolog facts.

1. relativity(einstein).   2. atom(bohr).

After you have completed the program by writing the predicates and domains sections, run the program and have it answer the following questions.

1. Did Watson discover DNA?
2. Did Crick discover DNA?
3. Is it true that Newton discovered the laws of motion?
4. Did Mickey Mouse write symphonies?
5. The model of the atom was developed by Mendel?
6. Did Jonas Salk discover the cure for polio?
7. Did Galileo discover the moons of Jupiter?

2-4. Rewrite the data base presented in problem 2-3 with more than one object per clause. In this case, use the verb as the predicate. For example, the first fact in the data base is that Einstein discovered the laws of relativity. Discovered is the verb, and the two objects of interest are Einstein and the laws of relativity. Writing this fact in terms of two objects and a verb-like predicate results in

discovered(einstein,relativity).

As you can see, the fact now includes information about the relationship between the objects.

Save the program from problem 2-3. Then use the **New file** command to clear the program in the Editor Window. Enter the new data base. Run the program and pose the same questions in the new predicate form.

Chapter 3
Variables

*Like other programming languages, Turbo Prolog uses variables to represent values stored in memory. In other computer languages, variables are assigned a value. However, in Turbo Prolog, variables are considered either to be **bound** to a value or to be **free** (unbound) of a value. Variables can represent more than one value during any one program. This chapter will introduce you to the use of variables, the anonymous variable, the concept of arity, and how to ask questions with variables. Tutorial 3-1, **Building an Intelligent Data Base**, will guide you through the writing of a program that uses variables and poses questions using variables.*

Variables

As in other computer programming languages, Turbo Prolog uses variables to store values in the computer's memory. However, variables work differently in Turbo Prolog than in other languages. Turbo Prolog uses variables to represent objects. When a variable represents an object, that object is said to be bound to that variable. A variable in Turbo Prolog is any name that begins with a capital letter. An object in Turbo Prolog begins with a lower case letter. For example, **Person** is a variable; **person** is an object.

Binding and Unbinding Variables

Turbo Prolog uses pattern matching to solve problems. When given a goal containing a variable, Turbo Prolog looks for a clause with the same predicate. When found, the object in the clause is bound to that variable. The object becomes the value of the variable. Turbo Prolog then places a marker beside the clause. The marker identifies the clause where the binding occurs. This marker occurs in memory. You don't see it on your screen.

A variable is bound until Turbo Prolog unbinds it. When a variable becomes unbound, it is free to be bound to another object. Variables are either bound or free. If a variable is bound, Turbo Prolog knows its value. If a variable is free, Turbo Prolog does not know its value. A bound variable is treated exactly the same as the object it is bound to. Thus when we speak of the value of a variable, we mean the object to which it is bound. Some texts call a bound variable an **instantiated** variable and a free or unbound variable an **uninstantiated** variable. The Turbo Prolog User's Guide uses the terms *bound* and *free*. We will do the same.

Consider, as an example, the following data base:

Intelligent Persons Data Base

Fact	Turbo Prolog Clause
Helen is intelligent.	intelligent(helen).

Let's pose a question to this simple data base using a variable. You might ask "Who is an intelligent person?" Person is the variable. Expressed as a goal, you would type:

Goal:**intelligent(Person).**

Turbo Prolog searches the data base to match the goal's predicate **intelligent** to a clause with the same predicate. The first clause [intelligent(helen).] has **intelligent** as its predicate. The goal matches this clause. The variable **Person** is then bound to the object **helen**. Remember, **Person** is a variable because it begins with a capital letter. From this point on, Turbo Prolog considers the variable **Person** to have the value **helen**. This binding continues until Turbo Prolog frees or unbinds the variable. Turbo Prolog would answer **Person=helen**.

Asking Questions with Variables

Variables are useful when asking a question in Turbo Prolog. If a variable is used in place of an object in a goal statement, it is bound to the object in a corresponding position of a matching clause. The following example shows you how to use a variable in a goal statement.

Let's expand the Intelligent Persons Data Base:

Intelligent Persons Data Base

Fact	Turbo Prolog Clause
Helen is intelligent.	intelligent(helen).
Jane is intelligent.	intelligent(jane).
Jim is intelligent.	intelligent(jim).
John is average.	average(john).

Suppose the question is, "Who are all the intelligent people?" Stated as a Turbo Prolog Goal this question would be:

Goal:**intelligent(Person).**

Turbo Prolog responds with:

> Person=helen
> Person=jane
> Person=jim
> 3 Solutions.

Turbo Prolog declares three people to be intelligent and displays their names. How is it possible for the variable Person to have three values? To understand the answer, you must know how Turbo Prolog searches a data base. Turbo Prolog starts the search at the top of the data base. When it finds a matching fact, a mark is internally placed next to the fact. This happens in your computer's memory; you can't see the mark. The variable becomes bound to the object with the result printed in your Dialog Window. From this point on, the variable represents the object it is bound to. However, the variable may become free to be bound to other objects.

Turbo Prolog does not stop the search when it finds one answer. The inference engine that drives Turbo Prolog keeps searching the data base until it finds all possible solutions. After displaying the value of the object in the Dialog Window, the variable becomes unbound. Turbo Prolog continues its search with the next matching clause binding the variable to the next object. In this case the variable **Person** is bound to the object **jane** (Person=jane). This process continues until all corresponding matches have been found. Here are the steps Turbo Prolog takes to answer the question **intelligent(Person)**.

Step 1

Goal:**intelligent(Person).**

Data base:
    * **intelligent(helen)**.
    intelligent(jane).
    intelligent(jim).
    average(john).

Explanation:

1) The predicate **intelligent** in the goal matches the same predicate in the first clause.

2) Turbo Prolog marks the clause.

3) The variable **Person** is bound to **helen**. We say that **Person** is bound to the object **helen** or **Person** has the value **helen**.

4) Turbo Prolog prints the value of **Person** in the Dialog Window.

       Person=helen

5) The variable is unbound and the search continues. The variable **Person** has no value.

Step 2

Goal:**intelligent(Person).**

Data base:
        intelligent(helen).
    * **intelligent(jane).**
        intelligent(jim).
        average(john).

Explanation:

1) The search continues with the clause following the previously marked clause. Another match occurs with the second clause.

2) Turbo Prolog marks the second clause where the new match takes place.

3) **Person** is bound to **jane**.

4) Turbo Prolog prints the value of **Person** in the Dialog Window.

        Person=jane

5) The variable **Person** is unbound and the search continues with the next clause.

Step 3

Goal:**intelligent(Person).**

Data base:
        intelligent(helen).
        intelligent(jane).
    * **intelligent(jim).**
        average(john).

Explanation:

1) The predicate **intelligent** in the goal matches the third predicate.

2) Turbo Prolog marks the clause.

3) **Person** is bound to **jim**.

4) Turbo Prolog prints the value of **Person** in the Dialog Window.

        Person=jim

5) The variable **Person** is unbound and the search continues.

Step 4

Goal:**intelligent(Person).**

Data base:
                intelligent(helen).
                intelligent(jane).
                intelligent(jim).
                average(john).

Explanation:
                1) The predicate **intelligent** does not match any other
                predicates in the data base. The process stops. Turbo
                Prolog has found all the possible solutions and displays
                the number of solutions in the Dialog Window. Three
                solutions were found.

Anonymous Variables

Variables have two uses in Turbo Prolog. First, a free variable can match any object
in a matching clause. Second, free variables are bound to the matching objects.
However, there are times when you want to use the matching ability of a variable,
but you do not care about binding the variable to the object. For this purpose,
Turbo Prolog provides the **anonymous variable**. Used as part of a goal statement, the anonymous variable substitutes for any object in any fact that otherwise
matches. The underscore character [_] is the anonymous variable.

Again, using the Intelligent Persons Data Base, look at how the anonymous variable works. The new question becomes "Is there an intelligent person listed in this
data base?"

Question: Is there an intelligent person?

    Goal: **intelligent(_).**   <-_ *anonymous variable*

    Clauses: intelligent(helen).
                intelligent(jane).
                intelligent(jim).
                average(john).

    Result: **Yes**

How to Use the Anonymous Variable

The anonymous variable is the underscore character. When given the goal
intelligent (_). , Turbo Prolog begins searching the data base for a match. The
anonymous variable says, "I only want to see if a match exists, I don't care about
the details of that match." The predicate in the goal matches the predicate in the
first clause.

Since the goal has an anonymous variable, Turbo Prolog matches it with the object. The anonymous variable matches **helen**, but is not bound to it. No variables are bound, so Turbo Prolog does not print a value for the variable. At this point, you might think that the search continues. However, the question asks only if there is one intelligent person. Turbo Prolog found one. It displays Yes in the Dialog Window to indicate that it found a match and stops execution.

Now suppose you want to ask the question, "Are there any men?" The goal that asks this question is **man(_)**. However, the data base does not have a predicate called **man**. Rather than answering No because it cannot confirm the clause, Turbo Prolog responds with an error message.

404 Undeclared predicate or misspelling

It cannot find a matching predicate. Therefore, it cannot proceed and uses the error message to question the use of the non-matching predicate. You might think that Turbo Prolog would say No, but it requires that the goal predicate be defined in the predicates sections and be included in the clauses section.

Facts with Two or More Objects

So far, you have used only the simplest form of a Turbo Prolog clause. To write functional data bases, you must learn to represent facts with two or more objects.

Semantic Networks

Much of the current research in artificial intelligence focuses on how the brain represents knowledge. Cognitive psychologists suggest one model of knowledge representation called a semantic network. A semantic network (semantic net) is a picture of clusters of objects and the relationships between these objects.

Semantic networks consist of parts, called nodes, which represent objects. The links that connect the nodes show the relationships between the objects.

Below is a semantic net showing the knowledge one might have about a certain car. The car is a blue, 1985 Nissan Sentra owned by Ray. Here is the semantic net.

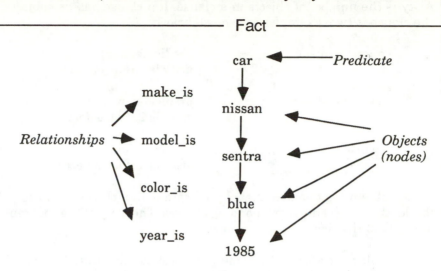

This semantic net shows how the objects (Nissan, Sentra, Blue, and 1985) relate to each other. The relationships are **make_is**, **model_is**, **color_is**, and **year_is**, respectively.

Recall from Chapter 2 that relationships can be stated as a Turbo Prolog predicate in the form:

> relationships(object1,object2,...,objectn.)

The above semantic net expressed as a Turbo Prolog clause becomes:

> **car(nissan,sentra,blue,1985).**

In this clause, **car** is the predicate, and **nissan**, **sentra**, **blue**, and **1985** are objects related to the predicate. Turbo Prolog does not know the relationships. You must keep **make_is**, **year_is**, and the other relationships in mind as you write your programs. You should write your predicates so they have meaning to you. This becomes important when you want to return to a Turbo Prolog program at a later date or when you have a large data base. If you use simple symbols such as x's and y's, your programs will be difficult to debug.

Turbo Prolog can represent information presented in a semantic network. The clause form depicts objects and the relationship between the objects. This is called the predicate form of representing facts. Many applications in Turbo Prolog stem from its ability to represent facts in a semantic network.

Arity

Arity is the number of objects in a clause. If a clause has two objects, the arity of the clause is two. Examples are shown below:

man(socrates).	predicate: man arity is 1 (one object)
owns(car,shannon).	predicate: owns arity is 2 (two objects)
owns(car,shannon,1987,blue).	predicate: owns arity is 4 (four objects)

When attempting to match a goal predicate with a clause predicate, Turbo Prolog checks the arity of the corresponding clauses. The arity of the goal must be equal to the arity of the clause.

Turbo Prolog 2.x allows the same predicate to have different arities, but Turbo Prolog 1.x does not. The rules for determining a match between a goal and clauses in the data base are summarized in Figure 3-1.

Figure 3-1: Rules for Matching Goals and Clauses

1) The predicate of the goal must match the predicate of the clause.

2) The arity of the goal must match the arity of the clause.

3) Objects in the goal match only the corresponding object in the clause. They must be spelled exactly the same and occur in the same position in both clauses.

4) Turbo Prolog treats bound variables as if they were the objects to which they are bound.

5) Unbound variables in the goal can be bound to corresponding objects in the clause.

6) The anonymous variable is free to match any object in a clause. No binding occurs.

If a goal and a clause meet all of the above conditions, a match occurs. Unbound variables are bound to the objects with which they correspond, and the goal succeeds.

Here are some examples of goals and facts and how Turbo Prolog goes about matching them.

Example 1

> Goal: car(buick,green,Make,1987).
>
> Clause: car(__,green,ford,1987).

1) Do the predicates match?   Yes. The goal matches the clause. The predicate of the goal is **car**. The predicate of the clause is also **car**. They match.

2) Do the arities match?   Yes. The number of objects in the goal is four (4). The number of objects in the clause is four (4). The arities match.

3) Do objects in the goal match the clause?   Yes. **green** and **1987** are exact objects in the matches.

4) Can the unbound variables in the goal be bound to corresponding objects in the clause?   Yes. **Make** is a variable and becomes bound to **ford**. The underline character (_) in the clause is an anonymous variable. The place is held, but no binding occurs.

Conclusion: The goal succeeds. The goal matches the clause. The variable **Make** is bound to **ford**, and the anonymous variable acts as a place keeper.

Example 2

> Goal: car(honda,grey,sold,1985).
>
> Clause: auto(honda,grey,_sold,1985).

1) Do the predicates match?   No. The predicate of the goal is **car**, while the predicate of the clause is **auto**. They do not match.

Conclusion: The goal fails. If this were part of an active program, Turbo Prolog would either go on to the next clause or stop execution.

Example 3

> Goal: car(buick,green,Year,ford).
>
> Clause: car(green,buick,Year,ford).

1) Do the predicates match?   Yes. **car** is the predicate of both the goal and the clause.

2) Do the arities match?   Yes. There are four objects in the goal and four objects in the clause.

3) Do the objects in the goal match the objects in the clause?   No. They are not in corresponding order.

Conclusion: No match occurs. The goal fails.

Now that you know how Turbo Prolog finds a match, you are ready to examine the steps used in creating a data base with clauses containing multiple objects. Tutorial 3-1 will guide you through this process. When you complete this tutorial, you will know how to create a relatively sophisticated, intelligent data base using Turbo Prolog.

Tutorial 3-1 Building an Intelligent Data Base

Boot your computer and enter the Turbo Prolog Editor Window.

The data base below contains facts about cars and trucks in a used car lot. These facts are shown below with their corresponding Turbo Prolog clauses:

Used Car Lot Data Base

Facts	Turbo Prolog Clauses
Cars	
1985,Blue,Ford,Mustang	car(1985,blue,ford,mustang).
1981,Red,Ford,Fairlane	car(1981,red,ford,fairlane).
1984,Blue,Buick,Electra	car(1984,blue,buick,electra).
1986,Red,Cadillac,Fleetwood	car(1986,red,cadillac,fleetwood).
1986,Yellow,Chevrolet,Nova	car(1986,yellow,chevrolet,nova).
Trucks	
1985,Red,Dodge,RAM	truck(1985,red,dodge,ram).
1983,Blue,Ford,Ranchero	truck(1983,blue,ford,ranchero).
1981,Yellow,Ford,Van	truck(1981,yellow,ford,van).

Type the automobile data base following the steps below. Don't forget to end each clause with a period.

Clauses Section

clauses ⏎

P <Tab>

car(1985,blue,ford,mustang).　⏎
car(1981,red,ford,fairlane).　⏎
car(1984,blue,buick,electra).　⏎
car(1986,red,cadillac,fleetwood).　⏎
car(1986,yellow,chevrolet,nova).　⏎
　⏎
truck(1985,red,dodge,ram).　⏎
truck(1983,blue,ford,ranchero).　⏎
truck(1981,yellow,ford,van).　⏎

Your monitor should show the following:

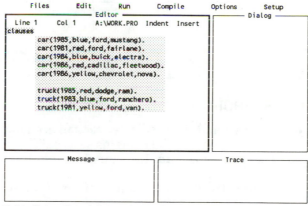

Predicates Section

The data base contains two predicates, **car** and **truck**. Turbo Prolog must be told that these are predicates. You must also tell Turbo Prolog the classes to which the objects belong. In this example, the classes are **year**, **color**, **make**, and **model**. Follow the steps on the next page to enter the predicates section.

Move the cursor to the upper left-hand corner of the Edit Window.

P ↵

Move the cursor to the upper left-hand corner of the Editor Window.

TYPE `predicates` ↵

P <Tab>

```
car(year,color,make,model)   ↵
truck(year,color,make,model)  ↵
```

Your Editor Window should appear as:

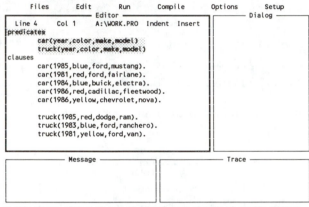

```
        Files      Edit      Run       Compile    Options    Setup
                        ┌──── Editor ────               ┌─── Dialog ───
         Line 4      Col 1      A:\WORK.PRO  Indent  Insert
        predicates
                   car(year,color,make,model)
                   truck(year,color,make,model)
        clauses
                   car(1985,blue,ford,mustang).
                   car(1981,red,ford,fairlane).
                   car(1984,blue,buick,electra).
                   car(1986,red,cadillac,fleetwood).
                   car(1986,yellow,chevrolet,nova).

                   truck(1985,red,dodge,ram).
                   truck(1983,blue,ford,ranchero).
                   truck(1981,yellow,ford,van).


          ┌──── Message ────             ┌──── Trace ────




        F1-Help F2-Save F3-Load F5-Zoom F6-Next F7-Xcopy F8-Xedit F9-Compile F10-Menu
```

Domains Section

 The clauses section and the predicates section are now complete. Before running the program, you must add the domains section. The domain type for **year** is integer. The domain type of **make**, **model**, and **color** is symbol.

 Move the cursor to the upper left-hand corner of the screen.

P {↵}

Move the cursor to the upper left-hand corner of the Editor Window.

TYPE `domains`   ↵

P <Tab>

```
color, make, model=symbol  ↵
year=integer
```

Your program should now include the domains, predicates, and clauses sections as shown below:

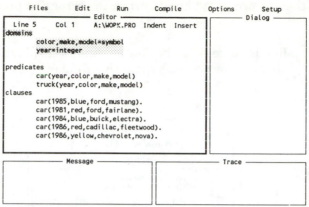

When writing a Turbo Prolog program, you should check several items before running the program.

1) Check for proper parentheses. Parentheses enclose the list of objects in predicates and clauses. The number of left-hand parentheses must be equal to the number of right-hand parentheses.

2) Each clause ends with a period. Domains and predicates do not require the period.

3) Each object begins with a lower case letter.

4) Variables begin with an upper case letter.

Now return the cursor to the Main Menu by pressing the (Esc) key.

Running The Program

This program does not have an internal goal section, thus it will ask you for a goal when it runs. Follow the steps below to run the program.

Select the **Run** command. Either press the letter **R** key, or move the cursor so that it highlights the **Run** command. Then press the (Enter) key.

Turbo Prolog compiles and executes your program. If an error occurs, Turbo Prolog will stop compiling and return the cursor to the Editor Window. The cursor will be located at the point where the compiler detected the error. Compare your screen with the one presented here. Correct the error and press {F10} to continue compiling.

If compiling is successful, the Dialog Window displays the Goal: prompt. The Dialog Window now becomes the active window.

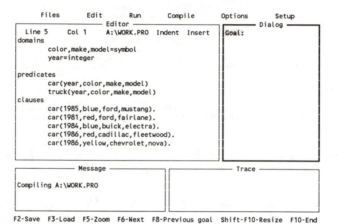

Now ask Turbo Prolog to list the year, color, make, and model of every car in the data base. Enter the following goal.

TYPE   Goal: car(Year, Color, Make, Model).   ↵

All objects in the goal are variables. (They all begin with capital letters.) These variables will be bound to the objects in the clauses. Your screen now shows:

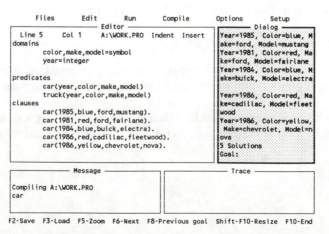

Turbo Prolog displays all the matches to the goal. It tells you the year, color, make, and model of all of the cars in the data base. After it displays the solutions, Turbo Prolog tells you how many solutions it found. It then displays the Goal: prompt to await your next question.

How Turbo Prolog Found the Answers

When you enter a goal, Turbo Prolog looks for a match to the predicate. Look at the first clause and recall the rules for matching. The first fact has **car** as the predicate. All of the variables in the goal are unbound. Thus, they can be bound to the corresponding objects in the clause. For the first clause, **Year** is bound to **1985**, **Color** is bound to **blue**, **Make** to **ford**, and **Model** to **mustang**. Turbo Prolog displays each variable along with the object to which it is bound. The first step is shown below:

Goal:**car(Year,Color,Make,Model).**

clauses

                       ***car(1985,blue,ford,mustang).**
                       car(1981,red,ford,fairlane).
                       car(1984,blue,buick,electra).
                       car(1986,red,cadillac,fleetwood).
                       car(1986,yellow,chevrolet,nova).
                       truck(1985,red,dodge,ram).
                       truck(1983,blue,ford,ranchero).
                       truck(1981,yellow,ford,van).

Turbo Prolog finds all possible solutions to the goal. After a match, Turbo Prolog frees all variables in the goal and moves to the next clause. Using the same rules for matching, the goal and second clause match. **Year**, **Color**, **Make**, and **Model** are bound to the new values: **1981**, **red**, **ford**, and **fairlane**, respectively. Turbo Prolog displays this result in the Dialog Window. The second match is illustrated below:

Goal:**car(Year,Color,Make,Model).**

clauses

                       car(1985,blue,ford,mustang).
                       ***car(1981,red,ford,fairlane).**
                       car(1984,blue,buick,electra).
                       car(1986,red,cadillac,fleetwood).
                       car(1986,yellow,chevrolet,nova).

                       truck(1985,red,dodge,ram).
                       truck(1983,blue,ford,ranchero).
                       truck(1981,yellow,ford,van).

This process continues through the first five clauses. In each case, the predicates match and the variables are bound to the objects. Turbo Prolog displays the values in the Dialog Window, frees the variables, and continues the search. When Turbo Prolog gets to the sixth clause, the predicates do not match (**car** does not match **truck**), so variable binding does not occur. Turbo Prolog moves on to the remaining clauses. None of the remaining predicates match. Turbo Prolog displays the number of successful matches (5 solutions) and stops execution.

Using the Anonymous Variable

The anonymous variable, which is the underline character [_], matches any object in a clause without binding a variable to the object. Suppose you wanted to ask the question, "Are there any trucks on the lot?" Expressed as a Turbo Prolog goal, the question becomes:

Goal:**truck(_,_,_,_).**

Enter the goal **truck(_,_,_,_).** in the Dialog Window and view the result on your monitor screen.

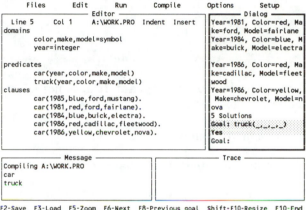

This goal uses four anonymous variables. Because there are two clauses that match the predicate, the anonymous variables match the objects in the truck clauses. No binding occurs, and Turbo Prolog displays nothing. The goal tells Turbo Prolog, "I don't care about the details, just tell me if there are any trucks." Since Turbo Prolog found a match, it prints Yes. This confirms that there is a truck on the lot.

 The anonymous variable is handy when information about a specific object is not required. For example, suppose you want to know the year of all cars on the lot. You could use the goal **car(Year,Color,Make,Model)**. However, not only will you see the year, but also the color, make, and model displayed. Turbo Prolog offers a better way – the anonymous variable. The goal would be:

Goal:car(Year,_,_,_).

TYPE

Goal:**car(Year,_,_,_).** ↵

Your screen displays:

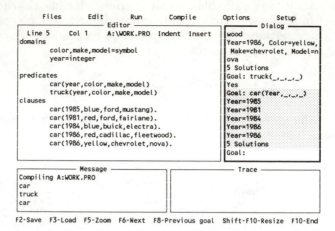

```
        Files       Edit      Run       Compile      Options      Setup
                          ─ Editor ─                          ─ Dialog ─
      Line 5      Col 1      A:\WORK.PRO  Indent  Insert      wood
domains                                                        Year=1986, Color=yellow,
          color,make,model=symbol                               Make=chevrolet, Model=n
          year=integer                                         ova
                                                              5 Solutions
predicates                                                    Goal: truck(_,_,_,_)
          car(year,color,make,model)                          Yes
          truck(year,color,make,model)                        Goal: car(Year,_,_,_)
clauses                                                       Year=1985
          car(1985,blue,ford,mustang).                        Year=1981
          car(1981,red,ford,fairlane).                        Year=1984
          car(1984,blue,buick,electra).                       Year=1986
          car(1986,red,cadillac,fleetwood).                   Year=1986
          car(1986,yellow,chevrolet,nova).                    5 Solutions
                                                              Goal:
                    ─ Message ─                          ─ Trace ─
Compiling A:WORK.PRO
car
truck
car

F2-Save  F3-Load  F5-Zoom  F6-Next  F8-Previous goal  Shift-F10-Resize  F10-End
```

Turbo Prolog displays only the years. It does not show the objects matched to the anonymous variables.

Now try some more examples.

How can you ask the question, "What is the color of all the Fords?"

The Turbo Prolog goal is **car(_,Color,ford,_)**.

The first and last objects are the anonymous variable [_]. As you have seen, objects that match anonymous variables are not displayed. **Color** is a variable and **ford** is an object. Thus, matches will be found with the cars in the lot that are Fords. Each color is displayed as Turbo Prolog searches through the clauses section looking for a match to **ford**. This goal, then, has two anonymous variables, one unbound variable and one object name. Try it.

/TYPE\ Goal: **car(_,Color,ford,_)**. ↵

Your screen will display:

```
        Files       Edit      Run       Compile      Options      Setup
                       ─── Editor ───                    ─── Dialog ───
    Line 5    Col 1      A:\WORK.PRO  Indent  Insert  truck(_,_,_,_)
domains                                                Yes
          color,make,model=symbol                     Goal: car(Year,_,_,_)
          year=integer                                Year=1985
                                                      Year=1981
predicates                                            Year=1984
          car(year,color,make,model)                  Year=1986
          truck(year,color,make,model)                Year=1986
clauses                                               5 Solutions
          car(1985,blue,ford,mustang).                Goal: car(_,Color,ford,_
          car(1981,red,ford,fairlane).                )
          car(1984,blue,buick,electra).               Color=blue
          car(1986,red,cadillac,fleetwood).           Color=red
          car(1986,yellow,chevrolet,nova).            2 Solutions
                                                      Goal:

                ─── Message ───                           ─── Trace ───
Compiling A:\WORK.PRO
car
truck
car

   F2-Save  F3-Load  F5-Zoom  F6-Next  F8-Previous goal  Shift-F10-Resize  F10-End
```

Two Fords were found, one blue and the other red.

To satisfy this goal, Turbo Prolog follows the rules of matching. First, it looks for a clause that has the same predicate. The predicate of the first clause matches. The object **ford** (lower case f) in the goal matches the object **ford** in the clause. The variable **Color** is free to be bound to **blue**. The two anonymous variables in the goal match the two objects in the clause, but no binding occurs. The result is displayed in the Dialog Window. Turbo Prolog then unbinds the variable **Color** and continues the search with the next clause. The second clause also matches. **Color** is now bound to **red**, with the second result displayed in the Dialog Window. **Color** is unbound and the search continues with the next clause. None of the remaining clauses match because none are Ford cars. Turbo displays the number of solutions and stops execution.

Turbo Prolog can have compound goals. You can use this feature in asking questions. Suppose you want Turbo Prolog to list the make and model of all the cars and trucks on the lot. The goal that would ask this question is:

car(_,_,Make,Model) or truck(_,_,Make,Model).

Compound goals are discussed in detail in the next chapter. For now, try a few to see how they work.

This goal says, "If it is a car or a truck, display its make and model." Try the goal as shown below:

TYPE `Goal:car(_,_,Make,Model) or truck(_,_,Make,Model).` ⏎

Turbo Prolog lists the make and model of all of the cars and trucks in the data base, as shown in the screen display:

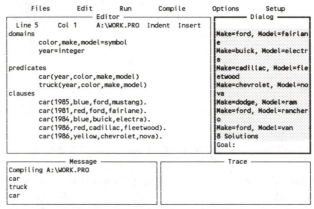

Notice that part of the answer scrolled off the Dialog Window. Later you will learn how to expand this window.

Practice

Try the following questions. First, convert the question to a Turbo Prolog goal. Then enter the goal and note the results. To get you started, look at the first two examples provided below:

Questions	Turbo Prolog Goals
What is the year of the trucks?	truck(Year,_,_,_).
Are there any Chevrolet cars?	car(_,_,chevrolet,_).
What is the make of the yellow truck?	
What are the makes of all the trucks?	
What cars are red?	
List all the information about 1986 cars.	
Is there a yellow truck on the lot?	
Is there a green Buick Electra?	
Is there a blue Cadillac Fleetwood?	
List all the years of the cars and trucks.	
List everything in the data base.	

This completes Chapter 3. Complete the exercises and problems and then move on to Chapter 4 where you will learn about compound goals and backtracking.

Exercises

3-1.   How does Turbo Prolog recognize an object as a variable?

3-2.   What is the term for a variable that has not been matched to an object?

3-3.   What is the term for a variable that has been matched to an object?

3-4.   What is the name for a diagram that shows objects and relationships?

3-5.   What character is used for the anonymous variable?

3-6.   What is the function of an anonymous variable?

3-7.   Define the term *arity*. What is its importance in Turbo Prolog?

3-8.   List the rules (process) for matching a goal to a predicate.

3-9.   Do the following goals match the corresponding predicates?

Goal	Predicate	Match (Y/N)
likes(X,george).	likes(mary,george)	
sky(blue,cloudy,_).	sky(blue,cloudy,storm,rain)	
grades(A,B,C,D).	gpa(98,35,78,68)	
grades(A,_,_,_).	grades(35,99,97,88)	

Problems

3-1. Four fighter aircraft are observed to have different flight characteristics that make each aircraft suitable for a particular mission. Write a Turbo Prolog program that will specify the correct aircraft for a requested mission. The aircraft and the type of missions suitable for each aircraft are shown below:

AD-6 Skyraider	Low-level bombing. Infantry support. Carrier based.
P-51 Mustang	Air-to-air combat. Infantry support. Land based.
TBF Avenger	Torpedo delivery. Sea support. Carrier based.
FAC Piper Cub	Forward air control. Land support. Land based.

As the Commander of a war zone, ask your computer to supply answers to the following questions.

a. Specify aircraft for low-level bombing.

b. Which aircraft can fly as a forward air controller?

c. Which aircraft are on an aircraft carrier?

d. Which aircraft are based in North Africa?

e. You want to launch a torpedo attack against enemy ships. Which aircraft can do the job?

f. The Marines need help. Dispatch an aircraft to support their position. Which aircraft will you dispatch?

3-2. Write a Turbo Prolog program that will tell the principal of a school whether a certain course is available at a period, on a certain day, and with a certain teacher. For example suppose Joe Student wants to take English at third period on Wednesday with Dr. Asimov. Is this possible? The data base is listed below. Translate the information into Turbo Prolog clauses and pose questions to the data base.

Data Base

Course	Period	Teacher	Day
English	1	Hemingway	Monday
English	3	Steinbeck	Wednesday
English	2	Asimov	Thursday
Mathematics	4	Von Neuman	Monday
Mathematics	5	Godel	Thursday
Chemistry	2	Pauling	Thursday
Physics	5	Einstein	Tuesday
Geography	3	Columbus	Friday
Geography	4	Drake	Thursday

Possible Questions:

Who teaches English?
Who teaches English on Thursday?
Who teaches English on Wednesday and during what period?
What does Godel teach?
What does Godel teach and during which days and periods?
What courses are offered on Thursday?
What courses are offered in period 5?
What courses are offered in period 5, who teaches them, and on what days are they offered?
Does Einstein teach English?
Is Physics offered on Tuesdays?
What courses are offered on Fridays and who teaches them?
Is Oceanography offered at this school?

Variables

Chapter 4
Compound Goals and Backtracking

*Compound goals and the use of logical operators are introduced in this chapter. Backtracking is the single most important concept in Turbo Prolog programming. This chapter spends considerable time on backtracking. Tutorial 4-1, **Example of Backtracking**, guides you through this important concept.*

Compound Goals and Backtracking

In the previous chapters, you learned to write simple goals with one predicate. Recall some of those questions. Is Socrates a man? What are the colors of the Ford cars? Who are the intelligent people? Turbo Prolog can also solve goals with more than one predicate. Suppose you wanted to know the make of all the cars that are blue and manufactured after 1984. Or perhaps you want to list either the people that are intelligent or those who are average. These are examples of compound goals. A compound goal consists of two or more goals, called **subgoals**, joined by the logical operators **AND** or **OR**.

The AND Operator

The form of a compound goal with the AND logical operator is:

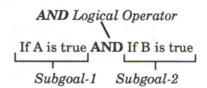

The compound goal is True if both Subgoal-1 and Subgoal-2 are True.

*To successfully satisfy a compound goal with the logical operator **AND**, each of the subgoals must be satisfied.*

The OR Operator

You can also form a compound goal with the connective word **OR**. Examples are: The president of the bank **OR** an officer of the bank. Who is the owner of the car **OR** the driver of the car? The **OR** operator connects two or more subgoals.

The form of a compound goal using the **OR** operator is:

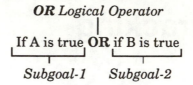

OR Logical Operator

If A is true **OR** if B is true

Subgoal-1   Subgoal-2

This compound goal is true if either Subgoal-1 or Subgoal-2 is true.

*To satisfy a goal with the logical operator **OR**, only one of the subgoals need be satisfied.*

Other Symbols Used for AND and OR

To be compatible with other versions of Prolog, Turbo Prolog allows the use of the symbols comma **[,]** and semi-colon **[;]** as substitutes for the **AND** and **OR** logical operators, respectively. The following interchangeable expressions of compound goals would be acceptable to Turbo Prolog:

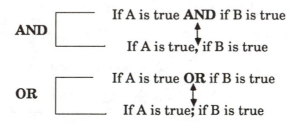

AND   If A is true **AND** if B is true

If A is true, if B is true

OR   If A is true **OR** if B is true

If A is true; if B is true

While the comma and semicolon are perfectly acceptable to Turbo Prolog, we recommend that you use **AND** and **OR** instead of the symbols, until you become more familiar with Turbo Prolog.

Mathematical Operators

Turbo Prolog utilizes mathematical operators as well as logical operators. These are the standard algebraic operators used in all other computer languages. They are shown below:

Mathematical Operators

>	Greater than	/	Divided by
<	Less than	*	Multiplied by
=	Equal to	>=	Greater than or equal to
+	Plus	<=	Less than or equal to
-	Minus	<>	Not equal to

Expressing Compound Goals in Turbo Prolog

Recall the used car lot data base from Chapter 3 which is reproduced below.

```
car(1985,blue,ford,mustang).
car(1981,red,ford,fairlane).
car(1984,blue,buick,electra).
car(1986,red,cadillac,fleetwood).
car(1986,yellow,chevrolet,nova).

truck(1985, red,dodge,ram).
truck(1983,blue,ford,ranchero).
truck(1981,yellow,ford,van).
```

This data base contains facts which describe the year, color, make, and model of the five cars and three trucks.

Using the AND Operator

Suppose you want to know the make and year of all cars manufactured in 1985 or later. That is, you want a list of vehicles that meet two criteria. The vehicle must be a car, and it must be made in the year 1985 or later.

Expressed as a Turbo Prolog compound goal it would be:

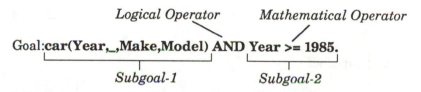

The goal asks Turbo Prolog to list the make and model of all cars manufactured in 1985 or later. In this example, the anonymous variable represents the color of the car. When Turbo Prolog displays the results, the color will not be displayed. A variable name could be used instead, and the color would be displayed.

If this goal were used, the result would be:

```
Year=1985,Make=ford,Model=mustang
Year=1986,Make=cadillac,Model=fleetwood
Year=1986,Make=chevrolet,Model=nova
3 Solutions.
```

Three cars were manufactured in 1985 or later.

Using the OR Operator

Compound goals may also be formed by using the logical operator **OR**. Using the same automobile data base, suppose you want to know the colors and models of all 1981 Fords on the lot (cars or trucks). Expressed as a Turbo Prolog compound goal, this question becomes:

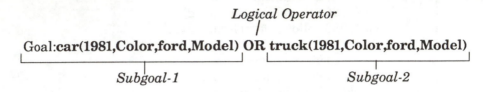

Logical Operator

Goal:**car(1981,Color,ford,Model) OR truck(1981,Color,ford,Model)**

Subgoal-1   *Subgoal-2*

Given this goal, Turbo Prolog would search through the data base looking for either a 1981 Ford car or a 1981 Ford truck. It would find and display the following:

> Color=blue,Model=ranchero
> Color=yellow, Model=van

The goal is satisfied if either one of the subgoals is satisfied.

Summary

Turbo Prolog forms a compound goal by connecting two or more subgoals with the logical operators **AND** and **OR**.

To satisfy a goal formed with **AND**, all subgoals must succeed.

To satisfy a goal formed with the **OR** operator, only one of the subgoals must be satisfied.

Turbo Prolog allows you to replace the word **AND** with the comma [,] and the word **OR** with a semicolon [;]. This makes Turbo Prolog compatible with other versions of Prolog. Use the words until you are familiar with the operation of the logical operators.

Backtracking

To understand how Turbo Prolog satisfies compound goals, you must learn the rules of backtracking. Recall the compound goal that asked Turbo Prolog to list the cars built during or after 1985.

Goal:**car(Year,_,Make,_) AND Year >= 1985.**

Here, a compound goal is formed by joining two subgoals with the logical operator **AND**. For the goal to succeed, both subgoals must succeed. The two subgoals are:

Subgoal-1:   car(Year,_,Make,_)

and

Subgoal-2:   Year >= 1985

In contrast to traditional procedural languages, the path that a Turbo Prolog program follows is not determined by the programmer. Instead it is determined by Turbo Prolog's inference engine. This path is called the **flow of satisfaction**.

Flow of Satisfaction and Backtracking

When given a compound goal, Turbo Prolog attempts to satisfy the leftmost subgoal first. When a match is found, the variables of that subgoal are bound, and Turbo Prolog moves to the second subgoal. If the second subgoal succeeds, Turbo Prolog moves to the third subgoal attempting to find a match. If the third subgoal fails, Turbo Prolog backtracks to the second subgoal, attempting to find an alternate match. This process continues until all possible matches to the goal are found. If this sounds a bit complicated, it's simply because it is. The ability of Turbo Prolog to backtrack is at the very core of the inference engine that drives it. One way to get a feel for how backtracking works is to experiment with it. Let's look at an example to see how Turbo Prolog does it.

Below is a step-by-step explanation of how Turbo Prolog goes about solving this goal. Study these steps. They outline the flow of satisfaction (backtracking) that Turbo Prolog uses to solve a compound goal. The compound goal is:

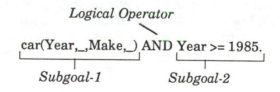

In each diagram, the top box represents Subgoal-1, and the bottom box represents Subgoal-2. The arrows indicate the flow of satisfaction. When the program starts, the flow of satisfaction begins with the first subgoal (entering the diagram from the top). When Turbo Prolog enters a goal from above, it is said to be calling the goal. Notice that the subgoal and clause under consideration are highlighted. When one or more of the goal's variables become bound to objects in a clause, a marker is placed beside that clause.

Step 1

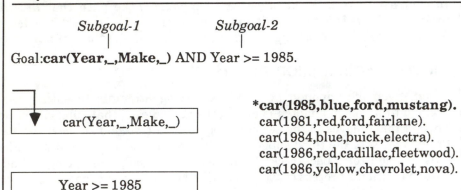

Subgoal-1   *Subgoal-2*

Goal:**car(Year,_,Make,_)** AND Year >= 1985.

| car(Year,_,Make,_) |

| Year >= 1985 |

> ***car(1985,blue,ford,mustang).**
> car(1981,red,ford,fairlane).
> car(1984,blue,buick,electra).
> car(1986,red,cadillac,fleetwood).
> car(1986,yellow,chevrolet,nova).

<u>Variables Bound</u>
Year=1985, Make=ford

Turbo Prolog starts with Subgoal-1. It first looks to match Subgoal-1 with a clause in the knowledge base starting at the top of the knowledge base.

Subgoal-1 matches the first clause. The predicate **car** of Subgoal-1 matches the predicate **car** of the first clause in the data base. There are four objects in Subgoal-1 and four objects in the first clause; thus, the arities match. Next, the variables **Year** and **Make** are then bound to **1985** and **ford**, respectively. Because Subgoal-1 found a match the with first clause, an asterisk (*) is placed next to the clause. This represents the internal mark that Turbo Prolog uses to indicate the clause which matches the sub-goal.

The flow of satisfaction now proceeds to Subgoal-2. Remember, for a compound goal with the logical operator **AND** to succeed, all subgoals must succeed. Thus, Subgoal-2 must be satisfied for the entire goal to succeed.

Step 2

Goal:car(Year,_,Make,_) AND **Year >= 1985.**

Subgoal-2 is entered from above; we say it is **called**.

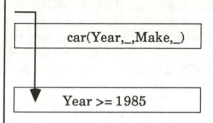

*car(1985,blue,ford,mustang).
car(1981,red,ford,fairlane).
car(1984,blue,buick,electra).
car(1986,red,cadillac,fleetwood).
car(1986,yellow,chevrolet,nova).

<u>Variables Bound</u>
Year=1985, Make=ford

Because the variable **Year** is already bound to **1985** from the first subgoal, the second subgoal reads it as 1985. That is, Turbo Prolog's inference engine sees Subgoal-2 as:

1985 >= 1985

This statement is true.

Because both subgoals succeed, the entire goal succeeds, and Turbo Prolog displays the results in the Dialog Window (Year=1985, Make=ford).

At this point, one solution has been found. However, Turbo Prolog is not satisfied with just one solution. It wants to look through the entire data base. Therefore, the inference engine retreats to Subgoal-1 to try for another solution. This backwards movement is called **backtracking**.

Step 3

Goal:**car(Year,_,Make,_)** AND Year >= 1985.

When Turbo Prolog backtracks to a previous subgoal to look in the data base for another solution, the bound variables for that subgoal are unbound. Beginning at the marker, Turbo Prolog attempts to find a match with the next clause (Subgoal-1 is again active; **Year** and **Make** are unbound). Turbo Prolog moves to the clause immediately following the marker, and a match is found with the second clause. **Year** is now bound to **1981** and **Make** to **ford**. The mark moves from Clause-1 to Clause-2 to indicate that the variables of Subgoal-1 have been bound to the objects in the second clause.

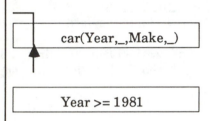

car(1985,blue,ford,mustang).
*car(1981,red,ford,fairlane).
car(1984,blue,buick,electra).
car(1986,red,cadillac,fleetwood).
car(1986,yellow,chevrolet,nova).

Variables Bound
Year=1981, Make=ford

Step 4

At Subgoal-2, the variable **Year** is bound to the object **1981**. Turbo Prolog thus sees Subgoal-2 as:

1981 >= 1985

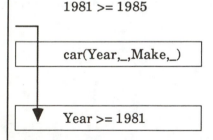

car(1985,blue,ford,mustang).
*car(1981,red,ford,fairlane).
car(1984,blue,buick,electra).
car(1986,red,cadillac,fleetwood).
car(1986,yellow,chevrolet,nova).

Variables Bound
Year=1981, Make=ford

The variable **Year** is already bound to **1981**. When the comparison is made in Subgoal-2, **Year** is not greater than or equal to 1985. Turbo Prolog evaluates the expression **1981 >= 1985** as false. Subgoal-2 fails. As a result, the entire goal fails, and Turbo Prolog backtracks to Subgoal-1 to find another solution.

Step 5

Turbo Prolog frees the bound variables and backtracks to Subgoal-1. Subgoal-1 now matches Clause-3. **Year** is bound to **1984**, and **Make** is bound to **buick**.

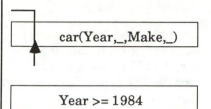

car(1985,blue,ford,mustang).
car(1981,red,ford,fairlane).
*car(1984,blue,buick,electra).
car(1986,red,cadillac,fleetwood).
car(1986,yellow,chevrolet,nova).

<u>Variables Bound</u>
Year=1984, Make=buick

Subgoal-1 is again satisfied, and Turbo Prolog moves to Subgoal-2.

Step 6

Looking at Subgoal-2, Turbo Prolog now sees Subgoal-2 as:

1984 >= 1985.

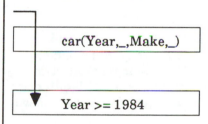

car(1985,blue,ford,mustang).
car(1981,red,ford,fairlane).
* car(1984,blue,buick,electra).
car(1986,red,cadillac,fleetwood).
car(1986,yellow,chevrolet,nova).

<u>Variables Bound</u>
Year=1984, Make=buick

Subgoal-2 is false, so it fails. When a subgoal fails, the entire goal fails, backtracking occurs, the variables of Subgoal-1 are unbound, and the flow of satisfaction reverses back to Subgoal-1.

Step 7

Subgoal-1 next looks to Clause-4 for a match. **Year** is bound to **1986**, and **Make** is bound to **cadillac**. Subgoal-1 succeeds, and Clause-4 is marked (*).

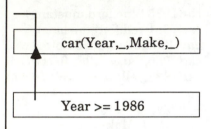

car(1985,blue,ford,mustang).
car(1981,red,ford,fairlane).
car(1984,blue,buick,electra).
*car(1986,red,cadillac,fleetwood).
car(1986,yellow,chevrolet,nova).

<u>Variables Bound</u>
Year=1986, Make=cadillac

Turbo Prolog proceeds to Subgoal-2.

Step 8

Because **Year** is greater than or equal to **1985**, Subgoal-2 succeeds, and the entire goal succeeds. Turbo Prolog displays the answer in the Dialog Window.

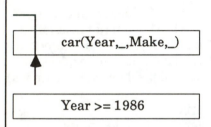

car(1985,blue,ford,mustang).
car(1981,red,ford,fairlane).
car(1984,blue,buick,electra).
*car(1986,red,cadillac,fleetwood).
car(1986,yellow,chevrolet,nova).

<u>Variables Bound</u>
Year=1986, Make=cadillac

Turbo Prolog backtracks to Subgoal-1 to search for more matches. The variables are unbound, and the search continues with the clause following the marked (*) clause.

Step 9

Subgoal-1 matches Clause-5. **Year** is bound to **1986**, and **Make** is bound to **chevrolet**. Clause-5 is marked.

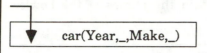

car(1985,blue,ford,mustang).
car(1981,red,ford,fairlane).
car(1984,blue,buick,electra).
car(1986,red,cadillac,fleetwood).
*car(1986,yellow,chevrolet,nova).

Variables Bound
Year=1986, Make=chevrolet

Having succeeded with Subgoal-1, Turbo Prolog moves to Subgoal-2.

Step 10

Subgoal-2 succeeds because Subgoal-2 is seen by Turbo Prolog as:

> 1986 >= 1985

Subgoal-2 is indeed true, and the entire goal succeeds. The results are displayed in the Dialog Window.

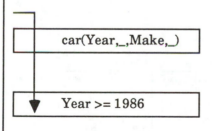

car(1985,blue,ford,mustang).
car(1981,red,ford,fairlane).
car(1984,blue,buick,electra).
car(1986,red,cadillac,fleetwood).
*car(1986,yellow,chevrolet,nova).

Variables Bound
Year=1986, Make=chevrolet

The marked clause is the last clause in the data base. Since there are no more solutions to find, Turbo Prolog reports 3 solutions found and stops execution of the program.

This has been a brief introduction to the use of compound goals, flow of satisfaction, and backtracking. The ability to backtrack is at the core of the inference engine that drives Turbo Prolog. You can get a feel for backtracking by writing a program and running it. In Tutorial 4-1, you will input a simple program, give it a compound goal, and follow the steps to the solution by using the **Trace** command.

Tutorial 4-1 Example of Backtracking

Boot your computer and enter the Turbo Prolog Editor.

The data base considered in this example contains facts about four people in a bowling tournament. The clauses contain the names of the bowlers and their ranking.

Facts	Turbo Prolog Clauses
Ray is an expert bowler.	bowler(ray,expert).
Dan is a novice bowler.	bowler(dan,novice).
Francis is an expert bowler.	bowler(francis,expert).
Don is an expert bowler.	bowler(don,expert).

To enter the data base, type the clauses section as shown below.

    clauses   ↵

P   **<Tab>**

    bowler(ray,expert).   ↵
    bowler(dan,novice).   ↵
    bowler(francis,expert).   ↵
    bowler(don,expert).   ↵

Your monitor should display:

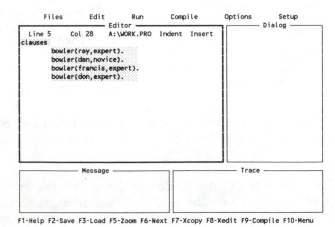

Chapter 4

Predicates Section

Now describe the **bowler** predicate in the predicates section. Use the terms **name** and **rank** to describe the objects.

Move the cursor to the upper left-hand corner of the Editor Window.

{↵} [Press the {Enter} key twice to insert blank lines]

Return the cursor to the upper left-hand corner.

predicates ↵

<Tab>

bowler(name,rank)

Your monitor will show:

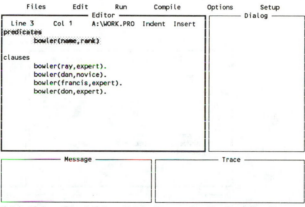

```
         Files      Edit     Run     Compile     Options     Setup
                            Editor                       Dialog
      Line 3      Col 1      A:\WORK.PRO   Indent   Insert
    predicates
            bowler(name,rank)

    clauses
            bowler(ray,expert).
            bowler(dan,novice).
            bowler(francis,expert).
            bowler(don,expert).




                       Message                      Trace



   F1-Help F2-Save F3-Load F5-Zoom F6-Next F7-Xcopy F8-Xedit F9-Compile F10-Menu
```

Compound Goals and Backtracking

Domains Section

Two sections of the program are now completed – the clauses section and the predicates section. Now input the domain type of the objects. Both of the objects, **name** and **rank**, are in the symbol domain. Enter this information in the domains section as shown in the next steps.

Move the cursor to the upper left-hand corner of the Editor Window.

[↵] [Press (Enter) key twice to make room for the domains section.]

Return the cursor to the upper left-hand top of the Editor Window.

TYPE   domains ↵

P   <Tab>

TYPE   name,rank=symbol

Your monitor displays:

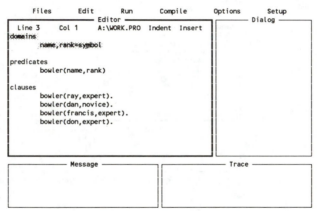

```
        Files       Edit       Run       Compile      Options       Setup
                          Editor                                  Dialog
    Line 3      Col 1      A:\WORK.PRO  Indent  Insert
domains
          name,rank=symbol

predicates
          bowler(name,rank)

clauses
          bowler(ray,expert).
          bowler(dan,novice).
          bowler(francis,expert).
          bowler(don,expert).




            Message                                   Trace



F1-Help F2-Save F3-Load F5-Zoom F6-Next F7-Xcopy F8-Xedit F9-Compile F10-Menu
```

Check your data base against that shown above. Check parentheses, periods after each clause, and commas. It is now time to run the program.

P   {Esc} [Moves the cursor to the Main Menu]

Choose the **Run** command in the Main Menu.

Your program now compiles and runs. If any errors are present, Turbo Prolog stops and displays the cursor at the location in the program where the error occurred.

Correct the error and continue compiling by pressing {F10}. When compilation is successful, the goal request will be displayed in the Dialog Window.

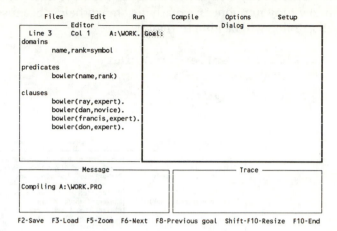

NOTE: We have expanded the Dialog Window so that you can follow the program more clearly. Your screen will look different from this one, but that is all right.

One possible use of the program is to match the expert players with each other to determine who should play whom. Player1 will be the variable to represent the first expert bowler, and Player2 represents the second player. The goal posed to the program is: "List all possible pairs of expert bowlers."

Posed as a Turbo Prolog Goal, this becomes:

```
bowler(Player1,expert) and
bowler(Player2,expert) and
Player1<>Player2.
```

This goal says:

    Player 1 is an expert and
    Player 2 is a expert and
    Player 1 is not the same as Player 2.

Enter the goal as shown below, and view the results in your Dialog Window. Do not press the {Enter} key until the entire goal is entered. As you type the goal, notice that Turbo Prolog wraps the words to the next line. What you type in your Dialog Window may not appear exactly as shown below because of the wrap around, but Turbo Prolog will be able to read it.

Goal:bowler(Player1,expert) and
      bowler(Player2,expert) and
      Player1<>Player2.   ↵

```
          Files      Edit      Run      Compile      Options      Setup
                  Editor                              Dialog
    Line 3     Col 1      A:\WORK.  Goal: bowler(Player1,expert) and bowler(Player
    domains                         2,expert) and Player1 <> Player2
            name,rank=symbol        Player1=ray, Player2=francis
                                    Player1=ray, Player2=don
    predicates                      Player1=francis, Player2=ray
            bowler(name,rank)       Player1=francis, Player2=don
                                    Player1=don, Player2=ray
    clauses                         Player1=don, Player2=francis
            bowler(ray,expert).     6 Solutions
            bowler(dan,novice).     Goal:
            bowler(francis,expert).
            bowler(don,expert).



                  Message                              Trace
    Compiling A:\WORK.PRO
    bowler


    F2-Save  F3-Load  F5-Zoom  F6-Next  F8-Previous goal  Shift-F10-Resize  F10-End
```

Turbo Prolog found six solutions to the goal.

Ray can play Francis and Don; Francis can play Ray and Don; and Don can play Ray and Francis. Dan, not an expert, cannot play anyone.

How Turbo Prolog Found the Answers

Understanding how Turbo Prolog solves this problem is critical to understanding the fundamentals of AI programming. The balance of this tutorial examines how Turbo Prolog uses backtracking to find the answers. To aid the discussion, the goal and data base are repeated below.

The compound goal is:

bowler(Player1,expert) and   *<— Subgoal-1*
bowler(Player2,expert) and   *<— Subgoal-2*
Player1<>Player2.   *<— Subgoal-3*

The data base is:

bowler(ray,expert).	<— *Clause-1*
bowler(dan,novice).	<— *Clause-2*
bowler(francis,expert).	<— *Clause-3*
bowler(don,expert).	<— *Clause-4*

Notice that the subgoals are joined with the **AND** operator. Thus, all subgoals must be satisfied for the entire goal to succeed.

The Trace feature of Turbo Prolog will be used to help you understand how Turbo Prolog finds the answers. To turn on the Trace Window, you must insert the word **Trace** as the first command of the program. The **Trace** command tells Turbo Prolog to execute the program one step at a time. You control the execution of the steps by use of the {F10} function key. Each time you press the key, the program executes one step. This permits you to see what is happening as the program runs. Each step is displayed in the Trace Window.

Press the {Esc} key to move the cursor to the Main Menu. Select the **Edit** command to move the cursor to the Editor Window.

Add the **Trace** command to the program by moving the cursor to the upper left-hand corner of the screen. Insert a blank line by pressing the {Enter} key. Return the cursor to the upper left-hand corner of Editor Window. Type the **Trace** command. When completed, your monitor should display the following:

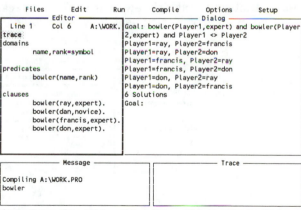

Compound Goals and Backtracking

Now run the edited version of the program. Move the cursor to the Main Menu (press {Esc} key). Select the **Run** command.

If your program is without errors, the goal request is displayed in the Dialog Window. If an error occurs, the cursor will be displayed in the Editor Window where the error occurs. Check the program for syntax errors. Correct the error(s), and continue by pressing {F10} key. When the goal request is displayed in the Dialog Window, type the goal again as shown below, or press the {F8} function key to recall the last goal.

/TYPE\   Goal:**bowler(Player1,expert) and**
              bowler(Player2,expert) and
              Player1 <> Player2.   ⏎

Recall that the comma [,] can replace the word **AND** when joining subgoals. You may use either the comma or the word **AND** for the logical operator. Using the words make the program easier to read, but the choice is up to you.

When you press the {Enter} key, Turbo Prolog begins running your program. It displays the first step in the Trace Window. To continue to the next step, press the {F10} key. Read the explanation in the Trace Window each time. At times, the cursor will be in the Editor Window at the location in the program related to the trace message. As you proceed, compare the trace message with the one shown in the book. Continue through the program one step at a time, reading the explanation in the boxes.

The first step is shown below and in the Trace Window on your display. Each step displayed in your Trace Window is also shown in the book at the beginning of the discussion of that step. Each time you are asked to press {F10}, we will explain the various operations Turbo Prolog uses to work through the program.

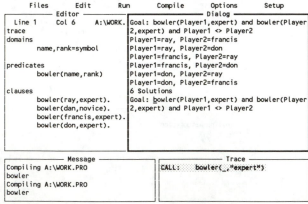

CALL:bowler(_,"expert")

CALL indicates that Turbo Prolog is solving a new goal. This means that the flow arrow enters the goal from the top (The cursor is flashing on Subgoal-1 in the Dialog Window). Turbo Prolog is looking for a match to Subgoal-1 and uses the anonymous variable as the first object. This means that it does not want to know the value of this object. It is looking for a match to **expert** only. Also note that Turbo Prolog converted the domain type of the object from symbol type to string type. This is indicated by the quote marks around the word "expert". Symbols and strings are treated the same in Turbo Prolog.

Goal: **bowler(Player1,expert)** and bowler(Player2,expert) and
        Player1 <> Player2

P {F10} [to continue]

```
        Files      Edit      Run      Compile      Options      Setup
        ┌─── Editor ───────────────┐┌──────── Dialog ──────────────────┐
        │Trace  Line 9   Col 9  A:\││Goal: bowler(Player1,expert) and bowler(Player│
        │domains                   ││2,expert) and Player1 <> Player2  │
        │        name,rank=symbol  ││Player1=ray, Player2=francis      │
        │                          ││Player1=ray, Player2=don          │
        │predicates                ││Player1=francis, Player2=ray      │
        │        bowler(name,rank) ││Player1=francis, Player2=don      │
        │                          ││Player1=don, Player2=ray          │
        │clauses                   ││Player1=don, Player2=francis      │
        │        bowler(ray,expert).││6 Solutions                      │
        │        bowler(dan,novice).││Goal: bowler(Player1,expert) and bowler(Player│
        │        bowler(francis,expert).││2,expert) and Player1 <> Player2│
        │        bowler(don,expert).││                                  │
        │                          ││                                  │
        └──────────────────────────┘└──────────────────────────────────┘
        ┌──── Message ─────────────┐┌──────── Trace ───────────────────┐
        │Compiling A:\WORK.PRO     ││CALL:    bowler(_,"expert")       │
        │bowler                    ││                                  │
        │Compiling A:\WORK.PRO     ││                                  │
        │bowler                    ││                                  │
        └──────────────────────────┘└──────────────────────────────────┘
     F1-Help F2-Save F5-Zoom  F10-Step  Shift-F10-Resize  Alt-T-Trace on/off  Esc-End
```

The cursor moves to the first clause in the Editor Window.

The goal matches the first clause. The cursor is under the letter "b" in Clause-1 in the Editor Window to indicate this. No new message appears in the Trace Window. A match of predicates has been found.

bowler(Player1,expert) and
bowler(Player2,expert) and Player1<>Player2.

<u>Variables Bound</u>   **bowler(ray,expert).**
Player 1=unbound   bowler(dan,novice).
Player 2=unbound   bowler(francis,expert).
                                          bowler(don,expert).

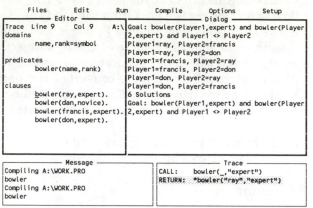

```
         Files      Edit      Run     Compile     Options    Setup
       ┌──────── Editor ────────┐┌──────────── Dialog ──────────────┐
       │Trace  Line 9   Col 9  A:\││Goal: bowler(Player1,expert) and bowler(Player│
       │domains                  ││2,expert) and Player1 <> Player2              │
       │        name,rank=symbol ││Player1=ray, Player2=francis                  │
       │                         ││Player1=ray, Player2=don                      │
       │predicates               ││Player1=francis, Player2=ray                  │
       │        bowler(name,rank)││Player1=francis, Player2=don                  │
       │                         ││Player1=don, Player2=ray                      │
       │clauses                  ││Player1=don, Player2=francis                  │
       │        bowler(ray,expert).  ││6 Solutions                               │
       │        bowler(dan,novice).  ││Goal: bowler(Player1,expert) and bowler(Player│
       │        bowler(francis,expert).││2,expert) and Player1 <> Player2        │
       │        bowler(don,expert).  ││                                          │
       │                         ││                                              │
       │                         ││                                              │
       └─────────────────────────┘└──────────────────────────────────────────────┘
       ┌──────── Message ────────┐┌──────────── Trace ───────────────┐
       │Compiling A:\WORK.PRO     ││CALL:     bowler(_,"expert")      │
       │bowler                    ││RETURN:   *bowler("ray","expert") │
       │Compiling A:\WORK.PRO     ││                                  │
       │bowler                    ││                                  │
       └─────────────────────────┘└──────────────────────────────────┘
   F1-Help F2-Save F5-Zoom  F10-Step  Shift-F10-Resize  Alt-T-Trace on/off  Esc-End
```

RETURN:*bowler("ray","expert")

Turbo Prolog marks the first clause and binds the variable **Player1** to **ray**.

bowler(Player1,expert) and
bowler(Player2,expert) and Player1<>Player2.

<u>Variables Bound</u>   ***1**   **bowler(ray,expert).**
Player1=ray   bowler(dan,novice).
Player2= unbound   bowler(francis,expert).
                                        bowler(don,expert).

```
         Files      Edit       Run      Compile     Options      Setup
 ┌─────── Editor ─────────┐┌──────────── Dialog ────────────────┐
 │Trace  Line 9    Col 9   A:\││Goal: bowler(Player1,expert) and bowler(Player│
 │domains                  ││2,expert) and Player1 <> Player2     │
 │       name,rank=symbol  ││Player1=ray, Player2=francis         │
 │                         ││Player1=ray, Player2=don             │
 │predicates               ││Player1=francis, Player2=ray         │
 │       bowler(name,rank) ││Player1=francis, Player2=don         │
 │                         ││Player1=don, Player2=ray             │
 │clauses                  ││Player1=don, Player2=francis         │
 │       bowler(ray,expert).││6 Solutions                         │
 │       bowler(dan,novice).││Goal: bowler(Player1,expert) and bowler(Player│
 │       bowler(francis,expert).││2,expert) and Player1 <> Player2  │
 │       bowler(don,expert).││                                     │
 └─────────────────────────┘└─────────────────────────────────────┘
 ┌─────── Message ────────┐┌──────────── Trace ─────────────────┐
 │Compiling A:\WORK.PRO    ││CALL:     bowler(_,"expert")         │
 │bowler                   ││RETURN:  *bowler("ray","expert")     │
 │Compiling A:\WORK.PRO    ││CALL:     bowler(_,"expert")         │
 │bowler                   ││                                     │
 └─────────────────────────┘└─────────────────────────────────────┘
 F1-Help F2-Save F5-Zoom  F10-Step  Shift-F10-Resize  Alt-T-Trace on/off  Esc-End
```

CALL:bowler(_,"expert")

The program moves to Subgoal-2. Recall that CALL means Turbo Prolog is
looking for the first solution to this subgoal.

bowler(Player1,expert) and
bowler(Player2,expert) and Player1 <> Player2.

<u>Variables Bound</u>	*1	**bowler(ray,expert).**
Player1=ray		bowler(dan,novice).
Player2= still unbound		bowler(francis,expert).
		bowler(don,expert).

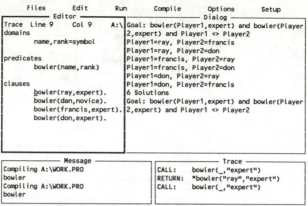

```
        Files      Edit      Run     Compile      Options     Setup
              Editor                          Dialog
Trace  Line 9     Col 9    A:\ Goal: bowler(Player1,expert) and bowler(Player
domains                          2,expert) and Player1 <> Player2
        name,rank=symbol         Player1=ray, Player2=francis
                                 Player1=ray, Player2=don
predicates                       Player1=francis, Player2=ray
        bowler(name,rank)        Player1=francis, Player2=don
                                 Player1=don, Player2=ray
clauses                          Player1=don, Player2=francis
        bowler(ray,expert).      6 Solutions
        bowler(dan,novice).      Goal: bowler(Player1,expert) and bowler(Player
        bowler(francis,expert).  2,expert) and Player1 <> Player2
        bowler(don,expert).



              Message                           Trace
Compiling A:\WORK.PRO           CALL:    bowler(_,"expert")
bowler                          RETURN:  *bowler("ray","expert")
Compiling A:\WORK.PRO           CALL:    bowler(_,"expert")
bowler

F1-Help F2-Save F5-Zoom F10-Step  Shift-F10-Resize  Alt-T-Trace on/off  Esc-End
```

There is nothing new in the Trace Window.

The cursor moves to the first clause in the Editor Window, indicating that the search begins at the top of the data base.

The cursor shows that the goal matches Clause-1 in the Editor Window.

bowler(Player1,expert) and
bowler(Player2,expert) and Player1 <> Player2

Variables Bound	*1	bowler(ray,expert).
Player1=ray		bowler(dan,novice).
Player2=unbound		bowler(francis,expert).
		bowler(don,expert).

Chapter 4

```
         Files      Edit      Run      Compile      Options      Setup
                  Editor                          Dialog
Trace  Line 9     Col 9    A:\ Goal: bowler(Player1,expert) and bowler(Player
domains                        2,expert) and Player1 <> Player2
        name,rank=symbol       Player1=ray, Player2=francis
                               Player1=ray, Player2=don
predicates                     Player1=francis, Player2=ray
        bowler(name,rank)      Player1=francis, Player2=don
                               Player1=don, Player2=ray
clauses                        Player1=don, Player2=francis
        bowler(ray,expert).    6 Solutions
        bowler(dan,novice).    Goal: bowler(Player1,expert) and bowler(Player
        bowler(francis,expert).2,expert) and Player1 <> Player2
        bowler(don,expert).

              Message                              Trace
Compiling A:\WORK.PRO            RETURN:   *bowler("ray","expert")
bowler                          CALL:     bowler(_,"expert")
Compiling A:\WORK.PRO           RETURN:   *bowler("ray","expert")
bowler

F1-Help F2-Save F5-Zoom  F10-Step  Shift-F10-Resize  Alt-T-Trace on/off  Esc-End
```

RETURN:*bowler("ray","expert")

Turbo Prolog marks the clause and binds **Player2** to **ray**.

bowler(Player1,expert) and
bowler(Player2,expert) and Player1 <> Player2.

Variables Bound	*1 *2	**bowler(ray,expert).**
Player1=ray		bowler(dan,novice).
Player2=ray		bowler(francis,expert).
		bowler(don,expert).

Each subgoal places its own marker in the data base. Thus, Clause-1 satisfies Subgoal-1 and also Subgoal-2. Turbo Prolog then moves to Subgoal-3. At this point, **Player1** is bound to **ray**, and **Player2** is bound to **ray**. Subgoal-3 fails because **ray** is equal to **ray**.

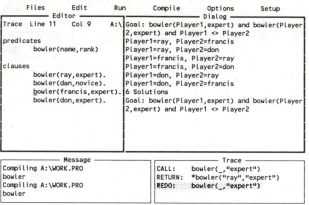

```
        Files       Edit       Run      Compile        Options      Setup
              Editor                          Dialog
Trace  Line 11    Col 9     A:\  Goal: bowler(Player1,expert) and bowler(Player
                                 2,expert) and Player1 <> Player2
predicates                       Player1=ray, Player2=francis
        bowler(name,rank)        Player1=ray, Player2=don
                                 Player1=francis, Player2=ray
clauses                          Player1=francis, Player2=don
        bowler(ray,expert).      Player1=don, Player2=ray
        bowler(dan,novice).      Player1=don, Player2=francis
        bowler(francis,expert).  6 Solutions
        bowler(don,expert).      Goal: bowler(Player1,expert) and bowler(Player
                                 2,expert) and Player1 <> Player2




                    Message                            Trace
Compiling A:\WORK.PRO                 CALL:    bowler(_,"expert")
bowler                                RETURN:  *bowler("ray","expert")
Compiling A:\WORK.PRO                 REDO:    bowler(_,"expert")
bowler

  F1-Help F2-Save F5-Zoom  F10-Step  Shift-F10-Resize  Alt-T-Trace on/off  Esc-End
```

REDO:bowler(_,"expert")

Turbo Prolog does not show you that Subgoal-3 failed. When a subgoal fails, backtracking occurs. In this case, Turbo Prolog moves back to Subgoal-2 and attempts to find another solution. In terms of the flow of satisfaction, the arrow is backing into Subgoal-2 from Subgoal-3. The term in the Trace Window that describes an attempt to re-satisfy a subgoal is REDO.

Turbo Prolog looks for a new solution for Subgoal-2. Notice that Subgoal-2 begins its search with the clause following the *1 marker. Notice also that Player2 is now unbound.

bowler(Player1,expert) and
bowler(Player2,expert) and Player1 <> Player2.

<u>Variables Bound</u>   *1 *2   **bowler(ray,expert).**
Player1=ray   bowler(dan,novice).
Player2=unbound   bowler(francis,expert).
                                      bowler(don,expert).

```
        Files      Edit      Run      Compile      Options      Setup
        ─── Editor ───                   ─── Dialog ───
Trace  Line 9    Col 9    A:\│Goal: bowler(Player1,expert) and bowler(Player
domains                      │2,expert) and Player1 <> Player2
        name,rank=symbol     │Player1=ray, Player2=francis
                             │Player1=ray, Player2=don
predicates                   │Player1=francis, Player2=ray
        bowler(name,rank)    │Player1=francis, Player2=don
                             │Player1=don, Player2=ray
clauses                      │Player1=don, Player2=francis
        bowler(ray,expert).  │6 Solutions
        bowler(dan,novice).  │Goal: bowler(Player1,expert) and bowler(Player
        bowler(francis,expert).│2,expert) and Player1 <> Player2
        bowler(don,expert).  │

        ─── Message ───              ─── Trace ───
Compiling A:\WORK.PRO           │RETURN:  *bowler("ray","expert")
bowler                          │CALL:     bowler(_,"expert")
Compiling A:\WORK.PRO           │RETURN:  *bowler("francis","expert")
bowler                          │

F1-Help F2-Save F5-Zoom F10-Step  Shift-F10-Resize  Alt-T-Trace on/off  Esc-End
```

RETURN:*bowler("francis","expert")

The cursor in the Editor Window shows that Subgoal-2 matches Clause-3. Turbo Prolog marks the clause and binds **Player2** to **francis**.

bowler(Player1,expert) and
bowler(Player2,expert) andPlayer1 <> Player2.

<u>Variables Bound</u>   *1   bowler(ray,expert).
Player1=ray   bowler(dan,novice).
Player2=francis   ***2**   **bowler(francis,expert).**
                               bowler(don,expert).

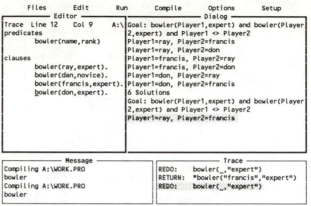

```
                Files      Edit      Run      Compile      Options      Setup
                        Editor                           Dialog
Trace  Line 12    Col 9         A:\  Goal: bowler(Player1,expert) and bowler(Player
predicates                            2,expert) and Player1 <> Player2
        bowler(name,rank)             Player1=ray, Player2=francis
                                      Player1=ray, Player2=don
clauses                               Player1=francis, Player2=ray
        bowler(ray,expert).           Player1=francis, Player2=don
        bowler(dan,novice).           Player1=don, Player2=ray
        bowler(francis,expert).       Player1=don, Player2=francis
        bowler(don,expert).           6 Solutions
                                      Goal: bowler(Player1,expert) and bowler(Player
                                      2,expert) and Player1 <> Player2
                                      Player1=ray, Player2=francis



                     Message                              Trace
 Compiling A:\WORK.PRO                 REDO:    bowler(_,"expert")
 bowler                                RETURN:  *bowler("francis","expert")
 Compiling A:\WORK.PRO                 REDO:    bowler(_,"expert")
 bowler

  F1-Help F2-Save F5-Zoom  F10-Step  Shift-F10-Resize  Alt-T-Trace on/off  Esc-End
```

REDO:bowler(_,"expert")

Subgoal-3 (**ray<>francis**) succeeds, so the entire goal succeeds. Turbo Prolog prints the result (Player1=ray, Player2=francis) in the Dialog Window. Now Turbo Prolog backtracks to Subgoal-2. The variable Player2 is unbound.

bowler(Player1,expert) and
bowler(Player2,expert) and Player1 <> Player2.

<u>Variables Bound</u>   *1   **bowler(ray,expert).**
Player1=ray   bowler(dan,novice).
Player2=unbound   *2   bowler(francis,expert).
                                      bowler(don,expert).

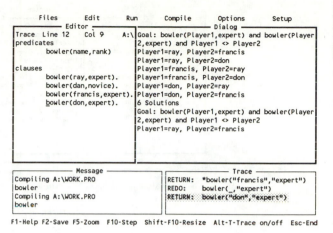

```
                  Files        Edit       Run      Compile     Options     Setup
              ┌──── Editor ─┐                  ┌──────── Dialog ─────────┐
              Trace Line 12   Col 9    A:\│Goal: bowler(Player1,expert) and bowler(Player
              predicates                     │2,expert) and Player1 <> Player2
                      bowler(name,rank)       │Player1=ray, Player2=francis
                                              │Player1=ray, Player2=don
              clauses                         │Player1=francis, Player2=ray
                      bowler(ray,expert).     │Player1=francis, Player2=don
                      bowler(dan,novice).     │Player1=don, Player2=ray
                      bowler(francis,expert). │Player1=don, Player2=francis
                      bowler(don,expert).     │6 Solutions
                                              │Goal: bowler(Player1,expert) and bowler(Player
                                              │2,expert) and Player1 <> Player2
                                              │Player1=ray, Player2=francis

              ┌──── Message ─┐                  ┌──────── Trace ─────────┐
              Compiling A:\WORK.PRO             │RETURN:  *bowler("francis","expert")
              bowler                            │REDO:     bowler(_,"expert")
              Compiling A:\WORK.PRO             │RETURN:  bowler("don","expert")
              bowler                            │
      F1-Help F2-Save F5-Zoom  F10-Step  Shift-F10-Resize  Alt-T-Trace on/off  Esc-End
```

RETURN:bowler("don","expert")

The cursor shows that Subgoal-2 matches Clause-4. Turbo Prolog marks the fact, and binds **Player2** to **don**.

bowler(Player1,expert) and
bowler(Player2,expert) and Player1 <> Player2.

<u>Variables Bound</u>	*1	bowler(ray,expert).
Player1=ray		bowler(dan,novice).
Player2=don		bowler(francis,expert).
	*2	**bowler(don,expert).**

{F10}

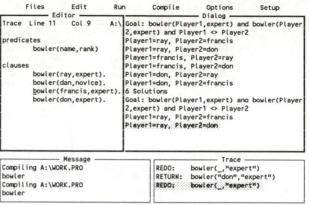

```
            Files      Edit      Run     Compile    Options    Setup
              ──── Editor ────              ──── Dialog ────
Trace  Line 11   Col 9    A:\  Goal: bowler(Player1,expert) and bowler(Player
                                2,expert) and Player1 <> Player2
predicates                      Player1=ray, Player2=francis
        bowler(name,rank)       Player1=ray, Player2=don
                                Player1=francis, Player2=ray
clauses                         Player1=francis, Player2=don
        bowler(ray,expert).     Player1=don, Player2=ray
        bowler(dan,novice).     Player1=don, Player2=francis
        bowler(francis,expert). 6 Solutions
        bowler(don,expert).     Goal: bowler(Player1,expert) and bowler(Player
                                2,expert) and Player1 <> Player2
                                Player1=ray, Player2=francis
                                Player1=ray, Player2=don

         ──── Message ────             ──────── Trace ────────
Compiling A:\WORK.PRO           REDO:    bowler(_,"expert")
bowler                          RETURN:  bowler("don","expert")
Compiling A:\WORK.PRO           REDO:    bowler(_,"expert")
bowler
```

F1-Help F2-Save F5-Zoom F10-Step Shift-F10-Resize Alt-T-Trace on/off Esc-End

REDO:bowler(_,"expert")

Since the goal succeeded, the result is printed in the Dialog Window. No more solutions to Subgoal-2 are possible. Turbo Prolog backtracks to Subgoal-1. **Player1** is unbound. Subgoal-1 matches Clause-3.

bowler(Player1,expert) and
bowler(Player2,expert) and Player1 <> Player2.

<u>Variables Bound</u>		bowler(ray,expert).
Player1=unbound		bowler(dan,novice).
Player2=unbound	*1	**bowler(francis,expert).**
	*2	bowler(don,expert).

```
        Files        Edit        Run        Compile        Options      Setup
┌─────────────── Editor ───────┬──────────────── Dialog ────────────────┐
│Trace  Line 11    Col 9    A:\│Goal: bowler(Player1,expert) and bowler(Player│
│                              │2,expert) and Player1 <> Player2          │
│predicates                    │Player1=ray, Player2=francis              │
│        bowler(name,rank)     │Player1=ray, Player2=don                  │
│                              │Player1=francis, Player2=ray              │
│clauses                       │Player1=francis, Player2=don              │
│        bowler(ray,expert).   │Player1=don, Player2=ray                  │
│        bowler(dan,novice).   │Player1=don, Player2=francis              │
│        bowler(francis,expert).│6 Solutions                              │
│        bowler(don,expert).   │Goal: bowler(Player1,expert) and bowler(Player│
│                              │2,expert) and Player1 <> Player2          │
│                              │Player1=ray, Player2=francis              │
│                              │Player1=ray, Player2=don                  │
└──────────────────────────────┴──────────────────────────────────────────┘
┌─────────── Message ──────────┐┌──────────────── Trace ───────────────┐
│Compiling A:\WORK.PRO         ││RETURN:   bowler("don","expert")       │
│bowler                        ││REDO:     bowler(_,"expert")           │
│Compiling A:\WORK.PRO         ││RETURN:   *bowler("francis","expert")  │
│bowler                        ││                                       │
└──────────────────────────────┘└───────────────────────────────────────┘
   F1-Help F2-Save F5-Zoom  F10-Step  Shift-F10-Resize  Alt-T-Trace on/off  Esc-End
```

RETURN:*bowler("francis","expert")

The third clause is marked and **Player1** is bound to **francis**.

bowler(Player1,expert) and
bowler(Player2,expert) and Player1 <> Player2.

<u>Variables Bound</u>   bowler(ray,expert).
Player1=francis   bowler(dan,novice).
Player2=unbound   ***1**   **bowler(francis,expert).**
       bowler(don,expert).

F1-Help F2-Save F5-Zoom F10-Step Shift-F10-Resize Alt-T-Trace on/off Esc-End

CALL:bowler(_,"expert")

Turbo Prolog moves to Subgoal-2.

bowler(Player1,expert) and
bowler(Player2,expert) and Player1 <> Player2.

<u>Variables Bound</u>   bowler(ray,expert).
Player1=francis   bowler(dan,novice).
Player2=unbound   *1   **bowler(francis,expert).**
                                             bowler(don,expert).

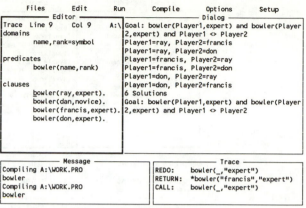

```
        Files      Edit      Run      Compile    Options    Setup
       ┌──────── Editor ────────┐   ┌──────────── Dialog ────────────┐
       Trace  Line 9    Col 9   A:\ Goal: bowler(Player1,expert) and bowler(Player
       domains                      2,expert) and Player1 <> Player2
               name,rank=symbol     Player1=ray, Player2=francis
                                    Player1=ray, Player2=don
       predicates                   Player1=francis, Player2=ray
               bowler(name,rank)    Player1=francis, Player2=don
                                    Player1=don, Player2=ray
       clauses                      Player1=don, Player2=francis
               bowler(ray,expert).  6 Solutions
               bowler(dan,novice).  Goal: bowler(Player1,expert) and bowler(Player
               bowler(francis,expert). 2,expert) and Player1 <> Player2
               bowler(don,expert).
       └────────────────────────┘   └────────────────────────────────┘
       ┌──────── Message ────────┐   ┌──────────── Trace ────────────┐
       Compiling A:\WORK.PRO         REDO:     bowler(_,"expert")
       bowler                        RETURN:  *bowler("francis","expert")
       Compiling A:\WORK.PRO         CALL:     bowler(_,"expert")
       bowler
       └─────────────────────────┘   └────────────────────────────────┘
       F1-Help  F2-Save  F5-Zoom  F10-Step  Shift-F10-Resize  Alt-T-Trace on/off  Esc-End
```

The cursor moves to the first clause in the Editor Window to show that the clause matches Subgoal-2.

bowler(Player1,expert) and
bowler(Player2,expert) and Player1 <> Player2.

<u>Variables Bound</u>   bowler(ray,expert).
Player1=francis   bowler(dan,novice).
Player2=unbound   *1   **bowler(francis,expert).**
                                                bowler(don,expert).

```
        Files      Edit      Run      Compile      Options      Setup
 ┌──────── Editor ────────┐ ┌──────── Dialog ────────┐
 │Trace  Line 9    Col 9  A:\│Goal: bowler(Player1,expert) and bowler(Player
 │domains                 │2,expert) and Player1 <> Player2
 │      name,rank=symbol  │Player1=ray, Player2=francis
 │                        │Player1=ray, Player2=don
 │predicates              │Player1=francis, Player2=ray
 │      bowler(name,rank) │Player1=francis, Player2=don
 │                        │Player1=don, Player2=ray
 │clauses                 │Player1=don, Player2=francis
 │      bowler(ray,expert).   │6 Solutions
 │      bowler(dan,novice).   │Goal: bowler(Player1,expert) and bowler(Player
 │      bowler(francis,expert).│2,expert) and Player1 <> Player2
 │      bowler(don,expert).│
 └────────────────────────┘ └────────────────────────┘
 ┌──────── Message ────────┐ ┌──────── Trace ────────┐
 │Compiling A:\WORK.PRO   │ │RETURN:  *bowler("francis","expert")│
 │bowler                  │ │CALL:     bowler(_,"expert")        │
 │Compiling A:\WORK.PRO   │ │RETURN:  *bowler("ray","expert")    │
 │bowler                  │ │                                    │
 └────────────────────────┘ └────────────────────────┘
   F1-Help F2-Save F5-Zoom  F10-Step  Shift-F10-Resize  Alt-T-Trace on/off  Esc-End
```

RETURN:*bowler("ray","expert")

Subgoal-2 places a mark next to Clause-1. **Player1** is still bound to **francis**, while **Player2** is now bound to **ray**.

bowler(Player1,expert) and
bowler(Player2,expert) and Player1 <> Player2.

Variables Bound		
	*2	**bowler(ray,expert).**
Player1=francis		bowler(dan,novice).
Player2=ray	*1	bowler(francis,expert).
		bowler(don,expert).

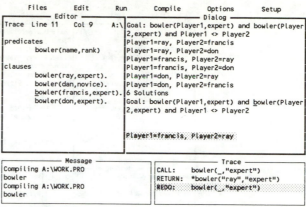

```
          Files      Edit      Run     Compile      Options    Setup
                 Editor                          Dialog
Trace  Line 11    Col 9    A:\  Goal: bowler(Player1,expert) and bowler(Player
                                 2,expert) and Player1 <> Player2
predicates                       Player1=ray, Player2=francis
        bowler(name,rank)        Player1=ray, Player2=don
                                 Player1=francis, Player2=ray
clauses                          Player1=francis, Player2=don
        bowler(ray,expert).      Player1=don, Player2=ray
        bowler(dan,novice).      Player1=don, Player2=francis
        bowler(francis,expert).  6 Solutions
        bowler(don,expert).      Goal: bowler(Player1,expert) and bowler(Player
                                 2,expert) and Player1 <> Player2


                                 Player1=francis, Player2=ray

              Message                              Trace
Compiling A:\WORK.PRO            CALL:    bowler(_,"expert")
bowler                          RETURN:  *bowler("ray","expert")
Compiling A:\WORK.PRO           REDO:    bowler(_,"expert")
bowler

F1-Help F2-Save F5-Zoom  F10-Step  Shift-F10-Resize  Alt-T-Trace on/off  Esc-End
```

REDO:bowler(_,"expert")

The result (Player1=francis,Player2=ray) is printed. Turbo Prolog backtracks
to Subgoal-2. **Player2** is unbound.

  bowler(Player1,expert) and
  bowler(Player2,expert) and Player1 <> Player2.

<u>Variables Bound</u>		*2	bowler(ray,expert).
Player1=francis			bowler(dan,novice).
Player2=unbound	*1		**bowler(francis,expert).**
			bowler(don,expert).

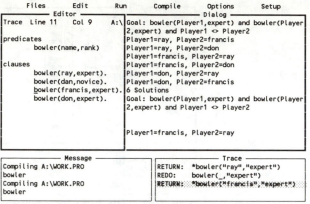

RETURN:*bowler("francis","expert")

Subgoal-2 matches Clause-3. **Player2** is bound to **francis**. But Subgoal-3 fails, because **francis** is equal to **francis**.

bowler(Player1,expert) and
bowler(Player2,expert) and Player1 <> Player2.

<u>Variables Bound</u>   bowler(ray,expert).
Player1=francis   bowler(dan,novice).
Player2=francis   *1   *2   **bowler(francis,expert).**
                                        bowler(don,expert).

Thus, the entire goal fails.

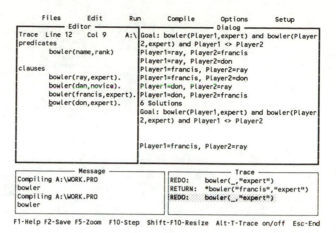

REDO:bowler(_,"expert")

Turbo Prolog again backtracks to Subgoal-2, unbinding **Player2**. **Player1** is still bound to **francis**.

bowler(Player1,expert) and
bowler(Player2,expert) and Player1 <> Player2.

Variables Bound		
Player1=francis		bowler(ray,expert).
Player2= unbound		bowler(dan,novice).
	*1 *2	bowler(francis,expert).
		bowler(don,expert).

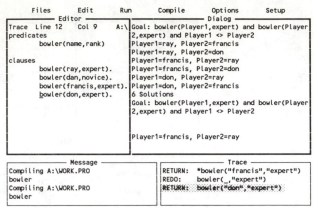

```
         Files       Edit       Run      Compile      Options      Setup
        ─ Editor ─────────────────      ─ Dialog ────────────────────────
Trace  Line 12    Col 9     A:\   Goal: bowler(Player1,expert) and bowler(Player
predicates                        2,expert) and Player1 <> Player2
       bowler(name,rank)          Player1=ray, Player2=francis
                                  Player1=ray, Player2=don
clauses                           Player1=francis, Player2=ray
       bowler(ray,expert).        Player1=francis, Player2=don
       bowler(dan,novice).        Player1=don, Player2=ray
       bowler(francis,expert).    Player1=don, Player2=francis
       bowler(don,expert).        6 Solutions
                                  Goal: bowler(Player1,expert) and bowler(Player
                                  2,expert) and Player1 <> Player2

                                  Player1=francis, Player2=ray

        ─ Message ─────────────          ─ Trace ─────────────────────
Compiling A:\WORK.PRO              RETURN:  *bowler("francis","expert")
bowler                             REDO:    bowler(_,"expert")
Compiling A:\WORK.PRO              RETURN:  bowler("don","expert")
bowler

  F1-Help F2-Save F5-Zoom  F10-Step  Shift-F10-Resize  Alt-T-Trace on/off  Esc-End
```

RETURN:*bowler("don","expert")

Clause-4 is marked by Subgoal-2 (*2). **Player2** is bound to **don**.

    bowler(Player1,expert) and
    bowler(Player2,expert) and Player1 <> Player2.

Variables Bound		
Player1=francis		bowler(ray,expert).
Player2=don		bowler(dan,novice).
	*1	bowler(francis,expert).
	***2**	**bowler(don,expert).**

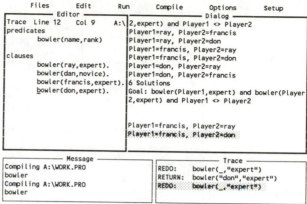

```
        Files      Edit      Run     Compile      Options     Setup
                 Editor                            Dialog
Trace  Line 12    Col 9   A:\  2,expert) and Player1 <> Player2
predicates                     Player1=ray, Player2=francis
        bowler(name,rank)      Player1=ray, Player2=don
                               Player1=francis, Player2=ray
clauses                        Player1=francis, Player2=don
        bowler(ray,expert).    Player1=don, Player2=ray
        bowler(dan,novice).    Player1=don, Player2=francis
        bowler(francis,expert).6 Solutions
        bowler(don,expert).    Goal: bowler(Player1,expert) and bowler(Player
                               2,expert) and Player1 <> Player2

                               Player1=francis, Player2=ray
                               Player1=francis, Player2=don
                 Message                            Trace
Compiling A:\WORK.PRO          REDO:    bowler(_,"expert")
bowler                         RETURN:  bowler("don","expert")
Compiling A:\WORK.PRO          REDO:    bowler(_,"expert")
bowler
  F1-Help F2-Save F5-Zoom  F10-Step  Shift-F10-Resize  Alt-T-Trace on/off  Esc-End
```

REDO:bowler(_,"expert")

Subgoal-3 succeeds. The results are displayed in the Dialog Window. There are no more solutions for Subgoal-2, Turbo Prolog backtracks again to Subgoal-1. **Player1** is unbound. **Player2** is unbound.

bowler(Player1,expert) and
bowler(Player2,expert) and **Player1 <> Player2**.

Variables Bound		bowler(ray,expert).
Player1=unbound		bowler(dan,novice).
Player2=unbound	*1	bowler(francis,expert).
	***2**	**bowler(don,expert).**

{F10}

```
            Files      Edit      Run     Compile     Options    Setup
            ── Editor ──                      ── Dialog ──
Trace  Line 12   Col 9    A:\  2,expert) and Player1 <> Player2
predicates                      Player1=ray, Player2=francis
        bowler(name,rank)       Player1=ray, Player2=don
                                Player1=francis, Player2=ray
clauses                         Player1=francis, Player2=don
        bowler(ray,expert).     Player1=don, Player2=ray
        bowler(dan,novice).     Player1=don, Player2=francis
        bowler(francis,expert). 6 Solutions
        bowler(don,expert).     Goal: bowler(Player1,expert) and bowler(Player
                                2,expert) and Player1 <> Player2

                                Player1=francis, Player2=ray
                                Player1=francis, Player2=don
            ── Message ──                    ── Trace ──
Compiling A:\WORK.PRO            RETURN:  bowler("don","expert")
bowler                          REDO:    bowler(_,"expert")
Compiling A:\WORK.PRO           RETURN:  bowler("don","expert")
bowler
  F1-Help F2-Save F5-Zoom  F10-Step  Shift-F10-Resize  Alt-T-Trace on/off  Esc-End
```

RETURN:bowler("don","expert")

The search begins at the Subgoal-1 marker. Subgoal-1 matches Clause-4.

bowler(Player1,expert) and
bowler(Player2,expert) and Player1 <> Player2.

<u>Variables Bound</u>   bowler(ray,expert).
Player1=don   bowler(dan,novice).
Player2=unbound   bowler(francis,expert).
                          *1   **bowler(don,expert).**

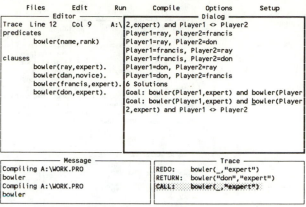

```
      Files       Edit      Run      Compile      Options     Setup
 ─────── Editor ──────              ───────── Dialog ─────────
Trace  Line 12    Col 9   A:\ 2,expert) and Player1 <> Player2
predicates                     Player1=ray, Player2=francis
        bowler(name,rank)      Player1=ray, Player2=don
                               Player1=francis, Player2=ray
clauses                        Player1=francis, Player2=don
        bowler(ray,expert).    Player1=don, Player2=ray
        bowler(dan,novice).    Player1=don, Player2=francis
        bowler(francis,expert). 6 Solutions
        bowler(don,expert).    Goal: bowler(Player1,expert) and bowler(Player
                               Goal: bowler(Player1,expert) and bowler(Player
                               2,expert) and Player1 <> Player2


 ──────── Message ────────        ────────── Trace ──────────
Compiling A:\WORK.PRO           REDO:    bowler(_,"expert")
bowler                          RETURN:  bowler("don","expert")
Compiling A:\WORK.PRO           CALL:    bowler(_,"expert")
bowler
 F1-Help F2-Save F5-Zoom  F10-Step  Shift-F10-Resize  Alt-T-Trace on/off  Esc-End
```

CALL:bowler(_,"expert")

Look for a new solution for Subgoal-2. Turbo Prolog displays the goal in the Dialog Window and indicates it is working on Subgoal-2.

bowler(Player1,expert) and
bowler(Player2,expert) and Player1 <> Player2.

<u>Variables Bound</u>   bowler(ray,expert).
Player1=don   bowler(dan,novice).
Player2=unbound   bowler(francis,expert).
                          *1   **bowler(don,expert).**

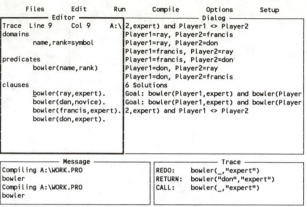

The cursor moves to the first clause in the Editor Window.

Subgoal-2 matches Clause-1 (shown in Editor Window).

bowler(Player1,expert) and
bowler(Player2,expert) and Player1 <> Player2.

<u>Variables Bound</u>   **bowler(ray,expert).**
Player1=don   bowler(dan,novice).
Player2=unbound   bowler(francis,expert).
                 *1   bowler(don,expert).

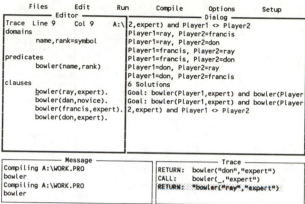

```
                Files      Edit      Run      Compile      Options      Setup
                ┌──────── Editor ────────┐ ┌──────────── Dialog ────────────┐
                │Trace Line 9    Col 9  A:\│ │2,expert) and Player1 <> Player2│
                │domains                   │ │Player1=ray, Player2=francis     │
                │       name,rank=symbol    │ │Player1=ray, Player2=don         │
                │                          │ │Player1=francis, Player2=ray     │
                │predicates                │ │Player1=francis, Player2=don     │
                │       bowler(name,rank)   │ │Player1=don, Player2=ray         │
                │                          │ │Player1=don, Player2=francis     │
                │clauses                   │ │6 Solutions                      │
                │       bowler(ray,expert). │ │Goal: bowler(Player1,expert) and bowler(Player│
                │       bowler(dan,novice). │ │Goal: bowler(Player1,expert) and bowler(Player│
                │       bowler(francis,expert).│ │2,expert) and Player1 <> Player2│
                │       bowler(don,expert). │ │                                 │
                └──────────────────────────┘ └─────────────────────────────────┘
    ┌──────── Message ────────┐        ┌────────── Trace ──────────┐
    │Compiling A:\WORK.PRO     │        │RETURN:  bowler("don","expert")│
    │bowler                    │        │CALL:    bowler(_,"expert")    │
    │Compiling A:\WORK.PRO     │        │RETURN:  *bowler("ray","expert")│
    │bowler                    │        └───────────────────────────┘
    └──────────────────────────┘
    F1-Help F2-Save F5-Zoom  F10-Step  Shift-F10-Resize  Alt-T-Trace on/off  Esc-End
```

RETURN:*bowler("ray","expert")

The clause is marked and **Player2** is bound to **ray**.

bowler(Player1,expert) and
bowler(Player2,expert) and Player1 <> Player2.

<u>Variables Bound</u>   ***2   bowler(ray,expert).**
Player1=don   bowler(dan,novice).
Player2=ray   bowler(francis,expert).
                              *1   bowler(don,expert).

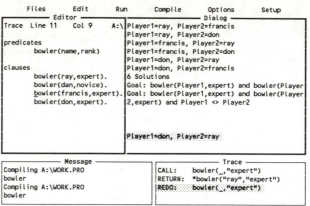

```
        Files      Edit      Run     Compile     Options      Setup
         Editor                           Dialog
Trace  Line 11   Col 9    A:\  Player1=ray, Player2=francis
                               Player1=ray, Player2=don
predicates                     Player1=francis, Player2=ray
        bowler(name,rank)      Player1=francis, Player2=don
                               Player1=don, Player2=ray
clauses                        Player1=don, Player2=francis
        bowler(ray,expert).    6 Solutions
        bowler(dan,novice).    Goal: bowler(Player1,expert) and bowler(Player
        bowler(francis,expert).Goal: bowler(Player1,expert) and bowler(Player
        bowler(don,expert).    2,expert) and Player1 <> Player2


                               Player1=don, Player2=ray

         Message                              Trace
Compiling A:\WORK.PRO          CALL:    bowler(_,"expert")
bowler                         RETURN:  *bowler("ray","expert")
Compiling A:\WORK.PRO          REDO:    bowler(_,"expert")
bowler

F1-Help F2-Save F5-Zoom  F10-Step  Shift-F10-Resize  Alt-T-Trace on/off  Esc-End
```

REDO:bowler(_,"expert")

Subgoal-3 succeeds. The results are displayed in the Dialog Window. Turbo
Prolog backtracks to Subgoal-2, unbinding the value from **Player2**.

bowler(Player1,expert) and
bowler(Player2,expert) and **Player1 <> Player2**.

<u>Variables Bound</u>   ***2   bowler(ray,expert).**
Player1=don   bowler(dan,novice).
Player2=unbound   bowler(francis,expert).
                                        *1   bowler(don,expert).

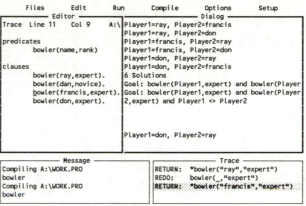

```
       Files      Edit       Run      Compile      Options      Setup
         ─── Editor ───                       ─── Dialog ───
Trace  Line 11   Col 9    A:\ Player1=ray, Player2=francis
                              Player1=ray, Player2=don
predicates                    Player1=francis, Player2=ray
      bowler(name,rank)       Player1=francis, Player2=don
                              Player1=don, Player2=ray
clauses                       Player1=don, Player2=francis
      bowler(ray,expert).     6 Solutions
      bowler(dan,novice).     Goal: bowler(Player1,expert) and bowler(Player
      bowler(francis,expert). Goal: bowler(Player1,expert) and bowler(Player
      bowler(don,expert).     2,expert) and Player1 <> Player2


                              Player1=don, Player2=ray


      ─── Message ───                        ─── Trace ───
Compiling A:\WORK.PRO          RETURN:   *bowler("ray","expert")
bowler                         REDO:     bowler(_,"expert")
Compiling A:\WORK.PRO          RETURN:   *bowler("francis","expert")
bowler
```

F1-Help F2-Save F5-Zoom F10-Step Shift-F10-Resize Alt-T-Trace on/off Esc-End

RETURN:*bowler("francis","expert")

Subgoal-2 matches Clause-3. Clause-3 is marked by Subgoal-2 (*2), and
Player2 is now bound to **francis**.

bowler(Player1,expert) and
bowler(Player2,expert) and Player1 <> Player2.

<u>Variables Bound</u>   bowler(ray,expert).
Player1=don   bowler(dan,novice).
Player2=francis   ***2**   **bowler(francis,expert)**
                                 *1   bowler(don,expert).

```
              Files      Edit      Run      Compile      Options      Setup
                    Editor                                Dialog
  Trace  Line 12    Col 9    A:\  Player1=ray, Player2=don
  predicates                      Player1=francis, Player2=ray
          bowler(name,rank)       Player1=francis, Player2=don
                                  Player1=don, Player2=ray
  clauses                         Player1=don, Player2=francis
          bowler(ray,expert).     6 Solutions
          bowler(dan,novice).     Goal: bowler(Player1,expert) and bowler(Player
          bowler(francis,expert). Goal: bowler(Player1,expert) and bowler(Player
          bowler(don,expert).     2,expert) and Player1 <> Player2


                                  Player1=don, Player2=ray
                                  Player1=don, Player2=francis

                  Message                              Trace
  Compiling A:\WORK.PRO            REDO:    bowler(_,"expert")
  bowler                          RETURN:  *bowler("francis","expert")
  Compiling A:\WORK.PRO           REDO:    bowler(_,"expert")
  bowler

  F1-Help F2-Save F5-Zoom  F10-Step  Shift-F10-Resize  Alt-T-Trace on/off  Esc-End
```

REDO:bowler(_,"expert")

Subgoal-3 succeeds. The results are displayed in the Dialog Window. Again, backtracking to Subgoal-2 occurs with **Player2** becoming unbound.

> bowler(Player1,expert) and
> bowler(Player2,expert) and **Player1 <> Player2**.

Variables Bound		
Player1=don		bowler(ray,expert).
Player2=unbound		bowler(dan,novice).
	*2	**bowler(francis,expert).**
	*1	bowler(don,expert).

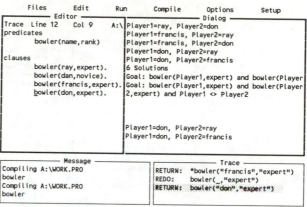

```
        Files      Edit      Run      Compile      Options      Setup
            ───── Editor ─────                     ───── Dialog ─────
Trace Line 12    Col 9    A:\ │Player1=ray, Player2=don
predicates                    │Player1=francis, Player2=ray
        bowler(name,rank)     │Player1=francis, Player2=don
                              │Player1=don, Player2=ray
clauses                       │Player1=don, Player2=francis
        bowler(ray,expert).   │6 Solutions
        bowler(dan,novice).   │Goal: bowler(Player1,expert) and bowler(Player
        bowler(francis,expert).│Goal: bowler(Player1,expert) and bowler(Player
        bowler(don,expert).   │2,expert) and Player1 <> Player2
                              │
                              │
                              │
                              │Player1=don, Player2=ray
                              │Player1=don, Player2=francis
        ───── Message ─────              ───── Trace ─────
Compiling A:\WORK.PRO          │RETURN:   *bowler("francis","expert")
bowler                         │REDO:     bowler(_,"expert")
Compiling A:\WORK.PRO          │RETURN:   bowler("don","expert")
bowler                         │
```
F1-Help F2-Save F5-Zoom F10-Step Shift-F10-Resize Alt-T-Trace on/off Esc-End

RETURN:bowler("don","expert")

Subgoal-2 matches Clause-4. **Player2** is bound to **don**. Clause-4 is marked by Subgoal-2 (*2).

bowler(Player1,expert) and
bowler(Player2,expert) and Player1 <> Player2.

<u>Variables Bound</u>   bowler(ray,expert).
Player1=don   bowler(dan,novice).
Player2=don   bowler(francis,expert).
                            *1   *2   **bowler(don,expert).**

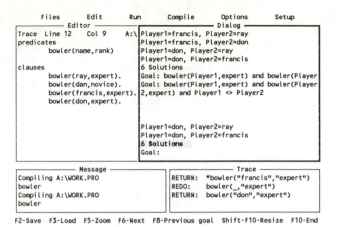

```
       Files      Edit      Run      Compile      Options      Setup
              Editor                           Dialog
Trace  Line 12    Col 9    A:\  Player1=francis, Player2=ray
predicates                      Player1=francis, Player2=don
        bowler(name,rank)       Player1=don, Player2=ray
                                Player1=don, Player2=francis
clauses                         6 Solutions
        bowler(ray,expert).     Goal: bowler(Player1,expert) and bowler(Player
        bowler(dan,novice).     Goal: bowler(Player1,expert) and bowler(Player
        bowler(francis,expert). 2,expert) and Player1 <> Player2
        bowler(don,expert).

                                Player1=don, Player2=ray
                                Player1=don, Player2=francis
                                6 Solutions
                                Goal:
              Message                           Trace
Compiling A:\WORK.PRO           RETURN:   *bowler("francis","expert")
bowler                          REDO:     bowler(_,"expert")
Compiling A:\WORK.PRO           RETURN:   bowler("don","expert")
bowler

F2-Save  F3-Load  F5-Zoom  F6-Next  F8-Previous goal  Shift-F10-Resize  F10-End
```

Subgoal-3 fails. The goal fails. There are no more solutions. Turbo Prolog displays the number of solutions it found.

This is the end of the tutorial about compound goals and backtracking. Step by step, you have followed Turbo Prolog on its inexorable search for solutions. A rather uncomplicated data base interrogated by a compound goal produced a modest amount of information without any instructions from you about how to do it. All you had to do was give it "the facts" and ask the question. That is the beauty of an object-oriented language such as Turbo Prolog.

Now, there was one small problem with the solutions found in the bowler example. Six solutions were found when only three were necessary. Turbo Prolog was so inquisitive that it not only matched **ray** with **francis**, but it also matched **francis** with **ray** and similarly matched the other players. That is one of the consequences of backtracking. Clearly, in our bowling tournament, matching **ray** with **francis** is the same as matching **francis** with **ray**. There is a way to take care of this, and you will learn how to stop Turbo Prolog from becoming too inquisitive in Chapter 6.

This past exercise in the Tutorial was intended to demonstrate the process of goal satisfaction and backtracking by showing you how Turbo Prolog searches for all possible solutions. Remember backtracking is the process through which Turbo Prolog backs up through a set of goals (we called them subgoals) to find all possible solutions to a stated compound goal.

For more practice, move on to the exercises and problems next in this chapter. You will get more practice in formulating Turbo Prolog programs from information and extracting answers from that information. In Chapter 5, you will learn how to add rules to a data base making it into a knowledge base. The power of Turbo Prolog really shines through when rules are added.

Exercises

4-1.   Name two logical operators and their symbols.

4-2.   What do we call goals with more than one subgoal?

4-3.   To successfully satisfy a compound goal joined with the logical operator _____, all of the subgoals must succeed.

4-4.   To satisfy two or more goals joined with the logical operator _____, only one of the subgoals must succeed.

4-5.   What is the path Turbo Prolog follows when solving a problem?

4-6.   What is the feature that requires Turbo Prolog to find all possible solutions to a goal?

4-7.   Where do you place the **Trace** command and what does it do?

4-8.   A compound goal connected by the logical operator **OR** is satisfied under what conditions?

4-9.   Give a short definition or explanation of backtracking.

4-10.   List seven fundamental mathematical operators used by Turbo Prolog.

Problems

4-1.   Consider the following data base. Using the specified goal, prepare the
        data base as a Turbo Prolog program. Enter and run the program. Ex-
        plain the steps that Turbo Prolog uses to satisfy the goal.

        Data base: Tom reads Shakespeare.
                      Mary reads Hemingway.
                      Poe is read by Henry.
                      John also reads Poe.
                      Tom also reads Hemingway.
                      Henry reads Tennyson.

        Goal: Which authors do Tom and John read?

4-2.   Given the following information, prepare a Turbo Prolog program to
        answer the presented goals.

        The information in this data base is concerned with the learning ability of
        various students in specific subject-matter areas. There are six students;
        three learning levels (level-1, level-2, level-3); and three subject-matter
        areas (mathematics, physics, and English). The students should also be
        identified by gender.

        Male Students
                Joe's ability is level-1 in mathematics.
                George's ability is level-2 in mathematics.
                Harry's ability is level-2 in mathematics.
                Joe's ability is level-1 in English.
                George's ability is level-1 in English.
                Harry's ability is level-3 in English.
                Joe's ability is level-2 in physics.
                George's ability is level-3 in physics.
                Harry's ability is level-1 in physics.

        Female Students
                Susan's ability is level-2 in physics.
                Melinda's ability is level-3 in physics.
                Marta's ability is level-1 in physics.
                Susan's ability is level-1 mathematics.
                Melinda's ability is level-1 in mathematics.
                Marta's ability is level-1 in mathematics.
                Susan's ability is level-2 in English.
                Melinda's ability is level-2 in English.
                Marta's ability is level-3 in English.

Transform this information into a Turbo Prolog data base and pose the following questions to the data base.

1. Who are the girls at level-1 in mathematics and English?

2. Which students are at level-3 and level-2 in physics?

3. Name the best students in English, assuming level-3 is the highest ability level.

4. List the ability levels in all subject-matter areas for Marta.

5. So that they can study together, pair up students according to ability level within each subject-matter area.

6. List all students who are male and at level-1 in mathematics.

7. List all students who are level-2 and display the subject-matter areas.

Chapter 5
Rules

*When you add rules to a data base, the data base becomes a knowledge base ready to answer questions about the information it contains. Through use of the if-then model of formal logic, you will learn how Turbo Prolog infers conclusions from known facts and rules. Semantic networks are used to help you formulate the logic and relationships in a program. Tutorial 5-1, **Using Rules**, shows you how to write a Turbo Prolog program from a semantic network.*

Rules

A Closer Look at Logic

In the last chapter, you learned to form compound goals using the logical operators **AND** and **OR**. This chapter takes a closer look at logic and how Turbo Prolog uses logical operations in the construction of rules.

In logic, the **AND** and **OR** operations are important. When either of these operations is used with two or more logical expressions, the result is always a logical expression. As you will recall, logical expressions have a value of either TRUE or FALSE. Thus, a logical expression formed by joining two or more expressions with the **AND** or **OR** operator has a value of either TRUE or FALSE.

Table 5-1 shows the possible combinations of two logical expressions **p** and **q**. Such a table is called a **truth table**. A truth table has the same relationship to logic that a multiplication table has to arithmetic. It is a way of determining the value of logical exressions.

Table 5-1: Truth Table

p	q	p and q	p or q
TRUE	TRUE	TRUE	TRUE
TRUE	FALSE	FALSE	TRUE
FALSE	TRUE	FALSE	TRUE
FALSE	FALSE	FALSE	FALSE

The first two columns in Table 5-1 represent the possible truth values of the logical expressions **p** and **q**. Both expressions may be true, the first true and the second false, the first false and the second true, or both could be false. The remaining columns represent the values of the logical expressions formed by joining the first two expressions with **AND** and **OR**. For example, row 2 shows that if **p** is true and **q** is false, then **p and q** is false, but **p or q** is True.

In Turbo Prolog logical expressions are represented by clauses in the data base. To solve complex problems, Turbo Prolog must be able to **infer** information not specified in the data base. To do this, Turbo Prolog uses the rules of logic.

Inferring Facts

Standard computer languages have a limited ability to infer facts. The logic of most computer programming languages is limited to the IF...THEN model of formal logic. This form of logic is called **implication**. A programmer using a language such as BASIC or Pascal uses structures like IF... THEN... ELSE to specify the conditions necessary to perform an action. These languages provide a simple way to use the **AND** and the **OR** operations to arrive at logical conclusions.

However, standard computer languages are **procedural**. This means that the programmer must specify each step in the problem-solving process. The procedure is predetermined by the programmer, and the program always follows these same steps in a predefined manner.

On the other hand, Turbo Prolog is driven by its inference engine which is never satisfied until all possible solutions are found. Turbo Prolog uses its own internal procedure (**backtracking**) to determine the steps needed to solve a logical problem. Thus, you do not have to tell Turbo Prolog the exact steps to follow.

Rather then telling Turbo Prolog each step needed to infer the steps in the problem-solving process, you tell it what you want done. You do this by adding to the data base the **rules** needed to solve the problems. In Turbo Prolog, rules are logical expressions that express relationships between facts. When you add rules to a Turbo Prolog data base, it becomes a knowledge base.

Turbo Prolog Rules

Turbo Prolog uses a form of logic called the **Horn clause** to express rules. In logic, the Horn clause uses the following form:

> Conclusion if
>> condition 1 and
>> condition 2 and
>> condition ...

The conclusion is a true statement if the conditions are met. Notice the similarity between a Turbo Prolog rule and a compound goal. Both are formed by joining smaller subgoals (or conditions) with the connectives **AND** or **OR**.

New definitions can be expressed through the use of rules. For example, assume you know the following facts:

Fact	Turbo Prolog Clause
The sky is blue.	sky(blue).
The weather is warm.	weather(warm).

Using these facts, you can derive a rule to express the conditions under which you will go to the beach.

Horn Clause	Turbo Prolog Rule
Go to the beach if the sky is blue and the weather is warm.	go_to_beach if sky(blue) and weather(warm).

Notice that the Turbo Prolog rule looks like any other clause. In fact, rules are part of the clauses section in a program and treated the same as any other fact. Assuming the above rule is part of a Turbo Prolog knowledge base, Turbo Prolog can infer whether or not you should go to the beach by matching the sky(blue) and weather(warm) parts of the rule with similar facts in the knowledge base.

Given the goal:	Goal:**go_to_beach**
Turbo Prolog responds:	Yes 1 Solution.

The answer **Yes** is inferred by Turbo Prolog because each of the conditions in the rule can be matched with a fact in the knowledge base.

Parts of a Rule

A Turbo Prolog rule has two parts – (1) a conclusion and (2) the conditions that must be met to satisfy the conclusion. The conclusion is called the **head** of the rule, and the conditions that must be met are called the **body** of the rule. In this example, the head of the rule is **go_to_beach**, and the body of the rule is **sky(blue) and weather(warm)**.

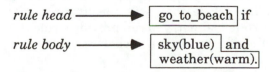

The rule is true (succeeds) because the conditions to satisfy the conclusion succeed. The sky, according to the facts in the knowledge base, is blue and the weather is warm; therefore, you can go to the beach. Consider a more complete example.

Using Turbo Prolog Rules

Assume the following data base has been entered as a Turbo Prolog program. Don't worry about the domains and predicates sections for now. Just follow along to see how the rules are created and evaluated.

```
clauses
    man(dan).
    man(ray).
    man(don).
    man(bob).
    woman(francis).
    woman(joan).
    woman(jane).
    unmarried(bob).
    unmarried(dan).
    unmarried(joan).
    unmarried(jane).
    married(francis).
    married(ray).
    married(don).
```

Using this data base, you could ask certain questions as shown in Table 5-2.

Table 5-2: Questions for the Married Data Base

Question	Goal	Answer
List the men.	man(Person)	dan,ray,don,bob
List the women.	woman(Person)	francis,joan,jane
List all the married people.	married(Person)	francis,ray,don
List the unmarried people.	unmarried(Person)	bob,dan,joan,jane

There are other questions that you might ask. For example, suppose you wanted to list all of the bachelors in the knowledge base. A look would tell you that Dan and Bob are unmarried men, thus they are bachelors. To conclude that Dan and Bob are bachelors, you applied a rule that said something like "a bachelor is an unmarried man." In the same manner, you can provide a rule to Turbo Prolog that would allow it to determine if a person is a bachelor or not.

This bachelor rule would be as follows:

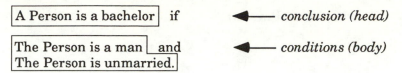

| A Person is a bachelor | if | ◄——— *conclusion (head)* |

The Person is a man and ◄——— *conditions (body)*
The Person is unmarried.

Expressed as a Turbo Prolog rule this horn clause becomes:

bachelor(Person) if ◄——— *conclusion (head)*
    man(Person) and ◄——— *conditions (body)*
    unmarried(Person).

This tells Turbo Prolog, "Conclude that a person is a bachelor if the person is a man and he is unmarried." In other words, "If you want to know who the bachelors are, find out who the unmarried men are." To add this rule to the data base, you would enter it the same way you would enter a fact. The rule added to the Bachelor data base is shown in Table 5-3. The data base now becomes a Turbo Prolog knowledge base.

Table 5-3: Rule for Bachelors

```
clauses
    man(dan).
    man(ray).
    man(don).
    man(bob).
    woman(francis).
    woman(joan).
    woman(jane).
    unmarried(bob).
    unmarried(dan).
    unmarried(joan).
    unmarried(jane).
    married(francis).
    married(ray).
    married(don).

    bachelor(Person) if
            man(Person) and
            unmarried(Person).
```

Now if you give Turbo Prolog the goal:

Goal:**bachelor(Person)**

Turbo Prolog replies:

Person=dan
Person=bob
2 Solutions.

Notice the parts of the bachelor rule. The rule head is **bachelor(Person).** It looks like and is a fact. A rule is a fact that is true only if the clauses in the rule body are true. In a sense, a fact is a rule without a body. Given a goal, Turbo Prolog first tries to match it with a fact. If there are no facts to match the goal, Turbo Prolog next looks for a matching rule head. When a matching rule head is found, Turbo Prolog tries to determine if the rule is true by finding the truth of the rule body.

Let's step through the process of determining who is a bachelor.

Assume we have the following bachelor knowledge base with nine facts and one rule. It is shown in Table 5-4.

Table 5-4: Bachelor Knowledge Base

man(dan).	*<—Fact-1*
man(ray).	*<—Fact-2*
man(don).	*<—Fact-3*
man(bob).	*<—Fact-4*
woman(francis).	*<—Fact-5*
unmarried(bob).	*<—Fact-6*
unmarried(dan).	*<—Fact-7*
married(ray).	*<—Fact-8*
married(don).	*<—Fact-9*

bachelor(Person) if
    man(Person) and
    unmarried(Person).
	<—Rule-1

Again, the goal that would list the bachelors is:

Goal:**bachelor(Person)**

To answer this goal, Turbo Prolog starts at the top of the knowledge base and tries to find a match for the goal. The goal eventually matches with the rule head of the bachelor rule. Now to satisfy the rule, the facts in the rule body must now be satisfied.

Below are the steps Turbo Prolog uses to solve this goal. Recall how Turbo Prolog found solutions in Chapter 4. The process is the same here, except that a rule has been added.

Step 1

Goal:**bachelor(Person)**

man(dan).	*<—Fact-1*
man(ray).	*<—Fact-2*
man(don).	*<—Fact-3*
man(bob).	*<—Fact-4*
woman(francis).	*<—Fact-5*
unmarried(bob).	*<—Fact-6*
unmarried(dan).	*<—Fact-7*
married(ray).	*<—Fact-8*
married(don).	*<—Fact-9*
bachelor(Person) if	*<—Rule-1*
man(Person) and	*<—Subgoal-1*
unmarried(Person).	*<—Subgoal-2*

1. The goal matches the rule head. That is, the predicate of the goal is the same as the predicate of the rule – **bachelor** matches **bachelor**.

2. Next, Turbo Prolog attempts to solve the first subgoal of the bachelor rule body, which is **man(Person)**. Looking for a match, Turbo Prolog starts at the top of the knowledge base looking to match Subgoal-1 **man(Person)** to a corresponding fact. Subgoal-1, in fact, becomes a new goal.

3. At this point, the variable **Person** is unbound.

Step 2

Goal:**man(Person)**

*1	**man(dan).**	*<—Fact-1*
	man(ray).	*<—Fact-2*
	man(don).	*<—Fact-3*
	man(bob).	*<—Fact-4*
	woman(francis).	*<—Fact-5*
	unmarried(bob).	*<—Fact-6*
	unmarried(dan).	*<—Fact-7*
	married(ray).	*<—Fact-8*
	married(don).	*<—Fact-9*
	bachelor(Person) if	*<—Rule-1*
	man(Person) and	*<—Subgoal-1*
	unmarried(Person).	*<—Subgoal-2*

1. This new goal **man(Person)** matches Fact-1 in the knowledge base. The fact is marked in memory.

2. The variable **Person** is then bound to the object **dan**.

3. Because Subgoal-1 has been satisfied, Turbo Prolog next moves on to Subgoal-2. This subgoal, **unmarried(Person)**, becomes the new goal.

Step 3

Goal:**unmarried(Person).**

The value of the variable **Person** is **dan**. Thus, Turbo Prolog actually sees this goal as **unmarried(dan).**

*1	man(dan).		<—*Fact-1*
	man(ray).		<—*Fact-2*
	man(don).		<—*Fact-3*
	man(bob).		<—*Fact-4*
	woman(francis).		<—*Fact-5*
	unmarried(bob).		<—*Fact-6*
*2	**unmarried(dan).**		<—*Fact-7*
	married(ray).		<—*Fact-8*
	married(don).		<—*Fact-9*
	bachelor(Person) if		<—*Rule-1*
	man(Person) and		<—*Subgoal-1*
	unmarried(Person).		<—*Subgoal-2*

1. This goal matches Fact-7. Because both conditions for the rule are now satisfied, Turbo Prolog concludes that Dan is a bachelor. Both subgoals succeed, hence the rule is satisfied, and Turbo Prolog displays the results in the Dialog Window as:
   Person=dan.

3. Now Turbo Prolog frees the variable **Person** and backtracks to Subgoal-1 [**man(Person)**] in an attempt to re-satisfy this subgoal. Remember, Turbo Prolog attempts to find all possible solutions.

4. The search to re-satisfy Subgoal-1 continues with the fact immediately following the marked fact where it had been previously satisfied. In this case, it continues with Fact-2.

Step 4

Goal:**man(Person).**

	man(dan).	*<—Fact-1*
*1	**man(ray).**	*<—Fact-2*
	man(don).	*<—Fact-3*
	man(bob).	*<—Fact-4*
	woman(francis).	*<—Fact-5*
	unmarried(bob).	*<—Fact-6*
*2	unmarried(dan).	*<—Fact-7*
	married(ray).	*<—Fact-8*
	married(don).	*<—Fact-9*
	bachelor(Person) if	*<—Rule-1*
	man(Person) and	*<—Subgoal-1*
	unmarried(Person).	*<—Subgoal-2*

1. Subgoal-1, **man(Person)**, matches Fact-2, which is **man(ray)**.

2. The variable **Person** is now bound to **ray** with a marker placed next to the fact where the variable was bound. Turbo Prolog again moves on to the second subgoal and attempts to find a match for Subgoal-2, **unmarried(Person)**, which Turbo Prolog sees as **unmarried(ray)**.

Step 5

Goal:unmarried(Person)

The variable **Person** is still bound to **ray**. However, Turbo Prolog now sees Subgoal-2 as **unmarried(ray).**

		man(dan).	*←—Fact-1*
*1		**man(ray).**	*←—Fact-2*
		man(don).	*←—Fact-3*
		man(bob)	*←—Fact-4*
		woman(francis).	*←—Fact-5*
		unmarried(bob).	*←—Fact-6*
	*2	unmarried(dan).	*←—Fact-7*
		married(ray).	*←—Fact-8*
		married(don).	*←—Fact-9*
		bachelor(Person) if	*←—Rule-1*
		man(Person) and	*←—Subgoal-1*
		unmarried(Person).	*←—Subgoal-2*

1. The fact **unmarried(ray)** is not in the knowledge base. No match occurs. When any one of the subgoals in a rule fails, the entire rule fails. Failing always causes backtracking.

2. Turbo Prolog frees the variable **Person**. It then backtracks to re-satisfy the subgoal **man(Person)**. The search continues with the fact below the marked fact. In this case, the search starts with Fact-3 and binds **Person** to **don**.

3. Turbo Prolog continues to Subgoal-2 and attempts to find a match with **unmarried(don)**. No match is found, and Turbo Prolog backtracks to Subgoal-1, frees the variable **Person**, and continues this process of satisfying subgoals and backtracking until all solutions are found. The final solutions are:

   Person = dan
   Person = bob.

Try this small knowledge base on your computer. Don't forget to describe the predicates in the predicate section and define the domain types in the domains section. The rule **bachelor(Person)** is described in the predicates section in the same way a fact is described. The program is shown in Table 5-5. When you run the program, enter **bachelor(Person)** at the goal request.

Table 5-5: Bachelor Knowledge Base

/* BACHELOR KNOWLEDGE BASE */ ◄——— *This is a comment in Turbo Prolog. It is ignored by the compiler.*

domains
       person = symbol

predicates
       man(person)
       woman(person)
       unmarried(person)
       married(person)
       bachelor(person)

clauses

/* Fact Section ——————————— */

       man(dan).
       man(ray).
       man(don).
       man(bob).

       woman(francis).

       unmarried(bob).
       unmarried(dan).

       married(ray).
       married(don).

/* Rule Section ——————————— */

       bachelor(Person) if
            man(Person) and
            unmarried(Person).

Now let's look at a more complex example.

A Semantic Network in Turbo Prolog

To demonstrate Turbo Prolog's power to make inferences based on rules, look at a semantic network that expresses the relationship between members of a family. The ability of Turbo Prolog to represent a semantic network is essential to its power. This semantic network is shown in Table 5-6.

Table 5-6: Semantic Network of Familial Relationships

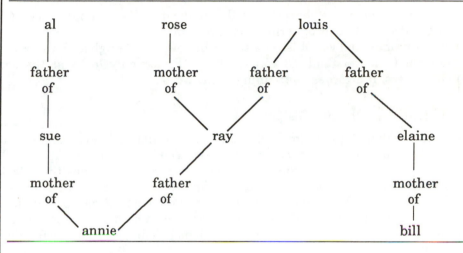

Explicit Relationships

A number of familial relationships are explicitly shown in the network. These are represented by the lines between the names. These explicit relationships are:

1. al is the father of sue.
2. sue is the mother of annie.
3. rose is the mother of ray.
4. louis is the father of ray.
5. ray is the father of annie.
6. louis is the father of elaine.
7. elaine is the mother of bill.

Expressed as Turbo Prolog facts, these relationships are:

1. father_of(sue,al)
2. mother_of(sue,annie)
3. mother_of(ray,rose)
4. father_of(ray,louis)
5. father_of(annie,ray)
6. father_of(elaine,louis)
7. mother_of(bill,elaine)

Notice the underline character in the predicates. For example, look at the predicate **father_of**. The underline character makes it possible to write predicates, object names, and variables in a somewhat everyday English. This makes it easier for you to understand. Of course, Turbo Prolog only looks at the sequence of characters. It attaches no meaning to the words.

Implicit Relationships

Other relationships are implied in the semantic network. For example, you can see that elaine and ray are brother and sister. You know this because they both have the same father and because you know the rule that defines the relationship of brother and sister. It is possible to define these implicit relationships as Turbo Prolog rules. In Tutorial 5-1, you will learn how Turbo Prolog determines that two people are brother and sister if they have the same mother and father. You will also create other rules about the relationships implied in the family semantic network.

In this tutorial, you will learn how to represent the family semantic network as a Turbo Prolog knowledge base. You will enter the knowledge base facts and rules and follow Turbo Prolog as it executes the program. The semantic network is repeated below for reference.

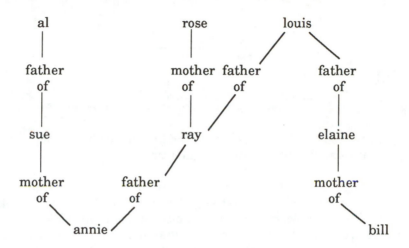

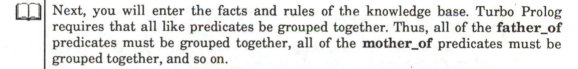

Boot your computer and move the cursor to the Turbo Prolog Editor Window.

Next, you will enter the facts and rules of the knowledge base. Turbo Prolog requires that all like predicates be grouped together. Thus, all of the **father_of** predicates must be grouped together, all of the **mother_of** predicates must be grouped together, and so on.

Enter the knowledge base into the Editor Window as shown. Don't forget to type the **clauses** heading and the periods at the end of each fact. The knowledge base has been arranged with all like predicates grouped together.

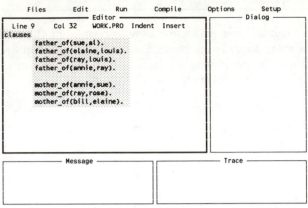

Notice that the number of clauses in the knowledge base is equal to the number of explicit relations (bonds) in the semantic network.

Even though the only relationships that are explicitly stated in the semantic network are mother_of and father_of, a number of additional relationships are implicit. For example, consider the relationship parent_of. You can see that sue is the parent of annie because you know that sue is annie's mother. Generally then, given any two people, call them Person1 and Person2, you know that:

Rule-1   Person2 is the parent of Person1
                              if
               Person2 is the mother of Person1.

You can also see that ray is the parent of annie. This is true because ray is annie's father. Expressing this as a rule, you would say that:

Rule-2   Person2 is the parent of Person1
                              if
               Person2 is the father of Person1.

These relationships can be expressed as two Turbo Prolog rules, they are:

Rule-1   parent_of(Person1,Person2) if
                       mother_of(Person1,Person2).

Rule-2   parent_of(Person1,Person2) if
                       father_of(Person1,Person2).

Add these rules to the knowledge base, as shown below.

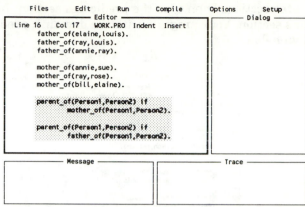

```
         Files      Edit      Run      Compile      Options    Setup
                 ┌─ Editor ─────────────────────┐  ┌─ Dialog ─────────┐
         Line 16    Col 17    WORK.PRO  Indent  Insert
                father_of(elaine,louis).
                father_of(ray,louis).
                father_of(annie,ray).

                mother_of(annie,sue).
                mother_of(ray,rose).
                mother_of(bill,elaine).

                parent_of(Person1,Person2) if
                     mother_of(Person1,Person2).

                parent_of(Person1,Person2) if
                     father_of(Person1,Person2).
                 └──────────────────────────────┘  └──────────────────┘
                 ┌─ Message ────────────┐  ┌─ Trace ──────────────┐
                 │                      │  │                      │
                 │                      │  │                      │
                 └──────────────────────┘  └──────────────────────┘
```

F1-Help F2-Save F3-Load F5-Zoom F6-Next F7-Xcopy F8-Xedit F9-Compile F10-Menu

Running the Program

Before you can execute the program, you must add the predicates and domains sections. To see a larger portion of the Editor Window, press the {F5} key sequence. You can expand any window using this command. Just place the cursor in the window and press {F5}. To return to the regular window size, press the {F5} key sequence again. This key sequence acts as a toggle switch between the enlarged screen and the regular screen.

{F5}   This enlarges the Editor Window to full screen size.

Move the cursor in the Editor Window to the upper left-hand corner of the window and press the {Enter} key several times to make space in the window for the predicates section. Then type the predicates section. In the same fashion type the domains section. Your program with the domains, predicates, and clauses sections is shown below.

```
           Files      Edit      Run      Compile    Options    Setup
                                 ─ Editor ─
  Line 7     Col 9     WORK.PRO  Indent  Insert
  domains
       person=symbol

  predicates
       mother_of(person,person).          father_of(person,person).
       parent_of(person,person).

  clauses
          father_of(sue,al).
          father_of(elaine,louis).

          father_of(ray,louis).
          father_of(annie,ray).

          mother_of(annie,sue).
          mother_of(ray,rose).
          mother_of(bill,elaine).

          parent_of(Person1,Person2) if
                  mother_of(Person1,Person2).

          parent_of(Person1,Person2) if
                  father_of(Person1,Person2).
```
F1-Help F2-Save F3-Load F5-Zoom F6-Next F7-Xcopy F8-Xedit F9-Compile F10-Menu

 If you have entered the three Turbo Prolog sections (clauses, predicates, and domains) correctly, your program is ready to run.

 {Esc} to return the cursor to the Main Menu.

 With the cursor in the main menu, select the **Run** command.

If there are no errors, you should see the goal request displayed in the Dialog Window.

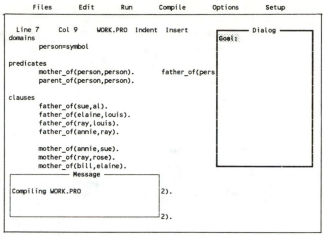

If the goal request is not in the Dialog Window, check the error messages and observe where the cursor is located in the Editor Window. The cursor will be near the location of an error. Check for typographical errors and make sure that the facts and rules end with periods. Check for opening and closing parentheses in the statements. When you correct the error, press the {F10} function key to continue.

Below are a series of questions that can be answered by this knowledge base. The Turbo Prolog goal is shown in the right column.

Question	Turbo Prolog Goal
Is Sue the mother of Annie?	mother_of(sue,annie).
Is Annie the mother of Sue?	mother_of(annie,sue).
List the names of the mothers.	mother_of(_,Mom).
Who are Louis' children?	parent_of(Who,louis).
List the parents.	parent_of(_,Parent).

Enter the first two questions at the goal prompt. The answers to the first two goals are presented below.

```
      Files       Edit       Run       Compile     Options     Setup

    Line 7     Col 9      WORK.PRO  Indent  Insert          ┌─── Dialog ───
domains                                                     │Goal: mother_of(sue,anni
        person=symbol                                       │e)
                                                            │No
predicates                                                  │Goal: mother_of(annie,su
        mother_of(person,person).    father_of(pers         │e)
        parent_of(person,person).                           │Yes
                                                            │Goal:
clauses
        father_of(sue,al).
        father_of(elaine,louis).
        father_of(ray,louis).
        father_of(annie,ray).

        mother_of(annie,sue).
        mother_of(ray,rose).
        mother_of(bill,elaine).
    ┌──────── Message ────────┐
    │                         │         2).
    │Compiling WORK.PRO       │
    │mother_of                │
    │                         │         2).
    └─────────────────────────┘

  F2-Save  F3-Load  F5-Zoom  F6-Next  F8-Previous goal  Shift-F10-Resize  F10-End
```

The answer to the first goal, **mother_of(sue,annie)**, is **No**. Do you know why? It is because there is no match for the objects **sue** and **annie** in the order specified in the goal.

Look at the answer to the second question. Is Annie the mother of Sue? It is true because the objects in the goal statement now match one of the facts in the knowledge base.

The remaining answers are shown below. Your screen will differ slightly because we have expanded the Dialog Window and placed all of the answers in this expanded window. Check your answers with the ones shown here. Your answers should agree if you have entered the knowledge base and goals as shown.

```
┌──────────────────── Dialog ────────────────────┐
│  Goal:mother_of(sue,annie).                     │
│  No                                             │
│  Goal:mother_of(annie,sue).                     │
│  Yes                                            │
│  Goal:mother_of(_,Mom).   <── Who are the mothers?
│  Mom=sue                                        │
│  Mom=rose                                       │
│  Mom=elaine                                     │
│  3 Solutions                                    │
│  Goal:parent_of(Who,louis)  <── Who are louis's children?
│  Who=elaine                                     │
│  Who=ray                                        │
│  2 Solutions                                    │
│  Goal:parent_of(_,Parent)  <── Who are the parents?
│  Parent=sue                                     │
│  Parent=rose                                    │
│  Parent=elaine                                  │
│  Parent=al                                      │
│  Parent=louis                                   │
│  Parent=louis                                   │
│  Parent=ray                                     │
│  7 Solutions                                    │
│  Goal:parent_of(Child,_)  <── Who are the children?
│  Child=annie                                    │
│  Child=ray                                      │
│  Child=bill                                     │
│  Child=sue                                      │
│  Child=elaine                                   │
│  Child=ray                                      │
│  Child=annie                                    │
│  7 Solutions                                    │
│  Goal:                                          │
└─────────────────────────────────────────────────┘
```

By adding additional facts, you can express more relationships. Since many relationships between people depend upon their gender, this information can be added to the knowledge base.

Add the gender information, using the predicates **male** and **female**, to the knowledge base. Don't forget to declare the predicates in the predicates section. The amended program is shown on the next page.

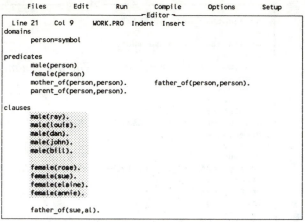

```
          Files      Edit       Run      Compile      Options      Setup
                                ┌─Editor─┐
     Line 21    Col 9      WORK.PRO  Indent  Insert
 domains
         person=symbol

 predicates
         male(person)
         female(person)
         mother_of(person,person).          father_of(person,person).
         parent_of(person,person).

 clauses
         male(ray).
         male(louis).
         male(dan).
         male(john).
         male(bill).

         female(rose).
         female(sue).
         female(elaine).
         female(annie).

         father_of(sue,al).
```

F1-Help F2-Save F3-Load F5-Zoom F6-Next F7-Xcopy F8-Xedit F9-Compile F10-Menu

Since Turbo Prolog can determine if someone is another person's parent, you can use the **parent_of** rule in other definitions of relationships. Try to think of a rule that describes the relationship brother.

One approach is to look at the part of the semantic network that shows the brother-sister relationship of ray and elaine. It is shown in Table 5-7.

Table 5-7: Brother-Sister Relationship

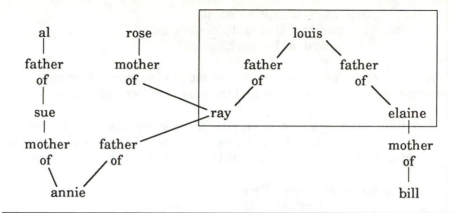

The boxed part of the semantic network shows that ray is the brother of elaine, because they both have louis as a father.

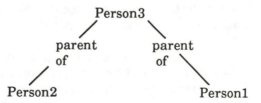

Let's define a general rule to describe all brother relationships. To do this, you can substitute variables for the names in the semantic network. It looks like the following:

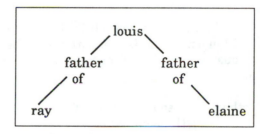

From this semantic network, you can now specify a Horn clause that describes the relationships. That is, if Person2 and Person1 have the same father or parent, they are related as brother and sister. The Horn clause is:

        Person2 is the brother of Person1 if
            Person3 is the parent of Person1 and
            Person3 is the parent of Person2.

The Turbo Prolog rule looks like this:

        brother_of(Person1,Person2) if
                parent_of(Person1,Person3) and
                parent_of(Person2,Person3).

Stated another way, this rule says that the brother of Person1 is Person2 if the parent of Person1 is Person3 and the parent of Person2 is also Person3.

This rule is not complete, however. There is no way to tell whether Person1 or Person2 is male or female. As stated **brother_of** could be a sister. Thus, we have to add information to the rule that tells us that Person2 must be a male.

        brother_of(Person1,Person2) if
                male(Person2) and
                parent_of(Person1,Person3) and
                parent_of(Person2,Person3).

To complete this rule, you must tell Turbo Prolog not to select the same person as Person1 and Person2. That is, Person1 cannot be the same person as Person2. As in the Famous Bowlers knowledge base, use the not-equal-to notation [<>] to indicate this.

        brother_of(Person1,Person2) if
                male(Person2) and
                parent_of(Person1,Person3) and
                parent_of(Person2,Person3) and
                Person1 <> Person2.

This completes the **brother_of** rule. It says that the brother of Person1 is Person2 if Person2 is a male, the parent of Person1 is Person3, the parent of Person2 is also Person3, and, finally, that Person1 is not Person2.

How about a **sister_of** rule? Can you write a rule that specifies that one person is the sister of another person? Of course you can. Just change the **male(Person2)** to the **female(Person2)** predicate. A **sister_of** rule would be :

        sister_of(Person1,Person2) if
                female(Person2) and
                parent_of(Person1,Person3) and
                parent_of(Person2,Person3) and
                Person1 <> Person2.

Add these two new rules to the clauses section. Remember to keep like predicates together. Also, keep the rules together. Don't forget to describe the **brother** and **sister** predicates in the predicates section.

When you have entered the new rules and defined the predicates of **brother** and **sister,** check your program against the one program listed below.

```
─────────────────── Editor ───────────────────
domains
        person=symbol

predicates
        male(person)
        female(person)
        mother_of(person,person)
        father_of(person,person)
        parent_of(person,person)
        brother_of(person,person)
        sister_of(person,person)

clauses
        male(ray).
        male(louis).
        male(dan).
        male(john).
        male(bill).

        female(rose).
        female(sue).
        female(elaine).
        female(annie).

        father_of(sue,al).
        father_of(elaine,louis).
        father_of(ray,louis).
        father_of(annie,ray).

        mother_of(annie,sue).
        mother_of(ray,rose).
        mother_of(bill,elaine).

parent_of(Person1,Person2) if
        mother_of(Person1,Person2).
parent_of(Person1,Person2) if
        father_of(Person1,Person2).

brother_of(Person1,Person2) if
        male(Person2) and
        parent_of(Person1,Person3) and
        parent_of(Person2,Person3) and
        Person1<>Person2.

sister_of(Person1,Person2) if
        female(Person2) and
        parent_of(Person1,Person3) and
        parent_of(Person2,Person3) and
        Person1<>Person2.
```

Run the program and answer the following questions:

1. Who is Ray's sister?
2. Elaine is the sister of whom?
3. Does Ray have a brother?
4. Does Elaine have a brother?

The goals and their answers are shown in Table 5-8.

Table 5-8: Answers to Brother and Sister Goals

1.   Goal:sister_of(ray, Who)
      Who = elaine
      1 solution

2.   Goal:sister_of(Who,elaine)
      Who = ray
      1 solution

3.   Goal:brother_of(ray,Who)
      No Solution

4.   Goal:brother_of(elaine,Who)
      Who=ray
      1 solution

Adding More Relationships

Look at how the grandfather relationship can be inferred from the semantic network.

This semantic net shows that louis is the grandfather of bill.

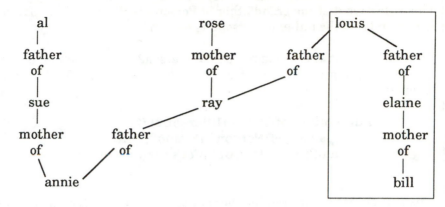

Creating a Grandfather and Grandmother Rule

To make the specific rule that louis is the grandfather of bill into a general rule that would work for other family trees, first replace the **mother_of** relationship between elaine and bill to a **parent_of** rule.

Notice that louis must be a father to be a grandfather. Only people that are fathers can be grandfathers, so we don't change this rule. However, we want to change the **mother_of** to **parent_of** because it is more general. It does not matter whether elaine is a mother or father, louis is still the grandfather. Substituting variables for names, the semantic net becomes:

Original Semantic Net	Revised Semantic Net	Generalized Semantic Net
louis	louis	Person2
father of	father of	father of
elaine	elaine	Person3
mother of	parent of	parent of
bill	bill	Person1

Expressing this semantic net in Turbo Prolog, the grandfather rule is:

grandfather_of(Person1,Person2) if
      parent_of(Person1,Person3) and
      father_of(Person3,Person2).

This rule says that the grandfather of Person1 is Person2 if the parent of Person1 is Person3 and the father of Person3 is Person2.

Now, how about the grandmother? If Person2 is the mother of Person3, then Person2 is the grandmother of Person1. Expressed as a Turbo Prolog rule this becomes:

grandmother_of(Person1,Person2) if
      parent_of(Person1,Person3) and
      mother_of(Person3,Person2).

This rule says that the grandmother of Person1 is Person2 if the parent of Person1 is Person 3 and the mother of Person3 is Person2.

Add these rules to the family knowledge base. Also, don't forget to add the **grandfather_of(person,person)** and **grandmother_of(person,person)** predicate definitions to the predicates section. Your program should now look like the one on the next page.

```
                              ── Editor ──────────────
    domains
            person=symbol

    predicates
            male(person)
            female(person)
            mother_of(person,person)
            father_of(person,person)
            parent_of(person,person)
            brother_of(person,person)
            sister_of(person,person)
            grandfather_of(person,person)
            grandmother_of(person,person)

    clauses
            male(ray).
            male(louis).
            male(dan).
            male(john).
            male(bill).

            female(rose).
            female(sue).
            female(elaine).
            female(annie).

            father_of(sue,al).
            father_of(elaine,louis).
            father_of(ray,louis).
            father_of(annie,ray).

            mother_of(annie,sue).
            mother_of(ray,rose).
            mother_of(bill,elaine).

    parent_of(Person1,Person2) if
            mother_of(Person1,Person2).
    parent_of(Person1,Person2) if
            father_of(Person1,Person2).

    brother_of(Person1,Person2) if
            male(Person2) and
            parent_of(Person1,Person3) and
            parent_of(Person2,Person3) and
            Person1<>Person2.

    sister_of(Person1,Person2) if
            female(Person2) and
            parent_of(Person1,Person3) and
            parent_of(Person2,Person3) and
            Person1<>Person2.

    grandfather_of(Person1,Person2) if
            parent_of(Person1,Person3) and
            father_of(Person3,Person2).

    grandmother_of(Person1,Person2) if
            parent_of(Person1,Person3) and
            mother_of(Person3,Person2).
```

 Try these goals:

grandfather_of(Grandchild,Grandpa)
grandmother _of(Grandchild,Grandma)

Adding an Aunt Rule

Looking again at the familial semantic network, we can see that elaine is the aunt of annie. How do we know that? We know that because ray and elaine are brother and sister, and elaine will be an aunt to any of ray's children. annie is ray's daughter; therefore, elaine is annie's aunt. The trick now is to translate this relationship into Turbo Prolog.

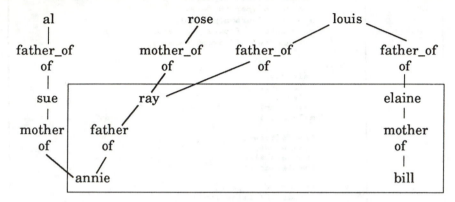

The relationship between ray and elaine is already known, they are brother and sister. You also know that ray is annie's parent. We can express this in another net.

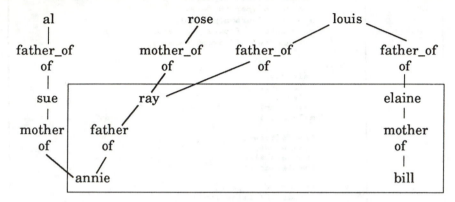

From this it is clear that elaine is annie's aunt. Using this semantic net, substitute variables for the specific names. The resulting semantic net is:

Person3—— sister_of —— Person2
|
parent_of
|
Person1

From this semantic net above, we can see that elaine is the aunt of annie, or Person3 is the aunt of Person1. The Turbo Prolog rule showing the general aunt relationship is:

aunt_of(Person1,Person3) if
sister_of(Person2,Person3) and
parent_of(Person1,Person2).

Add this rule to the clauses section of your data base. Also add the **aunt** predicate to the predicates section. When completed, your knowledge base should be as follows:

```
domains
        person=symbol

predicates
        male(person)
        female(person)
        mother_of(person,person)
        father_of(person,person)
        parent_of(person,person)
        brother_of(person,person)
        sister_of(person,person)
        grandfather_of(person,person)
        grandmother_of(person,person)
        aunt_of(person,person)

clauses
        male(ray).
        male(louis).
        male(dan).
        male(john).
        male(bill).

        female(rose).
        female(sue).
        female(elaine).
        female(annie).

        father_of(sue,al).
        father_of(elaine,louis).
        father_of(ray,louis).
        father_of(annie,ray).

        mother_of(annie,sue).
        mother_of(ray,rose).
        mother_of(bill,elaine).

parent_of(Person1,Person2) if
        mother_of(Person1,Person2).
parent_of(Person1,Person2) if
        father_of(Person1,Person2).

brother_of(Person1,Person2) if
        male(Person2) and
        parent_of(Person1,Person3) and
        parent_of(Person2,Person3) and
        Person1<>Person2.

sister_of(Person1,Person2) if
        female(Person2) and
        parent_of(Person1,Person3) and
        parent_of(Person2,Person3) and
        Person1<>Person2.

grandfather_of(Person1,Person2) if
        parent_of(Person1,Person3) and
        father_of(Person3,Person2).

grandmother_of(Person1,Person2) if
        parent_of(Person1,Person3) and
        mother_of(Person3,Person2).

aunt_of(Person1,Person3) if
        sister_of(Person2,Person3) and
        parent_of(Person1,Person2).
```

Now run the program and input a goal to ask who is annie's aunt. The goal would be:

Goal:**aunt_of(annie,Who).**

 The following result will appear in your Dialog Window showing that elaine is annie's aunt.

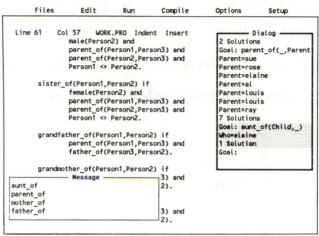

This is the end of Tutorial 5-1 and Chapter 5.

Complete the exercises and problems, and then move on to Chapter 6, where you will learn how to control Turbo Prolog programs through input and output commands, device commands, and predicates that can make your programs user friendly.

Exercises

5-1.   What are the parts of a rule?

5-2.   Explain the difference between a data base and a knowledge base.

5-3.   Turbo Prolog recognizes two symbols for the if conjunction. What are these symbols?

5-4.   What is the first part of a Turbo Prolog rule declaration called?

5-5.   What is the part of a rule statement that contains the subgoals?

5-6.   What determines if a rule head succeeds?

Problems

5-1.   Write a program that determines who might drive to the movies next Saturday. The facts that are known are:

John has a license.	Jane has a license.
Sally has a license.	Jim has a license.
Bob has a license.	Sally has a car.
Fred has a car.	John has a car.
Jane can borrow a car.	Bob can borrow a car.
John has insurance.	Sally has insurance.
Jane has insurance.	Bob has insurance.

Two rules determine whether a person can drive. The first says, "A person can drive if that person has a license and has a car and has insurance."

The second rule says, "A person can drive if that person has a license and can borrow a car and has insurance."

Write the facts and rules as Turbo Prolog clauses and enter them in the Editor. The output of the program should look like this:

Goal:can_drive_to_movies(Who).
Who=john, Who=sally
Who=jane, Who=bob

5-2.   Your friend Karen has asked you to write a program to help her decide who she might like to date. She has several facts about some gentlemen she knows:

Mike is tall.	Joe has a sense of humor.
Joe is tall.	Danny has a sense of humor.
Chuck is tall.	Bill has a sense of humor.
Bill is tall.	

Fred is good looking.	Bill has a good personality.
Joe is good looking.	Danny has a good personality.
Bill is good looking.	Joe has a good personality.
Danny is good looking.	Chuck has a good personality.

Obviously, Karen wants to date men who are tall and good looking and have a good sense of humor and have a good personality. Translate the facts and rule into Turbo Prolog clauses. The output of the program should be:

Goal:**karen_wants_to_date(Who).**
Who=joe, Who=bill

5-3.   Write a program to help a personnel manager to decide who to hire for a job. Here are the facts:

Joanne has a college degree.
Gina has a college degree.
Sherry has a college degree.
Greg has a college degree.
Lenny has a college degree.

Sherry has work experience.
Greg has work experience.
John has work experience.
Lenny has work experience.

Lenny has references.
Gina has references.
Greg has references.
John has references.

Naturally, only persons with a college education, work experience, and references will be considered. Represent the facts and rule in Turbo Prolog clauses. The output of the program looks like this:

Goal:will_hire(Who).
Who=greg, Who=lenny

Chapter 6
Controlling Turbo Prolog Programs

The presentation of a program to the user is an important facet of programming in any language. This chapter will show you how to use internal goals, set the graphics on the screen, make windows, change colors, send information to a printer, accept replies from the user, write information on the monitor, and use sound commands. Also in this chapter is an introduction to the concept of recursion which begins a spiral approach to this important concept.

Controlling Turbo Prolog Programs

You have seen that in solving problems with Turbo Prolog, you must know how to ask a question in a way that makes sense to the language. In Turbo Prolog questions are called goals, and they must be stated in an exact manner. If you don't know Prolog, asking a question in the goal format is not something that is readily apparent.

Most computer languages provide a way for the user of the program to communicate with the computer in a natural, English-like manner. The ability to write messages on the screen and to accept information from the user is an essential part of developing any program for others to use. Turbo Prolog is no exception. It provides special predicates to accomplish these processes.

Computer languages are also expected to take advantage of the hardware capacity of the microcomputer. Turbo Prolog excels in this regard by providing internal predicates for computer graphics, sound, and music. It also provides internal predicates for complete control of the computer screen. This includes support for one or more windows and colors. In this chapter, you will learn about the Turbo Prolog predicates that accomplish these tasks.

Internal Goals

The goals studied so far are known as external goals. They exist outside of the program itself. When you ran a program, Turbo Prolog stopped, printed the word **Goal:** in the Dialog Window and waited for you to input the goal. You were then expected to type the goal in a format Turbo Prolog could understand.

Turbo Prolog also uses goals located within the program. These goals, called **internal goals**, are entered into a special section of the program called the **goal section**. This is done just as you would enter the clauses, predicates, and domains sections. The structure of a Turbo Prolog program that includes an internal goal is shown in Figure 6-1 on the next page.

Figure 6-1: Structure of Turbo Prolog Program with Internal Goal

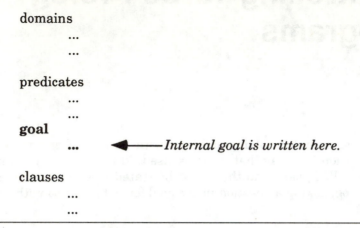

As you will see, internal goals behave somewhat differently than external goals. If you are accustomed to programming in procedural languages, it may be useful to think that internal goals act like the main procedure of a program while the clauses are like subroutines. Turbo Prolog's internal backtracking mechanism prevents us from pushing this analogy too far, however. Nevertheless, some of the standard predicates introduced in this chapter will be stated as internal goals in the goal section of the programs.

Standard Predicates as Internal Goals

Suppose you were asked to write a computer program that executes the following steps:

1. Display a window in the middle of the screen with a title.
2. Provide a black background for the text in the window.
3. Make the borders of the window red and the text blue.
4. Ask for the user's name.
5. Get a reply.
6. Greet the user, using his/her name.

The following screen shows the result of a Turbo Prolog program that does this.

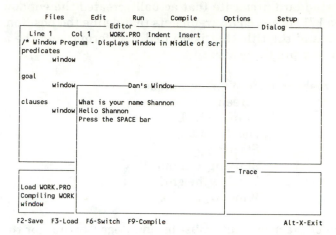

The program that causes the display of Dan's Window is shown in Figure 6-2. Writing this program in Turbo Prolog requires several of the standard built-in commands. These commands, like everything else in Turbo Prolog, are expressed as predicates. Turbo Prolog has a number of built-in predicates. They are called standard predicates. Since they are available from within the language, it is not required that they be defined in the predicates section.

Figure 6-2: Program to Display Window in Middle of Screen

/* Window Program - Displays Window in Middle of Screen */

predicates
      window
goal
      window.
clauses
      window if
            makewindow(1,1,4,"Dan's Window",8,15,16,40) and
            nl and
            write("What is your name? ") and
            readln(Name) and
            write("Hello, ",Name).

Four standard predicates are used in this program. They are **makewindow, nl, write,** and **readln.** The predicate **window** is the rule head of the rule in the clauses section. Since we have created it, it must be declared in the predicates section. We will examine each part of this program in detail.

The makewindow Predicate

This is the most complicated of the predicates to be discussed in this chapter. It is the standard predicate that actually created the window titled Dan's Window on page 171. It has eight arguments that define the position of the window, the colors used, and the title that is printed. The format and the arguments for the **makewindow** predicate are:

```
makewindow(Window_number,
           Screen_attribute,
           Frame_attribute,
           Header_attribute,
           Starting_row,
           Starting_column,
           Window_height,
           Window_width).
```

Each of the arguments must be an integer, except for the Header attribute which must be a string or symbol. Each of the arguments can be a variable if it is bound prior to execution of the predicate.

Window_number

The first argument of the **makewindow** predicate is an integer assigned to the window. Because several windows can be opened at one time, Turbo Prolog requires a way to identify each window. The **Window_number** variable is bound to this number. In the example, we have numbered the window as 1. Thereafter, this number can be used to refer to this particular window.

Screen_attribute

The **Screen_attribute** argument determines the colors of the window's background color and the text within the window. If you have a monochrome monitor, you have a choice of three attributes. Figure 6-3 presents the values used for monochrome monitors. Where it says white for the foreground colors, this may be green or amber, depending upon your type of monitor.

Figure 6-3: Values for Monochrome Monitors

Screen_attribute #	Background	Foreground	Type of Screen
0	Black	Black	Blank Screen
7	Black	White	Normal Video
112	White	Black	Inverse Video

As an example of setting the attributes for a monochrome monitor, suppose you want the text to be displayed in white (green or amber) on a black background. To accomplish this, you would add the value of 0 for the black background to the value of 7 for white (green or amber) text. If you want the text to blink, add 128 to the two previous values. Thus, a Screen_attribute value of 7 would display white (green or amber) text on a black background. If the value of the Screen_attribute is 135, then the text will blink. If you want inverse video, then assign a value of 112 to the Screen_attribute. For a blinking, inverse video, a value of 240 would be assigned to the Screen_attribute argument.

If you have a color monitor, you can choose colors for the background, the foreground, and the border. Figure 6-4 shows the colors and their respective attribute numbers.

Figure 6-4: Colors for Color Monitors

Foreground Colors	Number	Background Colors	Number
Black	0	Black	0
Blue	1	Blue	16
Green	2	Green	32
Cyan	3	Cyan	48
Red	4	Red	64
Magenta	5	Magenta	80
Brown	6	Brown	96
White	7	White	112
Gray	8		
Light Blue	9		
Light Green	10		
Light Cyan	11		
Light Red	12		
Light Magenta	13		
Yellow	14		
White (Hi-Intensity)	15		

To choose a value for the colors, select a background color and a foreground color. Add the corresponding numbers and use the result as the Screen_attribute value. For example, to have a window with a green background and yellow text, you would add the value of the green background (32) to the value of yellow foreground (14) for a result of 46. The Screen_attribute value would be 46. If you want the text on the screen to blink, then add 128 to the calculated Screen_attribute value. A Screen_attribute value of 174 would provide a green background with blinking yellow text.

Frame_attribute

The third argument in the **makewindow** predicate is the Frame_attribute value. This value determines the color of the border of the window. The values for the border are shown in Figure 6-5.

Figure 6-5: Border Frame_attribute Values

Color of Border	Frame_attribute Value
No border	0
Blue	1
Green	2
Light blue	3
Red	4
Magenta	5
Yellow	6
White	7
Brown	8
Blinking White	-1
Blinking Yellow	-2
Blinking Magenta	-3
Blinking Red	-4
Blinking Light Blue	-5
Blinking Light Green	-6
Blinking Blue	-7
Blinking Gray	-8

For a window with a blinking, light-green border, assign the value of -6 to the Frame_attribute argument. If you do not wish a border, the value would be 0.

Header_attribute

The Header_attribute is a string or symbol indicating a title for the window. If you do not want to title a window, then place opposing quotation marks ("")for the value of the Header_attribute. This is called a null attribute. In the example, we titled the window "Dan's Window". As you can see in the screen on page 171, the title is centered in the window.

Position and Size of Window

The last four arguments provide information about the size and position of the window. The Starting_row and Starting_column provide the coordinates for positioning the window, while the Window_height and Window_width arguments provide information about the size of the window.

Starting_row

The Starting_row attribute is an integer that denotes the starting row of the window. Your monitor screen is divided into 25 rows by 80 columns. Rows are numbered from 0 to 24. Columns are numbered from 0 to 79. If you want your window to start on the fifth row, then the value of the Starting_row attribute would be equal to 4. The value for the Starting_row attribute in the example is 8.

Starting_column

As stated, the number of columns on your monitor is 80, and they are numbered from 0 to 79. The value you assign to the Starting_column attribute determines where the left side of the window starts. In our example, the Starting_column value was set to 15.

Window_height

The total number of rows occupied by the window is specified by the Window_height attribute. This is an integer number with a maximum value of 25 — the total number of rows allowed on your screen. The value set in the example is 16. The window height is calculated using the Starting_row number and counting downward the number of rows specified by the Window_height attribute.

Window_width

The Window_width value is an integer indicating how many columns wide the window will be. The counting starts at the column number specified in the Starting_column attribute and moves to the right. The maximum value for the window width is 80. Our example specified a window width of 40 starting at column number 15. This would place the right hand margin of the window in the 55th column.

An error condition will result if you specify a value for the Window_height and/or Window_width attributes that would position the edge of the window beyond the limits of the screen. For example, if we had specified a Window_height of 23, this would place the bottom of the window in row 39. Since there is no row 39, Turbo Prolog would display an error message informing you that a parameter in the **makewindow** predicate is illegal.

The nl, write, and readln Predicates

The remainder of the internal predicates in the program are fairly straight-forward. The clauses section of our example program is reproduced in Figure 6-6 for your convenience. We have discussed the **makewindow** internal predicate, now we will look at the remaining internal predicates used in this example program.

Figure 6-6: Example Program

```
clauses
    window if
    makewindow(1,1,4,"Dan's Window",8,15,16,40) and
    nl and
    write("What is your name? ") and
    readln(Name) and
    write("Hello, ",Name).
```

The nl Predicate

The **nl** standard predicate is a predicate without any arguments. As such, it always succeeds. It means to move the cursor, or the printer head, to the next line. After the window is drawn by the **makewindow** predicate, the **nl** predicate moves the cursor to the next line.

The write Predicate – Sending Messages to the User

The **write** predicate is one of the more useful standard predicates in that it writes messages to the display or printer. It can include any number of constants or bound variables as its argument(s). The format of the **write** predicate is:

write("Arg1,Arg2,Arg3,...Argn")

Where Arg1, Arg2, Arg3,...Argn represent the arguments – objects, strings, and/or Turbo Prolog variables to be written.

Strings must be enclosed within quotation marks, and the variables must be bound prior to execution of the predicate. If you want your computer to communicate with the user of the program, you would use the **write** predicate. Here we ask for the user to type in his/her name.

write("What is your name?")

Turbo Prolog, when executing this standard predicate, would print the greeting as shown with a following space:

What is your name?

As seen, the **write** predicate displays on the screen the characters or words enclosed within the quotation marks. The quotation marks are not printed. You can also have Turbo Prolog write the values of variables, special control characters, and ASCII characters to your monitor. The **write** predicate is a very useful predicate. You will use it often. Other examples are shown in Figure 6-7:

Figure 6-7: Examples of the write Predicate

Example	Explanation
write("ABC587")	Displays the alphanumeric string ABC587.
write(Person)	Displays the value bound to the variable **Person**. Notice that the variable **Person** is not enclosed within quotes.
write('H')	Displays the character H on the screen.
write('\13')	Causes a line feed. The "\" symbol followed by a number prints the ASCII code associated with that number. A line feed is represented by the ASCII code 13.

Backslash \ Command

Turbo Prolog has three backslash \ commands that control the placement of the cursor on the screen or the printhead of the printer. These are: **backslash n**, **backslash b**, and **backslash t**. Stated in Turbo, they are **\n**, **\b**, and **\t**, respectively. When combined with the **write** command, they give the programmer significant control over how information is displayed on the screen and how information is printed on paper. These commands must be enclosed within either single or double quotation marks. They also may be included within strings that are surrounded by quotation marks. Examples are shown in Figure 6-8 on the next page.

Figure 6-8: Backslash Commands

Command	Description
write('\n') or write("\n")	Causes a line feed. The "\" symbol followed by the letter 'n' causes a new line to be printed. The result is the same as the standard predicate nl.
write('\b') or write("\b")	Causes a backspace. The "\" symbol followed by the small letter 'b' will cause the cursor to backspace one character.
write('\t') or write("\t")	The "\" symbol followed by the letter "t" causes the cursor to move to the next tab.
write("HELP\nME")	Prints the word HELP on one line and the word ME on the line following. The backslash command [\n] causes the cursor or printer head to move to the next line where the remainder of the string is printed.

You have no doubt noticed the use of the single and double quotes in the examples. Turbo Prolog treats them alike. As in most computer programming languages, letters, numbers, and symbols between the quotes are printed literally. If something is not between the single or double quotation marks, Turbo Prolog treats it as a variable or object and prints the value of the object bound to the variable.

The readln Predicate: Getting a Reply from the User

Transferring information from the user to the program is an important requirement of any computer language. One of the most important is Turbo Prolog's standard predicate the **readln** predicate. Its format is shown below:

readln(Argument)

The **readln** predicate has one argument, and this argument must be a variable. The **readln** predicate causes execution of the program to stop and waits for a response from the user. The response is then bound to the variable specified in the argument. The program then continues. As with the other standard predicates, the **readln** predicate does not have to be declared in the predicates section.

In our example, the **readln** predicate was written as:

readln(Name)

The **readln** predicate pauses and waits for the user to type in a name. We typed in the name Shannon causing the variable **Name** to be bound to the value **Shannon**. The following **write** predicate printed the contents between the quotes, which was Hello, followed by the value of the variable **Name**, which was Shannon (see the screen on page 171).

Variations of the readln Predicate

The **readln** predicate will always expect the input from the user to be either symbols or strings. However, Turbo Prolog provides other read predicates to accept input of other domain types. These additional predicates and their format are:

readchar(Variable)   *<—Read a Character*
readint(Variable)   *<—Read an Integer Number*
readreal(Variable)   *<—Read a Real Number*

The **readchar(Variable)** predicate reads a single character only. When the readchar predicate is presented, it will succeed when the first character is entered. It will not wait for more characters. This predicate is useful when you want single answers, such as Y for Yes or N for No.

The **readint(Variable)** predicate accepts integers only. Any other input will be rejected by the predicate.

The **readreal(Variable)** predicate accepts real numbers. This predicate is useful for computations and input requiring numbers with decimal points.

This completes the explanation of our example. However, there are more standard predicates, and you will learn about them next.

More Window Predicates

There are four other standard predicates that deal with windows. They are **clearwindow**, **shiftwindow**, **gotowindow**, and **removewindow**. They are, for the most part, self-explanatory, but we will discuss them briefly.

The clearwindow Predicate

The **clearwindow** predicate clears any text or graphics from the currently active window. The window remains intact. **Clearwindow** has no arguments. You can examine how it works by entering it as a goal the next time you are entering goals via the Dialog Window. At the goal prompt, just type **clearwindow**, and the window will be cleared. The format for the **clearwindow** predicate is:

    clearwindow

The shiftwindow Predicate

The **shiftwindow** predicate is used to shift the active window from one window to another. It allows windows to overlap when the current window is larger than the previous one. When one window overlaps other windows, the information in the overlapped windows is retained in memory, so it can be displayed again when a shift is made back to that window. You have observed this happening when you access selections from the Main Menu. The **shiftwindow** has one argument. The format for this predicate is as follows:

    shiftwindow(Window_number)

Where **Window_number** is the number of the window to which Turbo Prolog is to shift. This is the integer number specified in the **makewindow** predicate.

The gotowindow Predicate

The **gotowindow** predicate allows for a fast shift from one window to another window, if the windows do not overlap. This is similar to the **shiftwindow** predicate, except that it is faster. However, it does not accommodate overlapping windows. You should use this predicate to shift from window to window whenever overlapping windows are not a problem.

The **gotowindow** predicate has one argument. It is the number of the window to which the **gotowindow** predicate directs Turbo Prolog. The number is the number specified in the **makewindow** predicate. It will always succeed if the value for **Window_number** is valid. The format for the **gotowindow** predicate is:

    gotowindow(Window_number)

Where **Window_number** is the number of the window to which to go.

The removewindow Predicate

The **removewindow** predicate is just what is sounds like. It removes the currently active window and its contents from the display. If other windows are defined behind the removed window, they will be displayed. Turbo Prolog displays whatever was current prior to the removal of the active window. No arguments are required for the **removewindow** predicate. As such, it will always succeed. Its format is:

    removewindow

The cursor Predicate

Another standard predicate that comes in handy is the **cursor** predicate. This predicate positions the cursor in a specified window, or location, on your screen. The default cursor position in any window is in the upper left-hand corner of that window. However, you can place the cursor anywhere within a window. The **cursor** predicate has two arguments. Its format is:

cursor(Row_number, Column_number)

Where the argument **Row_number** is the number of the row upon which the cursor is to rest, and the **Column_number** is the column number. The Row_ and Column_numbers are calculated from the coordinates of the upper left-hand corner of the screen (0,0). If you attempt to place a cursor outside of the active window, Turbo Prolog will display an error message.

Sending Information to the Printer

Turbo Prolog provides a predicate to send information to the printer instead of the display. The predicate that accomplishes this is:

writedevice(Devicename)

This predicate has one argument which specifies the device to which the output is to be written. This argument **devicename** is either **printer, screen,** or a symbolic filename. When this goal is encountered, Turbo Prolog resets the output device to the device named in the argument. All subsequent output from the **write** predicate will be written to the new device.

To redirect Turbo Prolog's output to the printer, you would use the **writedevice** predicate as:

writedevice(printer) <——*Sends output to printer*

To redirect Turbo Prolog's output back to the display screen, the **writedevice** predicate would be written as:

writedevice(screen) <——*Sends output to monitor*

A Note of Caution – If you use the **writedevice(printer)** predicate, remember to reset the device to the screen before your program ends. If not, your computer will continue to send information to your printer. Also, your printer must be on for the **writedevice(printer)** to work. If Turbo Prolog executes this predicate when the printer is off-line, the computer system will "hang." If this happens, press [CTRL-BREAK] to regain control.

Setting Graphics and Color Mode

Note – The following discussion focuses on CGA (Color Graphics Adapter) monitors. If you have another type of color monitor and you are using Turbo Prolog version 2.0 (or a later version), refer to the Turbo Prolog User's Guide.

Turbo Prolog provides a standard predicate for setting the graphics mode. As with the **makewindow** predicate, the **graphics** predicate allows the use of color and drawings in many of your programs. The Towers of Hanoi program in Chapter 1 is an example of this capability.

The proper use of graphics and color in a program can enhance its use and display information in an attractive format. As such, the **graphics** predicate is an important part of Turbo Prolog. It should be mentioned, however, that the **graphics** predicate can be used only with color monitors.

The **dot** and **line** predicates give you the capability to draw figures on your display. These predicates will be discussed later in this section along with turtle graphics.

The graphics Predicate

The **graphics** predicate has three arguments – one to set the graphics mode, the second argument to set the color palette, and the third argument to set the background color. The predicate and its format are shown below:

graphics(Mode,Palette,Background)

Mode	*Palette*	*Background*
(1-5)	*(0-1)*	*(0-15)*
Graphics	*Color*	*Background*
Mode	*Palette Color*	

Mode

The **mode** argument is used to set the graphics mode. The value of this argument can range from 1 to 5. Each number represents a particular resolution of display on your monitor that is governed by the type of color graphics board installed on your computer. The most prevalent color standard is called CGA (Color Graphics Adapter). This mode is derived from the first color graphics board IBM used in its early PC's. Since then a number of higher resolution boards have been offered with IBM's standard EGA (Extended Graphics Adapter) being the most frequently imitated. With the introduction of the new PS/2 computers, IBM has introduced a new resolution standard called VGA. This new graphics mode will no doubt be the prevailing standard within a very short time.

The graphics modes available within Turbo Prolog and their mode numbers are shown in Figure 6-9. Each mode is shown with its particular resolution and the number of displayed colors. The definition of a graphics mode is made in units called pixels. Pixels are small picture elements on your display screen that can be turned on or off in colors specified by a particular mode. A graphics picture displayed on your screen is a collection of these pixels. The more pixels that can be controlled the finer will be the resolution of the image. Pixels are positioned on the video display in terms of horizontal and vertical lines. For example, mode 1 displays a resolution of 200 by 320 pixels. This means that the horizontal lines are made up of 320 pixels, and vertical lines are made up of 200 pixels. Figure 6-9 lists the possible graphics modes available from within Turbo Prolog.

Figure 6-9: Mode Settings

Mode	# Rows	# Col	Description	Text	Board
1	200	320	Medium resolution, 4 colors	40	CGA
2	200	640	High resolution, black & white	80	CGA
3	200	320	Medium resolution, 16 colors	40	EGA
4	200	640	High resolution, 16 colors	80	EGA
5	350	640	Enhanced resolution, 13 colors	80	EGA

Look at mode 1. The information in Figure 6-9 says that the pixel resolution is 200 by 320. This is called medium resolution and can display a maximum of 4 colors on the screen at one time. Mode 1 displays text in 40 columns across the screen. This is a large size text and is frequently used in programs written for younger children. Mode 2 displays text in an 80-column format and is the standard resolution of most IBM computers and their compatibles. Mode 2, however, has a higher number of pixels per vertical line and can display information with a finer resolution than mode 1.

If you have a CGA card and monitor, you can't use modes 3 through 5. If you try to use these modes, your system may crash. Unless you are sure that your system works with these modes, don't try them.

Palette Color

The second argument of the **graphics** predicate specifies the color of the palette. There are two palettes – palette 0 and palette 1. Each has its own color spectrum. The palettes and their color spectrums are shown in Figure 6-10.

Figure 6-10: Color Palettes for Medium Resolution

Palette	Color 1	Color 2	Color 3
0	Green	Red	Yellow
1	Cyan	Magenta	White

The palette determines which colors are available to draw a line or place a dot. If you choose palette 0, then the colors green, red, and yellow can be used. The color green would be selected by the number 1, red by 2, and yellow by 3. Palette 1 works in the same manner.

Background Color

The third argument of the graphics predicate tells Turbo Prolog the color to paint the background of your screen if you are using modes 1, 3, or 4. If you are using mode 2, the background is always black, and the number chosen for this argument determines the color of the foreground text, lines, dots, and window borders. There are 15 colors ranging from black to high intensity white. The codes and their corresponding colors are shown in Figure 6-11.

Figure 6-11: Background Colors (Modes 1, 2, 3, and 4)

Code	Color	Code	Color
0	Black	8	Grey
1	Blue	9	Light blue
2	Green	10	Light green
3	Cyan	11	Light cyan
4	Red	12	Light red
5	Magenta	13	Light magenta
6	Brown	14	Yellow
7	White	15	High-intensity White

Graphics mode 5, however, provides a choice of 13 different background colors. The code numbers are different from those shown in Figure 6-11. The mode 5 background colors are shown in Figure 6-12.

Figure 6-12: Background Colors for Mode 5

Code	Color	Code	Color
0	Black	7	White
1	Blue	8	Deep Green
2	Green	9	Light Blue
3	Cyan	10	Light Green
4	Red	11	Light Cyan
5	Magenta	12	Brown
6	Medium Green		

Now that you know the possible values for the three arguments of the **graphics** predicate, we will show you how to set the colors on the monitor using the **graphics** predicate in a small program. You will build a small program placing your commands in an internal goal statement. We will use values for CGA only. Follow the numbered steps.

If you haven't already done so, boot your computer and bring up the Main Menu of Turbo Prolog and enter the Editor Window. If you are continuing from the previous program, **clear** the program in the Editor Window to prepare for a new program.

1 - Graphics Predicate

To set the monitor to medium resolution with 4 colors (mode 1) and a blue background using palette 1, include the following predicate as part of a goal statement:

        graphics(1,1,1)

Note that since the **graphics** predicate is a standard predicate, it does not have to be declared in the predicate section of the program.

To start your program, type the goal section with the **graphics** predicate shown above as part of a goal. You will be adding additional goals to this statement, so type the **and** at the end of the **graphics** predicate as shown below.

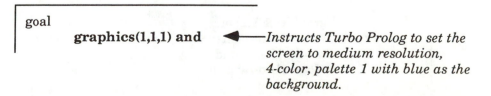

```
goal
        graphics(1,1,1) and
```
◀——*Instructs Turbo Prolog to set the screen to medium resolution, 4-color, palette 1 with blue as the background.*

2 - Adding a write Predicate to the Goal

The standard **write** predicate can be placed in a goal statement or in a rule definition. It works in both places. This time it is entered as part of a goal. Remember, standard predicates do not have to be declared in the predicates sections. Add the **write** predicate as shown.

goal

　　　graphics(1,1,1) and
　　　write("Please enter your name and press <Enter>　") and

note the space

3 - Getting a Reply from the User

Next, we want to receive the person's name. The **readln** predicate is used to accept input from the user. Again, it is a standard predicate and does not have to be declared in the predicates section. So far, we do not have a predicates section. All of the predicates declared are standard predicates.

Add the **readln** predicate as shown below. Add the logical operator **and** to the end of the predicate, because more predicates will be added.

goal

　　　graphics(1,1,1) and
　　　write("Please enter your name and press <Enter>　") and
　　　readln(Name) and

The **readln(Name)** predicate causes the program to stop and wait for the user to input his or her name. After the name is entered, **readln** binds the variable **Name** to whatever symbols the user types. In this case, it is his or her name. From this point on, the value of **Name** will be the user's name.

4 - Clearing the Window

The predicate **clearwindow** erases the contents of the active window. It always succeeds. Enter the **clearwindow** predicate along with the logical operator **and**. Adding the **clearwindow** clears the window for the next predicate.

goal

　　　graphics(1,1,1) and
　　　write("Please enter your name and press <Enter>") and
　　　readln(Name) and
　　　clearwindow and

5 - Adding Another write Predicate

Now add a second **write** predicate that greets the user and repeats the users name. To print the greeting "Nice to meet you" and the user's name, you will again use the **write** predicate. Recall that, unlike other predicates, the **write** predicate can take any number of arguments. When you use more than one argument in a **write** predicate, the arguments are separated with a comma such as:

write("Nice to meet you, ",Name)

Turbo Prolog will print the literal message "Nice to meet you, ". It prints everything between the quotes, including the space. The space is included at the end of the greeting to separate the name from the greeting when it writes the value of the variable **Name**. It knows that **Name** is a variable because it is not enclosed in quotes, and **Name** begins with an uppercase letter. Adding this **write** predicate to the program, you should have:

---

goal

    graphics(1,1,1) and
    write("Please enter your name and press <Enter>") and
    readln(Name) and
    clearwindow and
    write("Nice to meet you, ",Name) and

---

6 - How to Print a Blank Line

To print a blank line, Turbo Prolog provides the predicate **nl**. When Turbo Prolog encounters the **nl**, it moves the cursor to the next line. Like the **clearwindow** predicate, **nl** has no argument and no object to match. Therefore, it always succeeds. Its format and explanation is shown below. Don't forget to place the period at the end of **nl** indicating to Turbo Prolog that this is the end of the goal.

---

goal

    graphics(1,1,1) and
    write("Please enter your name and press <Enter>") and
    readln(Name) and
    write("Nice to meet you, ",Name) and
    nl.

You could have caused the new line just as easily by putting '**\n**' in the final **write** predicate. The result would be identical. If the '**\n**' were to be included in the

---

write predicate, it would cause the cursor to move to the next line after the user had typed in his/her name. The predicate would then be as follows:

write("Nice to meet you, ",Name,'\n').

Naturally, the final **nl** predicate would not be needed.

7 - Running the Program

Now run the program. Notice that the entire program consists of one goal. This will work if the goal does not have any predicates that require matching with clauses. The graphics command causes the screen background color to be blue, and the text is displayed in 40-column text mode in red.

If the program does not execute properly, check your typing and the syntax of the predicates. Check for quotes, parentheses, and periods. Correct the problem and run the program again.

When your program runs correctly, you will see the following displayed in your Dialog Window. We have used the name Chari to show you the results. If you type in your name, Turbo Prolog will greet you with your name.

Please enter your name and press <Enter>
Chari

Nice to meet you, Chari

Press the SPACE bar

Differences Between Internal and External Goals

When a program uses an external goal, Turbo Prolog executes the program until all possible solutions are found and displayed. The same program with the goal internal to the program will find one solution only and then stop.

To demonstrate this difference, input the following program with an external goal and run it. If the previous program exists in the Editor Window, **clear** it.

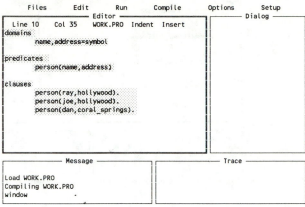

When the goal request is displayed in the Dialog Window, type in the following goal to ask the program to display all those who live in hollywood:

Goal:**person(Name,hollywood).** ⏎

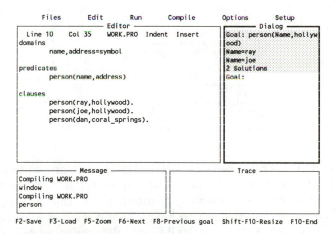

Two solutions are found. Ray and joe are found to live in hollywood. Turbo Prolog has found all possible answers to the goal.

Now, add the goal section to the program as shown below:

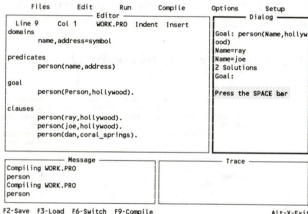

```
        Files        Edit       Run      Compile        Options      Setup
                        Editor                                Dialog
  Line 5      Col 32      WORK.PRO  Indent  Insert    Goal: person(Name,hollyw
domains                                                ood)
        name,address=symbol                           Name=ray
                                                      Name=joe
goal                                                  2 Solutions
        name(Person,hollywood).                       Goal:

predicates
        person(name,address)

clauses
        person(ray,hollywood).
        person(joe,hollywood).
        person(dan,coral_springs).

                   Message                                     Trace
Compiling WORK.PRO
window
Compiling WORK.PRO
person

F1-Help F2-Save F3-Load F5-Zoom F6-Next F7-Xcopy F8-Xedit F9-Compile F10-Menu
```

Run the program again. Your screen will show:

```
        Files        Edit       Run      Compile        Options      Setup
                        Editor                                Dialog
  Line 9      Col 1       WORK.PRO  Indent  Insert    Goal: person(Name,hollyw
domains                                                ood)
        name,address=symbol                           Name=ray
                                                      Name=joe
predicates                                            2 Solutions
        person(name,address)                          Goal:

goal
        person(Person,hollywood).                     Press the SPACE bar

clauses
        person(ray,hollywood).
        person(joe,hollywood).
        person(dan,coral_springs).

                   Message                                     Trace
Compiling WORK.PRO
person
Compiling WORK.PRO
person

F2-Save  F3-Load  F6-Switch  F9-Compile                          Alt-X-Exit
```

When Turbo Prolog sees an internal goal, it attempts to match it with the clauses in the same way as it does with an external goal. However, the value of the variable is not automatically printed. Thus, the only message displayed in the Dialog Window is **Press the SPACE bar**. This is an advantage, because it gives you, the programmer, the flexibility to determine what is displayed on the monitor or printed on the printer. To display the value of the variable, the **write** predicate is used.

Printing the Values of Internal Goal Variables

For Turbo Prolog to print the value of the variable, you must include a **write** predicate in the goal statement or rule definition. Add the **write** predicate as shown and run the program.

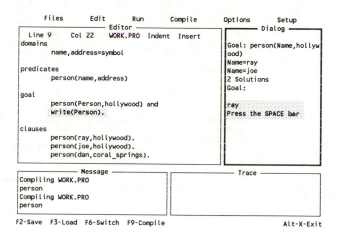

```
        Files        Edit        Run        Compile        Options       Setup
                           ── Editor ──                           ── Dialog ──
  Line 9      Col 22      WORK.PRO   Indent   Insert      Goal: person(Name,hollyw
domains                                                   ood)
        name,address=symbol                              Name=ray
                                                         Name=joe
predicates                                               2 Solutions
        person(name,address)                             Goal:

goal                                                     ray
        person(Person,hollywood) and                     Press the SPACE bar
        write(Person).

clauses
        person(ray,hollywood).
        person(joe,hollywood).
        person(dan,coral_springs).

                          ── Message ──                           ── Trace ──
Compiling WORK.PRO
person
Compiling WORK.PRO
person
 F2-Save  F3-Load  F6-Switch  F9-Compile                              Alt-X-Exit
```

The addition of the **write(Name)** predicate causes Turbo Prolog to write the object bound to the variable **Name** immediately after it is bound. However, not all possible solutions are printed. Only **ray** is printed as a solution. You know, however, that there are two people who live in hollywood. The result demonstrates another difference between an external and internal goal. If the goal is internal, Turbo Prolog stops looking for answers once it finds the first acceptable solution. That is, backtracking does not automatically take place. To find all the solutions, the standard predicate **fail** must be used as an internal subgoal. The **fail** predicate is explained next.

The fail Predicate

The **fail** predicate is a standard predicate that always fails. It has no argument. The result is to force backtracking. Add the **nl** and **fail** predicates to the program as shown below and then run the program. Your screen will now show the two names of **ray** and **joe**.

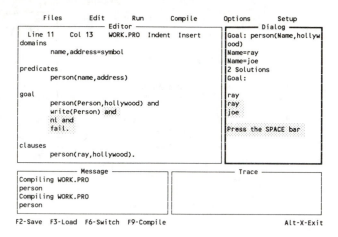

```
          Files      Edit      Run      Compile      Options      Setup
                          Editor                          Dialog
    Line 11    Col 13    WORK.PRO  Indent  Insert    Goal: person(Name,hollyw
domains                                              ood)
        name,address=symbol                          Name=ray
                                                     Name=joe
predicates                                           2 Solutions
        person(name,address)                         Goal:

goal
        person(Person,hollywood) and                 ray
        write(Person) and                            ray
        nl and                                       joe
        fail.
                                                     Press the SPACE bar
clauses
        person(ray,hollywood).


                   Message                                  Trace
Compiling WORK.PRO
person
Compiling WORK.PRO
person

F2-Save  F3-Load  F6-Switch  F9-Compile                        Alt-X-Exit
```

With the **fail** predicate in place, both **ray** and **joe** are found as matches to the goal, just as they were found when the goal was external. If the **fail** predicate was not there, only **ray** would be found, as was shown before. Again, the **fail** predicate always fails, forcing backtracking. In this example, both **ray** and **joe** are displayed in the Dialog Window. Because of the **fail** predicate, Turbo Prolog did not quit after finding one answer for the goal. The **fail** predicate caused the program to continue its search for a match to the **person(Name,hollywood)** predicate. In this case, the internal goal with the **fail** predicate produced the same result as the external goal **person(Name,hollywood)**. The important point to keep in mind is that the **fail** predicate always fails and forces backtracking to occur.

Clear the program in the Editor Window to prepare for the next example.

A User-Friendly Data Base

The next example demonstrates how standard predicates can be used to write an English-based interface to the used car data base used in chapter 3. If you saved the program back in chapter 3, load it into the Editor Window, if not enter it is as shown below.

```
domains
    make,model,color = symbol
    year = integer
predicates
    car(year,color,make,model)
clauses
    car(1985,blue,ford,mustang).
    car(1981,red,ford,fairlane).
    car(1984,blue,buick,electra).
    car(1986,red,cadillac,fleetwood).
    car(1986,yellow,chevrolet,nova).
```

If the goal is to determine the models of all of the Ford cars on the parking lot, it would be phrased in Turbo Prolog as:

```
goal:car(Year,Color,ford,Model).
```

If you recall, when you ran the program in chapter 3, you entered each goal in the Dialog Window. Let's use this same program, except the goal will be expanded and included within the program. In this manner, we can even make the program user-friendly. Enter the new internal goal as follows.

```
goal
        graphics(2,2,3) and
        write("Enter the make of the car you want to buy :") and
        readln(Make) and
        car(Year,Color,Make,Model) and
        nl and
        write("We have a ",Make,"\n") and
        write("It is a ",Year," ",Color, " ",Model) and
        nl and
        fail.
```

Add this goal statement to the used car data base as shown below.

domains
　　　make,model,color = symbol
　　　year = integer

predicates
　　　car(year,color,make,model)

goal
　　　graphics(2,2,3) and
　　　write("Enter the make of the car you want to buy :") and
　　　readln(Make) and
　　　car(Year,Color,Make,Model) and
　　　nl and
　　　write("We have a ",Make,"\n") and
　　　write("It is a ",Year," ",Color, " ",Model) and
　　　nl and
　　　fail.

clauses
　　　car(1985,blue,ford,mustang).
　　　car(1981,red,ford,fairlane).
　　　car(1984,blue,buick,electra).
　　　car(1986,red,cadillac,fleetwood).
　　　car(1986,yellow,chevrolet,nova).

Now run the program. At the request to enter the make of car, first enter ford, then try buick, then cadillac. For this limited program you must type in the names of the cars in lower case letters. If you capitalize a name such as Ford, the program will not be able to find a match and will respond with no answer. Likewise if you enter the name of a car that does not exist in the data base, there will be no matches found and, consequently, no response from the program. Compare your results to those shown in Figure 6-13.

Enter the make of the car you want to buy :**ford**

We have a ford
It is a 1985 blue mustang

We have a ford
It is a 1981 red fairlane

Press the SPACE bar

Enter the make of the car you want to buy :**buick**

We have a buick
It is a 1984 blue electra

Press the SPACE bar

Enter the make of the car you want to buy :**cadillac**

We have a cadillac
It is a 1986 red fleetwood

Press the SPACE bar

Including the goal as an internal part of the program and using built-in predicates results in a program that communicates more effectively with the user. **Clear** the used car data base program now in your Editor Window.

More Graphics Commands

Several additional predicates can be used to draw on the screen once the **graphics** predicate is used. These are the **dot, line,** and **turtle graphics** predicates.

The dot Predicate

The **dot** predicate has three arguments: Row, Column, and Color.

The format is:

dot(Row,Column,Color)   *(See palette chart for color, Fig. 6-10)*

(0-31,999)   (0-31,999)   (1-3)

The corner coordinates on the graphics screen are as follows:

```
(0,0)     <— upper left-hand corner           (0,31999)




(31999,0)                                      (31999,31999)
```

With your Editor Window clear, choose **Run** from the top menu line.

To set a white dot in the center of a blue screen (mode 1), try the following goal:

> goal
> > graphics(1,1,1) and
> > dot(16000,16000,3).

You will see a small dot placed in the middle of the screen. Press the {Space Bar} and **clear** the Editor Window to prepare for the line predicate.

The line Predicate

The **line** predicate requires that two points and a color be specified. The syntax of the **line** predicate is:

line(Row1,Column1,Row2,Column2,Color)

(coordinates   *(coordinates*   *(from palette chart, Fig. 6-10)*
for first point)   *for second point)*

This predicate draws a line from the first point (Row1,Column1) to the second point (Row2,Column2) in the specified color. Thus, to draw a red line from the upper left-hand corner of the screen to the lower right-hand corner the following goal would be used:

> goal
> > graphics(1,0,1) and
> > line(0,0,31999,31999,2).

Clear the Editor Window with the **New file** command.

Turtle Graphics

Turbo Prolog also provides support for turtle graphics. Turtle graphics is a term from the work of Seymour Papert in his development of the language LOGO. The turtle is a metaphor that represents the movement on a plane surface of an imaginary turtle with an imaginary pen attached to its body. Turtle predicates move this imaginary turtle about the plane either pressing the pen down and drawing lines or picking the pen up and moving about without tracing any lines. Within the LOGO language, children have very little trouble with the concept of turtle graphics. In a short amount of time, they become quite expert about the drawing of figures using turtle graphics.

Eight turtle graphics predicates are supported by Turbo Prolog. They are **pencolor**, **pendown**, **penup**, **penpos**, **forward**, **back**, **left**, and **right**. Turtle graphics coordinates are relative to the place where the turtle is at the time a turtle predicate is executed. Each of these commands is briefly described.

pencolor Predicate

The **pencolor** predicate specifies the color of the line that will be drawn by the turtle. The **pencolor** predicate has one argument. The format is:

    pencolor(Color)

Where **Color** is an integer number chosen from the color palette shown in Figure 6-10. If you had set the color palette to 1 using the **graphics** predicate, then the color chosen for pencolor could be cyan, magenta, or white with integer values of 1, 2, and 3, respectively.

pendown and penup Predicates

You can move the turtle anywhere on the screen. If the pen is down, then a line will be traced by the turtle as it moves. If the pen is up, the turtle can still move, but there will be no line traced onto the screen. These predicates have no arguments.

    pendown
    penup

penpos Predicate

The **penpos** predicate specifies a location on the screen to place the turtle. It has three arguments.

    penpos(Row,Column,Angle)

Where **Row** and **Column** are position numbers measured in pixels. The **Angle** argument causes the turtle to move at a specified angle. If the angle is 0 degrees, the turtle is in position to move toward the bottom of the screen. Contrary to the usual measure of a circle with 0 degrees at the top and 180 degrees at the bottom, 180 degrees in turtle graphics is toward the top of the screen, and 0 degrees is toward the bottom of the screen.

forward and back Predicates

As you might suspect, the **forward** and **back** predicates move the turtle forward and backward. These predicates have one argument, which is the number of steps to move the turtle. The format of these two predicates is:

> forward(Steps)   back(Steps)

The range of step size is 1 to 31,999. If you move a turtle past the borders of the screen, no error condition will occur. However, you will not be able to see the turtle.

right and left Predicates

The **right** and **left** predicates turn the turtle through a specified angle. These predicates have one argument. The format is:

> left(Angle)   right(Angle)

Angle is expressed in degrees. The predicate **right(38)** will turn the turtle to the right 38 degrees from its present position.

An Example of Turtle Graphics

To see how turtle graphics predicates work, look at how to draw a simple box. First, the required steps to draw the box are defined.

1. Move turtle forward X number of steps
   Make a 90 degree right turn
2. Move Turtle forward X number of steps
   Make a 90 degree right turn
3. Move turtle forward X number of steps
   Make a 90 degree right turn
4. Move turtle forward X number of steps

5. Stop.

These steps can be translated into a Turbo Prolog program through the construction of a rule. The rule for drawing a box can be expressed as a clause, where the number 5000 is the number of turtle steps to move. We will call the rule that draws a box **draw_a _box**. It is shown below:

```
draw_a_box if
        forward(5000) and
        right(90) and
        forward(5000) and
        right(90) and
        forward(5000) and
        right(90) and
        forward(5000) and
        right(90).
```

Placed into a program, the rule is as shown:

```
predicates
        draw_a_box
goal
        graphics(2,2,5) and
        draw_a_box.
clauses
        draw_a_box if
                forward(5000) and
                right(90) and
                forward(5000) and
                right(90) and
                forward(5000) and
                right(90) and
                forward(5000) and
                right(90).
```

Enter and execute the program. You will see a small box drawn in magenta color on a full screen with a black background.

Sound Commands

Turbo Prolog also provides predicates to make the computer beep or even play a song. The **beep** predicate may be placed in a rule definition or goal statement. The format of the **beep** predicate is:

```
beep
```

It has no arguments and just beeps when it is executed.

The **sound** predicate requires two arguments. The first argument specifies the duration of the tone, while the second argument tells the computer the frequency of the tone to play. The format of the sound predicate is:

sound(Duration, Frequency)

Duration is measured in hundredths of a second, and **Frequency** is the frequency of notes on the musical scale. Refer to the chart below for the frequencies related to each musical note.

Frequency	Note
131	C
139	C#
147	D
156	D#
165	E
175	F
185	F#

Frequency	Note
196	G
208	G#
220	A
233	A#
247	B
262	C

A Turbo Prolog rule that would cause the computer to beep twice could be:

```
beep_twice if
        beep and
        beep.
```

A Turbo Prolog program that would play the musical triad of C, E, G with each note played 0.10 second could be:

```
predicates
        triad
goal
        triad
clauses
        triad if
                sound(10,131)  and
                sound(10,165) and
                sound(10,196).
```

Introduction to Recursion

Recursion is an important feature of modern computer programming languages. Most sophisticated Turbo Prolog programs use recursion. While recursion is difficult to explain, you can get a feel for it if the process is used in a program. This section demonstrates how recursion works by executing two programs. We will visit recursion over and over again in later chapters.

Recursion is a method of defining an object or procedure in terms of itself. Nature uses recursion. Take, for example, a rosebush. A rosebush consists of a main stem, branches, leaves, and roses. As a working definition, it might be said that a rosebush is:

> a stem that has branches with leaves and flowers.

Looking closer, a branch could also be defined as

> a stem that has branches with leaves and flowers.

As it turns out, the definition of a branch is the same definition as the rosebush itself. This definition recurs again and again as the rosebush grows. As the plant gets larger, it duplicates itself over and over again until the duplication ends in a grouping of leaves and a flower. This ending point is important. If there were no ending points in the growth of the rosebush, it would grow to an infinite size, branches duplicating branches forever, eventually engulfing the world. Earth would become one large rosebush.

The ending point in recursion is called the boundary condition. This is the point where duplication ceases, and the recursion stops. The boundary condition is a stop sign. It is the place where the recursion stops.

In summary, there are two important concepts to understand in recursion:

1. Recursion is a process that calls itself as part of that process.

2. A boundary condition must be included in any recursive statement.

Tail Recursion

The simplest form of recursion is called tail recursion. This occurs when a rule definition calls itself at the end of the procedure. The result of tail recursion is like the execution of a loop. Consider the following program that asks you to input your name and then writes it on the screen:

Tail Recursion Program

```
domains
        name=symbol
predicates
        repeat_name(name)
goal
        graphics(1,1,8) and
        write("Enter your name ") and
        readln(Name) and
        repeat_name(Name).
clauses

        repeat_name(Name) if
            write(Name) and
            nl and
            repeat_name(Name).        <——This is recursion
```

Enter this program and run it. The program will not stop because it has no exit condition to stop it. It keeps calling itself over and over again and will continue to do so until you stop it. To stop the program press, the {Ctrl-Break} key sequence. The program will stop, and you will be returned to the Main Menu.

After running and stopping the program, insert the **Trace** command at the beginning of the program. Run the program again, pressing the {F10} key to follow each step that the program takes in executing the predicates.

Program Explanation

In this program, when Turbo Prolog gets to the last line of the **repeat_name** definition, it makes a copy of the whole definition (call it copy-2). It then attempts to satisfy copy-2. When it gets to the last line of copy-2, it makes copy-3. When the last line of copy-3 is encountered, copy-4 is made, and the process repeats itself over and over again until the program is stopped.

The result appears to be an infinite loop, but it is important to understand that recursive rules exist at various levels. Hence copy-2 of the program is identical to copy-1, but it exists as a separate entity in the computer's memory. As each copy is made, it is placed into the computer's memory. Eventually, the computer will run out of memory and cease operation. Fortunately, Turbo Prolog handles this situation of making copies by treating the tail recursion as if it were a loop, keeping memory intact. But keep in mind that all properly written Turbo Prolog programs that use recursion must have a method for terminating recursion. They must have a specified boundary condition.

Recursion with Graphics

The next program uses recursion to draw graphics on the screen. This graphics program will help you visualize the recursive process. The following program uses our prior definition of the **draw_a_box** rule and a recursive pattern rule:

Program–Recursion with Graphics

```
        Files      Edit      Run       Compile      Options      Setup

   Line 1      Col 1      WORK.PRO  Indent  Insert
predicates
        draw_a_box
        pattern

goal
        graphics(1,2,8) and pattern.

clauses
        draw_a_box if
                forward(5000) and right(90) and
                forward(5000) and right(90) and
                forward(5000) and right(90) and
                forward(5000) and right(90).

        pattern if
                draw_a_box and
                right(20) and
                pattern.
```

Enter the program as shown and run it. There is no boundary condition to this program, so you will have to stop it with the {Ctrl-Break} key sequence. You will see the pattern in Figure 6-14 displayed on a gray background with the tracing of the figure in the color cyan.

Figure 6-14

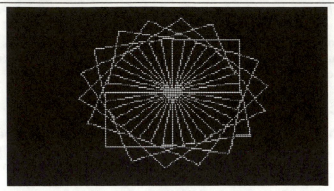

This completes your introduction to Turbo Prolog graphics, turtle graphics, the **sound** and **beep** predicates, the window predicates, and input and output graphics. This chapter has presented you with many new predicates, procedures, and a brief introduction to recursion. Try writing some of your own programs using these predicates. With practice, you can become quite proficient with them. Do the exercises and problems that follow, then move on to Chapter 7 where you will learn about doing arithmetic in Turbo Prolog.

Exercises

6-1.   Turbo Prolog has two types of goals. Name them and describe their operation.

6-2.   Turbo Prolog has a number of built-in predicates. These built-in predicates are called _____ predicates.

6-3.   The graphics standard predicate has three arguments. What are they and what do they do?

6-4.   Are you required to declare a standard predicate in the predicates section?

6-5.   What is the predicate that displays information on your monitor screen?

6-6.   What does the standard predicate **writedevice** do? How many arguments does it require? What are the possible values of these predicates?

6-7.   Write the standard predicate that switches output from the screen to the printer and vice versa.

6-8.   If a response is required from the user, name the standard predicate that receives the responses.

6-9.   What command clears the Dialog Window?

6-10.   How do you cause Turbo Prolog to advance to a new line?

6-11.   What predicate forces backtracking? Explain how this works.

6-12.   How many arguments does the **dot** predicate require? What are they?

6-13.   What is the predicate for drawing a line from point to point?

6-14.   The **sound** predicate requires two arguments. What are they?

6-15.   Explain recursion to a non-programmer.

Problems

6-1.   Write goal statements to set different characteristics of the **graphics** predicate. This predicate stated as in internal goal should be as:

goal
        graphics (1,1,11).

The only section that you need to write is the goal section. This is because the **graphics** predicate is a built-in predicate, and built-in predicates do not need to be defined in the predicates section.

When you execute the **graphics** predicate as indicated above, your screen will display the attributes of the **graphics** predicate. For example, if you use the **graphics** predicate with the arguments 1, 1, and 11, as shown above, your screen will show a background of light cyan with text in the 40 column mode displayed in magenta.

Execute the following goals and write the results in the space provided.

Predicate	Background	Text	Text Size
graphics(2,1,7) graphics(1,1,4) graphics(1,0,14) graphics(2,1,14) graphics(2,1,11) graphics(2,0,11)	black	white	80

6-2.   Write an interactive program that allows the user to input the three arguments for the **graphics** predicate.

*Hint: Use the **write** predicate to ask the user to input the values for each attribute. Use variables for the arguments of the **graphics** predicate. Use the **readint** predicate to accept the values.*

6-3.   Write a program that asks for the learner to type in his/her name, street address, city, zip code, and telephone number. Present the learner with a choice of where to send the information – to the printer or to the screen.

6-4.   Using the following data base, prepare a program to satisfy the stated goals. Try the program with both internal and external goals.

Discovery	Discoverer
1st Law of Motion	Newton
2nd Law of Motion	Newton
3rd Law of Motion	Newton
DNA Molecule	Watson
DNA Molecule	Crick
Uncertainty Principle	Heisenberg
Relativity Principle	Einstein

Goals:
1. Who discovered the structure of DNA?
2. What did Newton discover?
3. What was Heisenberg uncertain about?
4. Who discovered the principle of relativity?

6-5.   Write a program to draw lines on the screen. Use a different color for each line.

a.   Diagonal line from lower left-hand corner to upper right-hand corner
b.   Horizontal line from middle left to middle right
c.   Vertical line from middle upper to middle lower

6-6.   Using the turtle graphics predicates, write:

a.   A program to recursively draw and rotate a rectangle.
b.   A program to recursively draw and rotate a triangle.
c.   A program to recursively draw and rotate a hexagon.
d.   A program to recursively draw and rotate an octagon.

Chapter 7
Arithmetic in Turbo Prolog

Although Turbo Prolog is a language designed for the manipulation of symbols, it is also adept at mathematics. It can handle arithmetic expressions, compare numbers and words, and perform a host of mathematical functions. Turbo Prolog can also manipulate items at the bit level through the use of logical bit predicates. This chapter covers these topics. Also, another look at recursion is presented through a program about the child's game of tag and a simple counting loop.

Arithmetic in Turbo Prolog

All computer languages have particular strengths and weaknesses. Prolog has a reputation for not being particularly suited to number crunching applications. However, one of Turbo Prolog's strengths is its inclusion of a full range of arithmetic operations, relational operators, and mathematic functions. Other versions of Prolog do not offer the mathematical flexibility of Turbo Prolog.

If you have written programs in BASIC, Pascal, or any other programming language, you will find that Turbo Prolog's arithmetic, relational, and mathematical functions are similar. If you have not written programs in other languages, this chapter provides you with a brief introduction to these operations.

Arithmetic Expressions

Turbo Prolog arithmetic expressions can include real numbers, integers, arithmetic operators (+,-,*,/,>,<, etc.), and hexadecimal numbers. Hexadecimal numbers are represented by numbers preceded by a dollar sign.

Turbo Prolog provides six arithmetic operators. These operations, the domain of their operands, and the results of the operations are presented in Table 7-1.

Table 7–1: Arithmetic Operators in Turbo Prolog

```
                    Argument 1
                      /
       Integer =  2  + 3 ———— Argument 2
                  |      \
                  |       \
       Result        Operation
```

Operation	Name	Argument 1	Argument 2	Result
+	addition	integer	integer	integer
		real	integer	real
		integer	real	real
		real	real	real
-	subtraction	integer	integer	integer
		integer	real	real
		real	integer	real
		real	real	real
*	multiplication	integer	integer	integer
		real	integer	real
		integer	real	real
		real	real	real
/	division	integer	integer	real
		real	integer	real
		integer	real	real
		real	real	real
mod	modula division *(Gives the remainder of division)*	integer	integer	integer
div	integer division *(Gives the quotient of division)*	integer	integer	integer

Integers and Real Numbers

Integers are whole numbers (1, 6, 78334), while real numbers are numbers that include a decimal point (2.5, 145.67, .004). Here are some examples of the results of arithmetic operations with integers and real numbers:

1. Adding an integer to a real number results in an real number.

$$3 + 4.75 = 7.75$$
$$\text{integer} \quad \text{real} \quad \text{real}$$

2. Multiplying a real number by a real number results in a real number.

$$16.55 * 23.80 = 393.89$$
$$\text{real} \quad \text{real} \quad \text{real}$$

3. Division of integers results in a real number.

$$6 \;/\; 3 = 2.0$$
$$\text{integer} \quad \text{integer} \quad \text{real}$$

Order of Operations

Turbo Prolog follows standard arithmetic conventions in determining the order of operations used in evaluating arithmetic expressions. The order of operations is shown in Table 7-2.

Table 7-2: Order of Operations

		Operation	Symbol
P	1	parentheses	( )
R			
I	2	exponentiation	^
O			
R	3	multiplication and division	*, /
I			
T	4	mod & div	mod,div
Y			
	5	addition and subtraction	+,-

The first operation evaluated in an arithmetic expression is exponentiation (raising of a number to a power), then multiplication and division, followed by mod and div. The lowest priority is addition and subtraction.

If two operations have the same priority level, such as addition and subtraction, they are evaluated from left to right.

Changing the Order of Operations

The order of operations can be changed through the use of parentheses. Operations enclosed within parentheses are always executed first. If several pairs of parentheses are present, the operations in the innermost pair of parentheses are evaluated first followed by the operations in each successive pair of parentheses. The example below shows how parentheses can affect the order of operations and the answer.

Goal-1

```
Goal:Result= 2 + 2 * 2.
       Result = 6
       1 Solution
```

Goal-2

```
Goal:Result = (2 + 2) * 2.
       Result = 8
       1 Solution
```

In Goal-1, the multiplication (2*2=4) takes place first. The result (4) is added to the first 2 resulting in the integer 6. The Turbo Prolog variable **Result** is then bound to the value 6.

In Goal-2, the operation inside the parentheses is evaluated first. Thus, (2+2) is evaluated with the result of 4. Then, 4 is multiplied by the remaining 2. The variable **Result** is then bound to the integer value 8.

An Example of an Arithmetic Expression in Turbo Prolog

Suppose you wanted to write a program that translates degrees Fahrenheit to degrees Centigrade. The equation for this is:

$$C = \frac{5}{9} * (F - 32)$$

Where: C = Temperature in degrees Centigrade.
F = Temperature in degrees Fahrenheit.

To solve this equation, substitute the Fahrenheit degrees for the variable F, subtract 32 from this value, and multiply the result by 5. Then, divide the product of the multiplication by 9. The result will be the temperature in degrees Centigrade.

You can represent this process with a semantic net. The diagram below shows the process of solving the equation and translates into Turbo Prolog clauses. The semantic net for C = 5/9 * (F − 32) is:

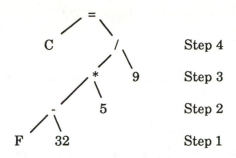

The steps in the semantic net represent a hierarchy of operations. They are performed from bottom to top. First, subtract 32 from **F**. Next, multiply the result by 5. This result is then divided by 9, with the **C** being bound to the value of the division. Look at a Turbo Prolog program written from this semantic net. The program is shown in Table 7-3.

Table 7-3

/* Fahrenheit to Centigrade Temperature Conversion Program */

        domains
                fahrenheit, centigrade = integer

        predicates
                degrees_centigrade(fahrenheit,centigrade)

        clauses
                degrees_centigrade(F,C) if
                C = 5/9 * (F -32).

/* End of Temperature Conversion Program */

Enter this program and run it. Enter the following goal to change 212 degrees Fahrenheit to degrees Centigrade. Type:

    Goal:degrees_centigrade(212,C).
    C = 100
    1 solution

How can you find the freezing point of water in degrees Centigrade? You know the freezing point of water is 32 degrees Fahrenheit. Type in this value as a goal, and Turbo Prolog will provide the answer.

```
Goal:degrees_centigrade(32,C).
C = 0
1 solution
```

Try other values. Modify the program so that it converts degrees Centigrade to degrees Fahrenheit.

Logical Operators

In addition to the standard arithmetic operators (+, -, *, /, ^, mod and div), Turbo Prolog offers an additional six logical operators. Logical operators provide a way to compare objects to determine equality or inequality.

These logical operators allow Turbo Prolog to compare one value with another, one word to another, or one object with another. Numbers may be compared with each other, and letters may be compared with each other. These operators are called logical operators because the result of expressions formed with them have values of either true or false. Table 7-4 shows the logical operators supported by Turbo Prolog.

Table 7-4: Logical Operators

Symbol	Meaning
<	less than
<=	less than or equal to
=	equal to
>	greater than
>=	greater than or equal to
<> or ><	not equal to

Comparing Numbers

Comparing one number with another is straightforward. Let's ask Turbo Prolog if 45 is less than 65. To try this goal, clear your Editor Window of all text. Then choose **Run** from the menu. Even though there is no program in the Editor Window, Turbo Prolog asks you for a goal. Type in the goal as shown below.

        Goal:45 < 65.
        Yes

Turbo Prolog replies **Yes**. Since you know that 65 is indeed greater than 45, this answer makes sense. Try it the other way, and ask Turbo Prolog if 65 is less than 45. It will answer **No**.

Comparing Letters

Letters and words can also be compared in Turbo Prolog. For example, compare the letters **C** and **G**. Is the letter **G** greater that the letter **C**? In computer jargon a letter is greater than another letter if it occurs later in the alphabet. The letter **G** occurs after the letter **C** in the alphabet; therefore, we would say that **G** is greater than **C**. Enter the following goal to test this assertion.

        Goal: "G" > "C".
        Yes

Or, to put it another way:

        Goal:"C" < "G".
        Yes

These examples show that Turbo Prolog can compare letters as well as numbers. How does Turbo Prolog know that the letter **C** occurs first in the alphabet when compared to the letter **G**? The answers lies in the ASCII code.

ASCII Code

ASCII (pronounced Ask-ee) is the acronym for American Standard Code for Information Interchange. The ASCII code is a standard way to represent letters, special characters, and control codes with numerical values. Since computers can only store binary digits, these codes are essential for the representation of text in a computer.

The ASCII value of the capital letter **C** is 67. The ASCII value of the capital letter **G** is 71. Thus, when you ask Turbo Prolog if **C** is less than **G**, it uses the ASCII codes to determine the answer. It compares 67 to 71. Since 67 is less than 71, Turbo Prolog declares that the letter **C** occurs before the letter **G**.

Comparing Words

Turbo Prolog also uses ASCII codes to compare words. Look at the following example.

> Goal:"boat" < "bean".
> No

To determine if the word **boat** is less than the word **bean**, Turbo Prolog compares the ASCII value of the first letter of each word.

> *word*——>   "b   o   a   t"   <   "b   e   a   n"
>
> *ASCII value*——>   98   111   97   116   98   101   97   110

The ASCII value of lower case **b** is 98. Because both words begin with **b**, Turbo Prolog sees them as equal and moves to the second letter. The second letter of **boat** is the lower case **o** which has an ASCII value of 111. The second letter of **bean** is **e**, with an ASCII value of 101. Turbo Prolog tests to see if **o** (111) is less than **e** (101). Turbo Prolog replies **No** to the comparison.

When comparing words using the logical operators, Turbo Prolog moves through the words from left to right comparing the ASCII values of the corresponding letters. When it finds a difference, the processing stops.

Mathematics in Turbo Prolog

To add the integer **2** to the integer **3** in Turbo Prolog, you would phrase the operation as a goal.

> Goal:Answer = 2 + 3.
> Answer = 5
> 1 solution

Turbo Prolog displays the result of the computation by binding the value of **5** to the variable **Answer**. In most computer languages, the equal sign means *is assigned to*. Thus, **Answer = 5** means that the value **5** is assigned to the variable **Answer**.

In Turbo Prolog, however, the equal sign represents *is bound to*. Thus, the result of the computation, which is **5**, is bound to the Turbo Prolog variable **Answer**. The variable remains bound to that value until Turbo Prolog unbinds it.

The arithmetic expressions of Turbo Prolog look the same as expressions in other computer languages. The example above is an example of an arithmetic procedure. Consider the following goal:

    Goal:Answer = 5 + X.
    501 Free variable in expression.

When you run this goal, an error message will be displayed in the Dialog Window indicating that **X** is an unbound variable. Since you want to control your mathematical procedures, you should make sure that all variables on the right side of the equal sign are bound prior to their being used. With a more extensive program, Turbo Prolog would start to backtrack if it did not have a value for **X** when it executed the equation. This can result in unexpected outcomes.

The mod and div Operators

The **mod** and **div** operators provide Turbo Prolog with the ability to obtain the remainder and the quotient of an arithmetic division. **Mod** returns the remainder, while **div** returns the quotient.

The mod Operation

The term **mod** performs modulo arithmetic. This form of integer division produces the remainder resulting from the division. The result of the **mod** operation is always an integer. To determine the remainder of a division using the **mod** operator of Turbo Prolog, enter the following goal:

    Goal:Remainder =32 mod 5.
    Remainder = 2
    1 solution

This shows that the remainder of the division of 32 by 5 is 2, and the variable **Remainder** is bound to the value **2**.

The div Operation

The **div** operation returns the quotient of a division between two arguments. As in the **mod** operation, the result is always an integer. The following shows the operation of the **div** operator:

> Goal:Quotient=32 div 5.
> Quotient = 6
> 1 solution

The **div** operation returns the value of the quotient of the division of the two arguments. In this example, the quotient of 32 divided by 5 is 6. Turbo Prolog binds the variable **Quotient** to the number **6** and reports one solution found.

Combining the mod and div Operations

You can combine the **mod** and **div** operators to provide both the quotient and the remainder of a division problem. Try this Turbo Prolog goal that divides 32 by 5 and responds with both the quotient and the remainder.

> Goal:Quotient = 32 div 5 and Remainder = 32 mod 5.
> Quotient = 6, Remainder = 2
> 1 solution

Turbo Prolog carries out the division and then binds the variables to their respective numbers. **Quotient** is bound to the value **6**, and **Remainder** is bound to the number **2**. This result is displayed in the Dialog Window, and 1 solution is reported.

Mathematical Functions

Unlike other versions of Prolog, Turbo Prolog has many built-in mathematical functions. These functions use the predicate form to represent the standard mathematical and trigonometric functions supported by most computer languages.

Table 7-5 shows these functions. A complete explanation of these functions is beyond the scope of this book. If you want more information about these functions, consult any college algebra and/or trigonometric text.

Table 7-5: Turbo Prolog Built-in Mathematical Functions

Functional Predicate	Name	Description
abs(Z)	Absolute Value	Returns the absolute value of Z
sqrt(Z)	Square Root	Returns the square root of Z
log(Z)	Logarithm to base 10	Returns the logarithm to the base 10 of Z
ln(Z)	Logarithm to base e	Returns the logarithm to the base e of Z
exp(Z)	Exponential Function	Returns the value of e raised to the Z power
cos(Z)	Cosine Function	Returns the cosine of angle Z (Z is expressed in Radians)
sin(Z)	Sine Function	Returns the sine of angle Z (Z is expressed in Radians)
tan(Z)	Tangent Function	Returns the tangent of angle Z (Z is expressed in Radians)
arctan(Z)	Arctangent Function	Returns the arctangent of the angle Z (Z is expressed in Radians)
X mod Z	Mod Function	Returns the remainder of X divided by Z
X div Z	Division Function	Returns the quotient of X divided by Z
random(Z)	Random Generate	Returns a random real number where $0 <= Z < 1$
round(Z)	Rounding Function	Returns rounded value of Z

Logical Bit Predicates

Turbo Prolog offers a set of logical bit predicates. These predicates manipulate data at the bit level and can be used to control the hardware components of your computer system. While the application of these bit predicates is beyond the scope of this book, a brief description and example of each predicate is presented. Most readers can skip this section.

The bit predicates are shown below. Each predicate has three arguments, except for the **bitnot** predicate. The X and Y arguments are bound to integer values which are then translated into signed, 16-bit binary numbers. The predicate operations (and, or, xor, not, left, right) are performed on these numbers with the result bound to the argument Z. The examples show how each function works. Although these predicates work with 16-bit binary words, the examples show only 8 bits.

If you already know about bit processing, skip the section about bit predicates.

Bit Predicates

> bitand(X,Y,Z)

*(The bitand function performs a logical **AND** between the X and Y arguments and returns the result to argument Z.)*

$$X = 01110011$$
$$Y = \underline{11100110}$$

(X AND Y) $Z = 01100010$

The **bitand** predicate compares the individual bits of each of the binary words. It returns a 1 when a 1 exists in both of the corresponding bit positions. Otherwise, it returns a 0. The resulting bits are bound to the argument **Z**.

> *bitor(X,Y,Z)*

*(The bitor function performs a logical **OR** between the X and Y arguments, returning the result to argument Z.)*

$$X = 01110011$$
$$Y = \underline{11100110}$$

(X or Y) $Z = 11110111$

The **bitor** predicate compares the individual bits of each binary string, much like the **bitand** predicate. However, a 1 is returned if a 1 exists either in **X** or **Y** or both. Otherwise, a 0 is returned.

| bitnot(X,Y) | *(The bitnot predicate performs a logical **NOT** to the X argument, returning the result to the Y argument.)* |

$$X = \underline{01110011}$$

NOT $X = 10001100$

The **bitnot** predicate negates the bits of the word bound to **X**. Every 0 bit is changed to a 1 bit, and every 1 bit is changed to a 0 bit. The **NOT X** result is bound to argument **Y**.

| bitxor(X,Y,Z) | *(The bitxor predicate performs the logical **Exclusive OR** between the X and Y values and returns the result to Z.)* |

$$X = 01110011$$
$$Y = \underline{11100110}$$

(X XOR Y) $Z = 10010101$

The **bitxor** predicate is almost the same as the **bitor** predicate except that the **XOR** returns a 1 only if a 1 exists in either argument, but not both arguments. Otherwise, it returns a 0. The result is bound to the argument **Z**.

| bitright(X,N,Z) | *(The bitright predicate shifts the bits of the X argument to the right N bits. The result is bound to the Z argument.)* |

Example: bitright(X,3,Z)

$$X = \underline{01110011}$$

(Shift X 3 bits to Right) $Z = 00001110$

The **bitright** predicate takes the value bound to **X** and shifts the bits to the right **N** times. The leftmost bits are replaced with zeros as the word is shifted to the right.

$$\boxed{\text{bitleft(X,N,Z)}}$$

(The bitleft predicate shifts the bits of the X argument N bits to the left. The result is bound to the Z argument.)

Example: bitleft(X,4,Z)

$$X = 01110011$$
(Shift X 4 bits to left) $$Z = 00110000$$

The **bitleft** predicate works like the **bitright** predicate except that the bit shift is to the left. The value bound to **X** is shifted to the left **N** number of bits. The right-most bit positions are replaced with zeros.

Another Look at Recursion

The last chapter introduced you to the concept of recursion. You will now take a second look at this important programming technique. You know that the easiest form of recursion, called **tail recursion**, resembles programming loops. However, it is important to understand the difference between recursion and looping.

To see how a loop is different from recursion, consider the child's game of tag. Here are two ways to play the game, the first uses a loop and the second recursion.

Loop Tag

Assume that some people want to play a game of tag. These people, though, have particularly poor memories. In fact, you must give them the rules for the game on paper. Their memories are so poor that, after each step in the game, they must read the next rule from the paper. The rules are shown in Table 7-6.

Table 7-6: How to Play Loop Tag

1. choose someone to be **it**
2. person who is **it** chases other players.
3. person who is **it** taps another player
4. the tapped player is **it**
5. if you are tired of the game, quit
6. if not tired go back to step 2

To start the game, someone is designated as **it**. Next, steps 2 through 6 are repeated over and over until the people become too tired to continue, at which time they quit. The rules of this game demonstrate important features of loops shown in Table 7-7.

Table 7-7: Features of Loops

1.	someone is it.	<— *entry condition*
2.	it chases other players.	<— *start of loop*
3.	it taps another player.	} *loop*
4.	player tapped is it.	} *body*
5.	if tired, quit.	<— *test* }
6.	go back to step 2.	<— *end of loop* }

Explanation of Steps

1. Loops have an entry condition. This represents the predetermined state of affairs that exists when the loop begins.

2. Loops have a starting point. This is the first step repeated each time the loop is executed.

3. The body of the loop determines the actions to be performed.

4. Loops must contain a test for an exit condition in the body of the loop. This allows a way to end the loop.

5. The ending point marks the end of the loop. In this example, the ending step sends the person back to repeat step 2 and the steps that follow.

Program Flow

Loops are procedural in nature with each step described in detail. The flow of control is defined in the steps of the game. This flow can be thought of as circular. Table 7-8 shows a picture of the tag looping algorithm with a description of a programming loop.

Table 7-8 : Looping Tag and Programming Loop

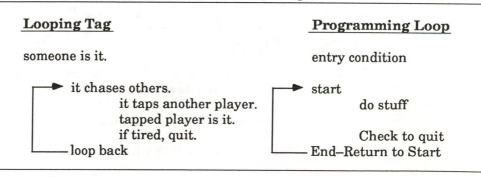

Looping Tag	Programming Loop
someone is it.	entry condition

┌──► it chases others.
      it taps another player.
      tapped player is it.
      if tired, quit.
└── loop back
	┌──► start
	            do stuff
	
	            Check to quit
	└── End–Return to Start

Now consider the game of recursive tag. To someone observing the game, it looks exactly like looping tag.

Recursive Tag

In this version of the game, each player is also given a list of instructions that describe the rules of tag. The instructions are shown in Table 7-9.

Table 7-9: Recursive Tag

---

1. someone is it.
2. person who is it chases other players.
3. person who is it taps another player.
4. the tapped player is it.
5. if you are tired of the game, quit.
6. play tag.

The players are told that each time they encounter the instruction to play tag, they must go to a copying machine and make a new copy of the rules of the game. They are instructed to set aside the original copy of the rules and follow the new rules. The players look as if they are playing the same game, but they are really playing a copy of the game. No looping is taking place. Since each copy of the rules is the same as the copy that produced it, the rules do not change. The rules of looping tag demonstrate important features of looping, and the rules of recursive tag demonstrate important features of recursion as shown in Table 7-10.

Table 7-10: Recursive Tag and Recursion

1.	person is it.	*<— entry condition*
2.	play tag.	*<— start of game of tag*
3.	it chases other players.	*{*
4.	it taps another player.	*{perform these actions*
5.	the tapped player is it.	
6.	if tired, quit.	*<— test for end*
7.	play tag.	*<— recursive call*

Explanation of Steps

1. Like the loop, a recursive call has an entry condition. Without a starting point, the rules do not make much sense.

2. This marks the start of the rules for tag.

3. The body of the procedure tells what actions must be performed.

4. Like the loop, recursive calls need an exit point.

5. This step is the real difference between a loop and recursion. In a loop, you end by returning to a previous location. In a recursive call, an entire new copy of the rules is made. While this may seem like a silly way to play tag, the idea that recursion involves making copies is important.

Program Flow

In recursive tag, the flow of the game is not circular as it was in looping tag. In recursive tag, the game has many levels. Each time a copy of the rules is created, a new game begins. A diagram of this flow might look like that shown in Table 7-11.

Table 7-11: Flow of Program

Game 1 - Level 1
1. person is it.
2. play tag.
3. it chases other players.
4. it taps another player.
5. the tapped player is it.
6. if tired, quit.
7. play tag.

Game 2 - Level 2
1. person is it.
2. play tag.
3. it chases other players.
4. it taps another player.
5. the tapped player is it.
6. if tired, quit.
7. play tag.

Game 3 - Level 3
1. person is it.
2. play tag.
3. it chases other players.
4. it taps another player.
5. the tapped player is it.
6. if tired, quit.
7. play tag.

The game of recursive tag shows two important aspects of recursion. First is the idea of making copies. When a procedure calls itself, a copy is made. This is why recursive calls are not circular definitions.

The second important idea is that recursive calls exist at different levels. Recursive calls submerge to lower levels. When the exit condition is met, the procedure returns to the level above. We say it emerges. In this case, the games, or recursive calls, submerge from level-1 to level-3. Thus, when the exit condition is met, the games must continue to be played until the copies emerge back to level-1. This process will be shown in detail in a later chapter where you will follow Turbo Prolog as it submerges and then emerges in the process of recursion.

A Counting Loop

Although Turbo Prolog is a declarative language, there may be times that you want to use a looping structure. Turbo Prolog uses tail recursion to implement loops. To understand how tail recursion is used to build a simple loop, consider a counting loop. Most computer languages implement a loop that counts to 3 in the manner shown in Table 7-12.

Table 7-12: Procedural Loop

Note: *This example is shown in an imaginary computer language.*

X = 1	*<——entry condition*	
start	*<——beginning of loop*	
print(X),		*loop body*
if X=3 then quit,	*<——test for exit condition*	*loop body*
make X=X+1,		*loop body*
end.	*<——end of loop*	

You can see that, as in the game of looping tag, the program flow is circular:

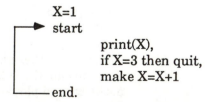

In recursive languages, procedures are generally given names. The entry condition is usually determined by values, or parameters, passed into the procedure when it is called. The recursive procedure shown in Table 7-13 is named **count_to_three** and performs like the counting loop. As in the example in Table 7-12, the language shown here is imaginary.

Table 7-13: Recursive Procedure of Counting

count_to_three(X)	<——*start procedure*	
print(X),		*loop body*
if X=3 then quit,	<——*test for exit*	*loop body*
count_to_three(X+1),	<——*recursive call*	*loop body*
end.	<——*end of procedure*	

This procedure is called with a value for **X** passed to the procedure. This is the initial value that is the entry condition. This example of recursion works like recursive tag. Each time the name **count_to_three** is encountered, a new copy of the entire procedure is created. As in all procedure calls, the calling procedure holds itself in abeyance, waiting until the copy of itself is completed before it completes it action.

Assume that the counting procedure is started as follows:

count_to_three(1)

The result printed would be 1,2,3.

To produce this result, the following steps occur:

1) The procedure called **count_to_three** is executed with X=1 as the entry condition.

2) The value of X (1) is printed.

3) A test is performed (if X=3 then quit), if not move to step 4.

4) This is the recursive call. A new copy of the **count_to_three** program is created. In this new copy, **X** now has a value of **2**. However, in copy 1, **X** still has a value of 1. How can a variable have two values **1** and **2**? Simple, these procedures are independent of each other. Remember the procedure called is a new copy of the program. Turbo Prolog views these as two independent programs. The **X** in the original program is not the same **X** as in the copy. **X** in the original is equal to 1, while **X** in the second copy is equal to 2. This is just like thinking. Can't you hold two equations in your head with the value of the **X** in the first equation different from the value of the **X** in the second equation? Of course you can, and so can Turbo Prolog. This is why Turbo Prolog is such an important language in the field of artificial intelligence, it mimics the way we think.

5) These steps continue until the exit condition is met. When that occurs, the procedure returns to the level above it (It emerges). In this particular case, there is no more work to be done at the next level, so the procedure is finished.

Arithmetic in Turbo Prolog

Here is a way to visualize the recursive procedure of counting process:

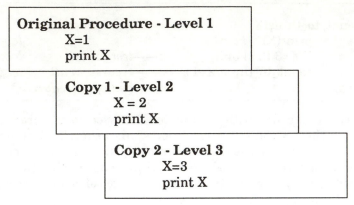

Original Procedure - Level 1
X=1
print X

Copy 1 - Level 2
X = 2
print X

Copy 2 - Level 3
X=3
print X

Now let's write a program as a counting loop in Turbo Prolog.

A Counting Loop in Turbo Prolog

Because Turbo Prolog supports recursion, you can use this form to implement a counting loop. However, there are significant differences that must be considered. First, Turbo Prolog uses the predicate form to express rules. To tell Turbo Prolog the rule for counting, you could use the predicate:

count_to_three(Num) if	*←——start of rule*	
write(Num) and		} *rule body*
nl and		} *rule body*
N=Num+1 and		} *rule body*
count_to_three(N).	*←——recursive call*	} *rule body*

Notice that this example does not provide an exit test. This is the second difference between Turbo Prolog and other languages. Turbo Prolog does not have an "IF..THEN.." construction to test the value of variables. To solve this problem, remember how Turbo Prolog solves goals. Each time the **count_to_three** predicate is encountered, a new copy of the rule is made. Then Turbo Prolog tries to satisfy this new copy before returning to the original procedure. The copy becomes a new goal to Turbo Prolog. Given a new goal, Turbo Prolog starts searching for matches at the top of the knowledge base. Therefore, we can put an exit condition at the beginning of the knowledge base.

In Turbo Prolog, the exit condition is called the **boundary condition**. This boundary condition is expressed as a fact placed above the recursive rule. Remember, that if a fact can satisfy a goal, the rule with the same predicate will not be invoked. When the exit condition occurs, the fact is activated and control passes back to the previous level. Each copy of the recursive call is implemented as the procedure emerges through the different levels created from the recursive call. This is an important new concept.

In searching a knowledge base, Turbo Prolog always begins at the top. If Turbo Prolog finds a fact that satisfies the goal, that fact fires, and Turbo Prolog does not continue to search for rules to satisfy the goal.

The fact that defines the boundary condition in the **count_to_three** predicate is:

count_to_three(4).

Notice that because of where the **count_to_three** rule calls itself (recursion), the boundary condition must be 4 rather than 3.

The complete program is shown in Table 7-14.

Table 7-14: count_to_three Program

```
domains
        counter = integer

predicates
        count_to_three(counter)

clauses
        count_to_three(4).              /* Boundary condition */
        count_to_three(Num) if          /* Rule               */
            write(Num) and
            nl and
            N=Num+1 and
            count_to_three(N).          /* Recursive Call  */
```

Enter the program in Table 7-14, and run it. At the goal request enter the following:

Goal:**count_to_three(1).** ↵

The result is shown below:

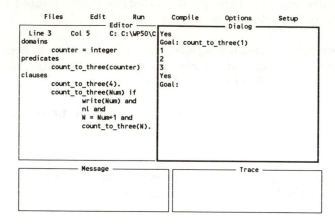

Explanation of count_to_three Program

When the goal is first presented to the program, a match is attempted with the first fact in the clauses section. This is the boundary condition fact. A match is not made because the object of the goal is **1**, and the object of the fact is **4**.

Next, Turbo Prolog attempts a match with the rule statement count_to_three(Num). **Num** is a variable and thus becomes bound to the value **1**. The rule body must be satisfied for the entire rule to succeed, so Turbo Prolog moves to the first subgoal which is the standard predicate **write** with **Num** as a variable. This predicate succeeds and writes the value of **Num**, which is **1**, in the Dialog Window. The next subgoal is also a standard predicate and succeeds by moving the cursor to the next line.

Next, the value **1** is added to the value of **Num** and binds the variable **N** to this new value, which is **2**. At this point, **Num** is bound to **1**, and **N** is bound to **2**. The last line of the program is now encountered causing a new copy to be made through a recursive call.

An attempt is now made to match the new goal **count_to_three(2)** with the first fact in the knowledge base. This fails with Turbo Prolog moving on to the head of the rule, binding **Num** to the value **2**, writing this value in the Dialog Window, moving the cursor to the next line, adding the value **1** to **Num**, which is **2**, and binding **N** to the result of this addition, **3**. The second recursive call is made.

An attempt is again made to match the new goal, which is now **count_to_three(3)**, to the fact **count_to_three(4)**. The match fails. Turbo Prolog moves on to the head of the rule. The new goal of **count_to_three(3)** is matched to the rule with **Num** being bound to the value **3**. This value is written in the Dialog Window, the cursor is moved to the next line, and **Num** is incremented by 1 with the result, which is **4**, bound to the variable **N**. The third recursive call is made.

Turbo Prolog now sees the goal as **count_to_three(4)**. An attempt to match this goal with the first fact in the knowledge base now succeeds. Thus, Turbo Prolog does not look any further in the knowledge base for satisfaction.

At this point, you might think that the program was finished, but not so. Remember the program submerged through three levels of recursion. It must now work its way up; that is, emerge from level-3 to the top level of the procedure. You can see this if you enter the **Trace** command at the top of the program and follow the program as it executes. You will see that after the three values have been printed on the screen, Turbo Prolog will show its emergence through the different levels of recursion in the Trace Window.

Add the **Trace** command and run the program again following the steps in the Trace Window. Make sure you understand each step of the execution process.

This completes Chapter 7. Do the exercises and problems and then move on to Chapter 8 where you will learn about data structures.

Exercises

7-1.   List and explain at least four of the arithmetic operators used by Turbo Prolog.

7-2.   Why are parentheses required in some mathematical formulas?

7-3.   Write a simple program that computes Newton's law of forces. The equation is:

$$F = MA$$

where: F = Force, M = Mass, and A = Acceleration.

Have your program solve for F given that Mass and Acceleration are known.

7-4.   Describe how Turbo Prolog compares letters to letters such as:

"B" < "E"

How does Turbo Prolog know this to be a true expression?

7-5.   What is ASCII?

7-6.   Below are several Turbo Prolog mathematical functions. What does each do?

sqrt(X)   random(X)   round(X)   abs(X)

7-8.   Describe an activity that is recursive. Think about nature, music, optics.

7-9.   Why does the recursive call require an exit condition to be specified?

7-10.   What are the two operators that deal with integers only?

Problems

7-1.   Write a series of rules that perform mathematical computations. There should be a rule for each of the following operations:

- add_to
- subtract_from
- multiply_by
- divide_by
- div_of
- mod_of

The user can then type in an external goal that performs the correct operation and prints the answer. For example:

Goal:add_to(3,5,Answer).
Answer=8

7-2.   Write a rule that calculates the area of a rectangle. The program will ask the user to type in the Length and Width and calculate the area by using the formula A = L * W. Turbo Prolog displays the answer. For example:

Goal:area_rec(3,4,Area).
Area=12

7-3.　Write an interactive program that lists a menu of mathematical functions and returns a value for user input values. Include the following functions:

1. absolute value
2. square root
3. logarithm to base 10
4. logarithm to base e
5. random number

7-4.　Write a program that rounds a number to two decimal places. The formula for rounding a number is:

Rounded Number = INT(100*N +.5)/100

Use both the above formula and the Turbo Prolog **round** function and compare the results.

7-5.　Write a program that displays the numbers 1 – 10 along with their respective square roots and squares.

7-6.　Change the program in problem 7-5 to ask the user how many numbers to calculate and display.

7-7.　Expand the program in problem 7-6 to include the logarithm of the number to base 10.

7-8.　Write a program that compares two words and displays them in alphabetic order.

7-9.　Write a program that displays the quotient and remainder resulting from the division of two numbers. Have your program request the user to supply the dividend and the divisor.

Chapter 8
Data Structures

*The term **data structures** refers to the concept of representing information in both simple and complex ways. Turbo Prolog can look at facts that are contained within other facts and make sense of the information. This chapter will help you develop complex data structures through the use of semantic networks. Tutorial 8-1, **Using Data Structures**, will show you how to use data structures to build a knowledge base of a library collection of books.*

Data Structures

Turbo Prolog Structures

In previous chapters you learned how to write Turbo Prolog facts in the predicate form. The predicate form helps you to represent the relationship between one or more objects. Some texts call this predicate form a data structure. A data structure is another term for the way you represent information as Turbo Prolog facts. Recall the form of a Turbo Prolog fact:

Fact ——> predicate(object1,object2...objectn).

Each object represents a single idea. We call these objects simple objects. However, the idea of simple objects in a fact can be expanded upon. You can form more complex objects by grouping two or more objects together. This allows you to treat these complex structures as single objects. The next section shows you how to build a data structure.

Example of a Data Structure

Suppose that you want to create a knowledge base that contains information about several coins in a collection. The information that you want to store is the value of the coin and the year the coin was minted. You want to represent this information as a Turbo Prolog fact.

Fact-1 ——> coin(value,year).

Look at the simple object **value**. Suppose that you want to represent some additional information related to the value of the coin. For example, you may want to know the condition of coin and the price paid for the coin. You could represent this information as another Turbo Prolog Fact:

Fact-2 ——> value(condition,price)

This new fact shows some of the things that determine the value of the coin – the price paid for the coin and its condition. In Fact-1, the value of the coin is a simple object. In Fact-2, you see some additional information about the value. You can now substitute Fact-2 for the simple object **value** in Fact-1. In this way, you have

---

expanded the knowledge about **value** in Fact-1. The following structure represents the result of replacing the simple object **value** with the data structure **value(condition,price)**. In effect, this combines the knowledge in Fact-1 and Fact-2.

Revised Fact-1 ——> coin(value(condition,price),year).

This revised fact illustrates the use of a data structure in Turbo Prolog. Structure allows us to treat two or more objects as if they were a single object. This permits the manipulation of related objects as if they were a single object.

Related Terms

In reading other texts on Turbo Prolog, you may encounter different terms that refer to the concept of data structure. Chapter 9 uses some of these terms in discussing the concept of lists. It is important to be familiar with these alternative terms.

The predicate is sometimes called the functor. The objects that relate to the functor are called the components of the functor. As you learned above, the relationship of the components to the functor is called a data structure. This is illustrated below with the coin data structure example:

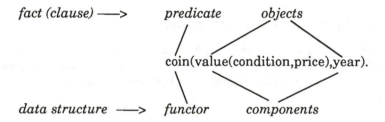

The predicate **coin** is a functor having the components **value** and **year**. You can see that **value** is a component of the functor **coin**. However, **value** is a functor also. It has its own components – **condition** and **price**.

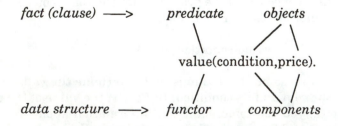

To expand the coin data structure example, suppose you want to represent additional information about the condition of each coin. You want to expand the object **condition** to represent the shininess of the coin and the degree of wear. As a Turbo Prolog fact this information could be represented by:

Fact-3 ———> condition(shininess,wear).

You can now incorporate this simple fact into the revised Fact-1. This creates a new data structure that represents all of the information in a single object. Recall the revised Fact-1:

Revised
Fact-1 ———> coin(value(condition,price),year).

Substituting the data structure **Fact-3** for the simple object **condition**, you obtain a new fact.

New
Fact ———> coin(value(**condition(shininess,wear)**,price),year).

As you can see, the new structure contains objects within objects. This new fact provides more information about the coin and includes a representation of the interrelationships between the different qualities of the coin.

The next section discusses how semantic networks can assist you in building Turbo Prolog data structures.

Using Semantic Nets to Develop Data Structures

In this section, you will learn how to develop a complex data network. You will first develop a basic, or skeleton, semantic network, then you will learn how to represent the semantic network as Turbo Prolog facts.

As you may have guessed, representing data in the form of data structures can get complicated. The degree to which you use data structures in your programming depends on your ability to organize the knowledge. Semantic nets are useful in this endeavor. For example, suppose that you want to represent several facts about things owned by Ray. To organize this information, assume the following semantic network represents the knowledge:

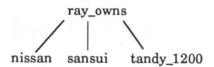

This semantic net says that:

>   Ray owns a Nissan.
>   Ray owns a Sansui.
>   Ray owns a Tandy 1200.

To represent these facts in Turbo Prolog, you could write:

>   ray_owns(nissan,sansui,tandy_1200).

In a large knowledge base, it is possible to have many statements like the one above. Because the objects have no context that give any hint as to what the objects are, confusion may result. A human being might know that a Nissan is a car, but computers need more specific information.

In the example above, the predicate (functor) **ray_owns** offers no information that tells what the objects are. Recall that Turbo Prolog attempts to help us represent knowledge in a context that resembles human thought. Humans usually do not think of objects as unrelated clusters. If you were asked to recall what kind of car Ray owns, you would search your memory for the relationship between **car** and **Ray**, not between **owns** and **Ray**.

Another approach might be to write some facts that clarify the meaning of the objects. You might add the following facts that define the objects:

Facts	Meaning
car(nissan).	Nissan is a car.
stereo(sansui).	Sansui is a stereo.
computer(tandy_1200).	Tandy 1200 is a computer.

Now you could write rules to describe the relationships:

Rule:rays_computer(Brand) if
                computer(Brand) and
                ray_owns(_,_,Brand).

This rule says that Ray's computer is a certain brand if the brand is a computer, and Ray owns that brand. At this point, you have several facts and one rule about some things that Ray owns. To make a query of this knowledge base about the type of computer Ray owns, you use the goal:

Goal:rays_computer(Brand).

If you were to use this goal in a Turbo Prolog program (after you had entered the knowledge base, of course), Turbo Prolog would respond with the following answer:

Brand = tandy_1200
1 solution

Turbo Prolog tells you that Ray's brand of computer is a Tandy 1200.

This knowledge base contained one rule. This rule described the relationship between Ray and a brand of computer. If you wanted to know what brand of stereo Ray owned, you would have to write another rule. Determining the name of Ray's car would require an additional rule about the car. This gets the job done but writing one rule for each relationship would be time consuming. This is particularly true in large knowledge bases.

Fortunately, Turbo Prolog offers a more elegant means to represent the knowledge. The key to this approach is to develop a semantic network that is much richer in context than those dealing with simple objects.

The Semantic Network Expanded

A more complex semantic net that represents all of the knowledge about things owned by Ray can be shown as:

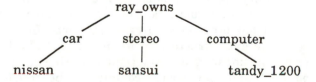

The first column says that Ray owns a car and that the car is a Nissan. The second column says that Rays owns a Sansui stereo, and the third says that Ray's computer is a Tandy 1200.

The advantage to this approach is that it treats the things owned by Ray and their logical relationship as a single object. The problem then becomes how to implement a data structure like this in Turbo Prolog.

Format of Data Structures

To understand how this works, recall the structure of a fact in Turbo Prolog:

functor(component1,component2,...,componentn).

or

predicate(object1,object2,...,objectn).

The structure of complex data structures is the same as the structure of a fact. The only new thing to remember is that each component of the structure can be a whole new structure in itself. This permits us to give a logical context (structure) to the items. These structures then represent a number of related objects as a single object.

To represent the facts about Ray in a data structure, we could represent the semantic network about Ray and his things as a Turbo Prolog fact like the following:

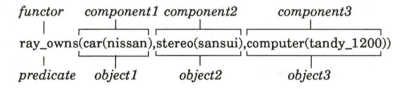

Objects 1, 2, and 3 are the components of the functor (predicate) **ray_owns**. These objects are functors themselves with their own components of **nissan**, **sansui**, and **tandy_1200**, respectively. This Turbo Prolog structure says that Ray owns a Nissan car, a Sansui stereo, and a Tandy 1200 computer. Compare this Turbo Prolog fact with the **ray_owns** semantic net shown previously.

Although this is a complex structure, this fact about Ray's things is no different from the simple facts described previously. All you need to remember is that arguments (also called objects or components) that follow any predicate can be either simple objects or other structures. Thus, the Turbo Prolog fact above is simply a structure that has other structures as its parts. In this example, each component is a complete data structure in its own right. The basic format of a Turbo Prolog fact remains unchanged. If you remember that each of the objects can be a structure, you will find it easy to write complex Turbo Prolog structures.

How to Build Data Structures

To understand why data structures are so useful, look at another example. Suppose that you were writing a knowledge base containing information about a record collection. An easy way to represent facts in the knowledge base might be to formulate a semantic network showing the relationship between the objects. The Turbo Prolog facts may then be derived from this semantic net.

Our first semantic network provides us with information about the recording artist and the name of the album. The corresponding Turbo Prolog fact is shown to the right of the semantic network.

The above representation works fine for this limited information. It provides a way to bring together the name of the artist and the name of the album. However, suppose you wanted to add information on the type of music, the album name, and the year the album was released. You must expand the semantic network. To do this, look at the object **album** in the semantic net. You can expand this simple object into a data structure that shows the type, name, and year associated with **album**. A semantic net that represents this knowledge might look like this:

The objects that follow the functor **album** describe more information about the album. You can now return to the original semantic net and replace the object **album** with the new data structure **album(type,name,year)**. The resulting semantic network and its corresponding Turbo Prolog Fact look like this:

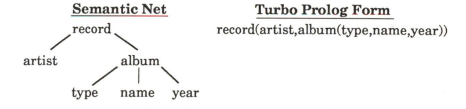

Now the **record** structure includes all of the information about the album. This is exactly what building data structures is all about. Notice the format of the corresponding Turbo Prolog fact:

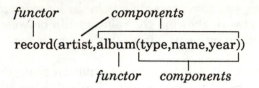

The functor **record** has the components **artist** and **album**. The functor **album** has the components **type, name,** and **year**. This new structure has a part that is not a simple object, but rather a structure on its own. As you might imagine, these structures can become highly complex.

Recall the chief advantages to this approach of representing knowledge as data structures.

1) Data structures are easier to read.
2) The relationships between the objects are apparent.
3) You can manipulate the entire data structure as a single object.

Data structures make Turbo Prolog a very powerful language. You will be using this concept in all of your Turbo Prolog activities.

Summary

The steps to build a semantic net are:

1) Create a simple semantic net that represents the basic knowledge you want to represent.

   In this example:

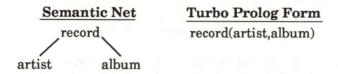

Semantic Net	**Turbo Prolog Form**

   record(artist,album)

2) Expand any of the simple objects to form a data structure to represent more knowledge. In this example, you expanded the object **album**.

   Semantic Net   **Turbo Prolog Form**

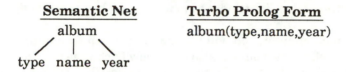

   album(type,name,year)

3) Substitute the new data structure for the original object. In this example, you substituted the data structure **album(type,name,year)** for the object **album**.

   Semantic Net   **Turbo Prolog Form**

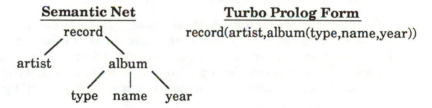

   record(artist,album(type,name,year))

Your can repeat steps 2 and 3 to further expand the semantic net.

Semantic Networks and the Flow of Satisfaction

You have seen how to use semantic networks to visualize the relationships between objects and how to express a semantic net in Turbo Prolog. Recall the semantic net in the record example:

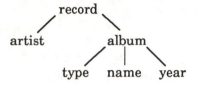

The network shows not only the relationships between the objects, but also shows the **flow of satisfaction** Turbo Prolog uses to match objects and variables. Turbo Prolog moves from top to bottom and then from left to right. This is called a **depth first** flow of satisfaction. Turbo Prolog first attempts to move vertically through the network before moving from left to right. Only when Turbo Prolog cannot find a match (fails) does it attempt to move up and horizontally (backtrack).

In the next chapter, you will see that this depth first approach may not always be the most efficient. You will also learn how to change the flow of satisfaction; that is, a way to force the program to follow a **breadth first** pattern. However, first you need some practice building and using data structures.

Tutorial 8-1 Using Data Structures

To illustrate how to use data structures, you will build a knowledge base that shows the advantages of using these structures. In this knowledge base, you will represent some information about some books in a library. You know from your visits to libraries that information may need to be retrieved in several different ways. You may wish to look up books on a certain subject, by a particular author, or with a known title.

Libraries solve this problem by creating separate files for titles, authors, and subjects. Computerized knowledge bases offer a more elegant solution. You want to set up a card catalog that contains the information about each book. Because each book is a single object, you want to use a complex data structure to represent the knowledge.

Recall the three steps used in developing complex semantic nets.

Step 1- Design the basic semantic net.

Step 2- Expand one or more of the simple objects into complex data structures.

Step 3- Replace the simple object with the new data structure.

Repeat steps 2 and 3 as necessary.

These steps are described in detail below:

Step 1–Design the basic semantic net

The basic facts you want to represent are the title, author, type, publisher, and reference number of each book. You will use a complex data structure because each book is an individual object and should be treated as such. The skeleton semantic network looks like this:

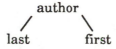

The Turbo Prolog clause that represents this knowledge is:

book(title,author,type,publisher,ref_num).

Notice that this is a simple structure. Each component is a single object. You may wish to specify more knowledge about the author.

Step 2–Expand part of the semantic net

Look at the object **author**. Represent the author's first and last names with a semantic network.

```
        author
       /      \
    last      first
```

The Turbo Prolog fact looks like this:

author(last,first)

Step 3- Replace the simple object (in this case author) with the data structure described above.

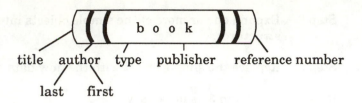

title   author   type   publisher   reference number

last   first

This can be represented by the Turbo Prolog fact:

book(title,**author(last,first)**,type,publisher,ref_num)

*this new structure replaces the object **author**.*

Notice that the semantic network has expanded. To expand further, repeat steps 2 and 3 (expansion and replacement) as necessary.

Step 2- Expand semantic net (repeated)

Suppose you also want to represent more information about the publisher. You will create a structure that contains the publisher's name, year, and location published. The semantic net is:

publisher

name   year   location

As a Turbo Prolog fact, this is represented as:

publisher(name,year,location).

Step 3- Replace the simple object with the data structure (repeated)

Again, you can substitute the newly created structure for the simple object. The new semantic net looks like this:

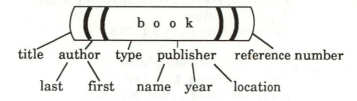

This can be represented by the Turbo Prolog fact:

book(title,author(last,first),type,
        publisher(pub_name,year,location),ref_num)

Step 2- Expand the semantic net (repeated)

Now add more information about where the book was published. This is a semantic net to associate the city and country to the object **location**.

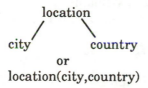

Step 3- Replace the simple object with the data structure (repeated)

Now you have the final representation of all of the facts found on each card in the catalog. The whole structure is:

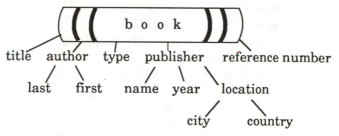

The full Turbo Prolog predicate is:

book(title,author(last,first),type,
        publisher(pub_name,year,**location(city,country)**),ref_num)

Below is the complete library knowledge base you will use in the next section.

Title: "Operating Manual for Spaceship Earth"
Author: Fuller, Buckminister
Publisher: Pocket Books, 1970, NY, USA
Type: Non-fiction
Reference Number: 69-15323

Title: "Understanding Media"
Author: McLuan, Marshall
Publisher: Signet, 1964, NY,USA
Type: Non-fiction
Reference Number: 11-11111

Title: "Henry IV"
Author: Shakespeare, William
Publisher: Wash. Square,1960,NY, USA
Type: Play
Reference Number: 22-22222

Title: "Julius Caesar"
Author: Shakespeare, William
Publisher: Wash. Square,1958, NY, USA
Type: Play
Reference Number: 33-33333

Title: "Robots and Empire"
Author: Asimov, Isaac
Publisher: Ballantine,1985, NY, USA
Type: Science Fiction
Reference Number: 85-1600

Title: "Robots of Dawn"
Author: Asimov, Isaac
Publisher: Ballantine, 1983, NY, USA
Type: Science Fiction
Reference Number: 83-8960

Boot your computer and enter the Turbo Prolog Editor Window. Enter the clauses as follows:

TYPE

```
--- Editor Window ---

clauses
    book("Operating Manual for Spaceship Earth",
    author("Fuller","Buckminister"),"Non-fiction",
    publisher("Pocket Books", 1970,location("NY","USA")),
    "69-15323").

    book("Understanding Media",
    author("McLuan","Marshall"),"Non-fiction",
    publisher("Signet",1964,location("NY","USA")),
    "11-11111").

    book("Henry IV",
    author("Shakespeare","William"),"Play",
    publisher("Wash. Square", 1960,location("NY","USA")),
    "22-22222").

    book("Julius Caesar",
    author("Shakespeare","William"),"Play",
    publisher("Wash. Square",1958,location("NY","USA")),
    "33-33333").

    book("Robots and Empire",
    author("Asimov","Isaac"), "Science Fiction",
    publisher("Ballantine",1985,location("NY","USA")),
    "85-1600").

    book("Robots of Dawn",
    author("Asimov","Isaac"),"Science Fiction",
    publisher("Ballantine",1983,location("NY","USA")),
    "83-8960").
```

Notice that you enter the objects with quote marks. Later in this chapter you will see why.

Now it is time to enter the predicates section. When you declare predicates, you enter each part of the declaration as a simple object. Even the objects that are data structures themselves are declared as simple objects. You will declare the data structures in the domain section. This follows the same pattern you used to build the data structure, so it will be easy.

Data Structures

Enter the predicates section as shown below.

```
predicates
        book(title,author,type,publisher,ref_num)

clauses
        book("Operating Manual for Spaceship Earth",
        author("Fuller","Buckminister"),"Non-fiction",
        publisher("Pocket Books", 1970,location("NY","USA")),
        "69-15323").
```

Note that the predicate declaration is the same as the original skeleton semantic net.

Now declare the domain types. Keep in mind that, although the predicate declaration is stated in the format shown above, the whole fact you want represented looks like this:

book(title,author(last,first),type,
publisher(pub_name,year,location(city,country)),ref_num).

The domains declared first are the ones in the inner parentheses. The objects in the inner parentheses are simple objects of the domain types you have learned (symbol, string, etc.). For this program, use the domain **string**, instead of **symbol**, to represent all of the objects but the year. The only difference between strings and symbols is that strings are enclosed in quotes. This is the reason you entered the names of the books as you did. Strings may begin with a capital letter, include spaces, and contain several words. They make a knowledge base more readable. The object **year** is an integer, while the remaining objects (**first, last, pub_name, city, country, type,** and **ref_num**) are strings.

Add the following domain declaration to the knowledge base.

```
domains
        title,first,last,pub_name,city,country,type,ref_num = string
        year=integer

predicates
        book(title,author,type,publisher,ref_num)
```

The compound data structures are user-defined data types. In other words, the data types **author**, **publisher**, and **location** are constructed from the standard data types.

The **author** object has two parts — the author's first name and last name. The objects **first** and **last** have already been declared, so you can use them to describe the new object data type as follows:

author = author(last,first)

Now Turbo Prolog knows that when it finds the **author** object in a predicate, it contains two other objects — **first** and **last**.

Add the new predicate definitions to the knowledge base.

```
                        --- Editor Window ---
domains
        title,first,last,pub_name,city,country,type,ref_num = string
        year=integer
        author = author(last,first)

predicates
        book(title,author,type,publisher,ref_num)
```

Because you must declare the structures in the inner parentheses first, you need to declare the meaning of the object **location**. You cannot declare the predicate **publisher** until **location** is declared. You must first declare the meaning of **location** so that you can use it to declare **publisher**. Adding the definition of **location** to the domain sections gives the following:

location=location(city,country)

Add the **location** domain as shown below.

```
                        --- Editor Window ---
domains
        title,first,last,pub_name,city,country,type,ref_num = string
        year=integer

        author = author(last,first)
        location = location(city,country)

predicates
        book(title,author,type,publisher,ref_num)
```

Now complete the definition of **publisher**.

publisher = publisher(pub_name,year,location)

Add the **publisher** domain as shown below.

```
                    --- Editor Window ---
domains
        title,first,last,pub_name,city,country,type,ref_num = string
        year=integer

        author = author(last,first)
        location = location(city,country)
        publisher = publisher(pub_name,year,location)
predicates
        book(title,author,type,publisher,ref_num)
```

The program is now complete.

Choose the Run option from the Main Menu. If you have any errors, compare the contents in your Editor Window with the complete program shown on the next page.

```
domains
    title,first,last,pub_name,city,country,type,ref_num = string
    year=integer

    author = author(last,first)
    location = location(city,country)
    publisher = publisher(pub_name,year,location)

predicates
    book(title,author,type,publisher,ref_num)

clauses
    book("Operating Manual for Spaceship Earth",
    author("Fuller","Buckminister"),"Non-fiction",
    publisher("Pocket Books", 1970,location("NY","USA")),
    "69-15323").

    book("Understanding Media",
    author("McLuan","Marshall"),"Non-fiction",
    publisher("Signet",1964,location("NY","USA")),
    "11-11111").

    book("Henry IV",
    author("Shakespeare","William"),"Play",
    publisher("Wash. Square", 1960,location("NY","USA")),
    "22-22222").

    book("Julius Caesar",
    author("Shakespeare","William"),"Play",
    publisher("Wash. Square",1958,location("NY","USA")),
    "33-33333").

    book("Robots and Empire",
    author("Asimov","Isaac"), "Science Fiction",
    publisher("Ballantine",1985,location("NY","USA")),
    "85-1600").

    book("Robots of Dawn",
    author("Asimov","Isaac"),"Science Fiction",
    publisher("Ballantine",1983,location("NY","USA")),
    "83-8960").
```

Data Structures

Enter the following goal statement to list the names of all the book titles:

```
                    --- Dialog Window ---
     Goal: book(Title,author(_,_),_,publisher(_,_,location(_,_)),_)
```

This goal produces the result:

```
                    --- Dialog Window ---

     Title=Operating Manual for Spaceship Earth
     Title=Understanding Media
     Title=Henry IV
     Title=Julius Caesar
     Title=Robots and Empire
     Title=Robots of Dawn
     6 Solutions
```

To make many queries that list the names of the books, you could write a rule to simplify your typing. Add the following rule to the clauses section of your knowledge base.

```
     book_titles(Title) if
             book(Title,author(_,_),_,
             publisher(_,_,location(_,_)),_).
```

Of course, you must declare the rule in the predicates section. Add the **book_titles** predicate as shown below:

```
predicates
        book(title,author,publisher,type,ref_num)
        book_titles(title)
```

Run the program and type the following goal:

Goal: `book_titles(Title)` ↵

```
                    --- Dialog Window ---

        Goal: book_titles(Title)

        Title=Operating Manual for Spaceship Earth
        Title=Understanding Media
        Title=Henry IV
        Title=Julius Caesar
        Title=Robots and Empire
        Title=Robots of Dawn
        6 Solutions
```

Type in the following goal to print the names and types of all of the books in the knowledge base:

```
                    --- Dialog Window ---

        Goal: book(Title,author(_,_),Type,publisher(_,_,location(_,_)),_).

        Title=Operating Manual for Spaceship Earth, Type=Non-fiction
        Title=Understanding Media, Type=Non-fiction
        Title=Henry IV, Type=Play
        Title=Julius Caesar, Type=Play
        Title=Robots and Empire, Type=Science Fiction
        Title=Robots of Dawn, Type=Science Fiction
        6 Solutions
```

Add a rule that queries the knowledge base about titles and type of work.

```
                    --- Editor Window ---

/*    Rules for Library Program Chapter 8    */

        book_titles(Title) if
                book(Title,author(_,_),_,
                publisher(_,_,location(_,_)),_).

        type_work(Title,Type) if
                book(Title,author(_,_),Type,
                publisher(_,_,location(_,_)),_).
```

Remember that you must add the description of the clause to the predicates section. Add the predicate description to the predicates section as shown below:

> predicates
>   book(title,author,publisher,type,ref_num)
>   book_titles(title)
>   **type_work(title,type)**

Run the program and pose the following goal:

```
           --- Dialog Window ---

Goal: type_work(Title,Type).

Title=Operating Manual for Spaceship Earth, Type=Non-fiction
Title=Understanding Media, Type=Non-fiction
Title=Henry IV, Type=Play
Title=Julius Caesar, Type=Play
Title=Robots and Empire, Type=Science Fiction
Title=Robots of Dawn, Type=Science Fiction
6 Solutions
```

To list all of the authors in the knowledge base, type in the following goal:

```
                  --- Dialog Window ---

Goal: book(Title,author(Last,First),_,publisher(_,_,location(_,_)),_).

Title=Operating Manual for Spaceship Earth, Last=Fuller, First=Buckminister
Title=Understanding Media, Last=McLuan, First=Marshall
Title=Henry IV, Last=Shakespeare, First=William
Title=Julius Caesar, Last=Shakespeare, First=William
Title=Robots and Empire, Last=Asimov, First=Isaac
Title=Robots of Dawn, Last=Asimov, First=Isaac
6 Solutions
```

To write a rule that makes this query easier, include a complex data structure in the head of the rule. The rule is:

> written_by(Title,author(Last,First)) if
>   book(Title,author(Last,First),_,
>   publisher(_,_,place(_,_)),_).

Add the rule and predicate description to the knowledge base. The predicate description and the rule are:

```
                --- Editor Window ---

predicates
        book(title,author,type,publisher,ref_num)
        book_titles(title)
        type_work(title,type)
        written_by(title,author)

/*    Rules for Library Program Chapter 8    */

        book_titles(Title) if
                book(Title,author(_,_),_,
                publisher(_,_,location(_,_)),_).

        type_work(Title,Type) if
                book(Title,author(_,_),Type,
                publisher(_,_,location(_,_)),_).

        written_by(Title,author(Last,First)) if
                book(Title,author(Last,First),_,
                publisher(_,_,location(_,_)),_).
```

Type in the goal:

```
                --- Dialog Window ---

Goal: written_by(Title,author(Last,First)).

Title=Operating Manual for Spaceship Earth, Last=Fuller, First=Buckminister
Title=Understanding Media, Last=McLuan, First=Marshall
Title=Henry IV, Last=Shakespeare, First=William
Title=Julius Caesar, Last=Shakespeare, First=William
Title=Robots and Empire, Last=Asimov, First=Isaac
Title=Robots of Dawn, Last=Asimov, First=Isaac
6 Solutions
```

```
/*    Complete Listing of Library Program for Chapter 8      */
domains
    title,first,last,pub_name,city,country,type,ref_num = string
    year=integer

    author = author(last,first)
    location = location(city,country)
    publisher = publisher(pub_name,year,location)
predicates
    book(title,author,type,publisher,ref_num)
    book_titles(title)
    type_work(title,type)
    written_by(title,author)

clauses
    book("Operating Manual for Spaceship Earth",
    author("Fuller","Buckminister"),"Non-fiction",
    publisher("Pocket Books", 1970,location("NY","USA")),
    "69-15323").

    book("Understanding Media",
    author("McLuan","Marshall"),"Non-fiction",
    publisher("Signet",1964,location("NY","USA")),
    "11-11111").

    book("Henry IV",
    author("Shakespeare","William"),"Play",
    publisher("Wash. Square", 1960,location("NY","USA")),
    "22-22222").

    book("Julius Caesar",
    author("Shakespeare","William"),"Play",
    publisher("Wash. Square",1958,location("NY","USA")),
    "33-33333").

    book("Robots and Empire",
    author("Asimov","Isaac"), "Science Fiction",
    publisher("Ballantine",1985,location("NY","USA")),
    "85-1600").
    book("Robots of Dawn",
    author("Asimov","Isaac"),"Science Fiction",
    publisher("Ballantine",1983,location("NY","USA")),
    "83-8960").

/*    Rules for Library Program Chapter 8    */

    book_titles(Title) if
            book(Title,author(_,_),_,
            publisher(_,_,location(_,_)),_).

    type_work(Title,Type) if
            book(Title,author(_,_),Type,
            publisher(_,_,location(_,_)),_).

    written_by(Title,author(Last,First)) if
            book(Title,author(Last,First),_,
            publisher(_,_,location(_,_)),_).
```

Write new rules that do the following:

1) list all the books in 1961

2) list the names of the authors who write science fiction

3) list the names of all the playwrights

Exercises

8-1. What is another name for the predicate part of a rule definition?

8-2. What is another name for the objects in a rule definition?

8-3. How does Turbo Prolog expand the usefulness of semantic nets?

8-4. Draw a semantic network for a knowledge base that describes your private record collection as shown in this chapter. Add further information that specifies whether the record is a long playing record or a compact disc.

8-5. Specify three advantages of using a semantic network to represent a knowledge base.

Problems

8-1. Write a knowledge base that contains the following information about students in a school club:

Student Name	Birthday	Social Sec.	Class
Mary Anderson	10/14/65	987-45-3456	Junior
John Jones	9/27/64	221-34-5676	Sophomore
Sam Johnson	4/7/67	234-54-3456	Freshman
Bill Barker	6/7/72	345-66-2345	Senior

Write a series of rules that give the knowledge base the ability to provide answers to the following goals:

> Goal:birthdate("Mary Anderson",Date).
> Date=10/14/65
>
> Goal:social_sec_num("Bill Barker",Number).
> Number=345-66-2345
>
> Goal:class("John Jones",Class).
> Class=Sophomore
>
> Goal:birthday(Who,When).
> Who="Mary Anderson", When=10/14/65
> Who="John Jones", When=9/27/64
> Who="Sam Johnson", When=4/7/67
> Who="Bill Barker", When=6/7/72

8-2. Write a program using the semantic network derived in Exercise question 8-4. Assume you number your records in sequential order as you buy them and store them in this order. For example, the first record you bought would be number 1, the second would be number 2, and so on. Add this information to the semantic net, and include it in this program. Create the knowledge base and pose your own goals to make inquires.

Chapter 9
Recursion: A Closer Look

*This chapter takes an in-depth look at recursion. You will learn about the recursive case, boundary conditions, and flow of satisfaction. You will be led step by step through a detailed explanation of the recursive case. Tutorial 9-1, **Using Recursion**, will show you how recursion works through the use of a program with embedded recursion.*

Recursion: A Closer Look

In Chapter 7, you learned how the simplest form of recursion (**tail recursion**) works. In this chapter, you will look at recursion in greater detail.

The Recursive Case and Boundary Conditions

Recall the example of tail recursion from Chapter 7. It is presented in Figure 9-1.

Figure 9-1: Example of Tail Recursion

```
Clauses
    count_to_three(4).              <——count_to_three fact
    count_to_three(Num) if          <——count_to_three rule
        write(Num) and
        nl and
        N=Num+1 and
        count_to_three(N).
```

The predicate **count_to_three** has two separate definitions – **count_to_three(4)** and **count_to_three(Num)**. The first definition is a fact, while the second is a rule. Turbo Prolog facts take precedence over rules. If Turbo Prolog can resolve a goal by matching it to a fact rather than to a rule, it will do so. This is the same way humans solve problems.

For example, suppose you want to calculate the answer to a mathematics problem like, "How much is 6x5?" If you knew a rule like **count by 5's six times,** you could calculate the answer. However, if you previously had memorized the fact that 6 x 5 = 30, you would not bother to use the rule.

Turbo Prolog works in a similar fashion. If you pose a goal that can be matched to a fact, Turbo Prolog will use the fact. In the **count_to_three** program, you are saying, "If you know that the goal matches a fact, don't bother using a rule to solve the goal. Don't backtrack." This is how to tell Turbo Prolog to terminate a recursive rule. It stops using the rule when it finds a matching fact. Turbo Prolog starts all searches at the top of the knowledge base. Thus, the fact used to stop recursion must be placed above the recursive rule in the knowledge base. Next, you will see why this is important.

When Turbo Prolog uses a fact to match a goal, it stops searching for solutions to that goal. Hence, the fact defines the exit condition, also called the **boundary condition**. It is a signal that tells Turbo Prolog to stop its inference mechanism. In the example shown in Figure 9-1, when the number **4** is bound to the variable **N**, Turbo Prolog stops looking for matches. Another term for a rule like the one shown in Figure 9-1 is the **recursive case**. Figure 9-2 shows this new terminology.

Figure 9-2: Example of Tail Recursion (new terminology)

Goal:count_to_three(1).

```
Clauses
    count_to_three(4).          <——boundary condition (fact)
    count_to_three(Num) if      <——recursive case (rule)
        write(Num) and
        nl and
        N=Num+1 and
        count_to_three(N).      <——recursive call
```

At some point in the recursive case, a boundary condition must be met. If not, Turbo Prolog will keep running until the {Ctrl-Break} key combination is pressed. Assume that you call the program in Figure 9-2 with the initial goal **count_to_three(1)**. Each time the rule is called, the value of **Num** increases by 1. When **N** is bound to the value 4, the fact will be satisfied; that is, the boundary condition will be met.

Flow of Satisfaction

Remember how rules work. If a goal is presented with the same predicate as the rule head, Turbo Prolog attempts to match the corresponding objects in the goal with the objects in the rule. In the **count_to_three** program, the goal is **count_to_three(1)**. Turbo Prolog tries to match this with the boundary condition, but the objects are not the same. The numeral **1** does not equal the numeral **4**. Because a match is not found with the first fact, Turbo Prolog moves down through the knowledge base and encounters the **count_to_three(Num)** rule.

The rule head of the recursive case has the unbound variable **Num** as an argument. Since the goal matches the rule head, the variable **Num** is bound to the value **1**, and Turbo Prolog moves to the right and attempts to resolve the subgoals. This order of searching is called the **flow of satisfaction** and continues until the boundary condition is met. We will examine this process in detail next.

How the Recursive Case Works

To understand how recursion works, consider an example of **embedded recursion**. Embedded recursion is slightly more complicated than tail recursion. In embedded recursion, the recursive call is somewhere other than at the end (tail) of the rule definition, as in Figure 9-3.

Figure 9-3: Example of Embedded Recursion

fact——>	count_to_three(4).	<——*boundary condition*
rule——>	count_to_three(Num) if	<——*recursive case*
	write(Num) and	
	nl and	
	N=Num+1 and	
	count_to_three(N) and	<——*this is the recursive call*
	nl and	
	write("Surprised").	

The knowledge base shown in Figure 9-3 consists of 2 clauses. The first clause is a fact, and the second clause is a rule. The rule has a recursive call that is not the last statement of the rule, but is embedded within the rule. This is why it is called embedded recursion.

Recall that, given a goal, Turbo Prolog attempts to match the goal with the facts and rules in its knowledge base. The search always begins at the top of the knowledge base and moves down through the knowledge base looking for a match for the stated goal. When a match is found, the unbound variables in the clause are bound to their corresponding values in the goal. Turbo Prolog then moves to the right within the clause attempting to satisfy the individual subgoals of the clause. This is called a **depth first** search and is the search pattern normally used by Turbo Prolog.

Example of a Depth First Search Pattern with Recursion

The following steps will demonstrate how Turbo Prolog solves a goal using the knowledge base in Figure 9-3. Keep in mind the values bound to the variables and which clause in the rule is being executed.

Goal:count_to_three(1).

Step 1

Goal:**count_to_three(1)**   <u>Knowledge Base</u>

                                            count_to_three(4).
Num = 1   count_to_three(Num) if
                                            write(Num) and
                                            nl and
N   =   unbound   N=Num+1 and
                                            count_to_three(N) and
                                            nl and
                                            write("Surprised").

1)   Turbo Prolog starts at the top of the knowledge base. In this case, the goal **count_to_three(1)** does not match the first clause **count_to_three(4)**.

2)   Turbo Prolog moves down (depth first) the knowledge base and encounters the head of the rule.

Step 2

Goal:**count_to_three(1)**	Knowledge Base
	count_to_three(4).
Num = 1	**count_to_three(Num) if**
	write(Num) and
	nl and
N = 2	N=Num+1 and
recursive call —>	count_to_three(N) and
	nl and
	write("Surprised").

1) The goal matches the rule head of the second clause.

2) The value **1** is bound to the variable **Num**.

3) Turbo Prolog moves to the right past the **if** statement and attempts to satisfy the rule body by:

   a. Writing the value of **Num** (1) in the Dialog Window,
   b. Printing a new line (nl) by moving the cursor down one line, and
   c. Adding 1 to Num (1+1=2) and binding the value to **N** so that **N = 2**.

4) Next, Turbo Prolog encounters the recursive call. A recursive call works like any other subgoal. The rule being satisfied must wait until its subgoals are satisfied before continuing. The difference in recursion is that the new subgoal is an exact copy of the goal by which it is called. To facilitate the discussion, the original goal is called level-1 and the first copy of the goal is called level-2. Level-1 of the goal still has some work to do, but it must wait until level-2 is satisfied. You will see this as you progress through these steps.

5) The new subgoal (level-2) is **count_to_three(N)**, where **N = 2**. This subgoal looks exactly the same as the original goal, but the values of the variables are different. Remember that the value of **N** is now established as **2**, or as we say in Turbo Prolog, the variable **N** is bound to the value **2**.

Step 3

Level-2 Goal: **count_to_three(N)**

<u>Knowledge Base</u>

count_to_three(4).
　count_to_three(Num) if
　write(Num) and
　nl and
　N=Num+1 and
　count_to_three(N) and
　l and
　write("Surprised").

Num= 1

N= 2

1) The recursive call is seen as a new goal by Turbo Prolog. So, the search begins again at the top of the knowledge base, and the new goal **count_to_three(N)**, where **N = 2**, is compared with the first fact.

2) At this point, the value of **N** is **2**. The predicate **count_to_three(N)** does not match **count_to_three(4)**, so the search continues down the knowledge base.

Step 4

Level-2 Goal: **count_to_three(N)**

<u>Knowledge Base</u>

count_to_three(4).
　count_to_three(Num) if
　write(Num) and
　nl and
　N=Num+1 and
　count_to_three(N) and
　nl and
　write("Surprised").

Num = 2

N= 3

1) The goal matches the rule head of the second clause.

2) The variable **Num** is bound to the value of **N**, which is **2**.

3) Turbo Prolog moves to the right and attempts to satisfy the rule body. To accomplish this, Turbo Prolog:

a. Writes the value of **Num** (2) in the Dialog Window,
b. Prints a new line (moves the cursor down one line), and
c. Binds the value **Num+1** (2+1=3) to **N**.

4) Turbo Prolog again encounters the recursive call. The new subgoal (call it level-3) is **count_to_three(N)** with **N** bound to the value **3**. Turbo Prolog makes a new copy of the rule and moves on to satisfy it.

Step 5

Level-3 Goal:**count_to_three(N)** Knowledge Base

Num= 2	count_to_three(4). count_to_three(Num) if write(Num) and nl and
N= 3	N=Num+1 and count_to_three(N) and nl and write("Surprised").

1) The recursive call is considered a new goal **count_to_three(N)** with **N = 3**. The search starts again at the top of the knowledge base.

2) This level-3 goal does not match the first clause, so the search moves to the rule head.

Step 6

Level-3 Goal:**count_to_three(N)** <u>Knowledge Base</u>

Num= 3	count_to_three(4). **count_to_three(Num)** if write(Num) and nl and
N= 4	N=Num+1 and count_to_three(N) and nl and write("Surprised").

1) The goal matches the rule head of the second clause with **Num** bound to the value **3**.

2) The rule body is now solved. Turbo Prolog:

a. Writes the value of **Num** (3),
b. Prints a new line, and
c. Binds the value **Num+1** (3+1=4) to **N**.

3) Turbo Prolog makes a new copy (level-4) of the rule and continues.

Step 7

Level-4 Goal:**count_to_three(N)**   <u>Knowledge Base</u>

	count_to_three(4).
Num = 3	count_to_three(Num) if
	write(Num) and
	nl and
N = 4	N=Num+1 and
	count_to_three(N) and
	nl and
	write("Surprised").

1) The level-4 goal finally matches the first clause. This is the boundary condition, and you might suspect that the program ceases execution. Not so, because there are three levels of recursion yet to be satisfied.

2) Turbo Prolog returns to the level-3 goal that is on hold. Level-3 was waiting for level-4 to finish, now it can continue.

2) When Turbo Prolog returns to the level-3 subgoal, it continues by moving to the right. Turbo Prolog writes a new line and prints the word "Surprised" in the Dialog Window.

3) Level-3 is now completed, and Turbo Prolog returns to level-2 and prints a new line and the word "Surprised" in the Dialog Window.

4) Turbo Prolog returns to level-1 (the top level). A new line and "Surprised" are printed again. The goal is now satisfied. The program ceases operation. The result of the recursion is that the word "Surprised" is printed three times in the Dialog Window – once for each level of the recursion from which Turbo Prolog emerges.

```
Goal:count_to_three(1).
1
2
3
Surprised
Surprised
Surprised
Yes
```

A Recursive Diagram for the Counting Problem

Another way to visualize embedded recursion is to look at a diagram that pictures the recursion. This diagram shows you how recursion submerges until the boundary condition is met. When this happens, the flow of satisfaction returns to the previous level to complete its work. It emerges upward. A diagram of the previous example is shown in Figure 9-4.

Figure 9-4: A Recursive Diagram for the Counting Problem

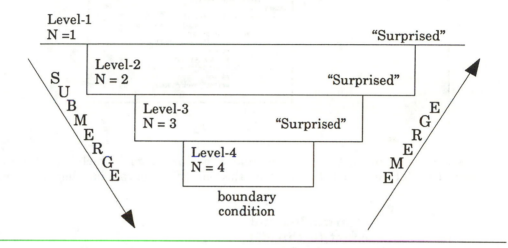

Tutorial 9-1 Using Recursion

It is important that you understand how recursion works. Tutorial 9-1 is designed to lead you step by step through this process. The example in the tutorial uses the more complex type of recursion, called **embedded recursion**, which you have been introduced to in the last example.

Recall that in embedded recursion the recursive call takes place in the middle of the rule, rather than at the end of the rule. As a result, each copy of the rule has additional tasks to perform when recursion returns to it. This is illustrated in the tutorial.

Enter the program below: [Reminder: You can expand the window to full size by pressing the [F5] key.]

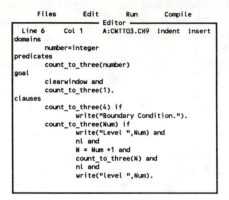

```
        Files        Edit        Run        Compile
                    Editor
  Line 6      Col 1        A:CNTTO3.CH9  Indent  Insert
domains
        number=integer
predicates
        count_to_three(number)
goal
        clearwindow and
        count_to_three(1).
clauses
        count_to_three(4) if
                write("Boundary Condition.").
        count_to_three(Num) if
                write("Level ",Num) and
                nl and
                N = Num +1 and
                count_to_three(N) and
                nl and
                write("level ",Num).
```

Before running this program, take a look at the goal which is part of the program. Recall that a goal stated within the body of a program is called an internal goal.

    goal
        clearwindow and
        count_to_three(1).

What do you think is the result of this goal? What would the output in the Dialog Window look like? Think about it before you proceed.

Compile and run the program. Here is the result:

```
         Files      Edit       Run      Compile      Options    Setup
                                                               ─ Dialog ─
  ┌─────────────────────────────────────────────┐    ┌──────────────────┐
  │ Line 18   Col 33    WORK.PRO  Indent  Insert │    │ Level 1          │
  │ goal                                         │    │ Level 2          │
  │         clearwindow and                      │    │ Level 3          │
  │         count_to_three(1).                   │    │ Boundary Condition.│
  │                                              │    │ level 3          │
  │ clauses                                      │    │ level 2          │
  │         count_to_three(4) if                 │    │ level 1          │
  │             write("Boundary Condition.").    │    │ Press the SPACE bar│
  │         count_to_three(Num) if               │    │                  │
  │             write("Level ",Num) and          │    │                  │
  │             nl and                           │    │                  │
  │             N = Num +1 and                   │    │                  │
  │             count_to_three(N) and            │    │                  │
  │             nl and                           │    │                  │
  │             write("level ",Num).             │    │                  │
  │                                              │    │                  │
  └─────────────────────────────────────────────┘    └──────────────────┘
  ┌──────────── Message ────────────┐    ┌──────────────────────────────┐
  │ Compiling WORK.PRO              │    │                              │
  │ Compiling WORK.PRO              │    │                              │
  │ Compiling WORK.PRO              │    │                              │
  │ count_to_three                  │    │                              │
  └─────────────────────────────────┘    └──────────────────────────────┘
    F2-Save  F3-Load  F6-Switch  F9-Compile                    Alt-X-Exit
```

Are you surprised at the result? Many people are. Embedded recursion illustrates the important features of how recursion works. In the above program, four complete copies of the predicate **count_to_three** exist. By the time the program is complete, all copies must be satisfied.

Each copy of the recursive case has further business to take care of. This business involves satisfying the subgoals **nl** and **write("level ",Num)** as highlighted below.

```
        count_to_three(4) if
            write("Boundary Condition.").
        count_to_three(Num) if
            write("Level ",Num) and
            nl and
            N=Num+1 and
            count_to_three(N) and
            nl and
            write("level ",Num).
```

When the boundary condition is met, **count_to_three(4)** is satisfied. Then Turbo Prolog starts to emerge from the three copies of the rule, eventually returning to level-1. As Turbo Prolog passes through each level, it executes these last two lines by issuing a new line and writing the level of the recursion in the Dialog Window. The "Press the SPACE bar" message at the end of the output means the program has completed its tasks.

Now you will step through this program using the **Trace** command. This may seem tedious, but understanding recursion is necessary if you want to write sophisticated Turbo Prolog programs.

Enter your Editor Window and add the **shorttrace** compiler directive at the top of your program. The Editor Window should look like this:

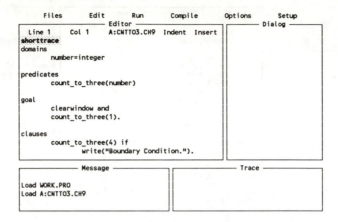

```
        Files      Edit      Run      Compile    Options    Setup
                            Editor                          Dialog
    Line 1      Col 1    A:CNTTO3.CH9   Indent  Insert
 shorttrace
 domains
         number=integer

 predicates
         count_to_three(number)

 goal
         clearwindow and
         count_to_three(1).

 clauses
         count_to_three(4) if
                 write("Boundary Condition.").

              Message                              Trace

 Load WORK.PRO
 Load A:CNTTO3.CH9
```

In the following steps, you will execute the program step by step. The **Trace** (or in this case the shorttrace) and the **shorttrace** commands will cause each step to be displayed in the Trace Window. Examine each step as it appears in the Trace Window and read the explanations accompanying each step in the tutorial. Be sure to notice where the cursor appears in the Editor Window. This provides additional information about the program's execution.

To step through the program, follow the **P** prompts in the tutorial, pressing the {F10} key where indicated. Pressing the {F10} key moves the execution of the program one step.

With the **shorttrace** command at the top of the program, run the program and follow each step as presented in the tutorial.

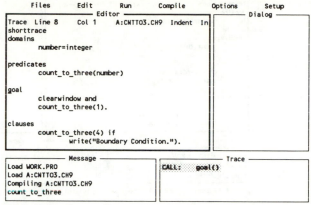

```
            Files       Edit       Run      Compile     Options     Setup
                    Editor                                      Dialog
Trace  Line 8    Col 1      A:CNTTO3.CH9   Indent  In
shorttrace
domains
        number=integer

predicates
        count_to_three(number)

goal
        clearwindow and
        count_to_three(1).

clauses
        count_to_three(4) if
                write("Boundary Condition.").

                Message                            Trace
Load WORK.PRO                              CALL:     goal()
Load A:CNTTO3.CH9
Compiling A:CNTTO3.CH9
count_to_three

F1-Help F2-Save F5-Zoom  F10-Step  Shift-F10-Resize  Alt-T-Trace on/off  Esc-End
```

CALL:**goal()**

Turbo Prolog has an internal goal; thus, it tries to satisfy that goal. No external goal request is displayed in the Dialog Window, and the flashing cursor is located on the goal statement in the Editor Window. The Trace Window shows a call for the goal.

{F10}

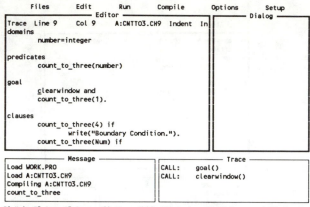

CALL:**clearwindow()**

The first statement of the goal is the standard predicate **clearwindow** which clears the Dialog Window. This command succeeds by clearing the Dialog Window. When you press {F10} the next time, the Dialog Window will be cleared.

{F10}

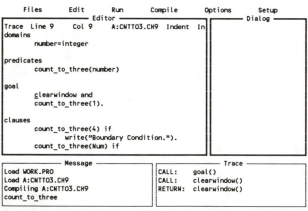

RETURN:**clearwindow()**

This executes the **clearwindow** command. The Dialog Window is cleared.

{F10}

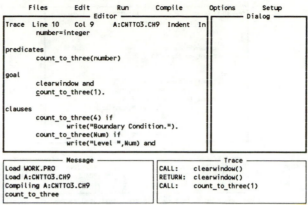

CALL:**count_to_three(1)**

The goal **count_to_three(1)** is called. The search to satisfy this goal begins at the top of the knowledge base.

{F10}

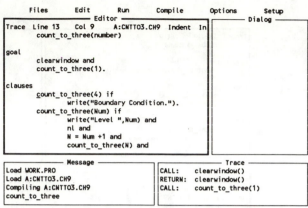

Notice that the cursor is located on the first clause. This first clause, **count_to_three(4)**, does not match the goal **count_to_three(1)**. Recall that this clause is the boundary condition. The search moves down the knowledge base.

**count_to_three(4) if
    write("Boundary Condition.").**
count_to_three(Num) if
    write("Level ",Num) and
    nl and
    N=Num+1 and
    count_to_three(N) and
    nl and
    write("level",Num).

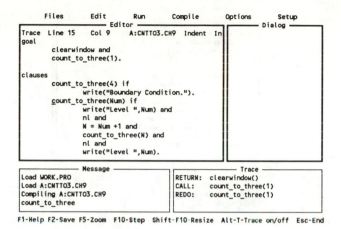

```
              Files      Edit      Run      Compile      Options      Setup
                               Editor                              Dialog
Trace  Line 15    Col 9      A:CNTTO3.CH9   Indent  In
goal
          clearwindow and
          count_to_three(1).

clauses
          count_to_three(4) if
                  write("Boundary Condition.").
          count_to_three(Num) if
                  write("Level ",Num) and
                  nl and
                  N = Num +1 and
                  count_to_three(N) and
                  nl and
                  write("level ",Num).

              Message                              Trace
Load WORK.PRO                        RETURN:  clearwindow()
Load A:CNTTO3.CH9                     CALL:    count_to_three(1)
Compiling A:CNTTO3.CH9                REDO:    count_to_three(1)
count_to_three
```

F1-Help F2-Save F5-Zoom F10-Step Shift-F10-Resize Alt-T-Trace on/off Esc-End

REDO:**count_to_three(1)**

Turbo Prolog attempts to solve the rule for **count_to_three(Num)**, where **Num** is an unbound variable. The rule succeeds by binding **Num** to the value **1** from the goal statement.

count_to_three(4) if
    write("Boundary Condition.").
count_to_three(Num) if   <——— *matched by*
    write("Level ",Num) and   *binding Num to 1*
    nl and
    N=Num+1 and
    count_to_three(N) and
    nl and
    write("level",Num).

The head of the second rule is satisfied. Turbo Prolog now tries to satisfy the subgoals for this rule at level-1.

Step 7

{F10}

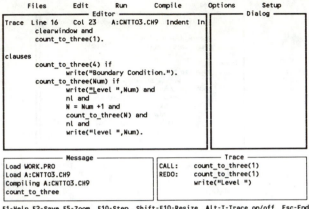

write("Level ")

The subgoal **write("Level ")** is called.

Step 8

{F10}

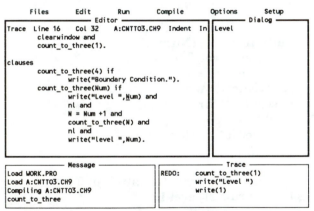

write(1)

The word **Level** is displayed in the Dialog Window.

{F10}

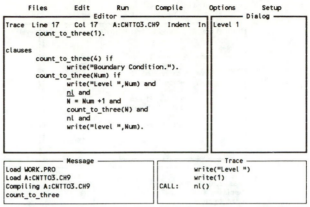

CALL:**nl()**

The value of **Num**, which is **1**, is written in the Dialog Window, and the standard predicate **nl** is called. The new line is really printed in the next step.

The subgoal **nl** always succeeds by printing a new line in the Dialog Window. It is a standard predicate that tells Turbo Prolog to advance one line.

Step 10

{F10}

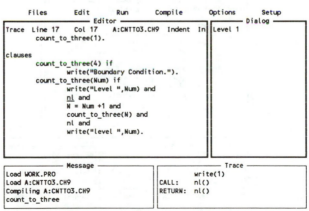

RETURN:**nl()**

You can't see it, but a new line is printed in the Dialog Window. The cursor has moved to the next line.

{F10}

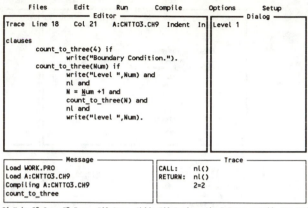

2=2

The third subgoal says, "Add 1 to the value of **Num** and bind the variable **N** to the result." At this point, **Num** is bound to **1**, and **N** is bound to **2**.

{F10}

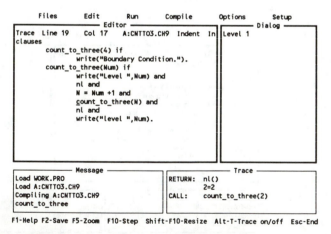

CALL:**count_to_three(2)**

This subgoal uses the rule **count_to_three(N)** and is recursive. The **count_to_three** predicate is called with the value **2** as its argument. It is important to recognize that this is a completely new goal. The CALL statement in the Trace Window shows that it is being treated as a new goal.

{F10}

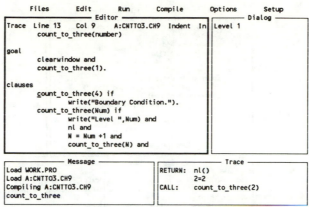

```
          Files        Edit        Run        Compile        Options        Setup
                  ─── Editor ───                              ─── Dialog ───
Trace  Line 13      Col 9      A:CNTTO3.CH9  Indent  In   Level 1
          count_to_three(number)

goal
          clearwindow and
          count_to_three(1).

clauses
          count_to_three(4) if
                  write("Boundary Condition.").
          count_to_three(Num) if
                  write("Level ",Num) and
                  nl and
                  N = Num +1 and
                  count_to_three(N) and

        ─── Message ───                       ─── Trace ───
Load WORK.PRO                          RETURN:  nl()
Load A:CNTTO3.CH9                                2=2
Compiling A:CNTTO3.CH9                  CALL:   count_to_three(2)
count_to_three

F1-Help F2-Save F5-Zoom  F10-Step  Shift-F10-Resize  Alt-T-Trace on/off  Esc-End
```

An attempt to solve this new goal is made. As with any new goal, the search begins at the top of the knowledge base. The predicate **count_to_three(4)** does not match because the value of $N = 2$, so no new message appears in the Trace Window.

count_to_three(4)   <————————*this does not match*

{F10}

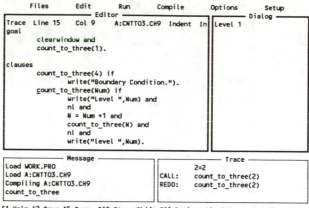

REDO:**count_to_three(2)**

An attempt is made to satisfy the **count_to_three** rule by trying to match the new goal with the second rule. It succeeds by binding **Num** to the value **2**. Recall that at level-1, **Num** has a value of **1**. How can this be? At the level-2 recursion, **Num** is bound to **2**. **Num** seems to have two values. This is one of the most important features of recursion. The same variable may have different values at different levels of recursion. Also, keep in mind that the top level of the rule is not completed as yet. It is on hold waiting for the copies of itself to be satisfied.

Step 15

{F10}

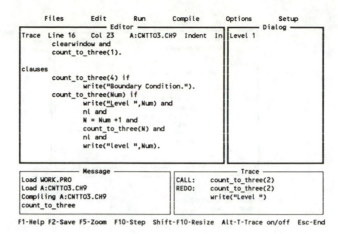

write("Level ")

The cursor is located on the **write("Level ",Num)** line in the Editor Window. This shows that this is the subgoal being processed.

Step 16

{F10}

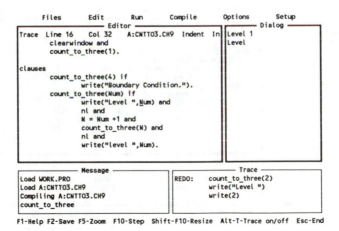

write(2)

The word "Level" is displayed in the Dialog Window, and the next subgoal **write(2)** is called.

Step 17

 {F10}

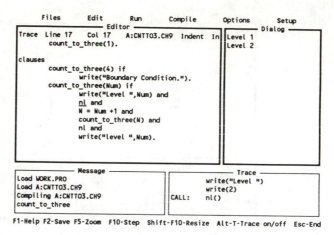

Call:**nl**()

The value of **Num** (2) is printed in Dialog Window, and the standard predicate **nl** is called.

Step 18

 {F10}

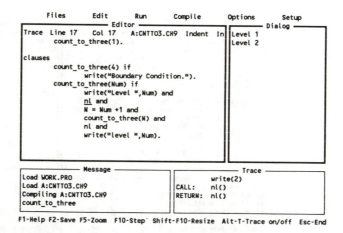

RETURN:**nl**()

The cursor moves to a new line in the Dialog Window.

Step 19

 {F10}

3=3

The next subgoal succeeds by binding **N** to the value of **Num**.

Step 20

 {F10}

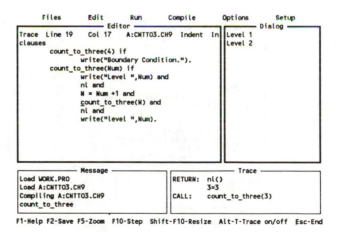

CALL:**count_to_three(3)**

A new copy of the **count_to_three** predicate is made. This is level-3 of the recursion with **N** bound to **3**.

Step 21

 {F10}

Turbo Prolog returns to the **count_to_three(4)** rule in an attempt to match the new goal of **count_to_three(3)**. They do not match. Turbo Prolog continues through the knowledge base.

Step 22

 {F10}

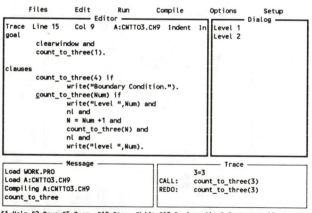

REDO:**count_to_three(3)**

The predicate **count_to_three(3)** matches **count_to_three(Num)** by binding **Num** to **3**. At level-3, **Num** is bound to the value **3**. Recall that at level-2, **Num** is still bound to **2**, and, at level-1, it is still bound to **1**.

Step 23

 {F10}

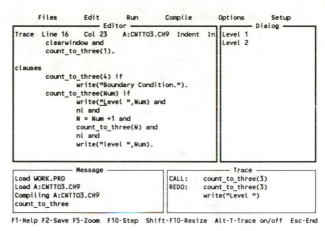

```
          Files      Edit       Run      Compile      Options      Setup
                       Editor                              Dialog
Trace  Line 16    Col 23    A:CNTTO3.CH9  Indent  In   Level 1
         clearwindow and                                Level 2
         count_to_three(1).

clauses
         count_to_three(4) if
                 write("Boundary Condition.").
         count_to_three(Num) if
                 write("Level ",Num) and
                 nl and
                 N = Num +1 and
                 count_to_three(N) and
                 nl and
                 write("level ",Num).



                     Message                           Trace
Load WORK.PRO                              CALL:   count_to_three(3)
Load A:CNTTO3.CH9                          REDO:   count_to_three(3)
Compiling A:CNTTO3.CH9                             write("Level ")
count_to_three
          F1-Help F2-Save F5-Zoom  F10-Step  Shift-F10-Resize  Alt-T-Trace on/off  Esc-End
```

write ("Level")

The next subgoal is called.

Step 24

 {F10}

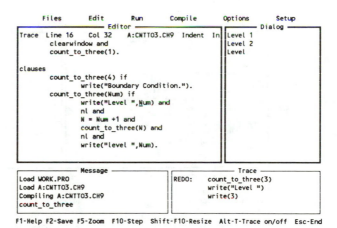

```
          Files      Edit       Run      Compile      Options      Setup
                       Editor                              Dialog
Trace  Line 16    Col 32    A:CNTTO3.CH9  Indent  In   Level 1
         clearwindow and                                Level 2
         count_to_three(1).                             Level

clauses
         count_to_three(4) if
                 write("Boundary Condition.").
         count_to_three(Num) if
                 write("Level ",Num) and
                 nl and
                 N = Num +1 and
                 count_to_three(N) and
                 nl and
                 write("level ",Num).


                     Message                           Trace
Load WORK.PRO                              REDO:   count_to_three(3)
Load A:CNTTO3.CH9                                  write("Level ")
Compiling A:CNTTO3.CH9                             write(3)
count_to_three
          F1-Help F2-Save F5-Zoom  F10-Step  Shift-F10-Resize  Alt-T-Trace on/off  Esc-End
```

write(3)

The word "Level" is displayed in the Dialog Window, and the next subgoal is called.

Recursion

{F10}

CALL:**nl()**

The **write** predicate succeeds by displaying its argument (3) in the Dialog Window, and the new line predicate is called.

{F10}

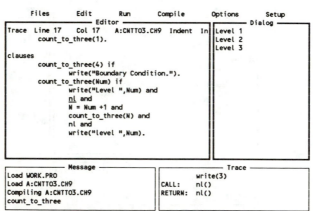

RETURN:**nl()**

The cursor moves down one line in the Dialog Window.

{F10}

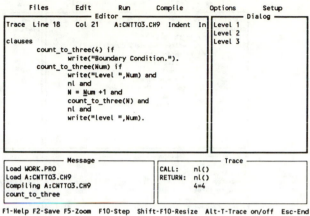

```
           Files       Edit      Run      Compile       Options      Setup
                         Editor                                    Dialog
Trace  Line 18    Col 21    A:CNTTO3.CH9   Indent   In  Level 1
                                                        Level 2
clauses                                                 Level 3
        count_to_three(4) if
                write("Boundary Condition.").
        count_to_three(Num) if
                write("Level ",Num) and
                nl and
                N = Num +1 and
                count_to_three(N) and
                nl and
                write("level ",Num).




                  Message                            Trace
 Load WORK.PRO                         CALL:     nl()
 Load A:CNTTO3.CH9                      RETURN:   nl()
 Compiling A:CNTTO3.CH9                           4=4
 count_to_three

 F1-Help F2-Save F5-Zoom  F10-Step  Shift-F10-Resize  Alt-T-Trace on/off  Esc-End
```

4=4

Num+1 is equal to **4**, so **N=Num+1** succeeds by binding **N** to **4**.

{F10}

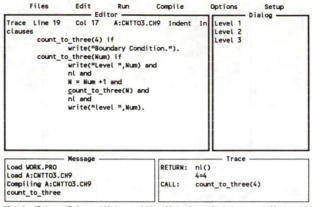

```
         Files      Edit      Run      Compile      Options     Setup
                   ── Editor ──                              ── Dialog ──
Trace  Line 19    Col 17    A:CNTTO3.CH9  Indent  In │Level 1
clauses                                              │Level 2
         count_to_three(4) if                        │Level 3
               write("Boundary Condition.").
         count_to_three(Num) if
               write("Level ",Num) and
               nl and
               N = Num +1 and
               count_to_three(N) and
               nl and
               write("level ",Num).



         ── Message ──                      ──────── Trace ────────
Load WORK.PRO                           │RETURN:  nl()
Load A:CNTTO3.CH9                        │         4=4
Compiling A:CNTTO3.CH9                   │CALL:    count_to_three(4)
count_to_three
```

F1-Help F2-Save F5-Zoom F10-Step Shift-F10-Resize Alt-T-Trace on/off Esc-End

CALL:count_to_three(4)

The final level of recursion occurs when this new goal is called. At this point, there are four separate goals and four separate values of **Num**. This is shown below.

Level	Goal	Value of Num
1	count_to_three(1)	1
2	count_to_three(2)	2
3	count_to_three(3)	3
4	count_to_three(4)	unchanged

{F10}

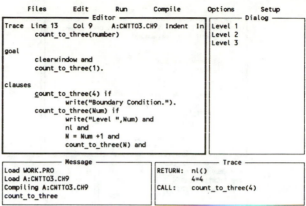

Because we have a new goal, a search for a match is again started at the top of the knowledge base. No new message appears in the Trace Window.

{F10}

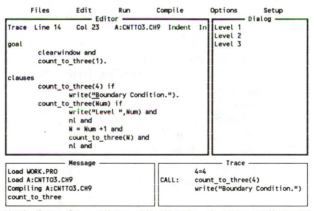

write("Boundary Condition.")

The first rule succeeds at level-4 of recursion. The rule then moves to the right to satisfy the subgoal.

{F10}

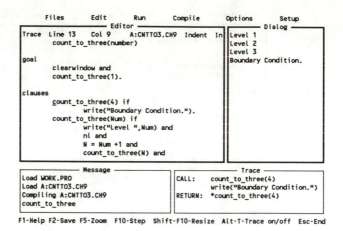

```
        Files      Edit      Run      Compile    Options      Setup
                        Editor                            Dialog
Trace  Line 13    Col 9       A:CNTT03.CH9  Indent  In │Level 1
        count_to_three(number)                           │Level 2
                                                         │Level 3
goal                                                     │Boundary Condition.
        clearwindow and
        count_to_three(1).

clauses
        count_to_three(4) if
                write("Boundary Condition.").
        count_to_three(Num) if
                write("Level ",Num) and
                nl and
                N = Num +1 and
                count_to_three(N) and
                Message                                Trace
Load WORK.PRO                          CALL:   count_to_three(4)
Load A:CNTT03.CH9                                write("Boundary Condition.")
Compiling A:CNTT03.CH9                  RETURN: *count_to_three(4)
count_to_three
```

F1-Help F2-Save F5-Zoom F10-Step Shift-F10-Resize Alt-T-Trace on/off Esc-End

> **RETURN:*count_to_three(4)**

Turbo Prolog now backtracks to the head of the rule. The words "Boundary
Condition." are displayed in the Dialog Window.

The new goal matches the clause. The boundary (exit) condition has been found.
Notice that **count_to_three(4)** is returned with an asterisk. This indicates that a
match has been found.

count_to_three(4) if
    write("Boundary Condition."). <── *this fact matches the*
count_to_three(Num) if   *new goal. The boundary*
    write("Level",Num) and   *condition is satisfied.*
    nl and
    N=Num+1 and
    count_to_three(N) and
    nl and
    write("level",Num).

{F10}

CALL:**nl()**

Because of the way recursion works, Turbo Prolog returns to the previous copy
(level-3) of the **count_to_three rule**. The value of **Num** is **3**. This copy has two
things that it has been waiting its turn to complete. These are the two standard
predicates **nl** and **write**. So, level-3 calls the predicate **nl**.

{F10}

RETURN:**nl()**

A new line is printed in Dialog Window.

{F10}

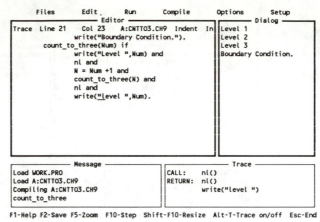

write("level ")

As Prolog emerges from recursive calls, it calls the next subgoal.

{F10}

write(3)

The word "level" is displayed in the Dialog Window, and the next subgoal is called.

Step 36

 {F10}

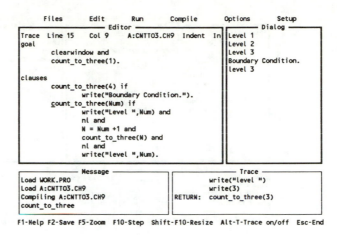

F1-Help F2-Save F5-Zoom F10-Step Shift-F10-Resize Alt-T-Trace on/off Esc-End

RETURN:count_to_three(3)

Level-3 prints the value of **Num** (3) in the Dialog Window. Turbo Prolog completes with level-3 of the recursion and moves to level-2 where **Num=2**.

Step 37

 {F10}

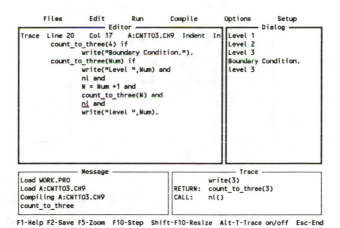

F1-Help F2-Save F5-Zoom F10-Step Shift-F10-Resize Alt-T-Trace on/off Esc-End

CALL:nl()

Turbo prolog emerges to level-2 of the rule. Level-2 will now complete its job.

       Recursion

Step 38

 {F10}

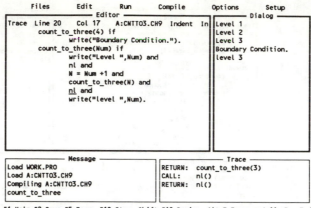

RETURN:**nl()**

A new line is printed in the Dialog Window.

Step 39

 {F10}

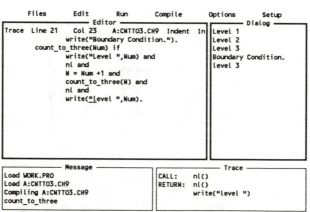

write("level")

The next subgoal (at level-2) is called.

{F10}

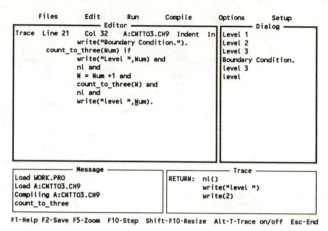

write(2)

The word "level " is printed in the Dialog Window, and the next subgoal is called.

Step 41

{F10}

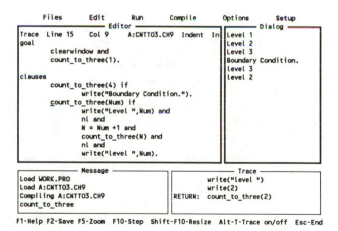

RETURN:**count_to_three(2)**

At level-2, the value of **Num** is **2**. This is printed in the Dialog Window. Level-2 is completed, and Turbo Prolog moves to level-1 where **Num=1**.

Step 42

 {F10}

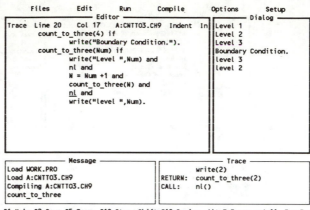

CALL:**nl**()

A call is made to the standard predicate **nl**.

Step 43

 {F10}

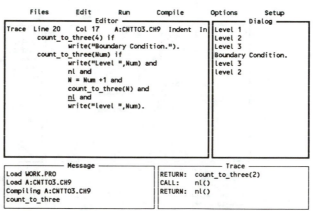

RETURN:**nl**()

A new line is printed in Dialog Window.

{F10}

write("level")

The next subgoal in level-1 is called.

{F10}

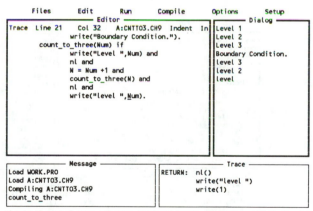

write(1)

Level-1 writes "level" in the Dialog Window.

{F10}

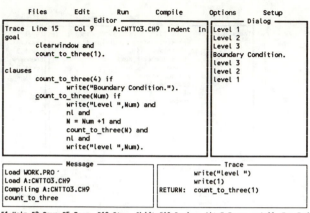

RETURN:**count_to_three(1)**

The value of **Num** is 1 at level-1. The numeral 1 is printed in the Dialog Window, and Turbo Prolog returns to the top level.

{F10}

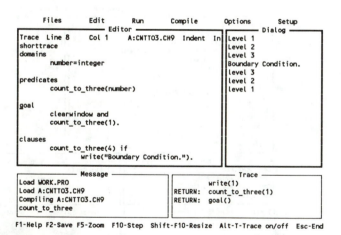

RETURN:**goal()**

Turbo Prolog returns to the internal goal to see if there is any more work to be done. There is none, so the program is complete.

{F10}

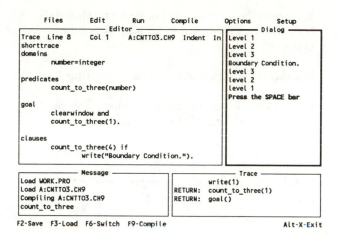

```
         Files      Edit      Run      Compile      Options      Setup
                        ── Editor ──                         ── Dialog ──
      Trace  Line 8      Col 1    A:CNTT03.CH9  Indent  In  Level 1
      shorttrace                                            Level 2
      domains                                               Level 3
              number=integer                                Boundary Condition.
                                                            level 3
      predicates                                            level 2
              count_to_three(number)                        level 1
                                                            Press the SPACE bar
      goal
              clearwindow and
              count_to_three(1).

      clauses
              count_to_three(4) if
                      write("Boundary Condition.").

                     ── Message ──                          ── Trace ──
      Load WORK.PRO                                                write(1)
      Load A:CNTT03.CH9                             RETURN:  count_to_three(1)
      Compiling A:CNTT03.CH9                        RETURN:  goal()
      count_to_three

      F2-Save  F3-Load  F6-Switch  F9-Compile                       Alt-X-Exit
```

The prompt "Press the SPACE bar" appears in the Dialog window. This tells you the program is complete. Press the {Space Bar} to complete the program.

This tutorial has guided you through the complicated procedure called recursion. At each step of the recursion, Turbo Prolog submerges by making a new copy of the rule, which is then executed. This process continues until the boundary condition is met at which time the recursion then emerges through each level generated during the submersion process. At each of these levels, variables can be bound to different values. A variable bound to more than one value at the same time demonstrates an important difference between Turbo Prolog and conventional computer languages.

You may want to save this program. If so, move to the **Files** command and choose the **Save** command. Name your program with a name you can remember. Be careful not to use any of the names of the files already existing on your Turbo Prolog disk. When these steps are completed, exit Turbo Prolog.

Exercises

9-1.   Recursion requires two clauses – one that defines the recursion and one that tells Turbo Prolog when to stop processing. What are the names of these clauses?

9-2.   What is the name of the order of searching Turbo Prolog uses to resolve goals?

9-3.   What is the kind of recursion where the recursive call appears somewhere other the last line of the recursive case?

9-4.   What is the normal search pattern followed by Turbo Prolog called?

9-5.   What is the diagram that represents the various levels of the recursive case called?

Problems

9-1.   Write a program that asks the user to type in his/her name and prints the name 20 times.

9-2.   Write a program that asks the user to type in a number greater than 1 and returns the sum of all the digits from 1 to the specified number. For example, if the user types in the number 4, the sum of the digits from 1 to 4 is 10 (1+2+3+4 = 10). Examples of Turbo Prolog goals to request this are:

        Goal:sum_to(4,Num)
        Num=10

        Goal:sum_to(5,Num)
        Num=15

9-3. Write a program that asks the user to type in a number and then prints the **factorial** of that number in theDialog Window. The factorial of a number is found by multiplying all the digits from 1 to that number. For example, the factorial of the number 4 is:

4! = 1*2*3*4 = 24.

5 factorial is:

5! = 1*2*3*4*5 = 120.

The ! sign after a number indicates the factorial of that number.

Goal:factorial(4,Num)
Num=24

Goal:factorial(5,Num)
Num=120

Recursion

Chapter 10
List Processing

*Turbo Prolog is particularly adept at processing information represented by symbols. To do this in an efficient manner, it uses a method called list processing. This chapter will introduce you to the concept of lists and list processing. Tutorial 10-1, **Lists and How They Are Used**, and Tutorial 10-2, **A Detailed Examination of List Predicates**, show you a number of predicates that manipulate lists in Turbo Prolog.*

List Processing

Computer languages used in Artificial Intelligence are more concerned with the manipulation of symbols than with the computation of numbers. They are concerned with information rather than data. To manipulate symbols, Turbo Prolog and other AI languages use a method called list processing. List processing treats sets of objects as a group. In Turbo Prolog, you can separate lists into their component elements, append one list to another, or reverse the order of a list. You can also print lists or see if an element is a member of a given list. This chapter will show you how these operations are performed.

What Is a List?

A list is an ordered set of objects. In Turbo Prolog, lists are represented as a series of objects separated by commas and are always enclosed in brackets []. The individual objects in a list are called members, or elements, of that list. As an example, consider a list of the colors of the rainbow. In Turbo Prolog, this list would be shown as:

[red,orange,yellow,green,blue,indigo,violet]

The objects "red", "orange", "yellow", "green", and so on, are the members, or elements, of the list and are separated by commas. Lists can also be made of data types other than symbols. For example, look at the rainbow list as strings.

["red","orange","yellow","green","blue","indigo","violet"]

A list may also consist of either real or integer numbers. However, you cannot mix different types of data within a list. In Turbo Prolog, all of the elements in a list must be of the same data type. To declare a list as a data type, a special notation is used. The * symbol is attached to the name of the list in the domains section.

The domains, predicates, and clauses sections for the rainbow example, as they might be entered into a Turbo Prolog program, are shown in Figure 10-1.

Figure 10-1: Rainbow Example

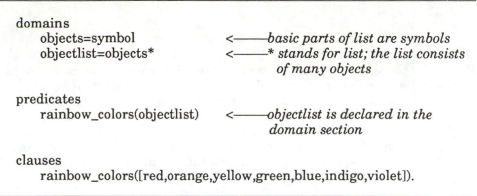

The predicate **rainbow_colors** contains a list of objects defined as the domain **objectlist**. In turn, **objectlist** is made up of objects in the form of a list, and these objects are symbols. The * symbol following the term **objects** defines **objectlist** as a list. The objects in this list are defined as symbols by the first statement in the domains section.

Empty List

Lists may have any number of elements or no elements at all. A list with no elements is called the empty list. The notation for the empty list is brackets with nothing inside.

[ ]

Lists as Elements

Individual elements of a list may be a single object or other lists. That is, the elements can be lists themselves. To show how this works, look at how you might change the original **rainbow_colors** predicate list.

As presently constructed, the list consists of 8 individual objects. Consider the first two objects – **red** and **orange**. You can treat these as one list with two objects **[red,orange]** and include this list in the original **rainbow_colors** list:

rainbow_colors([[**red,orange**],yellow,green,blue,indigo,violet]).

Now you have a list within a list, with each list enclosed by the bracket symbols [ ]. This new **rainbow_colors** predicate consists of six elements. The first element is the list **[red,orange]**, while the rest of the elements are single objects.

Next, form the list **[green,blue,indigo,violet]** and include it. The **rainbow_colors** predicate now becomes a predicate with three objects. The first object is a list, the second an object, and the third a list.

rainbow_colors([[red,orange],yellow,**[green,blue,indigo,violet]**]).

Look at the third object **[green,blue,indigo,violet]**. It can be broken into smaller segments by forming a list with some of its elements. You might want to consider the elements **green**, **blue**, and **indigo** as a list. The **rainbow_colors** predicate then becomes:

rainbow_colors([[red,orange],yellow,[[green,blue,indigo],violet]]).

This new list still has three elements, but now the third element is a list. A diagram showing the objects and the lists for the **rainbow_colors** predicate is shown in Figure 10-2.

Figure 10-2: Diagram of the rainbow_colors Example

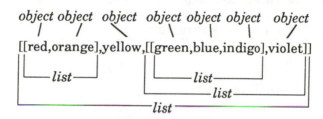

When using complex lists like the one above, always check the number of left brackets to be sure that it equals the number of right brackets. In the **rainbow_colors** predicate, there are four left brackets and four right brackets.

Special List Notation

All lists consist of two parts – the **head** of the list and the **tail** of the list. The head of the list is the first element in the list, and the tail is what is left of the list after the head has been removed. In the original **rainbow_colors** predicate, **red** is the head of the list with the remaining objects comprising the tail.

[red,orange,yellow,green,blue,indigo,violet]

Head= [red]
Tail= [orange,yellow,green,blue,indigo,violet]

Turbo Prolog uses a special notation (|) to show the head and tail of lists. Figure 10-3 shows the use of this symbol that divides the head from the tail.

Figure 10-3: The Vertical Bar Symbol

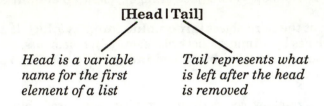

[Head | Tail]

Head is a variable
name for the first
element of a list

Tail represents what
is left after the head
is removed

Sample Program Showing Head|Tail Notation

The use of head and tail as variables is illustrated below as it might appear in a Turbo Prolog program. Any variable names can be used in place of **Head** and **Tail**. You may want to enter the program shown in Figure 10-4 and run it. Of course, don't include the explanations.

Figure 10-4: Rainbow Example

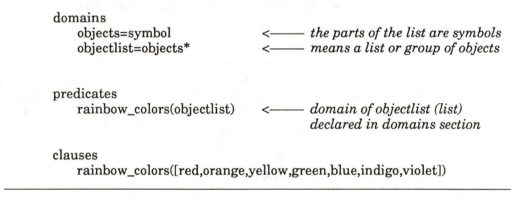

```
domains
    objects=symbol                  <——— the parts of the list are symbols
    objectlist=objects*             <——— means a list or group of objects


predicates
    rainbow_colors(objectlist)      <——— domain of objectlist (list)
                                         declared in domains section

clauses
    rainbow_colors([red,orange,yellow,green,blue,indigo,violet])
```

Now the goal

Goal:rainbow_colors([Head | Tail]).

shows the head and tail of the list.

```
        Files        Edit        Run        Compile      Options      Setup
                          Editor                        ┌─────── Dialog ───────
    Line 10    Col 36      WORK.PRO  Indent  Insert      │Goal: rainbow_colors([He│
domains                                                  │ad|Tail])               │
        objects = symbol                                 │Head=red, Tail=["orange"│
        objectlist = objects*                            │,"yellow","green","blue"│
                                                         │,"indigo","violet"]     │
predicates                                               │1 Solution              │
        rainbow_colors(objectlist)                       │Goal:                   │
                                                         │                        │
clauses                                                  │                        │
        rainbow_colors([red,orange,yellow,               │                        │
        green,blue,indigo,violet]).                      │                        │
                                                         │                        │
                                                         │                        │
                                                         │                        │

    ┌──────────── Message ────────────┐      ┌──────────── Trace ────────────┐
    │rainbow_colors                   │      │                               │
    │                                 │      │                               │
    └─────────────────────────────────┘      └───────────────────────────────┘

    F2-Save  F3-Load  F5-Zoom  F6-Next  F8-Previous Line  Shift-F10-Resize  F10-End
```

The goal tells Turbo Prolog to bind the head of the list to **Head** and the tail to **Tail**. One solution is found. **Head** is bound to **red**, and **Tail** is bound to the remaining elements of the list. The **Tail** variable shows how more than one object can be bound to a variable. This is in contrast to the assignment of values to variables in procedural languages where only one value at a time can be assigned to a variable.

Examples of Head|Tail Notation

Figure 10-5 shows various lists and the results of the binding that occur by using the Head|Tail notation. Remember, a list can be empty, or it may have one or more elements. If a list has one element, the tail of that list is the empty set [ ]. If a list is empty, it has no head or tail.

Figure 10-5: Head | Tail Notation

List	Result of [Head	Tail]
[a,b,c,d,e]	Head=[a] Tail=[b,c,d,e]
[book,table,pen]	Head=[book] Tail=[table,pen]
[a,b,[c,d]]	Head=[a] Tail=[b,[c,d]]
[clock]	Head=[clock] Tail=[ ]
[ ]	no head,no tail

Tutorial 10-1 will show you some of the ways lists can be used. As you work through this tutorial, you will see how to print the elements in a list, how to find a given element, how to append one list to another, and how to reverse a list.

Enter the knowledge base shown below. At this point, don't worry about what it all means. In the next tutorial, you will examine each part and each step in detail by using the **Trace** command.

Figure 10-6: Examples of List Processing

```
domains
    list = element*
    element = symbol

predicates
    append(list,list,list)
    member(element,list)
    reverse(list,list)
    print_list(list)

clauses
```

/*Example 1- Printing the Elements of a List*/

```
    print_list([]).
    print_list([Head | Tail]) if
        write(Head) and nl and
        print_list(Tail).
```

/*Example 2- Determining if an Element is a Member of a List*/

```
    member(Element,[Element | _]).
    member(Element,[_ | Tail]) if
        member(Element,Tail).
```

/*Example 3- Appending One List to Another List*/

```
    append([],List,List).
    append([Head | List1],List2,[Head | List3]) if
        append(List1,List2,List3).
```

/*Example 4- Reversing the Order of Elements in a List*/

```
    reverse([],[]).
    reverse([Head | Tail],List) if
        reverse(Tail,List2) and
        append(List2,[Head],List).
```

In this brief tutorial, you will look at each example separately. First, you will enter goals for each predicate and observe the results each produces. In Tutorial 10-2, you will use the **Trace** command to examine each rule in detail.

Example 1- Printing the Elements of a List

Look at the **print_list** goal below. This goal requires one argument which must be a list. Compile and run the program. If any error messages occur, compare your entry with the one in the book. Enter the following goal and note the result.

Goal:**print_list([one,two,three]).** ↵

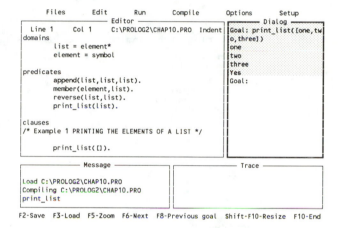

Turbo Prolog prints the list of **one, two,** and **three.** The **print_list** rule prints the elements of a list in the order given in the goal statement.

Example 2- Determining if an Element Is a Member of a List

The **member** predicate takes two arguments. The first must be a symbol and the second a list. If the element is a member of the list, Turbo Prolog displays **Yes**. If it is not, **No** is displayed. Try the following goals and observe their result.

Goal:**member(x,[x,y,z]).** ↵
Goal:**member(a,[x,y,z]).** ↵

Goal:**member(car,[boat,car,house]).** ↵

After you try all three goals, your screen should look like this:

The first goal, **member(x,[x,y,z])**, has the symbol **x** as the first element. The second argument of this goal is a list of the symbols **x**, **y**, and **z**. The **member** predicate determines if the first symbol is a member of the given list. In this case, **x** is a member of the list, and Turbo Prolog responds **Yes**, telling you that **x** is a member of the list of **[x,y,z]**.

Turbo Prolog responds **No** to the second goal. The symbol **a** is not a member of the given list of **[x,y,z]**.

The third goal is true because the object **car** is a member of the given list.

Example 3- Appending One List to Another List

The **append** predicate requires three arguments. All three of these arguments must be lists. The predicate takes the first list and the second list and joins them together to form the third list. The original lists remain unchanged. Try the following goal:

Goal:**append([a,b],[c,d],Newlist).** ↵

```
        Files      Edit      Run      Compile     Options     Setup
                        Editor                          Dialog
    Line 1     Col 1        C:\PROLOG2\CHAP10.PRO  Indent   three
domains                                                    Yes
        list = element*                                    Goal: member(x,[x,y,z])
        element = symbol                                   Yes
                                                           Goal: member(a,[x,y,z])
predicates                                                 No
        append(list,list,list).                            Goal: member(car,[boat,c
        member(element,list).                              ar,house])
        reverse(list,list).                                Yes
        print_list(list).                                  Goal: append([a,b],[c,d]
                                                           ,Newlist)
clauses                                                    Newlist=["a","b","c","d"
/* Example 1 PRINTING THE ELEMENTS OF A LIST */            ]
                                                           1 Solution
        print_list([]).                                    Goal:

                    Message                                     Trace
Compiling C:\PROLOG2\CHAP10.PRO
print_list
member
append

  F2-Save  F3-Load  F5-Zoom  F6-Next  F8-Previous goal  Shift-F10-Resize  F10-End
```

The first list is **[a,b]**, and the second list is **[c,d]**. The **append** predicate appends the second list to the end of the first list and assigns the resulting list to the variable **Newlist**. The first lists are unchanged, while the value assigned to **Newlist** is the list **["a","b","c","d"]**.

Example 4- Reversing the Order of Elements in a List

The **reverse** predicate requires two lists as arguments. The first list will be reversed and then bound as a list to the second argument. The first list remains unaltered. Type in the following goal:

Goal:**reverse([a,b,c,d],Newlist).** ↵

```
      Files       Edit      Run      Compile      Options      Setup
                        ┌─ Editor ──                    ┌─ Dialog ──
  Line 1      Col 1      C:\PROLOG2\CHAP10.PRO   Indent  No
domains                                                 Goal: member(car,[boat,c
        list = element*                                 ar,house])
        element = symbol                                Yes
                                                        Goal: append([a,b],[c,d]
predicates                                              ,Newlist)
        append(list,list,list).                         Newlist=["a","b","c","d"
        member(element,list).                           ]
        reverse(list,list).                             1 Solution
        print_list(list).                               Goal: reverse([a,b,c,d],
                                                        Newlist)
clauses                                                 Newlist=["d","c","b","a"
/* Example 1 PRINTING THE ELEMENTS OF A LIST */         ]
                                                        1 Solution
        print_list([]).                                 Goal:

                  ┌─ Message ──              ┌─ Trace ──
  print_list
  member
  append
  reverse

  F2-Save  F3-Load  F5-Zoom  F6-Next  F8-Previous goal  Shift-F10-Resize  F10-End
```

The elements of the first list are reversed in their order and then assigned to the variable **Newlist**. The variable **Newlist** becomes bound to the list ["d","c","b","a"]. The order of the first list has been reversed, while the original list remains unchanged.

Tutorial 10-2 uses the same knowledge base as this tutorial. If you are not continuing on immediately, be sure to save it.

Tutorial 10-2 A Detailed Examination of List Predicates

Tutorial 10-2 will look at each of these rules more carefully. You will learn not only how these predicates work, but also how Turbo Prolog uses recursion and backtracking to resolve the rules.

Add the **Trace** command to the knowledge base used in Tutorial 10-1 (see Figure 10-6).

Figure 10-6: Adding the Trace Command

trace

domains
    list = element*
    element = symbol

predicates
    append(list,list,list)
    member(element,list)
    reverse(list,list)
    print_list(list)

clauses

/*Example 1- Printing the Elements of a List*/

    print_list([]).
    print_list([Head | Tail]) if
        write(Head) and nl and
        print_list(Tail).

/*Example 2- Determining if an Element is a Member of a List*/

    member(Element,[Element | _]).
    member(Element,[_ | Tail]) if
        member(Element,Tail).

/*Example 3- Appending One List to Another List*/

    append([],List,List).
    append([Head | List1],List2,[Head | List3]) if
        append(List1,List2,List3).

/*Example 4- Reverse the Order of Elements in a List*/

    reverse([],[]).
    reverse([Head | Tail],List) if
        reverse(Tail,List2) and
        append(List2,[Head],List).

Example 1- Printing the Elements of a List

You will now trace through the **print_list** predicate in Example 1. When you enter the **print_list** goal, only the rules with the predicate **print_list** will match. The other rules will not be executed.

After each step, press the {F10} key to move to the next step. Explanations accompany each step.

In this tutorial, the size of the Trace Window has been expanded to show the results of the trace. You can do this by pressing {F6} to select the Trace Window and using the arrow keys to expand the window.

After you expand the Trace Window, run the program and enter the following goal:

Goal:**print_list([one,two,three]).**   ↵

The purpose of this goal is to print the elements of the list. The goal has one argument, the list that is to be printed. That list is **[one,two,three]**.

The first **print_list** fact defines the boundary condition. It tells Turbo Prolog to emerge from recursion when the list is empty.

> print_list([]).   *<——Boundary condition*

The **print_list** rule works by "pinching off" the head of the list and printing it. It then calls a copy of itself with the tail of the first list passed as the new list. This continues until the boundary condition is met (the list is empty).

> print_list([Head|Tail]) if   *<-——Recursive rule*
>   write(Head) and nl and
>   print_list(Tail).

Follow each step below as the execution of this rule is presented. Press {F10} where indicated to continue to the next step.

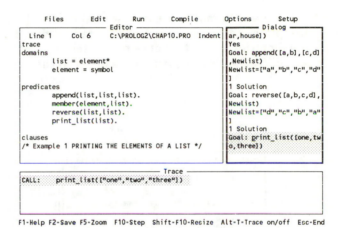

CALL:print_list(["one","two","three"]).

When Turbo Prolog calls a goal, it means it is trying to match that goal for the first time.

Step 2

{F10}

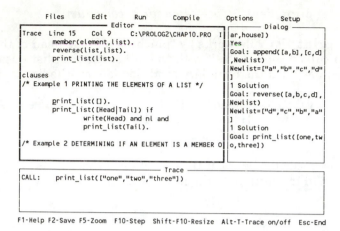

An attempt is made to match the goal with the first clause in the knowledge base in the Example 1 section. The first predicate is **print_list([])**. Because the argument in the fact (the empty list) does not match the argument of the goal, the first predicate fails. Turbo Prolog then moves down to the next **print_list** predicate.

Step 3

{F10}

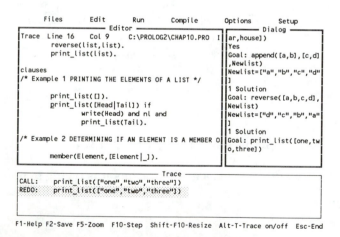

REDO: **print_list(["one","two","three"])**

Redo means to try to match the goal with the next predicate. In this case, the argument of the rule is the variable **Head|Tail**. Thus, a match can be made by binding **Head** to the first element in the list **[one]** and **Tail** to the remaining elements **[two,three]**. Because a match is found, Turbo Prolog moves to the right to solve the subgoals.

{F10}

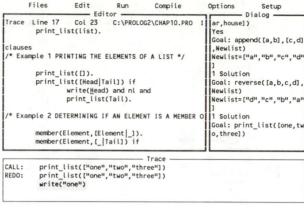

write("one")

The first subgoal is **write(Head)**. Because **Head** is bound to the list **[one]**, the goal succeeds by writing the value **one** in the Dialog Window. This is accomplished in the next step.

{F10}

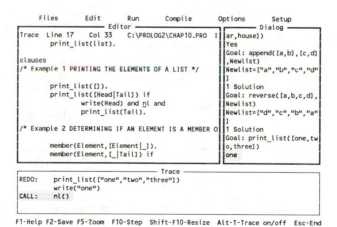

CALL: **nl()**

The value **one** is displayed in the Dialog Window. Turbo Prolog moves to the next subgoal, **nl**.

{F10}

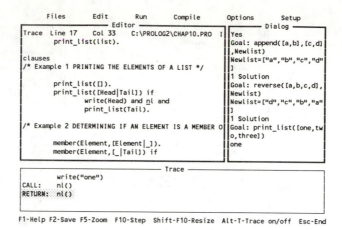

RETURN: **nl()**

The standard predicate **nl** succeeds by printing a new line in the Dialog Window.
Turbo Prolog is ready to move to the next subgoal.

 {F10}

CALL: **print_list(["two","three"])**

Call indicates a new goal. This recursive call creates a new copy of the rule that
must be solved. The list under consideration at level-1 of recursion is **["two","three"]**.
This is because the goal is called with the tail of the top level list. The recursive call
print_list(Tail) accomplishes this.

Step 8

 {F10}

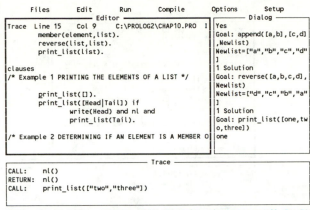

Because this call is a new goal, the search starts again at the top of the knowledge base. An attempt is made to match the **print_list([])** rule. The goal **print_list(["two","three"])** does not match.

Step 9

 {F10}

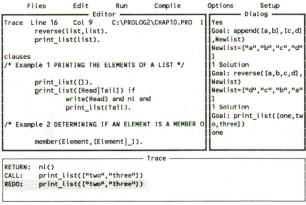

REDO: **print_list(["two","three"])**

Turbo Prolog tries to match the **print_list([Head|Tail])** rule. At level-1 of recursion the list is **["two","three"]**. Therefore, the variable **Head** is bound to **["two"]** and **Tail** to **["three"]**. Because a match is found, Turbo Prolog moves to the right in the rule to satisfy the subgoals.

List Processing

{F10}

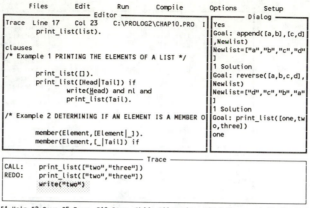

write("two")

Because **Head** is bound to the value **two**, the subgoal **write(Head)** means **write("two")**. At level-1 of recursion, **Head** has a value of **two** while at the top level it has a value of **one**. This is another case where a variable can have more than one value.

Step 11

{F10}

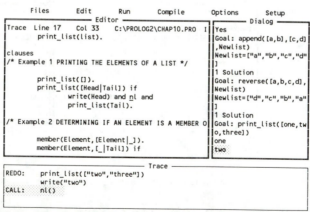

CALL: nl()

The symbol **two** is displayed in the Dialog Window, and the next subgoal **nl()** is called.

{F10}

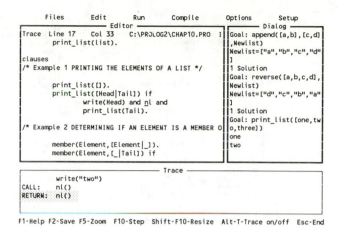

RETURN: **nl()**

A new line is printed in Dialog Window.

{F10}

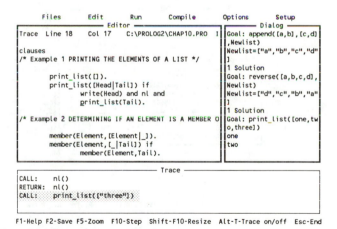

CALL: **print_list(["three"])**

The **print_list** rule recursively calls another copy of itself. This is level-2 of **print_list**. It is called with the **Tail** of the level-1 as its list. This is a new goal.

{F10}

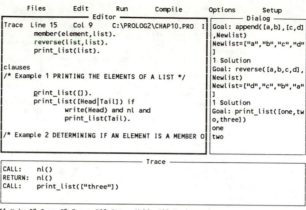

```
         Files      Edit      Run      Compile      Options      Setup
                      Editor                             Dialog
Trace  Line 15   Col 9      C:\PROLOG2\CHAP10.PRO  I   Goal: append([a,b],[c,d]
      member(element,list).                             ,Newlist)
      reverse(list,list).                              Newlist=["a","b","c","d"
      print_list(list).                                ]
                                                       1 Solution
clauses                                                Goal: reverse([a,b,c,d],
/* Example 1 PRINTING THE ELEMENTS OF A LIST */         Newlist)
                                                       Newlist=["d","c","b","a"
      print_list([]).                                   ]
      print_list([Head|Tail]) if                       1 Solution
            write(Head) and nl and                     Goal: print_list([one,tw
            print_list(Tail).                           o,three])
                                                       one
/* Example 2 DETERMINING IF AN ELEMENT IS A MEMBER O    two
                      Trace
CALL:    nl()
RETURN:  nl()
CALL:    print_list(["three"])
```

F1-Help F2-Save F5-Zoom F10-Step Shift-F10-Resize Alt-T-Trace on/off Esc-End

An attempt is made to match the **print_list** fact. It does not match, so the search moves down the knowledge base.

{F10}

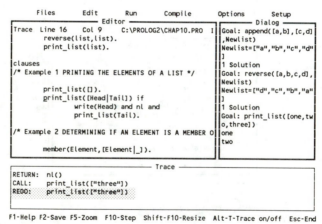

```
         Files      Edit      Run      Compile      Options      Setup
                      Editor                             Dialog
Trace  Line 16   Col 9      C:\PROLOG2\CHAP10.PRO  I   Goal: append([a,b],[c,d]
      reverse(list,list).                               ,Newlist)
      print_list(list).                                Newlist=["a","b","c","d"
                                                       ]
clauses                                                1 Solution
/* Example 1 PRINTING THE ELEMENTS OF A LIST */         Goal: reverse([a,b,c,d],
                                                        Newlist)
      print_list([]).                                  Newlist=["d","c","b","a"
      print_list([Head|Tail]) if                       ]
            write(Head) and nl and                     1 Solution
            print_list(Tail).                           Goal: print_list([one,tw
                                                        o,three])
/* Example 2 DETERMINING IF AN ELEMENT IS A MEMBER O    one
                                                        two
      member(Element,[Element|_]).
                      Trace
RETURN:  nl()
CALL:    print_list(["three"])
REDO:    print_list(["three"])
```

F1-Help F2-Save F5-Zoom F10-Step Shift-F10-Resize Alt-T-Trace on/off Esc-End

REDO: **print_list(["three"])**

This goal matches the rule for **print_list** by binding **Head** to **three** and **Tail** to the empty list. Now Turbo Prolog moves to the right to solve the subgoals.

{F10}

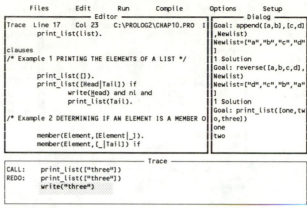

F1-Help F2-Save F5-Zoom F10-Step Shift-F10-Resize Alt-T-Trace on/off Esc-End

write("three")

The subgoal **write(Head)** prints the value bound to the variable **Head** at level-2 ("three").

{F10}

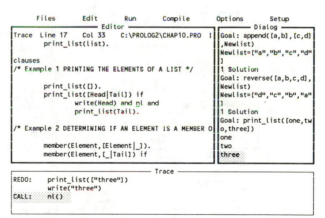

F1-Help F2-Save F5-Zoom F10-Step Shift-F10-Resize Alt-T-Trace on/off Esc-End

CALL: nl()

The **"three"** from the previous step is printed in the Dialog Window. The **nl()** predicate (still at level-2) is called.

{F10}

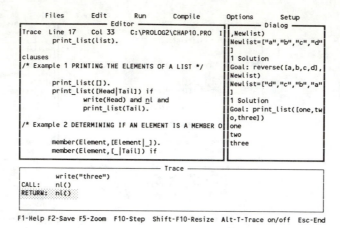

RETURN: **nl()**

A new line is printed in the Dialog Window.

{F10}

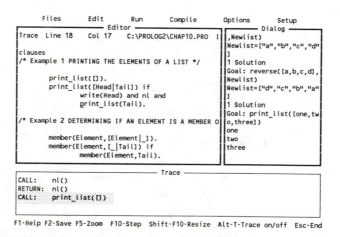

CALL: **print_list([])**

Turbo Prolog creates level-3 of recursion. At this level, the list is empty. That is, the head is [] and the tail is []. This is the boundary condition.

Step 20

{F10}

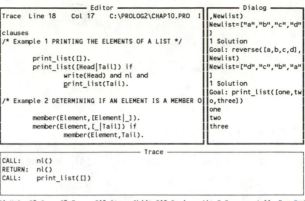

```
┌───────────────── Editor ─────────────────┐  ┌───────────── Dialog ──────────────┐
│Trace  Line 18   Col 17   C:\PROLOG2\CHAP10.PRO  I│ │,Newlist)                        │
│                                           │  │Newlist=["a","b","c","d"          │
│clauses                                    │  │]                                 │
│/* Example 1 PRINTING THE ELEMENTS OF A LIST */│  │1 Solution                      │
│                                           │  │Goal: reverse([a,b,c,d],          │
│        print_list([]).                    │  │Newlist)                          │
│        print_list([Head|Tail]) if         │  │Newlist=["d","c","b","a"          │
│                write(Head) and nl and     │  │]                                 │
│                print_list(Tail).          │  │1 Solution                        │
│                                           │  │Goal: print_list([one,tw          │
│/* Example 2 DETERMINING IF AN ELEMENT IS A MEMBER O│ │o,three])                     │
│                                           │  │one                               │
│        member(Element, [Element|_]).      │  │two                               │
│        member(Element, [_|Tail]) if       │  │three                             │
│                member(Element,Tail).      │  │                                  │
└───────────────────────────────────────────┘  └──────────────────────────────────┘
┌──────────────────────────────── Trace ──────────────────────────────────────────┐
│CALL:    nl()                                                                     │
│RETURN:  nl()                                                                     │
│CALL:    print_list([])                                                           │
└──────────────────────────────────────────────────────────────────────────────────┘
```

F1-Help F2-Save F5-Zoom F10-Step Shift-F10-Resize Alt-T-Trace on/off Esc-End

Because it has a new goal, Turbo Prolog begins at the top of the knowledge base. Since the goal now matches **print_list([])**, the boundary condition is met and no further matches need to be found.

Step 21

{F10}

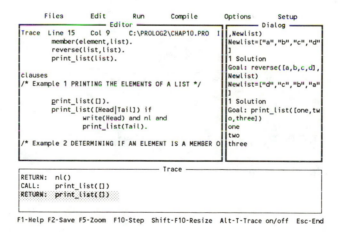

```
        Files      Edit      Run      Compile      Options      Setup
┌───────────────── Editor ─────────────────┐  ┌───────────── Dialog ──────────────┐
│Trace  Line 15   Col 9   C:\PROLOG2\CHAP10.PRO  I│ │,Newlist)                        │
│        member(element,list).              │  │Newlist=["a","b","c","d"          │
│        reverse(list,list).                │  │]                                 │
│        print_list(list).                  │  │1 Solution                        │
│                                           │  │Goal: reverse([a,b,c,d],          │
│clauses                                    │  │Newlist)                          │
│/* Example 1 PRINTING THE ELEMENTS OF A LIST */│  │Newlist=["d","c","b","a"        │
│                                           │  │]                                 │
│        print_list([]).                    │  │1 Solution                        │
│        print_list([Head|Tail]) if         │  │Goal: print_list([one,tw          │
│                write(Head) and nl and     │  │o,three])                         │
│                print_list(Tail).          │  │one                               │
│                                           │  │two                               │
│/* Example 2 DETERMINING IF AN ELEMENT IS A MEMBER O│ │three                         │
└───────────────────────────────────────────┘  └──────────────────────────────────┘
┌──────────────────────────────── Trace ──────────────────────────────────────────┐
│RETURN:  nl()                                                                     │
│CALL:    print_list([])                                                           │
│RETURN:  print_list([])                                                           │
└──────────────────────────────────────────────────────────────────────────────────┘
```

F1-Help F2-Save F5-Zoom F10-Step Shift-F10-Resize Alt-T-Trace on/off Esc-End

RETURN: **print_list([])**

Turbo Prolog has completed its work. However, because of recursion, each level (level-2, level-1, top level) must be revisited. These levels have no further tasks. As shown in Steps 22–24, you will have to press {F10} three times to complete the program.

{F10}

```
                              ┌──────── Trace ────────────────────────┐
                              │ CALL:   print_list([])                │
                              │ RETURN: print_list([])                │
                              │ RETURN: print_list(["three"])         │
                              └───────────────────────────────────────┘
```
F1-Help F2-Save F5-Zoom F10-Step Shift-F10-Resize Alt-T-Trace on/off Esc-End

RETURN:**print_list(["three"])**

This is a return to level-2 of recursion. Recall that at this level the list is **["three"]**.

 {F10}

```
                              ┌──────── Trace ────────────────────────┐
                              │ RETURN: print_list([])                │
                              │ RETURN: print_list(["three"])         │
                              │ RETURN: print_list(["two","three"])   │
                              └───────────────────────────────────────┘
```
F1-Help F2-Save F5-Zoom F10-Step Shift-F10-Resize Alt-T-Trace on/off Esc-End

RETURN:**print_list(["two," "three"])**

This is level-1 of recursion.

Step 24

{F10}

```
                                 ── Trace ───────────────────
RETURN:  print_list(["three"])
RETURN:  print_list(["two","three"])
RETURN:  print_list(["one","two","three"])
```

F1-Help F2-Save F5-Zoom F10-Step Shift-F10-Resize Alt-T-Trace on/off Esc-End

RETURN: **print_list (["one," "two," "three"])**

This is the top level.

Step 25

{F10}

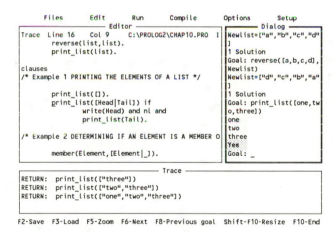

```
           Files      Edit       Run      Compile      Options      Setup
                    ── Editor ──                                  ── Dialog ──
Trace  Line 16   Col 9    C:\PROLOG2\CHAP10.PRO  I  Newlist=["a","b","c","d"
           reverse(list,list).                       ]
           print_list(list).                         1 Solution
                                                     Goal: reverse([a,b,c,d],
clauses                                              Newlist)
/* Example 1 PRINTING THE ELEMENTS OF A LIST */      Newlist=["d","c","b","a"
                                                     ]
           print_list([]).                           1 Solution
           print_list([Head|Tail]) if                Goal: print_list([one,tw
                 write(Head) and nl and              o,three])
                 print_list(Tail).                   one
                                                     two
/* Example 2 DETERMINING IF AN ELEMENT IS A MEMBER O  three
                                                     Yes
           member(Element,[Element|_]).              Goal: _
                                 ── Trace ──────────────────
RETURN:  print_list(["three"])
RETURN:  print_list(["two","three"])
RETURN:  print_list(["one","two","three"])
```

F2-Save F3-Load F5-Zoom F6-Next F8-Previous goal Shift-F10-Resize F10-End

Turbo Prolog prints **Yes** in the Dialog Window to show that at least one match was found.

Example 2- Determining if an Element Is a Member of a List

Now recall the **member** predicate in Example 2. This predicate determines if an element is a member of a list.

Goal:**member(z,[x,y,z])**

The rule takes two arguments – the first argument is an object and the second a list. It prints **Yes** if the object is a member of the list or **No** if it is not. The rule works by comparing the object to the head of the list and calls itself recursively, each time "pinching off" the head. This continues until the head of the list matches the element or the tail of the list is the empty list. The clause that defines the boundary condition is

member(Element,[Element | _]).   <—*boundary condition*

This clause says, "Exit if the object matches the head of the list."

At each level, the head is "pinched off" until the boundary condition is met.

member(Element,[_ | Tail]) if   <—*recursive rule*
        member(Element,Tail).

Now type in the following goal to see how the **member** predicate works.

Goal:**member(z,[x,y,z]).**   ↲

As before, follow the steps by running the program and pressing {F10} to move on to the next step.

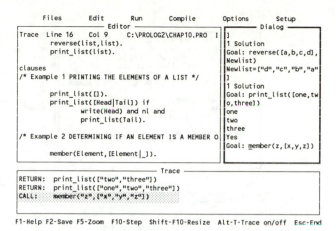

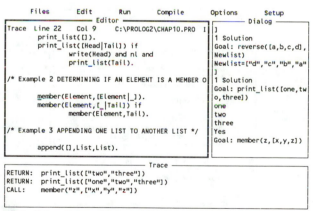

CALL:member("z",["x","y","z"])

The Call statement indicates a new goal. Turbo Prolog will begin the search with the first **member** predicate.

An attempt is made to match the **member** fact. This rule cannot succeed unless **z** is at the head of the list. Since it is not, the search continues down the knowledge base.

{F10}

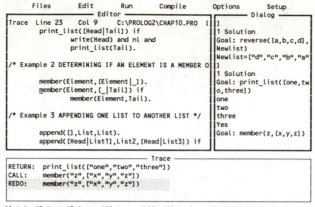

REDO: **member("z",["x","y","z"])**

This rule succeeds by binding **z** to **Element** and the list **["y","z"]** to **Tail**.

  {F10}

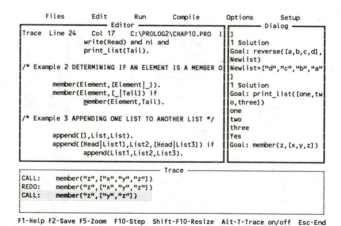

CALL: **member(["z",["y","z"])**

This goal succeeds by calling a copy (level-1) of itself. **Element** is still **z**, but at level-1 the list is the **Tail** of the top level list **["y","z"]**. Since this is a new goal, Turbo Prolog will start at the top of the knowledge base.

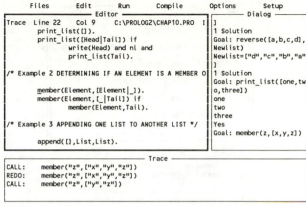

Turbo Prolog tries to match the **member** fact. Because this can succeed only when **z** is at the head of the list, the search continues down the knowledge base.

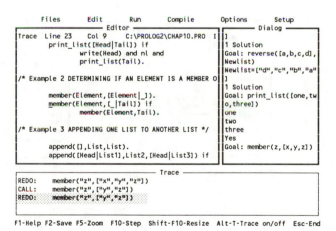

REDO: **member("z",["y","z"])**

This new attempt to solve the goal succeeds by binding **z** to the variable **Tail**.

{F10}

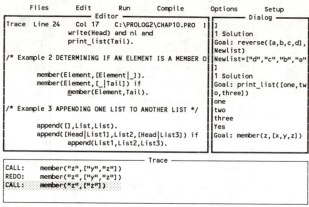

CALL:member("z",["z"])

A new copy (level-2) of the **member** predicate is made with **z** as the list under consideration.

 {F10}

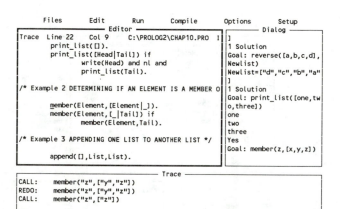

The object matches the head of the list. This is because **z** is the head of the list at level-2. The boundary condition has been met, and Turbo Prolog is now ready to emerge from recursion.

{F10}

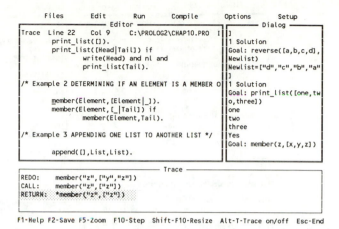

RETURN: ***member("z",["z"])**

The asterisk indicates that a match has been found at this level (level-2) of recursion and causes **Yes** to be displayed in the Dialog Window in step 12. If no match were found, **No** would be printed.

{F10}

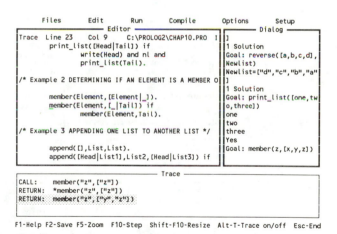

RETURN: **member("z",["y","z"])**

Turbo Prolog emerges to level-1 of recursion. The clause is not marked (*) because, at this level of recursion, no match was found. You may recognize that no purpose is served by returning to this level. There is no more work to do. In the next chapter, you will learn how to eliminate unnecessary backtracking.

{F10}

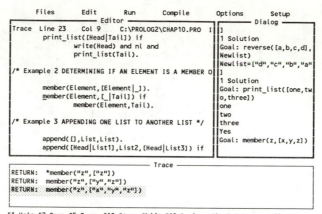

RETURN: **member("z",["x","y","z"])**

This is the top level.

{F10}

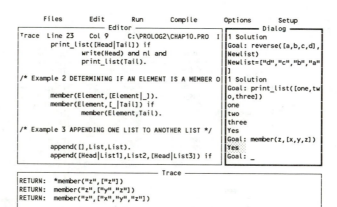

Yes

At least one match was found, so **Yes** is printed on the Dialog Window to indicate
that the object is in the list.

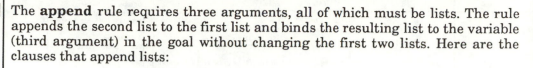

Example 3- Appending One List to Another List

The **append** rule requires three arguments, all of which must be lists. The rule appends the second list to the first list and binds the resulting list to the variable (third argument) in the goal without changing the first two lists. Here are the clauses that append lists:

```
append([],List,List).
append([Head | List1],List2,[Head | List3]) if
      append(List1,List2,List3).
```

This rule works by using the same technique as the **member** predicate. It "pinches off" the head of the first list at each level of recursion. When the boundary condition is met, the contents of the second list are copied to the third list. The boundary condition is met when the first list is empty. The fact that says this is

```
append([],List,List).     <——boundary condition
```

This fact says, "When the first list is empty, copy the contents of the second list to the third list."

As Turbo Prolog emerges from each level of recursion, the head of **List1** is put at the head of **List3**. This is accomplished by telling Turbo Prolog to make the head of **List1** (at each level) the head of **List3**. The first line of the append rule accomplishes this.

```
append([Head | List1],List2,[Head | List3])     <——recursive rule head
```

This says, "Take the head of **List1** (at each level) and put it on the top of **List3**." Recall that when the boundary condition was met, **List2** was copied to **List3**. Therefore, when processing is completed, **List1** and **List2** are unchanged. **List3** consists of **List2** (copied by the boundary condition) plus **List1** (added one element at a time by each level of recursion).

To demonstrate how the **append** predicate works, type in the following goal and follow the explanation. Press {F10} where indicated.

```
Goal:append([red,green,blue],
     [lions,tigers,bears],Newlist).  ↵
```

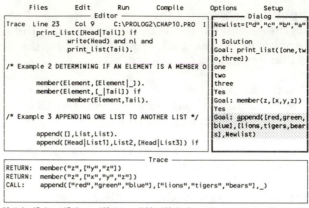

{F10}

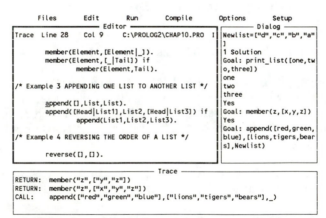

CALL: **append(["red","green","blue"],["lions","tigers","bears"],_)**

This is the first call to attempt to find a solution to the goal.

An attempt is made to match the goal to the first **append** predicate. This can succeed only when the first list is empty. Since no match is found, the search continues down the knowledge base.

Step 3

{F10}

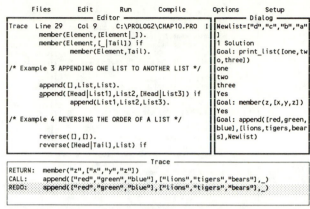

REDO: **append(["red","green","blue"],["lions","tigers", "bears"],_)**

A match is found with the second **append** predicate. The variables bound at this, level are:

> Head="red",
> List1=["red","green","blue"],
> List2=["lions","tigers","bears"], and
> List3= _   <——*(anonymous variable, no known value)*

List2 will never change and is passed as **List2** to each level. Thus, it will not be referred to as you progress through the rest of the program.

Figure 10-7 summarizes the values of each variable at each level of recursion. You may want to refer to this figure as you progress through the example.

Step 4

{F10}

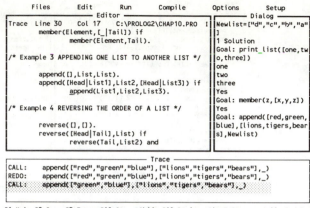

```
                    Files     Edit     Run     Compile     Options     Setup
                  ┌──────────────────── Editor ──────────────────┐ ┌───── Dialog ──────┐
                  │Trace  Line 30   Col 17   C:\PROLOG2\CHAP10.PRO  I│ │Newlist=["d","c","b","a"│
                  │      member(Element,[_|Tail]) if                │ │]                  │
                  │            member(Element,Tail).                │ │1 Solution         │
                  │                                                 │ │Goal: print_list([one,tw│
                  │ /* Example 3 APPENDING ONE LIST TO ANOTHER LIST */│ │o,three])         │
                  │                                                 │ │one                │
                  │      append([],List,List).                      │ │two                │
                  │      append([Head|List1],List2,[Head|List3]) if │ │three              │
                  │            append(List1,List2,List3).           │ │Yes                │
                  │                                                 │ │Goal: member(z,[x,y,z])│
                  │ /* Example 4 REVERSING THE ORDER OF A LIST */    │ │Yes                │
                  │                                                 │ │Goal: append([red,green,│
                  │      reverse([],[]).                            │ │blue],[lions,tigers,bear│
                  │      reverse([Head|Tail],List) if               │ │s],Newlist)        │
                  │            reverse(Tail,List2) and              │ │                   │
                  └─────────────────────────────────────────────────┘ └───────────────────┘
                  ┌──────────────────────── Trace ──────────────────────────────┐
                  │CALL:    append(["red","green","blue"],["lions","tigers","bears"],_)│
                  │REDO:    append(["red","green","blue"],["lions","tigers","bears"],_)│
                  │CALL:    append(["green","blue"],["lions","tigers","bears"],_)│
                  └─────────────────────────────────────────────────────────────┘
```

F1-Help F2-Save F5-Zoom F10-Step Shift-F10-Resize Alt-T-Trace on/off Esc-End

CALL: **append(["green","blue"],["lions","tigers","bears"],_)**

This call creates level-1. At this level, the tail of **List1** at top level becomes the new **List1**.

Step 5

{F10}

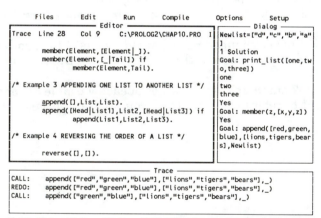

```
                    Files     Edit     Run     Compile     Options     Setup
                  ┌──────────────────── Editor ──────────────────┐ ┌───── Dialog ──────┐
                  │Trace  Line 28   Col 9    C:\PROLOG2\CHAP10.PRO  I│ │Newlist=["d","c","b","a"│
                  │                                                 │ │]                  │
                  │      member(Element,[Element|_]).               │ │1 Solution         │
                  │      member(Element,[_|Tail]) if                │ │Goal: print_list([one,tw│
                  │            member(Element,Tail).                │ │o,three])          │
                  │                                                 │ │one                │
                  │ /* Example 3 APPENDING ONE LIST TO ANOTHER LIST */│ │two               │
                  │                                                 │ │three              │
                  │      append([],List,List).                      │ │Yes                │
                  │      append([Head|List1],List2,[Head|List3]) if │ │Goal: member(z,[x,y,z])│
                  │            append(List1,List2,List3).           │ │Yes                │
                  │                                                 │ │Goal: append([red,green,│
                  │ /* Example 4 REVERSING THE ORDER OF A LIST */    │ │blue],[lions,tigers,bear│
                  │                                                 │ │s],Newlist)        │
                  │      reverse([],[]).                            │ │                   │
                  └─────────────────────────────────────────────────┘ └───────────────────┘
                  ┌──────────────────────── Trace ──────────────────────────────┐
                  │CALL:    append(["red","green","blue"],["lions","tigers","bears"],_)│
                  │REDO:    append(["red","green","blue"],["lions","tigers","bears"],_)│
                  │CALL:    append(["green","blue"],["lions","tigers","bears"],_)│
                  └─────────────────────────────────────────────────────────────┘
```

F1-Help F2-Save F5-Zoom F10-Step Shift-F10-Resize Alt-T-Trace on/off Esc-End

Again, an attempt to match the goal with the first append clause fails because **List1** is not empty. So, Turbo Prolog moves down the knowledge base.

{F10}

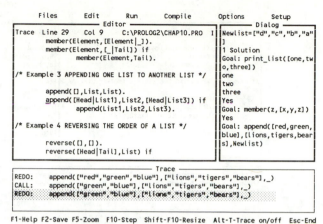

REDO: **append(["green","blue"],["lions","tigers","bears"],_)**

The goal matches the **append** rule. At level-1, the variables are

Head = ["green"]
List1 = ["green","blue"].

{F10}

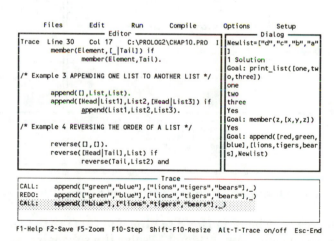

CALL: **append(["blue"],["lions","tigers","bears"],_)**

Level-2 of recursion is called. At this level, the list is **["blue"]**. The head is also
blue.

{F10}

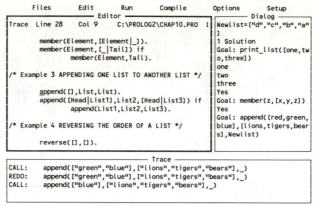

The goal tries to match the first **append** predicate clause. It does not match because the list is not empty.

{F10}

REDO: **append(["blue"],["lions","tigers","bears"],_)**

This succeeds by binding **Head** to **blue** and **List1** to the empty list []. Turbo Prolog moves to the right in an attempt to solve the subgoals.

{F10}

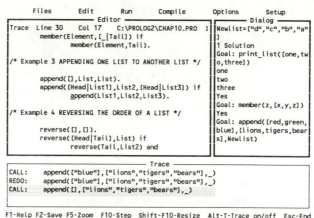

CALL: **append([],["lions","tigers","bears"],_)**

Level-3 of the **append** rule is called. At this level, **List1** (and therefore the head of **List1**) is empty. This is the exit condition.

{F10}

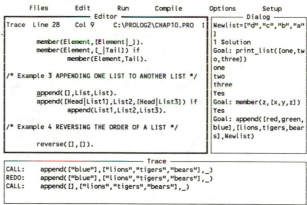

The first **append** clause now matches because the first argument of the goal is now the empty list. The boundary condition is met, and Turbo Prolog moves to the right in an attempt to solve the subgoals of the boundary clause. This succeeds by binding **List2** to the variable **Newlist**. This is shown in the next step.

{F10}

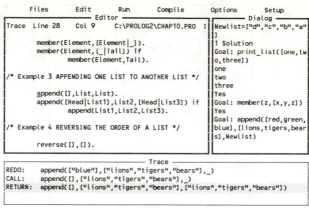

RETURN:**append([],["lions","tigers","bears"],["lions","tigers","bears"]**

Notice that **List2** has been copied to **Newlist** (List3). Turbo Prolog is ready to emerge from the levels of recursion. This level says, "Put nothing (the empty set) on the head of **List3**."

{F10}

RETURN: **append(["blue"],["lions","tigers","bears"],**
["blue","lions","tigers","bears"])

At level-2, the rule says, "Take the head of **List1** at level-2 (blue) and make it the head of **List3**." **Newlist** is now bound to **["blue","lions", "tigers","bears"]**.

{F10}

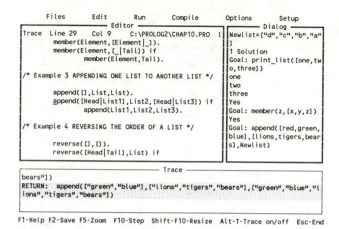

RETURN: **append(["green","blue"],["lions","tigers","bears"],
["green","blue","lions","tigers","bears"])**

Turbo Prolog returns to level-1 and takes the head of its **List1** and makes it the head of **List3**. The head is **green** at this level of recursion. At level-1, **Newlist** is now bound to **["green","blue","lions","tigers","bears"]**.

{F10}

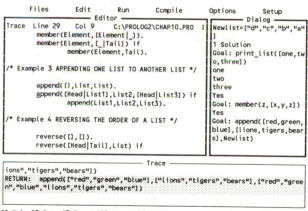

RETURN: **append(["red","green","blue"],["lions","tigers","bears"],
["red","green","blue","lions","tigers","bears"])**

The top level takes the head of **List1** and makes it the head of **List3**. **Head** is bound to **red** at top level, so **Newlist** becomes **["red","green","blue","lions", "tigers","bears"]**.

{F10}

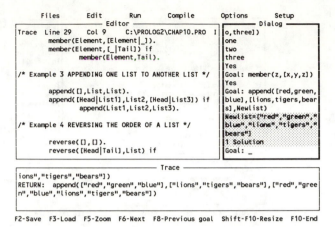

Newlist= ["red","green","blue","lions","tigers","bears"]

The value bound to **Newlist** is displayed in the Dialog Window. The second list has been appended to the first list to form the third list. Figure 10-7 reviews how this example worked.

Figure 10-7: A View of the append Predicate at Each Level of Recursion

Level	Values of Each Variable			
	List1	Head	List2	List3
Top	red,green,blue	red	lions,tigers,bears	–
1	green,blue	green	lions,tigers,bears	–
2	blue	blue	lions,tigers,bears	–
3	[]	[]	lions,tigers,bears	lions,tigers,bears
2	blue	blue	lions,tigers,bears	blue,lions, tigers,bears
1	green,blue	green	lions,tigers,bears	green,blue, lions,tigers,bears
Top	red,green,blue	red	lions,tigers,bears	red,green,blue, lions,tigers,bears

In this example, the head of **List1** is "pinched off" at each level of recursion. When the exit condition is met at level-3, the contents of **List2** are copied to **List3**. Then, as Turbo Prolog emerges from recursion, the head of **List1** at that level is placed at the head of **List3**. As a result, **List1** and **List2** are unchanged, and **List3** is formed by adding **List2** to **List1**.

Example 4- Reversing the Order of Elements in a List

The **reverse** predicate takes two arguments, both of which must be lists. Turbo Prolog reverses the order of the elements of the first list and outputs the result to the second list. In the goal statement, the second list will be a variable, and the reversed list is bound to that variable. For example, if you present the goal, **reverse([r,a,t],List)**, to the program, the list **[t,a,r]** will be bound to **List**.

You have probably already guessed that this example uses recursion to inspect each element of the list. At each level of recursion, the head of the list is "pinched off" as before. The value of the tail is bound to the variable **Tail** and passed on to each level of recursion until the boundary condition is met. The first clause of the reverse example defines the boundary condition. The search ceases when both lists are empty. The part of the rule that describes the boundary condition is

reverse([],[]).   <——*boundary condition*

As Turbo Prolog emerges from the recursion, the head of the list at each level is added to the list using the **append** predicate. Because you already know how append works, only the first part of the trace is shown. You should complete the trace on your own. It is a bit complicated since a recursive rule (append) is called at many levels of a recursive rule (reverse). More will be explained about this below.

The recursive rule that accomplishes this looks like this:

> reverse([Head | Tail],List) if   <—— *recursive rule*
>   reverse(Tail,List2) and
>   append(List2,[Head],List).

 Enter the following goal and run the program. Press {F10} where indicated.

> Goal:reverse([a,b,c],List).   ↵

Step 1

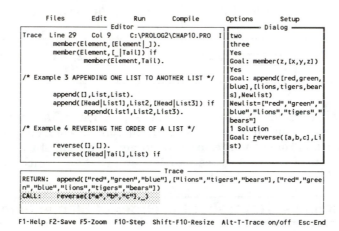

```
        Files      Edit      Run      Compile      Options      Setup
                    Editor                              Dialog
Trace  Line 29    Col 9      C:\PROLOG2\CHAP10.PRO  I  two
        member(Element,[Element|_]).                     three
        member(Element,[_|Tail]) if                      Yes
                member(Element,Tail).                    Goal: member(z,[x,y,z])
                                                         Yes
/* Example 3 APPENDING ONE LIST TO ANOTHER LIST */       Goal: append([red,green,
                                                         blue],[lions,tigers,bear
        append([],List,List).                            s],Newlist)
        append([Head|List1],List2,[Head|List3]) if       Newlist=["red","green","
                append(List1,List2,List3).               blue","lions","tigers","
                                                         bears"]
/* Example 4 REVERSING THE ORDER OF A LIST */            1 Solution
                                                         Goal: reverse([a,b,c],Li
        reverse([],[]).                                  st)
        reverse([Head|Tail],List) if
                                Trace
RETURN:   append(["red","green","blue"],["lions","tigers","bears"],["red","gree
n","blue","lions","tigers","bears"])
CALL:    reverse(["a","b","c"],_)
```

F1-Help F2-Save F5-Zoom F10-Step Shift-F10-Resize Alt-T-Trace on/off Esc-End

CALL: **reverse(["a","b","c"],_)**

Turbo Prolog begins to attempt to solve this goal. This is the first attempt to find a match, so the search will begin at the top of the knowledge base.

{F10}

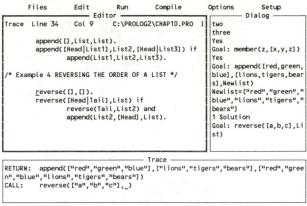

An attempt is made to match the goal with the first fact. The goal list is not empty, so there is no match. Turbo Prolog moves on to the next clause.

{F10}

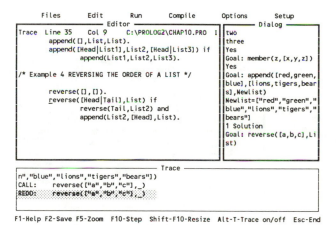

REDO: **reverse(["a","b","c"],_)**

Turbo Prolog finds a match with reverse rule. It succeeds by binding **Head** to the list **["a"]** and **Tail** to **["b","c"]**. The variable **List** is unbound and Turbo Prolog represents it with the anonymous variable (_).

{F10}

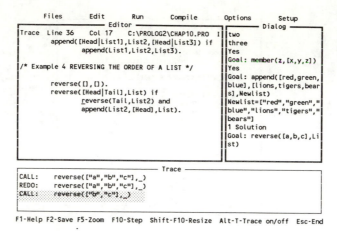

CALL: **reverse(["b","c"],_)**

The first order of business of the reverse rule is to make a copy of itself (level-1). This rule is called with the tail of the list at top level as the new list. The list being processed is **["b","c"]**.

{F10}

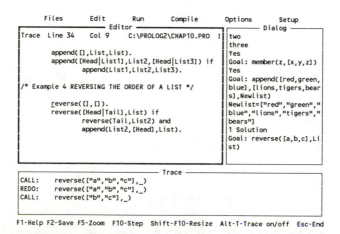

An attempt to match the first clause is attempted and fails because the first argument is not the empty list. No match can be made, so the list moves downward.

{F10}

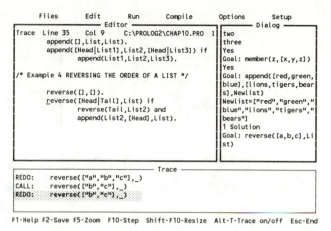

REDO: **reverse(["b","c"],_)**

Turbo Prolog continues down the knowledge base attempting to match the next **reverse** predicate. A match can be made by binding **Head** to ['b'] and **Tail** to ['c']. Turbo Prolog moves to the right to solve the subgoals.

Step 7

{F10}

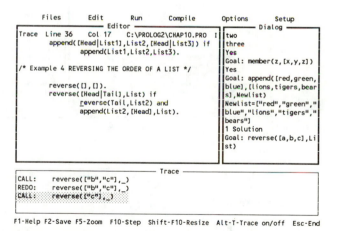

CALL:**reverse([c],_)**

This is level-2 with the value of **Tail** of the level-1 list as the new list. The list being processed is **["c"]**.

Step 8

{F10}

The list is not empty yet, so no match occurs with the clause. The search moves downward.

Step 9

{F10}

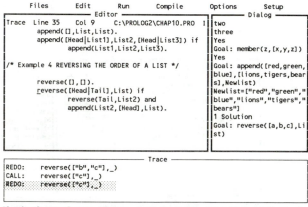

REDO: **reverse(["c"],_)**

The variable **Head** is bound to **["c"]**, and **Tail** is bound to []. Turbo Prolog moves to the right to solve the subgoals.

{F10}

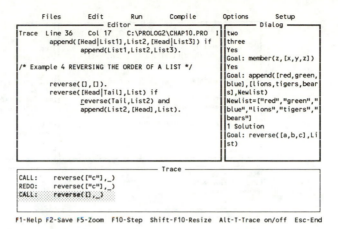

CALL: **reverse([],_)**

A new goal (level-3 of recursion) is called. At this level, the list being processed is the empty list ([]). This was the tail of the level-3 list.

{F10}

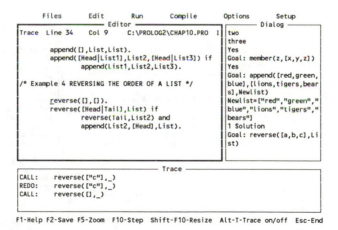

The new goal matches the first **reverse** predicate. The exit condition is met, and the program is ready to emerge.

{F10}

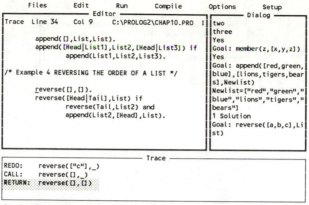

RETURN: **reverse([],[])**

Now that the exit condition is met, Turbo Prolog is ready to return to each level of recursion. As Turbo Prolog emerges from each level of recursion, it uses the **append** clause to attach the head of the list to the variable **List2** in reverse order. The remainder of the trace is not shown. You should continue through until you see the final answer. Be patient! It will take 25 presses of the {F10} key to complete the program.

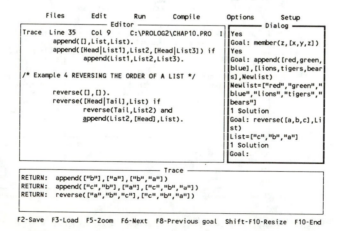

To visualize the way this example works, look at the diagram in Figure 10-8.

Figure 10-8: How the reverse Predicate Works

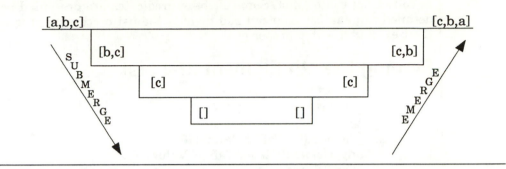

You can see how these predicates work. The head of the list is removed at various levels of recursion by the **reverse** rule. When the exit condition is met, the **append** predicate adds the head of the list at each level. Because this is done as Turbo Prolog is backing out of recursion, the list is formed in reverse order.

Tutorials 10-1 and 10-2 reviewed four list processing predicates. Of course, you may write additional predicates that can be useful in programs where list processing is required. Some of these are predicates to find the last element of a list, to determine the nth element of a list, to split a list into other lists, to sort a list, and to collect data into a list. Some of these predicates are presented below without detailed explanation. You can add them to the list processing program and trace their execution with a proper goal.

Finding the nth Element of a List

```
any_element([Head|_],1,Value] if
    Value = Head.
any_element([_|Tail],N,Value] if
    any_element([Head|Tail],N,Value] if
    NN=N-1 and
    any_element(Tail,NN,Value).
```

A goal to exercise this predicate rule might be:

Goal:**any_element([a,b,c,d,e],4,Value]).**

The first list is the list to be searched. The value following the list, in this case **4**, is the number of the element to be found. When located, the variable **Value** will be bound to the fourth element in the list. In this case, **Value** will equal **d**. The Dialog Window would look as shown below:

```
Goal:any_element([a,b,c,d,e],4,Value]).
Value = d
1 solution
```

Finding the Last Element of a List

```
last_element([Head|Last]) if
    Last = Head.
last_element([_|Tail],Last) if
    last_element(Tail,Last).
```

For example, the goal:

Goal:last_element([a,b,c])

Produces the result:

```
Last = "c"
1 Solution.
```

Splitting a List into Two Lists

```
split_list(Splitpoint,[Head|Tail],[Head|L1],L2) if
    Head <=Splitpoint and
    split_list(Splitpoint,Tail,L1,L2).
split_list(Splitpoint,[Head|Tail],L1,[Head|L2]) if
    split_list(Splitpoint,Tail,L1,L2) and
    Head > Splitpoint.
split_list(_,[],[],[]).
```

The goal:

```
Goal:split_list(50,[20,30,10,88,49,90,65],L1,L2.
L1 = [20,20,10,49] L2 = [88,90,65]
```

The first number (50) is the split point. All numbers equal to or below 50 are put in L1, while those over 50 are in L2.

There many possible list processing predicates. You should save the ones above (and any others you might obtain) in a file. That way, when you need to process lists, you can use the ones you have on disk.

Exercises

10-1.   What is a "list"?

10-2.   What is a list with no elements called?

10-3.   What is the notation for the empty list?

10-4.   Answer True or False:

    a.   Lists are enclosed by parentheses.

    b.   The individual items in a list are called elements.

    c.   The elements of a list are separated by the slash (/) symbol.

    d.   The elements of a list must be of the same data type.

    e.   To declare a list in the domains section, the symbol @ is attached to the name of the list.

    f.   A list can be an element of another list.

10-5. The first part of a list is called the _____.

10-6. The remainder of the list is called the _____.

10-7. The symbol that separates the head of a list from the remainder of the list is _____.

10-8. Write the head and tail of the following lists.

a. [1,2,3,4,5,8]
b. [wrench, screwdriver, [drill, bit], []]
c. [a]
d. [a,b]
e. []
f. [[a,b,c,d],e]
g. [hammer,[wrench,drill]]

Problems

10-1. Execute the **print_list** program from Tutorial 10-1 and input the following goal.

Goal:print_list[computer,memory,ram,rom,disk].

10-2. Write a program that accepts two inputs – an element and a list that contains that element – and then prints the position number that the element occupies in the list.

For example, the following goal requests the position number of the letter **c** in the list **[a,b,c,d]**. Of course, the answer is 3, but let Turbo Prolog find the answer.

Goal:find_position(c,[a,b,c,d],Position)
Position=3

10-3. Write a program that accepts two inputs – an integer **N** and a list of integers **List1** – and outputs two new lists. The first list (**List2**) contains all the elements of **List1** that are equal to or less than **N**, and the second new list (**List3**) contains all the elements that are above **N**. **List1**, the original list, will remain unchanged. For example, this goal says, "Bind all of the **List1** values that are less than or equal to 9 to the variable **List2**, and bind all of the values greater than 9 to the variable **List3**".

$$[\quad \text{List1} \quad]$$

Goal:split_list(9,[2,5,10,9,12,3,6,13],List2,List3).
List2=[2,5,9,3,6]
List3=[10,12,13]

10-4. Write a program that accepts a list as an input and prints the number of elements in the list. For example, the goal below says, "Tell me how many elements are in the list **[w,r,y,b,z]** and bind the variable **Number** to that value."

Goal:length([w,r,y,b,z],Number).
Number=5

10-5. Write a program that determines which members of a computer dating club might want to meet each other. The following information should be represented:

Name	Gender	Likes
Melinda	F	[tennis,movies,books,skiing]
Shannon	F	[books,dancing]
Chari	F	[programming,skiing]
Judy	F	[football,baseball,tennis]
Bob	M	[football,books]
Jim	M	[camping,hiking]
Sam	M	[programming,books,movies]
Paul	M	[skiing]

The facts about each person can be represented as follows:

gender(melinda,f).
likes(melinda,[tennis,movies,books,skiing]).

This knowledge base must also contain a rule that specifies that Person1 may date Person2 if they are of opposite gender and have at least one interest in common. For example, Melinda may date Bob, Sam, or Paul.

Goal:might_date(melinda,Who).
Who="bob"
Who="sam"
Who="paul"

10-6. Write a program which takes two arguments – an integer list and an integer variable. The program should use recursion to take the head of the list, add it to the variable, and print the sum of all integers in the list. For example:

add([4,5,6],Sum)
Sum=15

10-7. Write a program which accepts two integer lists as arguments. The second list should be a variable. The program should assign all positive elements in the first list to the second list. For example:

no_negatives([-5,7,9,-12,15,-4],Positives)
Positives=[7,9,15]

10-8. Write a program which takes two arguments – an integer variable and an integer list. The program should print the even numbers in the list. For example:

even_number(X,[1,2,3,4,5,6])
X=2
X=4
X=6

Chapter 11
The Cut

*The cut predicate stops backtracking. The fail predicate forces backtracking. This chapter introduces you to these concepts and shows you how they work. A program that processes loans is used to demonstrate the cut and fail predicates. Tutorial 11-1, **Using the Cut**, guides you through an exercise that uses the cut predicate in a program that contains information about members of a club and the interests of the members.*

The Cut

The Problem with Backtracking

The previous chapters praised the virtues of the backtracking mechanism that drives Turbo Prolog. While backtracking is an essential aspect of Prolog, there is one problem that arises. Backtracking, and for that matter recursion, can eat up large amounts memory very quickly. To understand why this happens, look at the "top" of a typical semantic network, as shown in Figure 11-1.

Figure 11-1: A Semantic Network

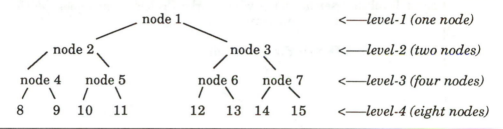

Notice that at each level the number of nodes doubles. This doubling uses memory quickly. As a matter of fact, a semantic net consisting of only 10 levels would have over 1,000 nodes. Since the nodes usually consist of strings or symbols, this represents a substantial amount of computer memory. This is one of the reasons that artificial intelligence applications have not been developed on microcomputers until recently.

In AI programming, the geometric progression described above is called the **combinatorial explosion**. There are many examples that demonstrate this phenomenon. You may be familiar with the following puzzle:

> "Suppose you give me a penny on November 1. On the second day, you give me double the amount of the first day (2 cents). Each day from then on you double the amount. How much money will you give to me on November 30?"

The answer is staggering. You would owe me over 5 million dollars ($5,368,709.10 to be exact). This demonstrates how Turbo Prolog's relentless pursuit of solutions can get out of hand.

The cut Predicate

This explosion of possibilities is particularly troublesome when you know in advance that searching some branches of the semantic network is unnecessary. In other words, there may be times that you do not wish to have backtracking occur. Turbo Prolog provides a standard predicate that says, "Do not backtrack."

This standard predicate is called the **cut** predicate. The symbol for the **cut** predicate is the exclamation point (!). The **cut** does not have any arguments, so it always succeeds. The effect of the cut is to "cut off" branches of the semantic network. This eliminates unnecessary searching.

How the cut Works

The cut is like a one-way valve. The flow of satisfaction goes through the cut in a single direction only. As you have seen, Turbo Prolog normally uses a depth first search pattern. Given the choice of branching to a lower node or to a node at the same level in a semantic network, Turbo Prolog always goes depth first. Look at the semantic network in Figure 11-2.

Figure 11-2: A Depth First Search

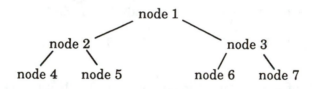

In this semantic network, if a subgoal in node 2 fails, backtracking occurs to node 1. Once an alternative match for node 1 is found, the search continues back to node 2 (depth first). If it moved to node 3, it would be called a **breadth first** search pattern. You can alter the flow of satisfaction by inserting a cut in the knowledge base as shown in Figure 11-3.

Figure 11-3: Changing the Flow of Satisfaction Using the cut

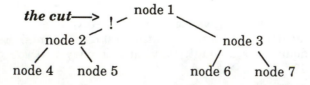

Now when the rule in node 2 fails, backtracking once again goes to node 1. At this point, the effect of the cut is demonstrated. Without the cut (Figure 11-2), Turbo Progog would move back to node 2 (depth first). In this case, the cut establishes that further inspection of node 2 and the nodes below it is unnecessary. So, Turbo Prolog moves to node 3 (breadth first).

The cut and the Flow of Satisfaction

Backtracking can occur freely above or below the cut. When Turbo Prolog encounters a cut, it may not be backed over. Note the following rule (The letters represent the goal and subgoals).

> A if
> > B and C and D and E.

To solve the rule, Turbo Prolog finds all of the values of **B**, **C**, **D**, and **E**. The flow of satisfaction is

> B <—> C <—> D <—> E.

The flow of satisfaction is free to re-evaluate all subgoals as many times as it can. This can lead to unnecessary backtracking. Suppose that you insert the cut between rules **C** and **D**. This changes the number of possible combinations.

> A if
> > B and C and ! and D and E

Placing the cut here produces the flow of satisfaction shown in Figure 11-4.

Figure 11-4: Effect of the cut on Flow of Satisfaction

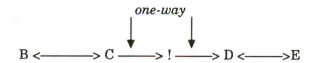

Turbo Prolog is free to backtrack between subgoals **B** and **C**. Once Turbo Prolog finds a solution to **B** and **C** , it crosses the fence, so to speak, when it encounters the cut. Alternate solutions to **D** and **E** are also possible, but subgoals **B** and **C** will never be re-evaluated. The current values of all the variables bound in subgoals **B** and **C** are frozen.

When to Use the cut

Typically, the cut is used in three situations. The first is when several clauses have the same predicate. The cut tells Turbo Prolog, "This is the right clause, don't backtrack to other clauses with the same predicate."

The second situation occurs within a rule definition when you want to freeze the choices made in solving a goal. It tells Turbo Prolog, "What you have found so far is correct, do not look for alternative solutions."

The third common use of the cut is in combination with the **fail** predicate. This tells Turbo Prolog, "What you have learned so far is enough to conclude that this goal has failed." The cut-fail combination eliminates rules that Turbo Prolog does not need to consider. Now take a closer look at the three ways to use the cut.

Preventing Backtracking to Another Rule

As you have seen, a knowledge base may contain more than one clause with the same head. For example, recall the clauses used to determine if a given element was a member of a given list. You defined **member** by saying, "The element is a member of the list if it is the head of the list or if it is in the tail of the list." This can be translated into the following Turbo Prolog clauses.

> member(Element,([Element | _]).   <——*member fact*
> member(Element,([_ | Tail]) if   <——*member rule*
>   member(Element,Tail).

Remember that Turbo Prolog finds the solution by matching the value of the variable **Element** with the head of the list. Once it matches the list head, there is no purpose in backtracking to the rule that defines **member**. However, Turbo Prolog always backtracks to prior goals. This is true even though there is no purpose in doing so which is what **member** did in the previous chapter. (If you don't remember, see Steps 10 and 11 in the tracing of the **member** predicate in Chapter 10.) To modify the rule so that this extra processing does not occur, add the cut as shown below.

> member(Element,([Element | _]) **if !.**   <——*member fact*
> member(Element,([_ | Tail]) if   <——*member rule*
>   member(Element,Tail).

When the **member** fact succeeds by matching the value of the variable **Element** with the rule head in the fact, Turbo Prolog will not backtrack to the **member** rule. While the new clauses save some processing time and space, it is of little consequence in this small example. As knowledge bases increase in size, judicious use of the cut can make the difference between a program that runs and one that does not.

It is also important to understand that the original rule and the revised rule are not the same. The original rule finds all occurrences of the **Element** in the list, while the revised rule stops once it finds a single match. If you need to find all of the matches, the fact without the cut is the correct choice.

Preventing Backtracking to a Previous Subgoal

To demonstrate the second use of the cut, consider an example that takes two lists and determines if they have any elements in common. For example, the lists **[a,b,c]** and **[d,e,f]** have no common elements, the lists **[a,b,c]** and **[c,d,e]** have one common element, and the lists **[a,b,c]** and **[b,c,d]** have two common elements.

The knowledge base works a bit like the **member** clauses in the previous chapter, which told you if a given element was a member of a given list. The clauses defined here tell if there are any elements of the first list in the second list.

The clauses take three arguments. The first two are the lists you want to compare, and the third is a variable that shows the elements that are common to both lists. In the program shown in Figure 11-5, the **in_common** predicate contains three arguments which are:

        List1 = First list,
        List2 = Second list, and
        Element=common Element.

Figure 11-5: in_common Program

```
domains
    element=string
    list=element*

predicates
    in_common(list,list,element)
    member(element,list)

clauses
    in_common(List1,List2,Element) is
        member(Element,List1) and
        member(Element,List2).

    member(Element,[Element|_]).
    member(Element,[_,Tail]) if
        member(Element,Tail).
```

This **in_common** rule says, "Two lists have common members if there are elements of the first list that are also elements of the second list." The rule works by binding the first element in List1 to the variable **Element**. Then it uses the **member** predicate to determine if that element is in the second list. Since you already know how the **member** clauses work, it will not be explained in detail here. Look at the examples shown in Figure 11-6.

Figure 11-6: Examples of the in_common Predicate

Example 1	Goal:in_common([a,b,c],[d,e,f],Common) No solution.
Example 2	Goal:in_common([a,b,c],[c,d,e],Common) Common=c 1 Solution.
Example 3	Goal:in_common([a,b,c],[b,c,d],Common) Common=b Common=c 2 Solutions.

Suppose that you only wanted to find the first common element in both lists. The **in_common** predicate as written forces Turbo Prolog to continue even after it finds a match. You can control this by using the cut predicate. Look at the new clause in Figure 11-7.

Figure 11-7: in_common Clauses with cut Predicate

```
clauses
    in_common(List1,List2,element) if
        member(Element,List1) and
        member(element, List2) and
        !.                              <——stop after one match
```

Once Turbo Prolog solves the subgoals, it runs into the cut. This says, "Do not backtrack to previous goals, you have found the solution." The first two examples above work the same way as before, but notice the difference in Example 3 of Figure 11-8 on the next page.

Figure 11-8: Example of the in_common Predicate with cut

Example 1	Goal:in_common([a,b,c],[d,e,f],Common) No solution.
Example 2 with cut	Goal:in_common([a,b,c],[c,d,e],Common) Common=c 1 Solution.
Example 3 with cut	Goal:in_common([a,b,c],[b,c,d],Common) Common=b 1 Solution.

Compare the results with those in Figure 11-7. In Example 3 above, Turbo Prolog stopped after it found that the lists had a member in common.

The cut-fail Combination

You may use the cut-fail combination to specify that some of the clauses in the knowledge base can be eliminated. In other words, you want to tell Turbo Prolog, "What you have learned so far is enough to conclude that goal should fail." Logically, you might think that using the predicate **fail** is enough to make a goal fail. However, remember that **fail** also causes backtracking. If you already know that a rule should fail, why cause backtracking in that rule? By placing the **cut** predicate immediately before **fail**, you can insure that a rule fails with no further backtracking. Thus, the cut-fail combination eliminates a rule from further consideration. The cut-fail combination should be used in large knowledge bases to eliminate clauses that you know do not have to be considered.

To understand how this works, assume you are writing an expert system that will assist a loan officer at a bank in determining if a person should be given a loan. The knowledge base would consist of several facts about the potential borrowers shown in Figure 11-9.

Figure 11-9: Loan Expert System

```
owns_home("Jim Smith").
owns_home("John Jones").

has_collateral("Jim Smith").
has_collateral("John Jones").

has_good_job("Jim Smith").
has_good_job("John Jones").
```

You might then write a rule that determines who can borrow money:

```
can_borrow_money(Person) if
    owns_home(Person) and
    has_collateral(Person) and
    has_good_job(Person).
```

The complete Turbo Prolog program is shown in Figure 11-10.

Figure 11-10: "Expert System" for Money Lenders

```
domains
    name=string

predicates
    owns_home(name)
    has_collateral(name)
    has_good_job(name)
    can_borrow_money(name)

clauses
    owns_home("Jim Smith").
    owns_home("John Jones").

    has_collateral("Jim Smith").
    has_collateral("John Jones").

    has_good_job("Jim Smith").
    has_good_job("John Jones").

    can_borrow_money(Person) if
        owns_home(Person) and
        has_collateral(Person) and
        has_good_job(Person).
```

To determine if a certain person can get a loan, you could enter the goal:

```
Goal:can_borrow_money(Who)
Who=Jim Smith
Who=John Jones
2 Solutions.
```

It might occur to you that this system isn't much of an expert. A real expert system would have a much larger knowledge base. Imagine your small example had several thousand facts and rules. When you want a list of people who can borrow money, all of these rules must be evaluated. However, what if you knew that some people had a poor credit rating? These people, despite whatever other qualifications, cannot borrow money. It is not efficient to evaluate several rules when you know you will deny the loan based upon one rule.

To do this, you might expand the knowledge base to include a list of people who had poor credit ratings. If a person is on this list, she will be denied credit no matter what the rest of the rules say. The facts representing people could be written like this is:

        deadbeat("Jim Smith").
        deadbeat("Sharon Johnson").

You would then write a rule that says, "If a person is a poor credit risk, deny him the loan." The new rule uses the cut-fail combination to accomplish this. The revised rule is shown in Figure 11-11.

Figure 11-11: can_borrow_money Rule with cut and fail Combination

        can_borrow_money(Person) if
            deadbeat(Person) and
            ! and
            fail.

        can_borrow_money(Person) if
            owns_home(Person) and
            has_collateral(Person) and
            has_good_job(Person).

Notice that this rule must be placed above the other **can_borrow_money** predicates. This is because of the top to bottom flow of satisfaction used by Turbo Prolog. This updated knowledge base is shown in Figure 11-12 on the next page.

Figure 11-12: Loan Expert System with Deadbeat Qualification

```
domains
    name=string

predicates
    owns_home(name)
    has_collateral(name)
    has_good_job(name)
    can_borrow_money(name)

clauses
    owns_home("Jim Smith").
    owns_home("John Jones").

    has_collateral("Jim Smith").
    has_collateral("John Jones").

    has_good_job("Jim Smith").
    has_good_job("John Jones").

    deadbeat("Jim Smith").
    deadbeat("Sharon Johnson").

    can_borrow_money(Person) if
    deadbeat(Person) and
    ! and
    fail.

    can_borrow_money(Person) if
        owns_home(Person) and
        has_collateral(Person) and
        has_good_job(Person).
```

Now apply the following goal:

    Goal:can_borrow_money(Who).

The result is

    Who="John Jones"
    1 Solution.

This goal produces the desired result without bothering to discover if Jim Smith or Sharon Johnson owns a home or has collateral. You eliminate them because they are poor credit risks.

Using the not Predicate

Most Prolog texts suggest that the cut-fail combination be replaced by the **not** operator where possible. The **not** operator has the following format:

> not(argument).

The predicate **not** reverses the result of the argument such that if the argument succeeds, the operation fails and vice versa. For example, the statement "George Washington was the first President of the United States" is true. The statement not("George Washington was the first President of the United States") is false and, thus, would fail.

If you typed in the goal **2=2**, Turbo Prolog would print the answer **Yes**. The goal **not(2=2)** produces the answer **No**.

In the example, you can modify the basic **can_borrow_money** predicate in the following way:

> can_borrow_money(Person) if
>   **not(deadbeat(Person))** and *←—replaces cut-fail*
>   owns_home(Person) and
>   has_collateral(Person) and
>   has_good_job(Person).

This form is logically more appealing than the cut-fail form and makes your knowledge base easier to read. It is important to understand the cut-fail combination because some texts use it. This text will use the **not** predicate wherever possible.

Tutorial 11-1 Using the cut

In this tutorial, you will develop a knowledge base that contains information about members of a computer club. The club wants to store each member's name along with their areas of interest in computers. Part of the knowledge base looks like this:

> club_member("Jim Smith").
> club_member("John Johnson").
> club_member("Sara Martin").
> club_member("Mary Malone").
> club_member("Al Marco").
>
> interests("Jim Smith",[apple,consultant,prolog,ai]).
> interests("John Johnson",[ibm,apple,ai,lisp]).
> interests("Sara Martin",[ibm,lisp,prolog,ai]).
> interests("Mary Malone",[apple,lisp,programmer]).
> interests("Al Marco",[consultant,ibm,prolog,basic]).

The club sends many different mailings each year. For instance, the club might wish to send a certain mailing to all those members who have an interest in artificial intelligence (ai). Or, perhaps, they might want to send a mailing to anyone interested in either LISP (lisp) or Prolog (prolog) programming. To accomplish this, you need to develop some rules that would allow the user to specify what interests they want considered in the mailing. Turbo Prolog will then search the knowledge base and print the names of any of those members who have matching interests.

To do this, you will use the **member** and **in_common** predicates you defined previously. These predicates compare two lists and determine if they have any common elements. Note that no cuts have been included at this point. You will add the cut later in the tutorial and see its effects.

You will also write a rule, as shown below, which allows the user to specify the interests they want included. These will be entered as a list.

```
mail_list(Name,Mylist) if
    club_member(Name) and
    interests(Name,Theirlist) and
    in_common(Mylist,Theirlist,_).
```

This rule supplies Turbo Prolog with a variable that represents the names of those members with certain interests. The second argument, **Mylist**, is the list of the interests you want to match. Figure 11-13 is the entire knowledge base, including the domain and predicate declarations.

```
domains
    element=symbol
    list=element*

predicates
    club_member(element)
    interests(element,list)
    member(element,list)
    mail_list(element,list)
    in_common(list,list,element)

clauses
    club_member("Jim Smith").
    club_member("John Johnson").
    club_member("Sara Martin").
    club_member("Mary Malone").
    club_member("Al Marco").

    interests("Jim Smith",[apple,consultant,prolog,ai]).
    interests("John Johnson",[ibm,apple,ai,lisp]).
    interests("Sara Martin",[ibm,lisp,prolog,ai]).
    interests("Mary Malone",[apple,lisp,programmer]).
    interests("Al Marco",[consultant,ibm,prolog,basic]).

in_common(List1,List2,Element) if
    member(Element,List1) and
    member(Element,List2).

member(Element,[Element|_]).
member(Element|[_,Tail]) if
    member(Element,Tail).

mail_list(Name,Mylist) if
    club_member(Name) and
    interests(Name,Theirlist) and
    in_common(Mylist,Theirlist,_).
```

Boot your computer and enter the Turbo Prolog Editor Window. Enter the clauses as shown. In the screens below, the Editor Window was expanded.

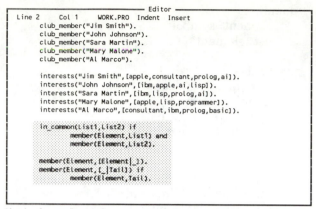

```
─────────────── Editor ───────────────
Line 2    Col 1    WORK.PRO  Indent  Insert
        club_member("Jim Smith").
        club_member("John Johnson").
        club_member("Sara Martin").
        club_member("Mary Malone").
        club_member("Al Marco").

        interests("Jim Smith",[apple,consultant,prolog,ai]).
        interests("John Johnson",[ibm,apple,ai,lisp]).
        interests("Sara Martin",[ibm,lisp,prolog,ai]).
        interests("Mary Malone",[apple,lisp,programmer]).
        interests("Al Marco",[consultant,ibm,prolog,basic]).

        in_common(List1,List2) if
              member(Element,List1) and
              member(Element,List2).

        member(Element,[Element|_]).
        member(Element,[_|Tail]) if
              member(Element,Tail).
```
F1-Help F2-Save F3-Load F5-Zoom F6-Next F7-Xcopy F8-Xedit F9-Compile F10-Menu

Add the domains and predicates section as shown in the beginning of Figure 11-13.

Press {Esc}, then {R} to run the program. If you have any errors, correct them and continue.

Type in the following goal:

Goal:`mail_list(Person,[ibm,prolog]).` ↵

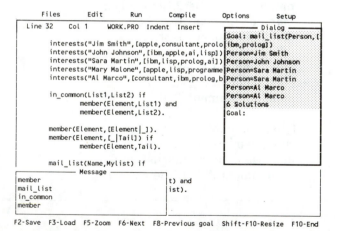

```
     Files      Edit      Run      Compile    Options    Setup
    Line 32   Col 1    WORK.PRO  Indent  Insert   ┌──── Dialog ────
                                                  │Goal: mail_list(Person,[
        interests("Jim Smith",[apple,consultant,prolo│ibm,prolog])
        interests("John Johnson",[ibm,apple,ai,lisp])│Person=Jim Smith
        interests("Sara Martin",[ibm,lisp,prolog,ai])│Person=John Johnson
        interests("Mary Malone",[apple,lisp,programme│Person=Sara Martin
        interests("Al Marco",[consultant,ibm,prolog,b│Person=Sara Martin
                                                  │Person=Al Marco
        in_common(List1,List2) if                 │Person=Al Marco
              member(Element,List1) and           │6 Solutions
              member(Element,List2).              │Goal:

        member(Element,[Element|_]).
        member(Element,[_|Tail]) if
              member(Element,Tail).

        mail_list(Name,Mylist) if
    ┌──── Message ────
    │member                          │t) and
    │mail_list                       │ist).
    │in_common
    │member
```
F2-Save F3-Load F5-Zoom F6-Next F8-Previous goal Shift-F10-Resize F10-End

Notice that several names are repeated more than once. If you were sending a letter to each person, you would be wasting money. Imagine how much money this kind of duplication would cost in a system containing thousands of names and perhaps dozens of interests! Now you will see how the cut can eliminate this duplication.

The reason that duplicate names were printed is in the definition of the **in_common** predicate. This predicate is written in such a way that Turbo Prolog must find all of the common interests in the two lists. Remember that Turbo Prolog does not stop until it finds all matches.

The cut tells Turbo Prolog, "What you have found is correct, do not backtrack." We can insert this cut at the end of the **in_common** rule definition like this:

> in_common(List1,List2,Element) if
>   member(Element,List1) and
>   member(Element,List2) **and !.**   <——*the cut*

Enter the Turbo Prolog editor. Make the additions shown to the knowledge base.

Figure 11.14: Club Member Knowledge Base with cut

```
domains
    element=symbol
    list=element*

predicates
    club_member(element)
    interests(element,list)
    member(element,list)
    mail_list(element,list)
    in_common(list,list,element)

clauses
    club_member("Jim Smith").
    club_member("John Johnson").
    club_member("Sara Martin").
    club_member("Mary Malone").
    club_member("Al Marco").

    interests("Jim Smith",[apple,consultant,prolog,ai]).
    interests("John Johnson",[ibm,apple,ai,lisp]).
    interests("Sara Martin",[ibm,lisp,prolog,ai]).
    interests("Mary Malone",[apple,lisp,programmer]).
    interests("Al Marco",[consultant,ibm,prolog,basic]).

    in_common(List1,List2,Element) if
        member(Element,List1) and
        member(Element,List2) and !.

    member(Element,[Element|_]).
    member(Element|[_,Tail]) if
        member(Element,Tail).

    mail_list(Name,Mylist) if
        club_member(Name) and
        interests(Name,Theirlist) and
        in_common(Mylist,Theirlist,_).
```

Now run the program and enter the same goal (Press {F8}) and note the result of the cut.

Goal:**mail_list(Person,[ibm,prolog]).** ↵

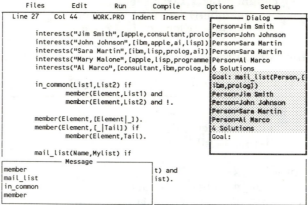

This knowledge base now works just the way you want it to. It finds all of the members who have the specified interests while avoiding duplication.

After the club used this program for awhile, they discovered one change they wanted to make. Some of the members became inactive for one reason or another. They did not want the information about the member removed, but they didn't want to send inactive members mailings. To modify the knowledge base, add the predicate **inactive** and modify the **mail_list** definition. Here is the new knowledge base.

Figure 11-15: Club Member Knowledge Base with Inactive Rule

```
domains
    element=symbol
    list=element*

predicates
    club_member(element)
    interests(element,list)
    member(element,list)
    mail_list(element,list)
    in_common(list,list,element)
    inactive(element)

clauses
    club_member("Jim Smith").
    club_member("John Johnson").
    club_member("Sara Martin").
    club_member("Mary Malone").
    club_member("Al Marco").
    inactive("John Johnson")

    interests("Jim Smith",[apple,consultant,prolog,ai]).
    interests("John Johnson",[ibm,apple,ai,lisp]).
    interests("Sara Martin",[ibm,lisp,prolog,ai]).
    interests("Mary Malone",[apple,lisp,programmer]).
    interests("Al Marco",[consultant,ibm,prolog,basic]).

in_common(List1,List2,Element) if
    member(Element,List1) and
    member(Element,List2) and !.

member(Element,[Element|_]).
member(Element|[_,Tail]) if
    member(Element,Tail).

mail_list(Name,Mylist) if
    club_member(Name) and
    not(inactive(Name)) and
    interests(Name,Theirlist) and
    in_common(Mylist,Theirlist,_).
```

Run the program and enter the goal again by pressing {F8}. Notice that the inactive members will not be sent a mailing.

Goal:**mail_list(Person,[ibm,prolog])** ↵

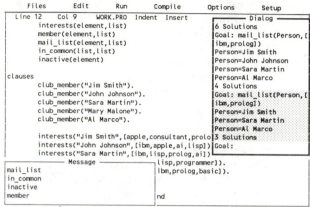

```
      Files     Edit      Run      Compile    Options      Setup
 ┌ Line 12   Col 9    WORK.PRO  Indent  Insert ┌──── Dialog ────┐
 │       interests(element,list)            │ 6 Solutions
 │       member(element,list)               │ Goal: mail_list(Person,[
 │       mail_list(element,list)            │ ibm,prolog])
 │       in_common(list,list)               │ Person=Jim Smith
 │       inactive(element)                  │ Person=John Johnson
 │                                          │ Person=Sara Martin
 │ clauses                                  │ Person=Al Marco
 │       club_member("Jim Smith").          │ 4 Solutions
 │       club_member("John Johnson").       │ Goal: mail_list(Person,[
 │       club_member("Sara Martin").        │ ibm,prolog])
 │       club_member("Mary Malone").        │ Person=Jim Smith
 │       club_member("Al Marco").           │ Person=Sara Martin
 │                                          │ Person=Al Marco
 │       interests("Jim Smith",[apple,consultant,prolo│ 3 Solutions
 │       interests("John Johnson",[ibm,apple,ai,lisp])│ Goal:
 │       interests("Sara Martin",[ibm,lisp,prolog,ai])│
 ┌───────── Message ─────────┐ lisp,programmer]).
 │ mail_list                 │ ibm,prolog,basic]).
 │ in_common                 │
 │ inactive                  │
 │ member                    │ nd
 └───────────────────────────┘
 F2-Save  F3-Load  F5-Zoom  F6-Next  F8-Previous goal  Shift-F10-Resize  F10-End
```

Summary

In this Tutorial, you saw two of the common uses of the cut. You added the cut to the **in_common** predicate to tell Turbo Prolog, "This answer is correct, don't look for another."

You also modified the **mail_list** predicate to eliminate some rules (branches of the semantic net) from consideration. You told Turbo Prolog, "This goal should fail, go no further." You used the **not** predicate to accomplish this, but you could have used the cut_fail combination.

The third use of the cut tells Turbo Prolog, "Everything you know at this point is correct, do not try to find alternative solutions." This was not part of the tutorial.

Exercises

11-1. The command that says "Do not backtrack" is _____. Its symbol is
_____.

11-2. List the three conditions under which the cut might be used.

_____

_____

_____

11-3. The fail predicate causes _____.

Problems

11-1. Write a knowledge base to determine who is allowed to check books out of the library. The following information must be represented:

People with Library Cards

sue
lynne
jim
tom
sherry
alex
greg
rick
mary
jill
al
robby

People with overdue books

sherry
alex
jill
al

The program should print "Yes" if the person can borrow a book and "No" if they cannot (use the cut-fail combination to eliminate these people). To borrow a book, the person must have a card and have no overdue books. For example:

Goal:can_borrow(jill)
No

Goal:can_borrow(rick)
Yes

Goal:can_borrow(roger)
No

11-2.   Notice that problem 11-1 does not work properly with the goal:

Goal:can_borrow(Who)

Modify the program by replacing the cut-fail combination with the **not** predicate so that it works properly.

11-3.   Players in a tennis club are divided into three leagues. Members may only play those who are in their own leagues. Write a program which displays all possible matches. Use the cut to eliminate unnecessary duplication. For example:

joe can_play jim
jim can_play joe
should not both be printed.

Chapter 12
Files

*Writing a program that performs one or more functions is indeed important. But if that information is to be retained for later use, storing the information collected by a program is equally important. Thus, the use of files is a vital concept in Turbo Prolog. This chapter will show you how to create a file, how to use the file, and how to save the file for later use. You will learn the symbolic filenames used by Turbo Prolog, how to open a file, how to build user-defined files, how to send information to a file, and how to read the information from a file. Tutorial 12-1, **Using Files**, will guide you through this process of creating and manipulating the contents of a file. You will also learn how to create a user friendly menu interface, in Tutorial 12-2, **Creating Menus**.*

Files

What Is a File?

A file is an organized collection of related information. You use many files in your life – telephone books, dictionaries, encyclopedias, and library card catalogs are examples.

Consider your personal telephone book, one in which you write the telephone numbers of your friends and relatives. This telephone book is a file. It contains related data – people's names and phone numbers. To make this file more useful to you, the information in it is organized by listing peoples' last names in alphabetic order. Alongside each person's name you place their telephone number.

Using your telephone book requires three actions. First, you must open the book. Once open, you search through the book for the last name of the person you want to call, and you retrieve the telephone number. When completed, you close the book and put it away.

Let's take a closer look at the steps required for setting up and using your phone book file.

1) Creating the file: This step involves setting up the general organization of the file. When you buy the telephone book, it is ready for you to enter the phone numbers organized by the last name. You only do this step once.

2) Using the file: Using the file requires three steps:

Step 1- Open the book.

Step 2- Use the book. There are several things you might want do with this book.

- look up a phone number
- add a new friend to the book
- change a phone number
- delete a name and phone number

Step 3- When you are through using the book, you close it and put it away.

As you will soon see, this is exactly how computer files work.

Computer Files

Most computer languages provide a way to create files on the disk. The advantage of these files is that computers are adept at searching large files quickly. Computer files work the same way as the telephone book file. First you must create the file, then you follow the same three steps to use the file:

Step 1- You open the computer file on the disk.

Step 2- Once you open it, you may use it.

Step 3- When you complete working with a computer file, you must close it.

Computer files have names. When you use a file, you must tell the computer the name of the file. This filename, called the **DOS filename**, follows the MS-DOS standard conventions. The filename may not exceed 8 letters or characters and may have up to a three letter extension.

Turbo Prolog Files

Turbo Prolog allows two kinds of file operations – file reading (input), and file writing (output). In fact, Turbo Prolog treats all program input or output as files. You will see how this works below.

Turbo Prolog provides a full complement of file handling predicates. There are predicates to

- create a file
- open a file
- retrieve information from a file
- add information to a file

Manipulating files on the disk is essentially a procedural problem. Therefore, file operations are not considered a strength of Prolog. In fact, many versions of Prolog do not provide the capacity to manipulate data files. However, this is not the case with Turbo Prolog.

In Turbo Prolog there are two types of files. The first type is the **predefined** file. As mentioned above, Turbo Prolog treats all of the input and output devices connected to your computer as files. The second type of file is the **user-defined** file. These are the disk files that you can create to store information.

Predefined Files

Turbo Prolog treats all input and output as files. It automatically takes input from the keyboard and writes output to the monitor. The keyboard is the default input device, while the monitor is the default output device. When you use the **write** predicate, Turbo Prolog writes the argument of the predicate on the **screen** file. In the same way, the **read** predicate looks for input from the default input file – the **keyboard**.

Since these files are predefined, you may use these files in any rule or clause without declaring them in the predicate section of the program. Notice that the keyboard can be used for input only. The monitor and the printer can be used only for output. The serial ports, called com1 and com2 by your computer, may be used for either input or output.

Figure 12-1 shows the standard devices and the symbolic filenames that Turbo Prolog uses to identify them.

Figure 12-1: Standard Devices

Symbolic Filename	Type of File
keyboard	the default input device
printer	output only
com1 or com2	serial port, input or output
screen	the default output device

These files are already created. You use them by opening them, performing some function, and then closing them. You close a predefined file by changing the active device. In other words, activating the screen turns off the printer as an output device.

Turbo Prolog provides special predicates to re-direct the input or output of the program to one of these standard devices. All read and write predicates go to the default devices unless otherwise specified.

Opening a File for Input

To open a device for reading, use the **readdevice** predicate:

predicate that changes the input device

readdevice(symbolic_filename)

name of the new input device
(keyboard or com1)

Figure 12-2: Examples of the readdevice Predicate

readdevice(keyboard)	Sets the keyboard as the input device. All further **read** predicates receive their input from the keyboard. The keyboard is the default input device.
readdevice(com1)	Sets the serial port com1 as the input device. To reactivate the keyboard, you must use **readdevice(keyboard)**.

The **readdevice** predicate changes the input device. Once the device is open, all further **read** predicates use the specified device (file). To return the read file to the keyboard, use the predicate

readdevice(keyboard).

Opening a File for Output

The **writedevice** predicate works the same way as the **readdevice** predicate.

predicate that changes the output device

writedevice(symbolic_filename)

name of the new output device
(screen or printer or com1)

When Turbo Prolog encounters this predicate, the output device changes to the specified device. The screen is the usual output device.

Figure 12-3: Examples of writedevice Predicate

writedevice(printer)	Sets the printer as the output device. All further **write** predicates send their output to the printer.
writedevice(screen)	Sets the screen as the output device. Screen is the default output device.
writedevice(com1)	Sets the serial port com1 as the output device.

The **writedevice** predicate changes the output device. Once the device is open, all further **write** predicates send their output to the specified device (file). To reactivate the monitor as the write device, use the predicate

writedevice(screen).

User-defined Output Files

The second type of Turbo Prolog files are the user-defined files. These are the files that store information on the disk. Turbo Prolog provides predicates for:

Creating a file —> openwrite
Opening a file —> writedevice
Writing to a file —> write
Closing a file —> closefile

Detailed explanations of each of these predicates follow.

1) Creating a file with the openwrite predicate

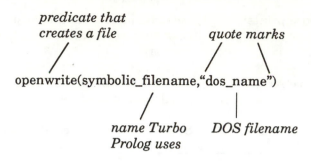

The **openwrite** predicate creates a file to which you can write information. Keep in mind that you need only create a file once. If you attempt to create an existing file with the **openwrite** predicate, Turbo Prolog assumes that you want to create a new file. Therefore, it will destroy the contents of the old file to make way for the new file.

The **openwrite** predicate requires two arguments. The first is the symbolic filename, and the second argument is the DOS filename in quotes.

Recall that Turbo Prolog is a language that manipulates objects. Files are considered objects in Prolog. In the predefined files, a standard symbolic filename (com1, keyboard, etc.) is used to refer to these files. With a user-defined file, you must supply the symbolic name. This name can be anything that you choose. The eight character DOS filename limitation does not apply. However, the second argument is the DOS filename in quotes and must, of course, correspond to the DOS rules for naming files. The **openwrite** predicate associates the symbolic filename specified in the first argument with the DOS filename specified in the second argument. Further references to the file in your program use the symbolic name in place of the DOS name. This provides for the use of more descriptive names for files than can be provided for under DOS.

Figure 12-4: Examples of the openwrite Predicate

openwrite(myfile,"names.txt")   *Creates a DOS text file called names.txt. The text file is given the symbolic filename myfile.*

openwrite(clubmembers,"b:mem.txt")   *Creates a DOS text file called mem.txt on the B drive. Turbo Prolog knows this file by its symbolic filename clubmembers.*

2) Writing to a file with the writedevice predicate

predicate that   *the symbolic*
directs output   *name of file for writing*

writedevice(symbolic_filename)

You have already seen how the **writedevice** predicate works with predefined files. It works the same way with user-defined files. When this predicate executes, the file (or device) specified as the argument (the symbolic filename) becomes the output file. All further **write** predicates write to this file until it is closed. The file must already exist for this predicate to succeed. Thus, you must use the **openwrite** predicate to create a file before using the **writedevice** predicate.

Figure 12-5: Examples of the writedevice Predicate

writedevice(myfile)	*Opens the file with the symbolic name myfile. Further output is directed to this file until it is closed.*
writedevice(clubmembers)	*Opens the existing file clubmembers for output.*

3) Using a file for writing with the write predicate

write(symbol)

You are already familiar with the **write** predicate. It writes (outputs) to a file or device. Once a file is opened with **openwrite**, all further output goes to that file. The opened file may be the default file or a file opened from within your program.

Figure 12-6: Examples of the write Predicate

write("Test")	*Writes the string "Test" to the active file.*
write(Name)	*Writes the value bound to the variable **Name** to the active file.*
write(car)	*Writes the symbol **car** to the file.*

4) Closing a file with the closefile predicate

predicate that   *symbolic name of*
closes a file   *file to be closed*

closefile(symbolic_filename)

The **closefile** predicate takes one argument, the symbolic filename of the file you want to close. When executed, closefile closes the file specified in argument. Once this occurs, information is no longer written to or read from the file.

Figure 12-7: **Examples of the closefile Predicate**

---

closefile(myfile)   *Closes the file called myfile.*

closefile(clubmembers)   *Closes the file called clubmembers.*

The next two tutorials provide specific examples of these steps. Tutorial 12-1 guides you through the basic steps in creating and writing data to a file. Tutorial 12-2 is an extended example. It includes techniques for creating a menu to make a file program that is user friendly.

Tutorial 12-1 Using Files

The knowledge base in this tutorial creates a file on your disk and writes the name of several chemicals to the file. The DOS filename is **chem.txt**, and the symbolic filename is **elements**. In this tutorial, you will learn how to

1) create a file.
2) open a file.
3) write information to a file.
4) close a file.

For this tutorial, it is assumed that you have a formatted data disk in the A drive. If you are using some other configuration, substitute the proper drive designation where appropriate.

Below is a rule called **use_file** that accomplishes the four steps to create a file in a Turbo Prolog program. The rule has four subgoals:

Subgoal-1 creates the file.
Subgoal-2 opens the file.
Subgoal-3 writes some data to the file.
Subgoal-4 closes the file.

The **use_file** predicate is

use_file if
    openwrite(elements,"chem.txt") and   *<— create the file*
    writedevice(elements) and   *<— open the file*
    write_some_stuff and   *<— write to the file*
    closefile(elements).   *<— close the file*

Subgoal-1 – Create the file

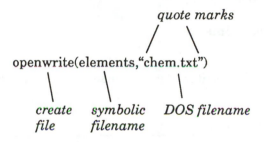

This subgoal creates a DOS file called **chem.txt**. Turbo Prolog refers to this file by its symbolic name **elements**.

Subgoal-2 – Open the file

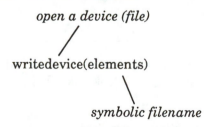

This predicate opens the file with the symbolic name **elements** so that information may be written to it. This sets the file **elements** as the output file. All further **write** predicates will send their information to this file until it is closed.

Subgoal-3 – Write to the file

To write some information to the file, you will create a new predicate. This predicate will be defined later.

> write_some_stuff
> \
> *calls a new rule named write_some_stuff*

As shown later, this predicate will write symbols to the file.

Subgoal-4 – Close the file

> *closefile predicate*
> /
> closefile(elements)
> \
> *symbolic filename*

This closes the file named **elements**.

You will now use this predicate in a Turbo Prolog Program. Boot your computer and enter the Turbo Prolog Editor. Add the **use_file** predicate to the clauses section as shown below.

Figure 12-8: use_file Predicate

```
clauses
    use_file if
        openwrite(elements,"a:chem.txt") and
        writedevice(elements) and
        write_some_stuff and
        closefile(elements).
```

With the clauses section complete, you are ready to create the predicate that writes to the file. The definition of **write_some_stuff** looks like this.

```
write_some_stuff if
    chemical(Name) and        <— find a chemical
    write(Name) and           <— write the name to the file
    flush(elements) and       <— forces the contents of the internal
    nl and fail.      <        buffer (memory) to be written to the file
                               new line and backtrack
```

Add the **write_some_stuff** and **chemical** predicates to your knowledge base. They are placed in the clauses section as shown in Figure 12-9.

Now we will add some objects to the knowledge base using the predicate **chemical**. This predicate writes each object to the file. Here are the chemical predicates. Enter these as shown in Figure 12-9.

```
chemical(oxygen).
chemical(boron).
chemical(iron).
chemical(chlorine).
chemical(uranium).
```

Figure 12-9: Clauses Section for Chemical Problem

```
clauses
    use_file if
        openwrite(elements,"a:chem.txt") and
        writedevice(elements) and
        write_some_stuff and
        closefile(elements).

    write_some_stuff if
        chemical (Name) and
        write(Name) and
        flush(elements) and
        nl and fail.

    chemical (oxygen).
    chemical(boron).
    chemical (iron).
    chemical(chlorine).
    chemical(uranium).
```

 Of course, before you can run the program, you must declare the predicates **chemical**, **use_file**, and **write_some_stuff** in the predicates section. The predicates section is shown in Figure 12-10. Add this to your program.

Figure 12-10: Predicates Section for Chemical Problem

```
predicates
    use_file
    write_some_stuff
    chemical (substance)
```

Neither **use_file** nor **write_some_stuff** requires any arguments. However, you must declare the data type of **substance** in the domains section. In addition to declaring **substance** as a symbol, you also need to tell Turbo Prolog that the object name **elements** refers to a file. Figure 12-11 shows the domains section. Add this section to your program.

Figure 12-11: Domains Section of Chemical Problem

```
domains
    file=elements
    substance=symbol
```

Turbo Prolog allows only one file declaration in the domains section of a program. However, more than one symbolic filename may be declared by separating them with a semicolon. If you had more than one file to declare, they would be written as shown below, where file1; file2...would be your filenames.

```
domains
    file=file1; file2; file3
```

The complete program, including the domains, predicates, and clauses sections, is shown in Figure 12-12.

Figure 12-12: Chemical Knowledge Base

```
domains
    file=elements
    substance=symbol

predicates
    use_file
    write_some_stuff
    chemical (substance)

clauses
    use_file if
        openwrite(elements,"a:chem.txt") and
        writedevice(elements) and
        write_some_stuff and
        closefile(elements).

    write_some_stuff if
        chemical (Name) and
        write(Name) and
        flush(elements) and
        nl and fail.

    chemical (oxygen).
    chemical(boron).
    chemical (iron).
    chemical(chlorine).
    chemical(uranium).
```

Run the program. If there are no errors, type the following goal. Notice that when you press the (Enter) key, the red light on your disk drive glows briefly. This indicates that the file is being created. This goal causes the **use_file** rule to write the chemical names to the specified file.

> Goal:use_file. ↵

The disk light should glow briefly as the names are written to the file. To indicate that it has finished, Turbo Prolog responds with the goal prompt:

> Goal:use_file.
> Goal:

Now you will verify that the proper elements were written to the file. Turbo Prolog saves text files the same way it saves program files. Thus, you can use the Turbo Prolog Editor to view the contents of the file. To do this, follow the steps below:

1) Save the file currently in the Editor Window.

Return to the Main Menu	<—— (Esc)
Select the Files Menu	<—— (F)
Select **Write** to command	<—— (W)

At this point, you will be asked to supply a filename for your program.

> Type A:CHEMFILE.PRO ↵

The program currently in the Editor Window (in this case, the CHEMFILE program) will be saved on the diskette in drive A with the name CHEMFILE.PRO. **Note**: if you are using a drive other than drive A to save your programs, replace the A designator with that designator.

2) Clear the Editor Window

Select the **New file** command from the Files Menu.

The program currently in the Editor Window will be deleted, leaving the cursor in the Editor Window waiting for you to enter a new program.

3) **Bring the newly created file (chem.txt) into the Editor Window.**

Return the cursor to the Main Menu   <——— {Esc}
Choose the Files Menu   <——— {F}
Choose the **Load** command   <——— {L}

A request for the filename will be displayed on your screen.

Type **A:CHEM.TXT**   ↵

The file **chem.txt** is shown in your Editor Window listing the chemicals.

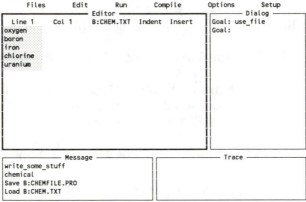

This shows that the program worked correctly. The chemical names were written to the file.

In this tutorial you will create a small, menu-driven data file program. You will first define a set of predicates that create, write, read, and modify disk files. Then you will write some predicates to create the menu-driven user interface.

You are going to create a file that contains the names of members of a club. You will only store the person's first name in this example. However, you should recognize that you could add other information such as their addresses and phone numbers. You could even add a list of interests like the ones in Tutorial 11-1.

This tutorial has six parts:

1) How to create a new file
2) How to get input from the keyboard and write it to a file
3) How to read a file
4) How to add data to an existing file
5) How to add a menu
6) How to add an internal goal

The complete program is shown in Figure 12-24. The next steps explain the rules of this program as they are added to make the completed program. Part 1 starts with creating the new file.

Part 1– How to Create a New File

Recall the steps required for using your personal telephone book:

1) Open the book.
2) Write information in the phone book.
3) Close the book.

Using a disk file requires the same three steps:

1) Open a file on the disk.
2) Write information to the file.
3) Close the file.

Of course, you must create the file before you can do any of these. Turbo Prolog provides special predicates to perform these steps. Study the examples below and the explanation that follows.

Figure 12-13: Rule to Create Members File

```
create_file if
    openwrite(members,"a:mem.txt") and        <—— step 1
    get_names and                             <—— step 2
    closefile(members).                       <—— step 3
```

Step 1. openwrite(members,"a:mem.txt").

This predicate creates the file on the disk in the A drive. Space is created on the disk for this file. The **openwrite** command requires two arguments. The first argument is the symbolic filename which will be declared in the domains section. The second argument is the DOS filename associated with the symbolic name. In this example, **members** is the symbolic name and **a:mem.txt** is the DOS filename.

Step 2. get_names

You will develop this predicate later in the tutorial. It will ask the user to type in the names. It then sets the write device to the file and writes the names to the file.

Step 3. closefile(members).

This predicate closes the file named **members**. When you finish using a file, you must close it. Failing to do this may result in the loss of data.

 If you have not already done so, clear your Editor Window. Type in the **create_file** rule as shown in Figure 12-14.

Figure 12-14: Rule to Create Members File

```
clauses
    create_file if
        openwrite(members,"a:mem.txt") and
        get_names and
        closefile(members).
```

Now declare the predicates **create_file** and **get_names** in the predicates section as shown in Figure 12-15.

Figure 12-15: Predicates Declaration for create_file Rule

---

        predicates
            create_file
            get_names

        clauses
            create_file if
                openwrite(members,"a:mem.txt") and
                get_names and
                closefile(members).

 The member file must be declared in the domains section. The file is declared with the symbolic filename **members**. Add the domains declaration as shown in Figure 12-16.

Figure 12-16: Domains Declaration for Members File

---

        domains
            file=members

        predicates
            create_file
            get_names

        clauses
            create_file if
                openwrite(members,"a:mem.txt") and
                get_names and
                closefile(members).

Next, you will add rules that allow the user to type in the names.

Part 2– How to Get Input from the Keyboard and Write it to a File

The rule **get_names** obtains input from the keyboard and writes it to the file. It sets **readdevice** to the **keyboard** and reads in the users response. It then calls another rule that actually writes the input to the file. The **get_names** rule is shown in Figure 12-17. Enter the rule as shown.

Figure 12-17: Predicate to Get Names and Write to File

```
get_names if
    writedevice(screen) and                          <–set screen
    write("Enter Name or <Return> to exit: ") and    <–prompt for name
    readdevice(keyboard) and                          <–set keyboard
    readln(Name) and                                  <–get name
    write_to_file(Name).                              <–write to file
                                          (You will define this later.)
```

Notice that the first subgoal of this rule sets the write device to the screen. Although the screen is the default write device, the get_name rule calls another rule **write_to_file** that changes the write device. Therefore, it is necessary to reset the proper input device.

Next, enter the new rule **write_to_file**. This rule has two jobs. The first is to check the input for the blank character. The user generates this character by pressing the {Return} key. This is the way the user signals that all the names have been entered. This is the exit condition. The rule that accomplishes this is

```
write_to_file("") if !.    <–if the user types in a blank return, end this
                              predicate.
```

If the user enters a blank carriage return, the cut (!) is encountered. Thus, both **write_to_file** and its calling routine **get_names** have completed their tasks.

The next rule tells Turbo Prolog what to do if the user enters a name (something other than a carriage return). Turbo Prolog will write this name to the file called **members**.

```
write_to_file(Name) if      <—if a name is typed in
    writedevice(members) and  <—open the members file
    write(Name,",") and       <—write Name and comma to the file
    get_names.                <—get the next name
```

Notice the second comma in the **write (Name,",")** predicate. When several names are written to a file, they must be separated by commas. You must tell Turbo Prolog to write the comma to the file.

 Enter these new predicates and complete the domains and predicates sections as shown in Figure 12-18.

Figure 12-18: write_to_file Predicates

```
domains
    file=members
    name=symbol

predicates
    create_file
    get_names
    write_to_file(name)

clauses
    create_file if
        openwrite(members,"a:mem.txt") and
        get_names and
        closefile(members).

    get_names if
        writedevice(screen) and
        write("Enter Name or <Return> to exit: ") and
        nl and
        readdevice(keyboard) and
        readln (Name) and
        write_to_file(Name).

    write_to_file("") if !.
    write_to_file(Name) if
        writedevice(members) and
        write(Name,",") and
        get_names.
```

Run this program. Type in the following goal:

> Goal:**create_file.** ↵

You will see the following in the Dialog Window:

> Enter Name or <Return> to exit:

Enter following names:

> **Fred** ↵
> **John** ↵
> **Bob** ↵
>   ↵   *<—blank carriage return*

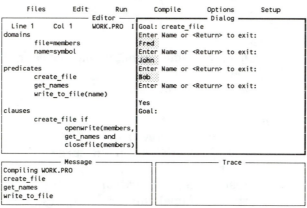

```
        Files      Edit      Run       Compile      Options      Setup
                        Editor                   Dialog
    Line 1    Col 1      WORK.PRO  I   Goal: create_file
  domains                                Enter Name or <Return> to exit:
           file=members                 Fred
           name=symbol                   Enter Name or <Return> to exit:
                                         John
  predicates                             Enter Name or <Return> to exit:
           create_file                   Bob
           get_names                     Enter Name or <Return> to exit:
           write_to_file(name)
                                         Yes
  clauses                                Goal:
           create_file if
                  openwrite(members,
                  get_names and
                  closefile(members)

                 Message                              Trace
  Compiling WORK.PRO
  create_file
  get_names
  write_to_file

  F2-Save  F3-Load  F5-Zoom  F6-Next  F8-Previous goal  Shift-F10-Resize  F10-End
```

Recall that the blank carriage return is the exit condition. This tells Turbo Prolog you are through entering names. If you want to check the file, you can use the technique used in the previous tutorial by reading the newly created file using the Turbo Prolog Editor. Part 3 of this tutorial shows you how to write a predicate that reads this file. If you decide to use the editor to view the file, remember to save the program first so that you can return to the tutorial. In the next part, you will learn how to read the file and display the information. The complete program is shown in Figure 12-24. The next steps explain the **read** and **print** rules..

Part 3– How to Read a File

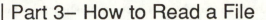

Reading the file requires two rule predicates. The first is **read_file**. This rule opens the "a:mem.txt" file and directs Turbo Prolog to obtain input from (read) the **mem.txt** file. Later, you will define a predicate called **print_file** to write the file on the screen. The **read_file** predicate is shown below.

> **read_file if**
>   **openread(members,"a:mem.txt") and** <— *open mem.txt for reading*
>   **readdevice(members) and**   <— *read from this file*
>   **clearwindow and**   <— *clear the window*
>   **print_file and**   <— *print the file*
>   **closefile(members).**   <—*close the file*

Once you open a file for reading, you want the items in it to be displayed or printed on the screen. Two rules called **print_file** handle this. The first **print_file** rule tells Turbo Prolog what to do if the end of the file has not been encountered. The second rule tells Turbo Prolog what to do when it finds itself at the end of the file. The first **print_file** rule is

> **print_file if**
>   **not(eof(members)) and** <— *if it's not end-of-file*
>   **readchar(Letter) and**   <— *read a letter*
>   **write(Letter) and**   <— *write the letter*
>   **print_file.**   <— *do it again*

The first clause of this rule fails if the next character is the end of the file marker. This causes Turbo Prolog to move down the knowledge base to the second **print_file** rule.

The second **print_file** rule tells Turbo Prolog what to do when the end of the file is encountered. This defines the boundary condition for the **print_file** rules. This predicate resets the read device to the keyboard and the write device to the screen. It tells the user that it is finished, waits for a key press, and then closes the file.

> **print_file if**
>   **nl and**   <—*print a new line*
>   **readdevice(keyboard) and**   <—*reset keyboard*
>   **writedevice(screen) and**   <—*reset screen*
>   **write("Press space bar ") and** <—*prompt user*
>   **readchar(_).**   <—*wait for key press*

To use these predicates, add them to the clauses section as shown below. Also add the new predicates to the predicate section. The new sections are shown in Figure 12-19.

Figure 12-19: The read_file and print_file Predicates

```
domains
    file=members
    name=symbol

predicates
    create_file
    get_names
    write_to_file(Nname)
    read_file
    print_file

clauses
    create_file if
        openwrite(members,"a:mem.txt") and
        get_names and
        closefile(members).

    get_names if
        writedevice(screen) and
        write("Enter Name or <Return> to exit: ") and
        readdevice(keyboard) and
        readln (Name) and
        write_to_file(Name).

    write_to_file("") if !.
    write_to_file(Name) if
        writedevice(members) and
        write(Name,",") and
        get_names.

    read_file if
        openread(members,"a:mem.txt") and
        readdevice(members) and
        clearwindow and
        print_file and
        closefile(members).

    print_file if
        not(eof(members)) and
        readchar(Letter) and
        write(Letter) and
        print_file.

    print_file if
        nl and
        readdevice(keyboard) and
        writedevice(screen) and
        write("Press space bar ") and
        readchar(_).
```

Now run the program and type in the following goal:

> Goal: **read_file.**   ↵

Here is the result:

> Goal:read_file.
> **Fred,John,Bob,**

Your program can now accept the names of club members, save those names to a disk file, and display the contents of the file on the screen. Next you will learn how to add names to an existing file. The complete program is shown in Figure 12-24. Part 4 will explain the new rules to add names to the file.

Part 4– How to Add Data to an Existing File

You cannot use the **create_file** rule to add new names to a file. The reason is that when you open a file for writing, Turbo Prolog destroys the contents of that file. Thus it is necessary to create a new rule which you will call **append_file**. This rule will open the members file for appending and preserve the original contents of the file.

The **append_file** rule is the same as **create_file** except that it opens the file for appending. It uses the standard predicate **openappend** to open the file. You will still use the **get_names** rule for processing the keyboard input.

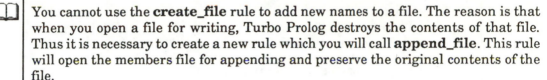

```
append_file if
    openappend(members,"a:mem.txt") and    <—new standard
    get_names and                                predicate
    closefile(members).
```

If you open a file for writing with **openwrite**, Turbo Prolog assumes it is a new file. If a file with the same name exists on the disk, Turbo Prolog destroys it. However, if you open a file for writing with **openappend**, Turbo Prolog assumes it is an existing file. This preserves the contents of the file. In order for this predicate to succeed, the file must exist on the disk prior to opening it with **openappend**.

Add the **append_file** rule to the clause section and predicates section.

Figure 12-20: The append_file Predicate

```
domains
    file=members
    name=symbol

predicates
    create_file
    get_names
    write_to_file(Name)
    read_file
    print_file
    append_file

clauses
    create_file if
        openwrite(members,"a:mem.txt") and
        get_names and
        closefile(members).

    append_file if
        openappend(members,"a:mem.txt") and
        get_names and
        closefile(members).
```

Run the program and type in the following goal:

Goal:**append_file.**   ⏎

You should see the following in the Dialog Window:

Enter Name or <Return> to exit

Add the names Tom and Al to the file.

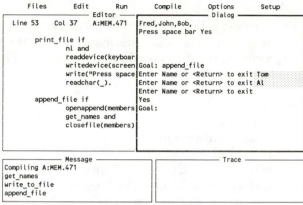

```
        Files      Edit      Run       Compile      Options      Setup
                       Editor                     Dialog
      Line 53    Col 37   A:MEM.471   Fred,John,Bob,
                                      Press space bar Yes
            print_file if
                nl and
                readdevice(keyboar   Goal: append_file
                writedevice(screen   Enter Name or <Return> to exit Tom
                write("Press space   Enter Name or <Return> to exit Al
                readchar(_).         Enter Name or <Return> to exit
                                     Yes
            append_file if           Goal:
                openappend(members
                get_names and
                closefile(members)


                    Message                        Trace
   Compiling A:MEM.471
   get_names
   write_to_file
   append_file

   F2-Save  F3-Load  F5-Zoom  F6-Next  F8-Previous goal  Shift-F10-Resize  F10-End
```

Now try the goal **read_file** to make sure that the new names have been added to the file.

Goal:**read_file.** ↵

```
        Files      Edit      Run       Compile      Options      Setup
                       Editor                     Dialog
      Line 53    Col 37   A:MEM.471   Fred,John,Bob,Tom,Al,
                                      Press space bar
            print_file if
                nl and
                readdevice(keyboar
                writedevice(screen
                write("Press space
                readchar(_).

            append_file if
                openappend(members
                get_names and
                closefile(members)


                    Message                        Trace
   write_to_file
   append_file
   read_file
   print_file

   F2-Save  F3-Load  F5-Zoom  F6-Next  F8-Previous goal  Shift-F10-Resize  F10-End
```

This shows that the new names were added to the file. Now you are ready to create your user-friendly menu. This is shown in Step 5 with the menu and repeat rules shown in Figure 12-21.

Part 5– How to Add a Menu

Now you will add a user-friendly menu to the program. This will make it easy for the non-expert user to use your Turbo Prolog program.

The first new rule is called **menu**. This predicate will display a menu that tells the user what the program does. The routine asks the user to input a choice. When the user enters a choice, the **do_it** predicate processes it. The **repeat** predicate (line 1) is explained below.

```
menu if
    repeat and                          <— set up a loop
    clearwindow and                     <— clear window
    nl and nl and nl and                <— blank lines
    write("    1. Create\n") and        <— choice 1
    write("    2. Append\n") and        <— choice 2
    write("    3. Read\n") and          <— choice 3
    write("    4. Exit") and            <— choice 4
    nl and nl and                       <— blank lines
    write("Enter Choice ") and          <— ask for choice
    readint(Choice) and                 <— read choice
    do_it(Choice).                      <— process choice
```

The first subgoal of the **menu** rule requires some explanation. In this example, you want the menu to reappear after each task. To do this, you need to use a loop structure. Unfortunately, Turbo Prolog does not have such a structure. Therefore, you must use a special technique to create a loop using recursion. The rule **repeat** is as follows:

```
repeat.
repeat if repeat.
```

These two repeat rules use recursion to force the entire **menu** rule to be repeated until the user chooses menu item 4 to exit.

Add the **menu** and **repeat** rules to the clause section and declare them in the predicates section as shown in Figure 12-21.

Figure 12-21: The menu and repeat Rules

```
domains
    file=members
    name=symbol

predicates
    create_file
    get_names
    write_to_file(Name)
    read_file
    print_file
    append_file
    menu
    repeat

clauses
    "
    "
    "
    menu if
        repeat and
        clearwindow and
        nl and nl and nl and
        write("      1. Create\n") and
        write("      2. Append\n") and
        write("      3. Read\n") and
        write("      4. Exit") and
        nl and nl and
        write("Enter Choice ") and
        readint(Choice) and
        do_it(Choice).
    repeat.
    repeat if repeat.
```

The **do_it** predicate processes the user's choice. It calls up the proper rules requested by the user. Here is how it looks.

```
do_it(1) if          <-- if the choice is 1
    create_file.     <-- create the file.
do_it(2) if          <-- if the choice is 2
    append_file.     <-- append to the file.
do_it(3) if          <-- if the choice is 3
    read_file.       <-- read the file.
do_it(4) if          <-- if the choice is 4
    exit.            <-- exit the program.
do_it(X) if          <-- any other choice
    X>4 and          <-- if the choice > 4
    error.           <-- give error message.
do_it(X) if          <-- any other choice
    X<1 and          <-- if the choice < 1
    error.           <-- give error message.
```

Notice the **exit** predicate in choice 4. This is a new standard predicate that succeeds by ending the program. If a number other than 1, 2, 3, or 4 is entered, the user must be informed of the error. The error rule shows how.

```
error if                              <-- error routine
    write("Choice not valid.") and    <-- give error message
    write("Try again\n ") and         <-- tell user "Try again"
    write("Press space bar ") and     <-- "Press space bar "
    readchar(_) and                   <-- wait for key press
    menu.                             <-- go back to menu
```

Think about how the error handling routine works. If the user chooses a number less than 1 or greater than 4 from the menu, the error routine informs the user that the choice was not valid. This technique is called **error trapping**.

Add the **do_it** and **error** rules, as shown above, to the program.

Next, add the **do_it** and **error** predicates to the predicates section and the choice type to the domains section. When completed, your domains and predicates section should be

```
domains
    file=members
    name=symbol
    choice=integer

predicates
    create_file
    get_names
    write_to_file(Name)
    read_file
    print_file
    append_file
    menu
    repeat
    do_it(Choice)
    error
```

Add the **do_it** and **error** rules to the clauses and predicates sections of your program. You must also declare the argument **choice** in the domains section. This argument is of the domain type **integer**. The complete domains and predicates sections are shown below, along with the two new clauses.

Figure 12-22: The do_it and error Predicates

```
domains
    file=members
    name=symbol
    choice=integer

predicates
    create_file
    get_names
    write_to_file(name)
    read_file
    print_file
    append_file
    menu
    repeat
    do_it(choice)
    error

clauses
    "
    "
    "
    do_it(1) if
        create_file.
    do_it(2) if
        append_file.
    do_it(3) if
        read_file.
    do_it(4) if
        exit.
    do_it(X) if
        X>4 and
        error.
    do_it(X) if
        X<1 and
        error.

    error if
        write("Choice not valid.") and
        write("Try again\n") and
        write("Press space bar ") and
        readchar(_) and
        menu.
```

Next, you must modify the predicates **create_file**, **read_file**, and **append_file** so that when they have completed their tasks, the user is returned to the menu. Below are the necessary modifications. Just add the **menu** predicate at the end of each section with the **and** operator as shown in Figure 12-23.

Figure 12-23: Modifications to Return to Menu

```
create_file if
    openwrite(members,"a:mem.txt") and
    get_names and
    closefile(members) and
    menu.

read_file if
    openread(members,"a:mem.txt") and
    readdevice(members) and
    clearwindow and
    print_file and
    closefile(members) and
    menu.

append_file if
    openappend(members,"a:mem.txt") and
    get_names and
    closefile (members) and
    menu.
```

Make the modifications and type in the following goal:

Goal:**menu.**　↵

Try each of the menu choices. Recall that when you choose number 1 (create a file), Turbo Prolog destroys the old file **mem.txt**. This is not a problem in this small knowledge base.

Part 6– How to Add an Internal Goal

Now you will tie it all together with an internal goal. You will enter **menu** as the internal goal by adding the following predicate to the goal section.

> **goal**
> **clearwindow and**
> **menu.**

Use the **clearwindow** command to clear the Dialog Window.

Now run the program which is shown in Figure 12-24. Try the various menu choices to create, read, append, and read the file again.

Remember, each time you choose menu choice 1, you destroy the existing members file. This is only practice, so it's no problem.

Figure 12-24: The Member Files Program

```
domains
    file=members
    name=symbol
    choice=integer

predicates
    create_file
    get_names
    write_to_file(name)
    read_file
    print_file
    append_file
    menu
    repeat
    do_it (choice)
    error

goal
    clearwindow
    and menu.

clauses
    menu if
        repeat and
        clearwindow and
        nl and nl and nl and
        write("     1. Create\n") and
        write("     2. Append\n") and
        write("     3. Read\n") and
        write("     4. Exit") and
        nl and nl and
        write("Enter Choice ") and
        readint(Choice) and
        do_it(Choice).

    do_it(1) if
        create_file.
    do_it(2) if
        append_file.
    do_it(3) if
        read_file.
    do_it(4) if
        exit.
    do_it(X) if
        X>4 and
        error.
    do_it(X) if
        X<1 and
        error.

    error if
        write("Choice not valid. ") and
        write("Try Again\n") and
        write("Press space bar") and
        readchar(_) and
        menu.
```

```
create_file if
    openwrite(members,"a:mem.txt") and
    get_names and
    closefile(members) and
    menu.

get_names if
    writedevice(screen) and
    write("Enter Name or <Return> to exit ") and
    readdevice(keyboard) and
    readln(Name) and
    write_to_file(Name).

write_to_file("") if !.
write_to_file(Name) if
    writedevice(members) and
    write(Name,",") and
    get_names.

read_file if
    openread(members,"a:mem.txt") and
    readdevice(members) and
    clearwindow and
    print_file and
    closefile(members) and
    menu.

print_file if
    not(eof(members)) and
    readchar(Letter) and
    write(Letter) and
    print_file.

print_file if
    nl and
    readdevice(keyboard) and
    writedevice(screen) and
    write("Press space bar ") and
    readchar(_).

append_file if
    openappend(members,"a:mem.txt") and
    get_names and
    closefile (members) and
    menu.

repeat.
repeat if repeat.
```

Exercises

12-1. The default input device is _____.

12-2. The default output device is _____.

12-3. What is the predicate that sends information to the output device.

12-4. What is the predicate that receives information from the input device.

12-5. Write the symbolic filenames for the following:

      a. The default input device.
      b. Hardcopy.
      c. The serial port.
      d. the default output device.

12-6. Explain each of the following predicates.

      a. readdevice(symbolic filename)
      b. writedevice(symbolic filename)
      c. openwrite(symbolic filename, DOS filename)
      d. closefile(symbolic filename)

Problems

12-1. Write a predicate (rule) that asks the user to type in a filename of an already created file. Write a rule that prints the contents of the file on the screen.

12-2. Modify problem 12-1 to direct the output to the printer.

12-3. Write a program that collects the names of birds observed on Discovery Island of Walt Disney World and stores them in a disk file. Write modules for printing this list from the diskfile and for displaying the list in the Dialog Window. Make up the bird names for this exercise or take a trip to Disney World to see the real birds.

Chapter 13
Dynamic Data Bases and Expert Systems

*This is where everything you have learned in previous chapters comes together, and you build a dynamic data base and an introductory Expert System. A dynamic data base is a data base that changes as it is used. A system that the user can modify provides a system that can be perceived as learning. This chapter will introduce you to this concept and show you how to build a dynamic data base using Turbo Prolog's built-in dynamic data base predicates. Tutorial 13-1, **Dynamic Data Base Predicates**, shows you these built-in predicates. Tutorial 13-2, **Expert Systems**, demonstrates how to write the basic parts of an expert system using information about French wines.*

Dynamic Data Bases and Expert Systems

Introduction

You have seen several ways to represent knowledge in Turbo Prolog. First, you saw how to represent a semantic network as Turbo Prolog clauses. These clauses are the facts and rules stored in a Turbo Prolog knowledge base. In the last chapter, you learned that Turbo Prolog also allows you to store data on a disk file. In this chapter you will learn yet another way to represent knowledge in Turbo Prolog — the **dynamic data base**.

You know some of the advantages of representing knowledge in the predicate form. Using this form, you can represent not only data, but also information about the relationships between the data. The major problem with this form of knowledge representation is that it is **static**. The user cannot readily modify the facts in a knowledge base. To add, remove, or modify the information in the knowledge base, you must be a Turbo Prolog programmer.

Many artificial intelligence applications require the creation of systems that the user can modify. Turbo Prolog's dynamic data base makes it easy to design systems that the user can revise.

By using the special dynamic data base predicates **assert** and **retract**, you can allow the user to assert new facts or retract old ones. These predicates allow easy modification of the knowledge base. However, Turbo Prolog allows only facts, not rules, to be asserted in a dynamic data base.

Turbo Prolog stores dynamic data bases in computer memory or on disk. Nevertheless, the facts are treated the same as if they were physically located in the clauses section. Dynamic data bases can be stored on the disk for retrieval at a later date.

Dynamic Data Base Predicates

Figure 13-1 shows a list of the special predicates that store facts in a dynamic data base.

Figure 13-1: Dynamic Data Base Predicates

Predicate	Function
asserta(fact)	adds a fact to top of data base
assertz(fact)	adds a fact to bottom of data base
retract (fact)	removes a fact from data base
save("dos_file")	saves the data base to disk
consult("dos_file")	loads the data base to RAM

Tutorial 13-1 explains how to use each of these predicates.

Tutorial 13-1 Dynamic Data Base Predicates

Asserting a New Fact

Turbo Prolog evaluates facts stored in a dynamic data base in exactly the same way that it evaluates facts in the clauses section. The major difference is that facts in a dynamic data base are stored in a **stack** in memory. Because they are stored in a stack in memory, it is easy to add new facts to the top or bottom of the stack. Turbo Prolog uses the predicate **asserta(fact)** to add an item to the top of the stack and the **assertz(fact)** predicate to add an item to the bottom of the stack. Because Turbo Prolog always searches from the top of the stack to the bottom, the placement of facts in the data base is an important consideration when searching through the data base.

Predicates used for data base operation are declared in a section called the data base section. This section works exactly the same as the predicates section and precedes the predicates section in the program.

```
database
    books(title,author)
```

Of course, you must declare the domain of each of the arguments in the domains section. A program may only have one database declaration. You declare multiple clauses in the data base by separating them with a semicolon:

```
database
     book(title,author);
     film(star,director);
     name(person)
```

Example of a Dynamic Data Base

To illustrate how to set up and use a dynamic data base, consider a simple example that stores a check number and the amount of that check.

Boot up Turbo Prolog and enter the checkbook dynamic data base as shown below.

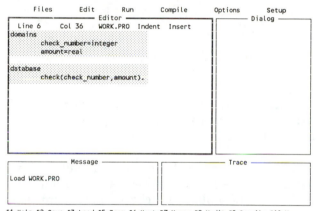

Dynamic Data Bases and Expert Systems

Run the program. Enter the following goal to add a check with the number **122** and the amount **$125.00**. The goal is:

Goal:**assertz(check(122,125.00).** ⏎

```
        Files      Edit      Run      Compile      Options      Setup
                        Editor                     Dialog
     Line 1     Col 1     WORK.PRO  Indent    Goal: assertz(check(122,125.00))
  domains                                     Yes
         check_number=integer                 Goal:
         amount=real

  database
         check(check_number,amount).




                        Message                           Trace
  Load WORK.PRO
  Compiling WORK.PRO


   F2-Save  F3-Load  F5-Zoom  F6-Next  F8-Previous goal  Shift-F10-Resize  F10-End
```

 Turbo Prolog responds by printing **Yes** and displaying the Goal statement request. The two items of information have been placed into the dynamic data base stack at the bottom of the stack.

If you ask Turbo Prolog to list the checks, it will. For example, suppose you were to enter a goal with the predicate check and a variable for the check number and a variable for the amount of the check. Turbo Prolog would list all of the check numbers and amounts entered into the data base.

Enter the goal below to request a listing of the check numbers and amounts of the checks existing in the data base using the variables **Number** and **Amount**.

Goal:**check(Number,Amount).** ↵

```
        Files        Edit       Run       Compile       Options       Setup
                         ── Editor ──              ── Dialog ──
   Line 1     Col 1     WORK.PRO   Indent  Goal: assertz(check(122,125.00))
domains                                    Yes
          check_number=integer             Goal: check(Number,Amount)
          amount=real                      Number=122,  Amount=125
                                           1 Solution
database                                   Goal:
          check(check_number,amount).



                 ── Message ──                        ── Trace ──

Load WORK.PRO
Compiling WORK.PRO
check

  F2-Save  F3-Load  F5-Zoom  F6-Next  F8-Previous goal  Shift-F10-Resize  F10-End
```

 Turbo Prolog displays the numbers and amounts for the checks existing in the data base. You have entered only one check so only one is reported.

Dynamic Data Bases and Expert Systems

Add another check to the knowledge base – check number 123 for $250.25.

Goal:**assertz(check(123,250.25)).** ↵

```
        Files      Edit      Run      Compile      Options      Setup
                         ─── Editor ───        ┌─── Dialog ───
    Line 1      Col 1      WORK.PRO  Indent     │Goal: assertz(check(122,125.00))
domains                                         │Yes
        check_number=integer                    │Goal: check(Number,Amount)
        amount=real                             │Number=122, Amount=125
                                                │1 Solution
database                                        │Goal: assertz(check(123,250.25))
        check(check_number,amount).             │Yes
                                                │Goal:




                     ─── Message ───            ─── Trace ───
Load WORK.PRO
Compiling WORK.PRO
check

F2-Save  F3-Load  F5-Zoom  F6-Next  F8-Previous goal  Shift-F10-Resize  F10-End
```

Turbo Prolog confirms that it has completed its task by writing **Yes** in the Dialog Window. Check number 123 for $250.25 has been added to the data base at the bottom of the stack.

Check the stack to see if this information has indeed been entered. Enter the following goal:

Goal:check(Number,Amount). ↵

```
        Files      Edit      Run      Compile      Options      Setup
                 ─ Editor ─                    ─ Dialog ─
 Line 1     Col 1      WORK.PRO  Indent  │Goal: assertz(check(122,125.00))
domains                                  │Yes
         check_number=integer            │Goal: check(Number,Amount)
         amount=real                     │Number=122, Amount=125
                                         │1 Solution
database                                 │Goal: assertz(check(123,250.25))
         check(check_number,amount).     │Yes
                                         │Goal: check(Number,Amount)
                                         │Number=122, Amount=125
                                         │Number=123, Amount=250.25
                                         │2 Solutions
                                         │Goal:


              ─ Message ─                         ─ Trace ─
Load WORK.PRO
Compiling WORK.PRO
check

F2-Save  F3-Load  F5-Zoom  F6-Next  F8-Previous goal  Shift-F10-Resize  F10-End
```

 The checks are listed showing the last check at the bottom of the data base as expected. Next, add a check to the top of the data base using the **asserta** predicate.

Enter the **asserta** goal as follows:

Goal:**asserta(check(121,135.54)).**   ↵

```
         Files      Edit      Run     Compile    Options    Setup
                    Editor ─────────┐  ┌─────────── Dialog ──────────┐
   Line 1     Col 1    WORK.PRO  Indent │Goal: assertz(check(122,125.00)) │
domains                                 │Yes                              │
        check_number=integer            │Goal: check(Number,Amount)       │
        amount=real                     │Number=122, Amount=125           │
                                        │1 Solution                       │
database                                │Goal: assertz(check(123,250.25)) │
        check(check_number,amount).     │Yes                              │
                                        │Goal: check(Number,Amount)       │
                                        │Number=122, Amount=125           │
                                        │Number=123, Amount=250.25        │
                                        │2 Solutions                      │
                                        │Goal: asserta(check(121,135.54)) │
                                        │Yes                              │
                                        │Goal:                            │
 ───────────────── Message ─────────────┘  ┌──────────── Trace ──────────┘

Load WORK.PRO
Compiling WORK.PRO
check

  F2-Save  F3-Load  F5-Zoom  F6-Next  F8-Previous goal  Shift-F10-Resize  F10-End
```

The reply of **Yes** assures you that the predicate succeeded.

List the checks in the data base to see if the last check was entered at the top of the data base. Enter the Goal:

Goal:**check(Number,Amount).** ↵

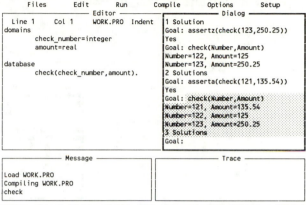

```
      Files      Edit      Run     Compile      Options      Setup
  ───────────────────── Editor ──────     ─────────── Dialog ───────────┐
  Line 1     Col 1     WORK.PRO  Indent │1 Solution
domains                                 │Goal: assertz(check(123,250.25))
        check_number=integer            │Yes
        amount=real                     │Goal: check(Number,Amount)
                                        │Number=122, Amount=125
database                                │Number=123, Amount=250.25
        check(check_number,amount).     │2 Solutions
                                        │Goal: asserta(check(121,135.54))
                                        │Yes
                                        │Goal: check(Number,Amount)
                                        │Number=121, Amount=135.54
                                        │Number=122, Amount=125
                                        │Number=123, Amount=250.25
                                        │3 Solutions
                                        │Goal:
  ─────────── Message ───────────     ──────────── Trace ────────────
Load WORK.PRO
Compiling WORK.PRO
check

F2-Save  F3-Load  F5-Zoom  F6-Next  F8-Previous goal  Shift-F10-Resize  F10-End
```

Check number 121 in the amount of $135.54 has been entered at the top of the data base. The **asserta** predicate worked exactly as advertised. The next section explains the procedure for removing facts from a data base.

Removing Facts from a Dynamic Data Base

The **retract** predicate removes an item or items from a dynamic data base. To remove check number 122, use the **retract** predicate as shown below.

Goal:**retract(check(122,_)).** ↵

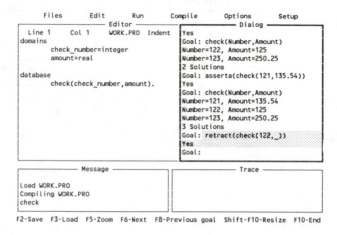

```
      Files       Edit       Run       Compile      Options      Setup
                ─ Editor ─                        ─ Dialog ─
   Line 1    Col 1      WORK.PRO  Indent   Yes
domains                                    Goal: check(Number,Amount)
         check_number=integer              Number=122, Amount=125
         amount=real                       Number=123, Amount=250.25
                                           2 Solutions
database                                   Goal: asserta(check(121,135.54))
         check(check_number,amount).       Yes
                                           Goal: check(Number,Amount)
                                           Number=121, Amount=135.54
                                           Number=122, Amount=125
                                           Number=123, Amount=250.25
                                           3 Solutions
                                           Goal: retract(check(122,_))
                                           Yes
                                           Goal:


             ─ Message ─                            ─ Trace ─
Load WORK.PRO
Compiling WORK.PRO
check

  F2-Save  F3-Load  F5-Zoom  F6-Next  F8-Previous goal  Shift-F10-Resize  F10-End
```

The response **Yes** in the Dialog Window confirms that the goal succeeded. Now interrogate the data base to see if the check was indeed removed by the **retract** predicate.

Enter the **check** predicate again to determine if check 122 was removed.

Goal:**check(Number,Amount).** ↵

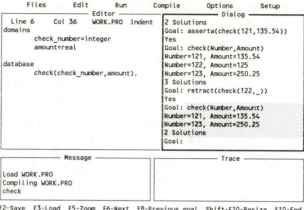

```
          Files        Edit      Run      Compile      Options      Setup
                       Editor                          Dialog
    Line 6    Col 36      WORK.PRO  Indent   2 Solutions
domains                                      Goal: asserta(check(121,135.54))
        check_number=integer                 Yes
        amount=real                          Goal: check(Number,Amount)
                                             Number=121, Amount=135.54
database                                     Number=122, Amount=125
        check(check_number,amount).          Number=123, Amount=250.25
                                             3 Solutions
                                             Goal: retract(check(122,_))
                                             Yes
                                             Goal: check(Number,Amount)
                                             Number=121, Amount=135.54
                                             Number=123, Amount=250.25
                                             2 Solutions
                                             Goal:

                     Message                               Trace
Load WORK.PRO
Compiling WORK.PRO
check

  F2-Save   F3-Load   F5-Zoom   F6-Next   F8-Previous goal   Shift-F10-Resize   F10-End
```

The **check** predicate now lists only two checks in the data base, 121 and 123. The **retract** predicate removed check 122 as expected.

Dynamic Data Base Disk Predicates

If the function of a dynamic data base were to store information in memory only, the data base would be of limited value. When a new program is run or when the computer is turned off, the information contained in the computer's memory is lost. As you might guess, Turbo Prolog has special predicates to save the information in a dynamic data base for later use. The **save** predicate saves the information in the dynamic data base to a DOS file. The **consult** predicate loads the information from a DOS file into memory.

The **save** predicate requires one argument – a DOS filename or a symbolic name bound to a DOS filename. For example:

save("checks.txt") <— *Saves dynamic data base. Uses the DOS filename* ***checks.txt***.

save(Myfile)   <— *The data base is saved with a DOS filename bound to the variable **Myfile** .*

To save the **check** dynamic data base currently residing in RAM to the disk in the A drive, enter the following goal:

> Goal:**save("a:checks.txt").** ↵

If you do not have a formatted disk in the A drive, substitute an appropriate drive specification.

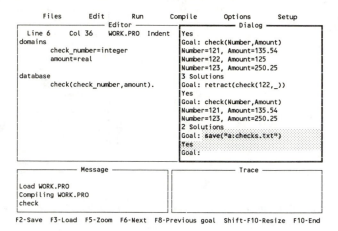

```
        Files       Edit        Run       Compile      Options      Setup
                    ┌─ Editor ─────────────┐┌─ Dialog ──────────────────┐
     Line 6    Col 36    WORK.PRO  Indent  │Yes                          │
    domains                               ││Goal: check(Number,Amount)   │
            check_number=integer          ││Number=121, Amount=135.54    │
            amount=real                   ││Number=122, Amount=125       │
                                          ││Number=123, Amount=250.25    │
    database                              ││3 Solutions                  │
            check(check_number,amount).   ││Goal: retract(check(122,_))  │
                                          ││Yes                          │
                                          ││Goal: check(Number,Amount)   │
                                          ││Number=121, Amount=135.54    │
                                          ││Number=123, Amount=250.25    │
                                          ││2 Solutions                  │
                                          ││Goal: save("a:checks.txt")   │
                                          ││Yes                          │
                                          ││Goal:                        │
                    └──────────────────────┘└───────────────────────────┘
                    ┌─ Message ────────────┐┌─ Trace ───────────────────┐
    Load WORK.PRO                          ││                            │
    Compiling WORK.PRO                     ││                            │
    check                                  ││                            │
                    └──────────────────────┘└───────────────────────────┘
        F2-Save  F3-Load  F5-Zoom  F6-Next  F8-Previous goal  Shift-F10-Resize  F10-End
```

Turbo Prolog responds **Yes** indicating that the operation is complete. You should have noticed that the red light on your disk drive was lit as the information was saved to the disk.

Now you can access this knowledge base when you need it. To demonstrate how this works, you will remove the two existing facts from the data base by using the **retract** predicate twice. The screen below shows the result of entering the **retract** predicate twice.

Goal:**retract(check(121,_)).** ↵
Goal:**retract(check(123,_)).** ↵

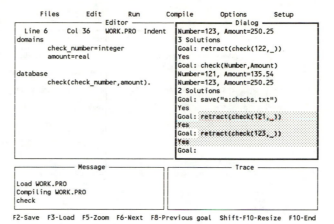

```
         Files      Edit      Run      Compile      Options      Setup
                    Editor                          Dialog
   Line 6     Col 36    WORK.PRO  Indent   Number=123, Amount=250.25
domains                                    3 Solutions
        check_number=integer              Goal: retract(check(122,_))
        amount=real                       Yes
                                          Goal: check(Number,Amount)
database                                  Number=121, Amount=135.54
        check(check_number,amount).       Number=123, Amount=250.25
                                          2 Solutions
                                          Goal: save("a:checks.txt")
                                          Yes
                                          Goal: retract(check(121,_))
                                          Yes
                                          Goal: retract(check(123,_))
                                          Yes
                                          Goal:

                    Message                          Trace
Load WORK.PRO
Compiling WORK.PRO
check

   F2-Save  F3-Load  F5-Zoom  F6-Next  F8-Previous goal  Shift-F10-Resize  F10-End
```

Check the dynamic data base by listing its contents using the **check** predicate.

Goal:**check(Number,Amount).** ↵

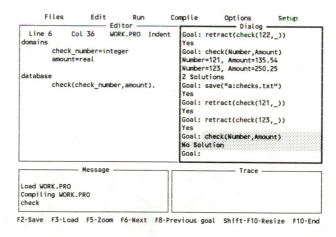

```
         Files      Edit      Run      Compile      Options      Setup
                    Editor                          Dialog
   Line 6     Col 36    WORK.PRO  Indent   Goal: retract(check(122,_))
domains                                    Yes
        check_number=integer              Goal: check(Number,Amount)
        amount=real                       Number=121, Amount=135.54
                                          Number=123, Amount=250.25
database                                  2 Solutions
        check(check_number,amount).       Goal: save("a:checks.txt")
                                          Yes
                                          Goal: retract(check(121,_))
                                          Yes
                                          Goal: retract(check(123,_))
                                          Yes
                                          Goal: check(Number,Amount)
                                          No Solution
                                          Goal:

                    Message                          Trace
Load WORK.PRO
Compiling WORK.PRO
check

   F2-Save  F3-Load  F5-Zoom  F6-Next  F8-Previous goal  Shift-F10-Resize  F10-End
```

The reply **No Solution** shows that the data base is empty.

The data base has previously been saved to the disk under the DOS filename **a:checks.txt**. To demonstrate how to load the data base from disk to memory, enter the **consult** predicate as follows:

Goal:**consult("a:checks.txt"),**   ↵

Again, if the **check.txt** file was saved on a different drive, substitute the correct drive designation.

```
        Files       Edit        Run     Compile      Options      Setup
                   ── Editor ──              ┌──── Dialog ─────────────────┐
   Line 6    Col 36    WORK.PRO  Indent      │Goal: check(Number,Amount)   │
domains                                      │Number=121, Amount=135.54    │
        check_number=integer                 │Number=123, Amount=250.25    │
        amount=real                          │2 Solutions                  │
                                             │Goal: save("a:checks.txt")   │
database                                     │Yes                          │
        check(check_number,amount).          │Goal: retract(check(121,_))  │
                                             │Yes                          │
                                             │Goal: retract(check(123,_))  │
                                             │Yes                          │
                                             │Goal: check(Number,Amount)   │
                                             │No Solution                  │
                                             │Goal: consult("a:checks.txt")│
                                             │Yes                          │
                                             │Goal:                        │
                                             └─────────────────────────────┘
              ── Message ──                       ──── Trace ────
Load WORK.PRO
Compiling WORK.PRO
check

F2-Save  F3-Load  F5-Zoom  F6-Next  F8-Previous goal  Shift-F10-Resize  F10-End
```

The confirmation **Yes** tells you that the goal has been successfully executed even though you can't see the results. The contents of the DOS file **checks.txt** have been loaded successfully into memory.

Once again, execute the **check** predicate to list the contents of the dynamic data base called **check**. Enter the goal:

Goal:**check(Number,Amount).** ↵

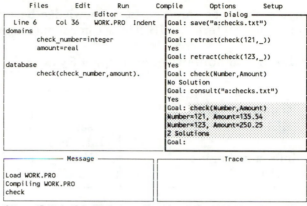

```
        Files      Edit      Run      Compile      Options      Setup
                      Editor                          Dialog
   Line 6     Col 36    WORK.PRO  Indent   Goal: save("a:checks.txt")
domains                                     Yes
        check_number=integer               Goal: retract(check(121,_))
        amount=real                        Yes
                                           Goal: retract(check(123,_))
database                                   Yes
        check(check_number,amount).        Goal: check(Number,Amount)
                                           No Solution
                                           Goal: consult("a:checks.txt")
                                           Yes
                                           Goal: check(Number,Amount)
                                           Number=121,  Amount=135.54
                                           Number=123,  Amount=250.25
                                           2 Solutions
                                           Goal:

                   Message                            Trace
Load WORK.PRO
Compiling WORK.PRO
check

 F2-Save  F3-Load  F5-Zoom  F6-Next  F8-Previous goal  Shift-F10-Resize  F10-End
```

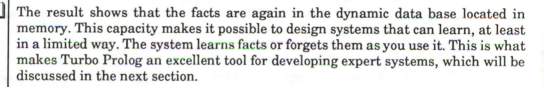

The result shows that the facts are again in the dynamic data base located in memory. This capacity makes it possible to design systems that can learn, at least in a limited way. The system learns facts or forgets them as you use it. This is what makes Turbo Prolog an excellent tool for developing expert systems, which will be discussed in the next section.

This tutorial has shown you how to set up and use a Turbo Prolog dynamic data base. You have used the **assertz** and the **asserta** predicates that add data to the bottom and the top of the data base, respectively. You have used the **retract** predicate to eliminate items of information from the dynamic data base. You have learned that the **save** predicate stores the contents of the data base to a disk file and that those contents can be retrieved through the use of the **consult** predicate. You have also seen how Turbo Prolog treats the facts in a dynamic data base exactly as if they were in the clauses section.

Turbo Prolog and Expert Systems

Developing a full blown expert system is beyond the scope of this book. However, you now have the fundamental skills to explore this exciting area of artificial intelligence. This section will introduce you to a simple expert system and the required programming principles.

An expert system has three parts, a knowledge base (KB), an inference engine (INE), and a user interface (UI). These components are shown in Figure 13-2.

Figure 13-2: Components of an Expert System

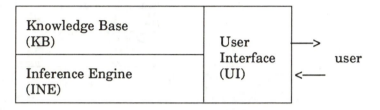

The knowledge base is the reservoir of facts and rules needed to solve a problem. In Turbo Prolog, these are clauses represented in the predicate form located in the clauses section. In the last section, you learned that Turbo Prolog also stores facts in dynamic data bases. The knowledge base of an expert system can exist in both forms with Turbo Prolog.

The **inference engine** contains the **heuristics** that determine how to search the knowledge base. A **heuristic** is a rule-of-thumb about how to solve problems. These heuristics are stated as Turbo Prolog rules. The inference engine then determines how to use the rules to make conclusions. In Turbo Prolog, the inference engine is driven by a built-in backtracking mechanism.

The user interface determines how the system communicates with the user. A well-designed expert system should allow a computer novice to use it easily. You cannot assume that the user knows how to phrase a Turbo Prolog goal. In the last chapter, you learned how to develop one type of user interface – a **menu**.

In Tutorial 13-2, you will build a system that is the beginning of an expert system on wines. It is important to recognize that this system is not an expert system. Expert systems contain hundreds (or thousands) of rules and take several man-years to develop. However, you will gain experience in the general structure of such systems and see how they are built.

This tutorial demonstrates how to write the basic parts of an expert system. This system will contain some information on French wines. While it is not an expert system, it demonstrates some of the principles of an expert system. The tutorial has three parts:

Part 1– How to add, find, list, and remove a wine from the data base

Part 2– How to save and load the data base

Part 3– How to add a user interface

The complete program is listed on pages 462–463.

Part 1– How to Add, Find, List, and Remove a Wine from the Data Base

First, you will create a rule that provides for the addition of information to the knowledge base. We will call this rule **add_to_kb**. It will ask the user to type in information about a French wine. The standard predicates **read** and **write** will retrieve the information, and the predicate **assertz** will add the items of information to the bottom of the data base.

If there is an existing program in your Turbo Prolog Editor, clear it out using the **New file** Editor command from the Files submenu.

Expand the Editor Window to the full screen size by entering the Turbo Prolog Editor and pressing the {F5} key. When you want to return to the four-window display, press the {F5} Zoom key again.

Enter the **add_to_kb** rule predicate in the clauses section.

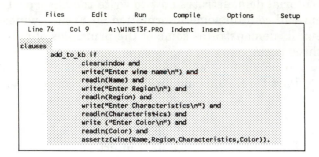

```
        Files       Edit        Run       Compile      Options      Setup

    Line 74    Col 9     A:\WINE13F.PRO   Indent   Insert

clauses
        add_to_kb if
                clearwindow and
                write("Enter wine name\n") and
                readln(Name) and
                write("Enter Region\n") and
                readln(Region) and
                write("Enter Characteristics\n") and
                readln(Characteristics) and
                write ("Enter Color\n") and
                readln(Color) and
                assertz(wine(Name,Region,Characteristics,Color)).
```

There are no new commands in this rule. However, lets examine each predicate as it appears.

The first predicate **clearwindow**, of course, clears the Dialog Window. The following **write** predicate displays in the Dialog Window the request to enter the name of the wine. The following **readln** predicate accepts the name the user enters and binds the variable **Name** to the name of the wine. This sequence of **write** and **readln** predicates continues asking for the region, characteristics, and color of the wine. The last predicate is the **assertz** predicate that places the values of the **Name**, **Region**, **Characteristics**, and **Color** variables into the dynamic data base called **wine**.

The next step is to declare the **wine** predicate as a dynamic data base. This is done in the section called data base. Add the data base section as shown below.

> **database**
> **wine(string,string,string,string)**

 Your screen should look like this:

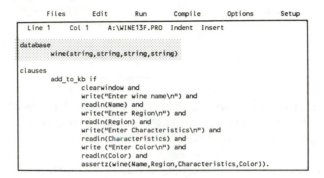

```
        Files        Edit        Run        Compile       Options      Setup

   Line 1      Col 1      A:\WINE13F.PRO   Indent   Insert

 database
         wine(string,string,string,string)

 clauses
         add_to_kb if
                 clearwindow and
                 write("Enter wine name\n") and
                 readln(Name) and
                 write("Enter Region\n") and
                 readln(Region) and
                 write("Enter Characteristics\n") and
                 readln(Characteristics) and
                 write ("Enter Color\n") and
                 readln(Color) and
                 assertz(wine(Name,Region,Characteristics,Color)).
```

 Notice the **wine** database declaration. The domains of the arguments are declared directly in the database section. This is a shortcut that Turbo Prolog allows in either a predicates or database declaration. If the arguments in a predicate or database declaration are of the standard domain types, they may be declared directly in the predicates or database sections. In this case, the domains of the objects in the **wine** dynamic data base are of the standard string type. Some comparisons and examples follow.

Figure 13-3: Ways to Declare Standard Domain Types – Example 1

Declaring the domains and the predicates the old way

> domains
>   name=string
>
> predicates
>   person(name,name)

is the same as declaring the objects in **person** in the predicates section with the string type.

> predicates
>   person(string,string)

Figure 13-4: Ways to Declare Standard Domain Types – Example 2

```
domains
    name,region,characteristics,color=string

predicates
    wine(name,region,characteristics,color)
```

This is the same as:

```
predicates
    wine(string,string,string,string)
```

Because the only purpose of the domains and predicates sections is to help the compiler, both forms are equivalent. Many texts, including the Turbo Prolog User's Guide, use this shortcut frequently.

Next add the predicate **find_a_wine**. This is a rule that allows the user to type in the name of a wine and then finds and lists information about that wine.

Enter the **find_a_wine** predicate rule as shown.

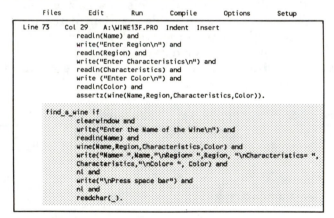

```
        Files       Edit       Run      Compile      Options      Setup

  Line 73    Col 29    A:\WINE13F.PRO   Indent   Insert
                readln(Name) and
                write("Enter Region\n") and
                readln(Region) and
                write("Enter Characteristics\n") and
                readln(Characteristics) and
                write ("Enter Color\n") and
                readln(Color) and
                assertz(wine(Name,Region,Characteristics,Color)).

            find_a_wine if
                clearwindow and
                write("Enter the Name of the Wine\n") and
                readln(Name) and
                wine(Name,Region,Characteristics,Color) and
                write("Name= ",Name,"\nRegion= ",Region, "\nCharacteristics= ",
                Characteristics,"\nColor= ", Color) and
                nl and
                write("\nPress space bar") and
                nl and
                readchar(_).

  F1-Help F2-Save F3-Load F5-Zoom F6-Next F7-Xcopy F8-Xedit F9-Compile F10-Menu
```

The **find_a_wine** predicate rule first clears the Dialog Window. It then uses the **write** and **readln** predicates to ask the user to "Enter the Name of the Wine..." and to assign the entered wine name to the variable **Name**. Next the dynamic data base is searched for this name. The **write** predicate then displays all the information about the wine. The rule concludes by telling the user to press the {Space Bar} to continue. This is important to assure that the user has sufficient time to read the answer.

Now add the predicate rules **list_all_wines** and **find_wine** to the program. The **list_all_wines** predicate is a rule that calls up another rule called **find_wine.** The **find_wine** predicate lists all the wines in the data base (Note the **find_wine** predicate is not the same as the **find_a_wine** predicate).

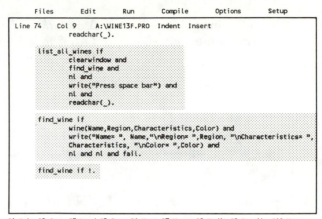

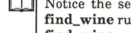 Notice the second **find_wine** rule (**find_wine if !.**). The need for this second **find_wine** rule is a side effect of how backtracking works. If you had only the first **find_wine** rule, the program would not work properly. Understanding the need for the second **find_wine** rule will help you understand how Turbo Prolog's backtracking mechanism works. Let's look at this process.

Figure 13-5 shows how you want this program to work:

Figure 13-5: The Desired Flow of Satisfaction

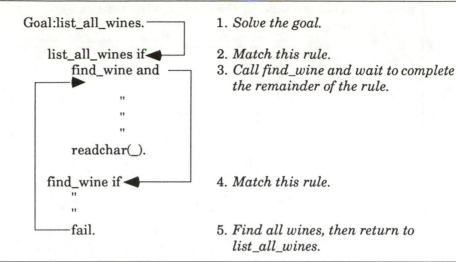

However, this is not what happens. Because the rule ends in a **fail** condition, Turbo Prolog does not return to the calling rule. Control only passes back to **list_all_wines** when **find_wine** completes its task, i.e., succeeds. When Turbo Prolog fails, it always backtracks. It looks for other rules with the **find_wine** predicate. Since there are none, Turbo Prolog backtracks to the original goal (**list_all_wines**) to see if there are any more subgoals to satisfy. There are not, so the program ends. The last lines of **list_all_wines** are not executed. The actual flow of satisfaction without the second **find_wine** predicate is shown in Figure 13-6.

Figure 13-6: The Flow of Satisfaction Without the Second find_wine Rule

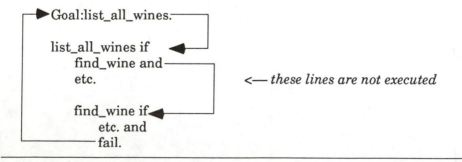

The solution to this problem depends on your knowing how Turbo Prolog matches goals. When the last subgoal of **find_wine** (fail) executes, Turbo Prolog first attempts to search for another **find_wine** predicate. Of course, there is no other **find_wine** predicate. Therefore, you need to add a second **find_wine** predicate. In the second predicate, there is only one subgoal – the **cut** (!). This predicate always succeeds, ensuring no further processing of the **find_wine** predicate. Because **find_wine** has successfully completed its task, control of the program passes back to the calling rule – **list_all_wines**. This is exactly what you want it to do. Below is a diagram of the flow of control with both **find_wine** predicates.

Figure 13-7: The Flow of Satisfaction with the Second find_wine Rule

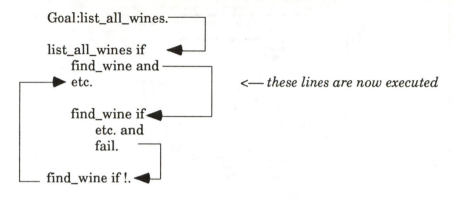

Goal:list_all_wines.

list_all_wines if
    find_wine and
    etc.   <— *these lines are now executed*

    find_wine if
        etc. and
        fail.

find_wine if !.

 Notice that the order of the predicates makes a big difference in this case. If the **find_wine** rules were reversed, the cut would prohibit the second rule from being evaluated.

The next predicate rule **retract_from_kb** removes a wine from the data base. This predicate rule asks the user to type in the name of the wine to delete and then retracts the wine from the data base.

Add the predicate rule **retract_from_kb** to the knowledge base as shown below.

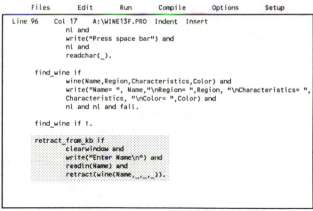

```
        Files      Edit      Run      Compile      Options      Setup
    Line 96    Col 17    A:\WINE13F.PRO   Indent   Insert
                    nl and
                    write("Press space bar") and
                    nl and
                    readchar(_).

            find_wine if
                    wine(Name,Region,Characteristics,Color) and
                    write("Name= ", Name,"\nRegion= ",Region, "\nCharacteristics= ",
                    Characteristics, "\nColor= ",Color) and
                    nl and nl and fail.

            find_wine if !.

            retract_from_kb if
                    clearwindow and
                    write("Enter Name\n") and
                    readln(Name) and
                    retract(wine(Name,_,_,_)).
```

F1-Help F2-Save F3-Load F5-Zoom F6-Next F7-Xcopy F8-Xedit F9-Compile F10-Menu

The last data base handling routine is **retract_all**. It deletes the contents of the data base. The use of **fail** ensures that each item in the data base is removed. Be careful using this option as it will erase the contents of your data base.

Add the **retract_all** predicate to the knowledge base as shown.

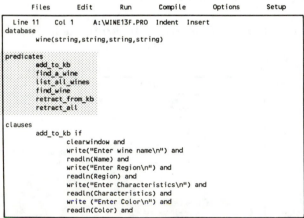

```
        Files      Edit      Run      Compile      Options      Setup

   Line 98    Col 48    A:\WINE13F.PRO   Indent   Insert
                 nl and
                 write("Press space bar") and
                 nl and
                 readchar(_).

        find_wine if
                 wine(Name,Region,Characteristics,Color) and
                 write("Name= ", Name,"\nRegion= ",Region, "\nCharacteristics= ",
                 Characteristics, "\nColor= ",Color) and
                 nl and nl and fail.

        find_wine if !.

        retract_from_kb if
                 clearwindow and
                 write("Enter Name\n") and
                 readln(Name) and
                 retract(wine(Name,_,_,_)).

        retract_all if
                 retract(wine(_,_,_,_)) and fail.
```

F1-Help F2-Save F3-Load F5-Zoom F6-Next F7-Xcopy F8-Xedit F9-Compile F10-Menu

To complete this section, enter all the predicate declarations in the predicates section. Your screen should look like this.

```
        Files      Edit      Run      Compile      Options      Setup

   Line 11    Col 1     A:\WINE13F.PRO   Indent   Insert
database
        wine(string,string,string,string)

predicates
        add_to_kb
        find_a_wine
        list_all_wines
        find_wine
        retract_from_kb
        retract_all

clauses
        add_to_kb if
                 clearwindow and
                 write("Enter wine name\n") and
                 readln(Name) and
                 write("Enter Region\n") and
                 readln(Region) and
                 write("Enter Characteristics\n") and
                 readln(Characteristics) and
                 write ("Enter Color\n") and
                 readln(Color) and
```

F1-Help F2-Save F3-Load F5-Zoom F6-Next F7-Xcopy F8-Xedit F9-Compile F10-Menu

Now experiment with these predicates. Run the program and follow the steps below.

First enter the information about a French wine. The wine is Medoc, a red wine from the Bordeau region. Medoc has a light body and a strong flavor. Type in the goal as shown:

Goal:**add_to_kb.**　　↲

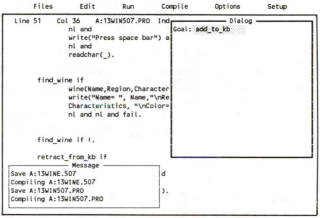

The next 4 screens show the steps in entering the information requested.

Step 1- Enter the name of the wine.

Medoc ↵

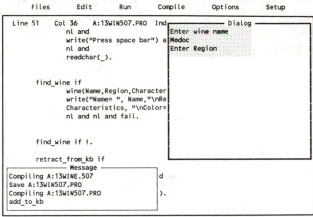

Step 2- Enter the region the wine comes from.

Bordeau ↵

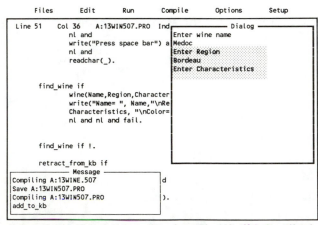

Step 3- Enter the wine characteristics.

light body, strong flavor ⏎

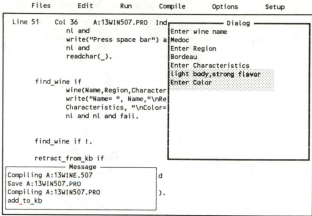

Step 4- Enter the color of the wine.

Red ⏎

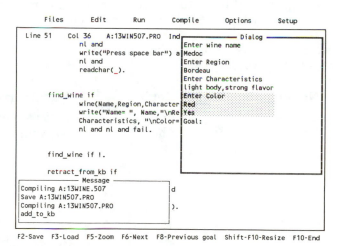

📖 You know that the goal succeeds because Turbo Prolog displays **Yes** in the Dialog Window.

To list the wines in the data base, enter a new goal

Goal:**list_all_wines.** ↵

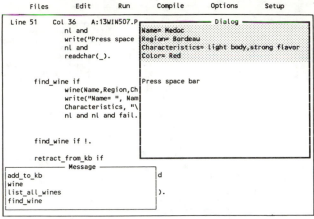

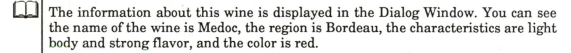

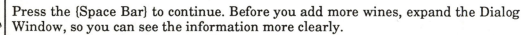

The information about this wine is displayed in the Dialog Window. You can see the name of the wine is Medoc, the region is Bordeau, the characteristics are light body and strong flavor, and the color is red.

Press the {Space Bar} to continue. Before you add more wines, expand the Dialog Window, so you can see the information more clearly.

Add two more wines using the information below. This will require typing the **add_to_kb** goal twice.

Name	Region	Characteristics	Color
Graves	Bordeau	not too sweet	Red
Beaujolais	Rhone	tasty and fruity	White

When you have finished, your screen should look like this:

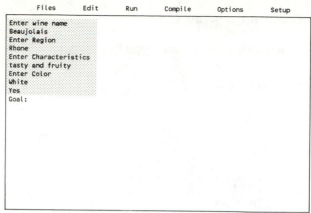

```
        Files      Edit      Run     Compile     Options     Setup
   Enter wine name
   Beaujolais
   Enter Region
   Rhone
   Enter Characteristics
   tasty and fruity
   Enter Color
   White
   Yes
   Goal:
```

F2-Save F3-Load F5-Zoom F6-Next F8-Previous goal Shift-F10-Resize F10-End

To check that you added the new wines properly, enter the goal **list_all_wines**.

Goal:**list_all_wines.** ↵

If you added the wines correctly, you will see:

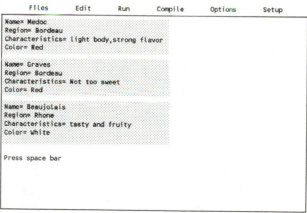

```
        Files      Edit      Run     Compile     Options     Setup
   Name= Medoc
   Region= Bordeau
   Characteristics= light body,strong flavor
   Color= Red

   Name= Graves
   Region= Bordeau
   Characteristics= Not too sweet
   Color= Red

   Name= Beaujolais
   Region= Rhone
   Characteristics= tasty and fruity
   Color= White


   Press space bar
```

F2-Save F3-Load F5-Zoom F6-Next F8-Previous goal Shift-F10-Resize F10-End

The Dialog Window lists the new wines in the data base.

This is a good time to test the **find_a_wine** predicate. Press the {Space Bar} as requested and type in the goal:

> Goal:**find_a_wine.** ↵

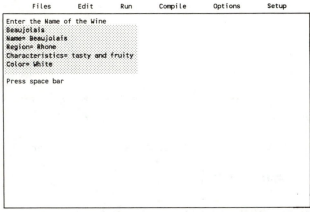 When you are asked for a wine, type Beaujolais.

> **Beaujolais** ↵

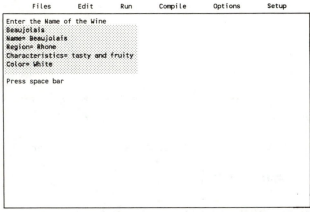

```
        Files       Edit      Run      Compile     Options     Setup

    Enter the Name of the Wine
    Beaujolais
    Name= Beaujolais
    Region= Rhone
    Characteristics= tasty and fruity
    Color= White

    Press space bar




    F2-Save  F3-Load  F5-Zoom  F6-Next  F8-Previous goal  Shift-F10-Resize  F10-End
```

Now test the **retract_from_kb** predicate. Press the {Space Bar} and type in the goal as indicated.

Goal:**retract_from_kb.** ↵

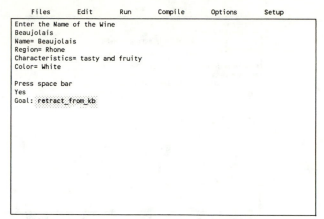

```
          Files      Edit      Run      Compile      Options      Setup
    Enter the Name of the Wine
    Beaujolais
    Name= Beaujolais
    Region= Rhone
    Characteristics= tasty and fruity
    Color= White

    Press space bar
    Yes
    Goal: retract_from_kb




    F2-Save  F3-Load  F5-Zoom  F6-Next  F8-Previous goal  Shift-F10-Resize  F10-End
```

 At the "Enter Name" prompt, tell Turbo Prolog to remove the wine called Graves.

Graves ↵

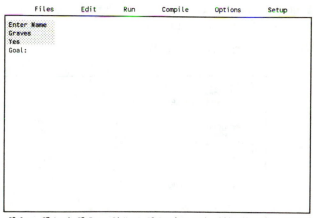

```
          Files      Edit      Run      Compile      Options      Setup
    Enter Name
    Graves
    Yes
    Goal:








    F2-Save  F3-Load  F5-Zoom  F6-Next  F8-Previous goal  Shift-F10-Resize  F10-End
```

 The response **Yes** shows that the wine called Graves has been removed from the data base.

Dynamic Data Bases and Expert Systems

To check that the Graves wine has been removed, enter the **list_all_wines** predicate.

Goal:**list_all_wines.** ↵

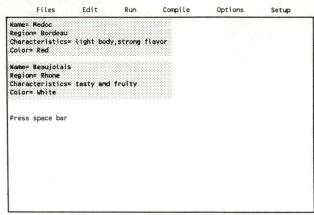

```
        Files      Edit      Run      Compile      Options      Setup

   Name= Medoc
   Region= Bordeau
   Characteristics= light body,strong flavor
   Color= Red

   Name= Beaujolais
   Region= Rhone
   Characteristics= tasty and fruity
   Color= White


   Press space bar




   F2-Save  F3-Load  F5-Zoom  F6-Next  F8-Previous goal  Shift-F10-Resize  F10-End
```

 The reply shows that the wines Medoc and Beaujolais remain in the data base, while Graves was removed.

 We will use the remaining facts in the data base later in this tutorial. To save yourself some typing, press the (Space Bar) and enter the **save** predicate to store the data base in the file called **a:wines.txt**. If you are not using drive A, substitute the appropriate drive abbreviation letter.

Goal:**save("a:wines.txt").** ↵

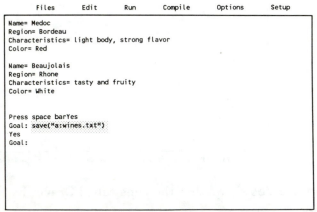

```
        Files      Edit      Run      Compile      Options      Setup

   Name= Medoc
   Region= Bordeau
   Characteristics= light body, strong flavor
   Color= Red

   Name= Beaujolais
   Region= Rhone
   Characteristics= tasty and fruity
   Color= White


   Press space barYes
   Goal: save("a:wines.txt")
   Yes
   Goal:



   F2-Save  F3-Load  F5-Zoom  F6-Next  F8-Previous goal  Shift-F10-Resize  F10-End
```

The response **Yes** in the Dialog Window shows the file is saved.

 Press (Esc) to return to the Main Menu. Enter the Editor and proceed to Part 2 – How to Save and Load the Data Base.

Part 2– How to Save and Load the Data Base

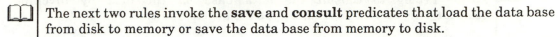

The next two rules invoke the **save** and **consult** predicates that load the data base from disk to memory or save the data base from memory to disk.

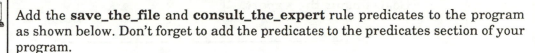

Add the **save_the_file** and **consult_the_expert** rule predicates to the program as shown below. Don't forget to add the predicates to the predicates section of your program.

```
        Files      Edit      Run      Compile      Options      Setup
   ┌─────────────────────────────────────────────────────────────────────┐
   │ Line 13    Col 9      A:\13WIN507.PRO  Indent  Insert                │
   │     find_a_wine                                                      │
   │     list_all_wines                                                   │
   │     find_wine                                                        │
   │     retract_from_kb                                                  │
   │     retract_all                                                      │
   │     save_the_file                                                    │
   │     consult_the_expert                                               │
   │                                                                      │
   │ clauses                                                              │
   │     save_the_file if                                                 │
   │          save("a:wines.txt").                                        │
   │                                                                      │
   │     consult_the_expert if                                            │
   │          consult("a:wines.txt").                                     │
   │                                                                      │
   │     add_to_kb if                                                     │
   │          clearwindow and                                            │
   │          write("Enter wine name\n") and                            │
   │          readln(Name) and                                           │
   │          write("Enter Region\n") and                               │
   │          readln(Region) and                                         │
   │          write("Enter Characteristics\n") and                      │
   └─────────────────────────────────────────────────────────────────────┘
   F1-Help F2-Save F3-Load F5-Zoom F6-Next F7-Xcopy F8-Xedit F9-Compile F10-Menu
```

When you last exited the program, you lost the data base in RAM. That is why you saved it to the disk using the **save** predicate as the goal. To be certain that the dynamic data base in RAM is empty, exit the Edit mode, run the program, and enter the following goal:

Goal:list_all_wines. ↵

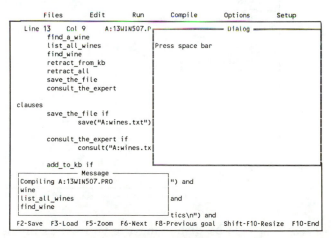

No wines are listed in the Dialog Window. This shows that the dynamic data base is empty.

As directed by the message in the Dialog Window, press the (Space Bar). Now tell Turbo Prolog to consult the data base on the disk by invoking the **consult_the_expert** predicate. Type the goal as shown.

Goal:**consult_the_expert.** ↵

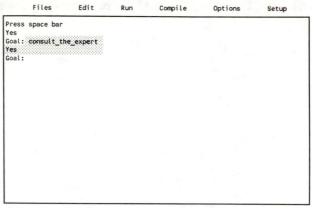

```
              Files    Edit     Run     Compile    Options    Setup

Press space bar
Yes
Goal: consult_the_expert
Yes
Goal:





F2-Save  F3-Load  F5-Zoom  F6-Next  F8-Previous goal  Shift-F10-Resize  F10-End
```

Turbo Prolog prints **Yes** to show that it consulted the data base and has loaded the specified file **a:wines.txt** into the memory of the computer. The list of wines is now in the dynamic data base.

Now list the wines by entering the **list_all_wines** predicate at the goal statement.

Goal:**list_all_wines.** ↵

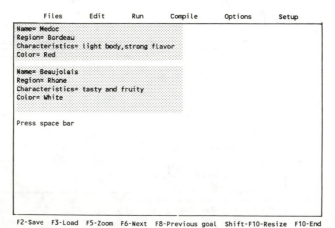

```
              Files    Edit     Run     Compile    Options    Setup

Name= Medoc
Region= Bordeau
Characteristics= light body,strong flavor
Color= Red

Name= Beaujolais
Region= Rhone
Characteristics= tasty and fruity
Color= White

Press space bar




F2-Save  F3-Load  F5-Zoom  F6-Next  F8-Previous goal  Shift-F10-Resize  F10-End
```

Turbo Prolog responds by displaying the two wines in the data base. Press the (Space Bar).

Below is a table of French wines. Add several of them to the data base. This will expand the knowledge base. You will need to type the goal **add_to_kb** for each wine added. To save time, you can press {F8} to tell Turbo Prolog to repeat the last goal.

Name	Region	Characteristics	Color
Pouilly-Fuisse	Saone-et-Loire	dry and heady	Red
Gewurztraminer	Alsasce	sweet and light	White
St. Emilion	Bordeau	full-bodied and dark	Red
Graves	Bordeau	not too sweet	White
Sauternes	Bordeau	sweet and fruity	White
Yonne	Burgundy	light and subtle	White
Muscadet	Loire	pale and delicate	White

If this were a real expert system, you would add information about new wines as you learned it. The system gets smarter the more often you use it.

Now save your additions to the knowledge base using the **save_the_file** predicate as the goal statement. Watch the red lights on your disk drives. When lit, they indicate that information is either being read to or from the disk in the drive. These cues help you in determining if operations related to the disk drives are occurring properly.

Goal:**save_the_file.** ↵

Turbo Prolog's reply of **Yes** shows that the contents of the dynamic data base have been saved to the file **a:wines.txt** on the disk.

You are now ready to go to Part 3. Press the {Esc} key to return to the Main Menu.

Part 3— How to Add a User Interface

This section uses the same techniques to develop a menu-driven user interface as was done in Tutorial 12-2. If you need some help recalling what each rule does, refer to the last chapter.

Enter the Editor Window and type the **menu** rule predicate as shown. The Editor Window has been expanded with the {F5} Zoom key.

```
          Files        Edit        Run        Compile      Options      Setup
       Line 9      Col 1      A:\WINE13F.PRO   Indent   Insert
              retract_from_kb
              retract_all
              save_the_file
              consult_the_expert

   clauses

              Menu if
                     repeat and
                     clearwindow and
                     write("Enter choice") and nl and nl and
                     write(" 1. Add a wine\n") and
                     write(" 2. Find a wine\n") and
                     write(" 3. List all the wines\n") and
                     write(" 4. Remove a wine\n") and
                     write(" 5. Delete Knowledge Base\n") and
                     write(" 6. Save the Knowledge Base\n") and
                     write(" 7. Consult the Knowledge Base\n") and
                     write(" 8. Exit\n\n") and
                     readint(Choice) and
                     do_it(Choice).

   F1-Help F2-Save F3-Load F5-Zoom F6-Next F7-Xcopy F8-Xedit F9-Compile F10-Menu
```

Now add the **do_it** rule predicates that will process the user's menu choice. Enter the **do_it** predicates following the menu rule.

```
          Files        Edit       Run      Compile      Options      Setup
      Line 30     Col 1        A:\WINE13F.PRO   Indent   Insert

          do_it(1) if
                  add_to_kb.
          do_it(2) if
                  find_a_wine.
          do_it(3) if
                  list_all_wines.
          do_it(4) if
                  retract_from_kb.
          do_it(5) if
                  retract_all.
          do_it(6) if
                  save_the_file.
          do_it(7) if
                  consult_the_expert.
          do_it(8) if
                  exit.
          do_it(X) if
                  X>8 and error.
          do_it(X) if
                  X<1 and error.

      F1-Help F2-Save F3-Load F5-Zoom F6-Next F7-Xcopy F8-Xedit F9-Compile F10-Menu
```

Now add the rule predicates **error** and **repeat**. Recall that **error** is the predicate that handles error trapping, and **repeat** uses recursion to set up a loop.

```
          Files        Edit       Run      Compile      Options      Setup
      Line 63     Col 1        A:\WINE13F.PRO   Indent   Insert
                  save_the_file.
          do_it(7) if
                  consult_the_expert.
          do_it(8) if
                  exit.
          do_it(X) if
                  X>8 and error.
          do_it(X) if
                  X<1 and error.

          error if
                  write("Not a valid choice - Try Again\n") and
                  write("Press space bar\n") and
                  readchar(_) and menu.

          repeat.
          repeat if repeat.

          save_the_file if
                  save("B:wines.txt").

      F1-Help F2-Save F3-Load F5-Zoom F6-Next F7-Xcopy F8-Xedit F9-Compile F10-Menu
```

Dynamic Data Bases and Expert Systems

You must add the predicates **menu, do_it, error,** and **repeat** to the predicates section. The **do_it** predicate has one argument, and it is an integer. Add them as shown below.

```
          Files      Edit       Run      Compile      Options      Setup

  Line 17    Col 9       A:\WINE13F.PRO  Indent  Insert
predicates
        add_to_kb
        find_a_wine
        list_all_wines
        find_wine
        retract_from_kb
        retract_all
        save_the_file
        consult_the_expert
        menu
        do_it(integer)
        error
        repeat

clauses

        Menu if
              repeat and
              clearwindow and
              write("Enter choice") and nl and nl and
              write(" 1. Add a wine\n") and
              write(" 2. Find a wine\n") and

 F1-Help F2-Save F3-Load F5-Zoom F6-Next F7-Xcopy F8-Xedit F9-Compile F10-Menu
```

Add an internal goal to clear the window and call the **menu** predicate as shown below.

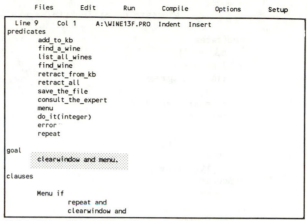

```
        Files        Edit        Run       Compile     Options      Setup

    Line 9     Col 1      A:\WINE13F.PRO  Indent  Insert
  predicates
          add_to_kb
          find_a_wine
          list_all_wines
          find_wine
          retract_from_kb
          retract_all
          save_the_file
          consult_the_expert
          menu
          do_it(integer)
          error
          repeat

  goal
          clearwindow and menu.

  clauses

          Menu if
                  repeat and
                  clearwindow and
```

F1-Help F2-Save F3-Load F5-Zoom F6-Next F7-Xcopy F8-Xedit F9-Compile F10-Menu

To have the program return to the presentation of the menu after each choice, add **and menu** to the end of each of the menu rule predicates. These rules are:

> save_the_file
> consult_the_expert
> add_to_kb
> find_a_wine
> list_all_wines
> fine_wine
> retract_from_kb
> retract_all

Type the **and menu** commands at the end of each of these predicates. Below is the **save_the_file** predicate modified with the **and menu** command. In the same manner, add the **and menu** commands to the remaining predicates listed above. Adding the **and menu** command to each of the predicates causes Turbo Prolog to return to the **menu** predicate after each choice.

> save_the_file if
>   save("a:wines.txt") and   <— *add*
>   menu.   <— *add*

Run the program. Choose menu item #3. List all the wines. If Turbo Prolog returns to the menu without displaying the list of wines, choose #7 (Consult the Knowledge Base) to load the data base into memory from the disk. Then try the other menu items. If you experience problems with operation of your program, check your program listing with the complete listing of the program on pages 462–463.

This completes Tutorial 13-2.

Figure 13-8: The Wine "Expert" System

```
database
            wine(string,string,string,string)

predicates
    add_to_kb
    find_a_wine
    list_all_wines
    find_wine
    retract_from_kb
    retract_all
    save_the_file
    consult_the_expert
    menu
    do_it(integer)
    error
    repeat
goal
    clearwindow and menu.
clauses
    Menu if
            repeat and
            clearwindow and
            write("Enter choice") and nl and nl and
            write(" 1. Add a wine\n") and
            write(" 2. Find a wine\n") and
            write(" 3. List all the wines\n") and
            write(" 4. Remove a wine\n") and
            write(" 5. Delete Knowledge Base\n") and
            write(" 6. Save the Knowledge Base\n") and
            write(" 7. Consult the Knowledge Base\n") and
            write(" 8. Exit\n\n") and
            readint(Choice) and
            do_it(Choice).
    do_it(1) if
            add_to_kb.
    do_it(2) if
            find_a_wine.
    do_it(3) if
            list_all_wines.
    do_it(4) if
            retract_from_kb.
    do_it(5) if
            retract_all.
    do_it(6) if
            save_the_file.
    do_it(7) if
            consult_the_expert.
    do_it(8) if
            exit.
    do_it(X) if
            X>8 and error.
    do_it(X) if
            X<1 and error.
```

```
            error if
                    write("Not a valid choice - Try Again\n") and
                    write("Press space bar\n") and
                    readchar(_) and menu.
        repeat.
        repeat if repeat.

        save_the_file if
                    save("B:wines.txt") and
                    menu.
        consult_the_expert if
                    consult("B:wines.txt") and
                    menu.
    clauses
        add_to_kb if
                    clearwindow and
                    write("Enter wine name\n") and
                    readln(Name) and
                    write("Enter Region\n") and
                    readln(Region) and
                    write("Enter Characteristics\n") and
                    readln(Characteristics) and
                    write ("Enter Color\n") and
                    readln(Color) and
                    assertz(wine(Name,Region,Characteristics,Color)) and
                    menu.
        find_a_wine if
                    clearwindow and
                    write("Enter the Name of the Wine\n") and
                    readln(Name) and
                    wine(Name,Region,Characteristics,Color) and
                    write("Name= ",Name,"\nRegion= ",Region, "\nCharacteristics= ",
                    Characteristics,"\nColor= ", Color) and
                    nl and
                    write("\nPress space bar") and
                    nl and
                    readchar(_) and
                    menu.
        list_all_wines if
                    clearwindow and
                    find_wine and
                    nl and
                    write("Press space bar") and
                    nl and
                    readchar(_) and
                    menu.
        find_wine if
                    wine(Name,Region,Characteristics,Color) and
                    write("Name= ", Name,"\nRegion= ",Region, "\nCharacteristics= ",
                    Characteristics, "\nColor= ",Color) and
                    nl and nl and fail and
                    menu.
```

```
find_wine if !.

retract_from_kb if
        clearwindow and
        write("Enter Name\n") and
        readln(Name) and
        retract(wine(Name,_,_,_)) and
        menu.
retract_all if
        retract(wine(_,_,_,_)) and fail and
        menu.
```

This chapter demonstrated the programming techniques required for part of building an expert system that has a user-friendly interface. Various predicates were constructed to perform tasks such as setting up a dynamic data base, presenting a menu to the user, saving the contents of the dynamic data base to disk, loading the contents of a file to the dynamic data base, adding and deleting information from the data base, and listing the contents of the data base.

From this basic framework, you now have the tools to expand this concept into a fairly sophisticated and intelligent knowledge base. Limited knowledge bases constructed from this foundation can be quite useful in many situations. Expert systems are already becoming accepted by many businesses. There are thousands of possibilities – business, education, industry, etc. You might wish to build your own knowledge base system. Of course, you will want to use Turbo Prolog. It is a powerful language that will prove itself over the next few years.

Exercises

13-1.   The major problem with only representing facts in the predicates section is that the data in this section is _____.

13-2.   What is the data structure that allows you to store facts in the computer RAM called?

13-3.   The predicate that allows you to add a fact to the top of a dynamic data base is _____.

13-4.   The predicate that allows you to add a fact to the bottom of a dynamic data base is _____.

13-5.   The predicate that allows you to remove a fact from dynamic data base is

_____.

13-6.   How would to tell Turbo Prolog to store a dynamic data base called **textbook.dat** on the disk in the B drive?

13-7.   How would you tell Turbo Prolog to retrieve a dynamic data base called **myjunk.txt** from the disk in the A drive?

13-8.   A dynamic data base must be declared in a separate part of the program called _____.

Problems

13-1.   Write a dynamic data base program that serves as an expert system on cheeses. Prepare a menu for the user as follows:

> 1. Add a cheese to the knowledge base
> 2. Find a cheese in the knowledge base
> 3. List all of the cheeses in the knowledge base
> 4. Remove a cheese from the knowledge base
> 5. Delete the cheese knowledge base
> 6. Save the knowledge base
> 7. Consult the knowledge base
> 8. Exit program

The expert system should have information on at least the following characteristics:

> 1. Name
> 2. Color
> 3. Consistency
> 4. Taste

Appendix A
Standard String Predicates

Strings in Turbo Prolog are defined as any collection of letters, symbols, and/or numbers grouped together within quotation marks. For example, the following statements are strings in Turbo Prolog:

"the cow jumped over the moon"
"A year has 399 days"
"Stardate 2504"
"987-4272"

Strings can be changed or converted in a Turbo Prolog program. To accomplish these changes, and to extract information from a particular string, Turbo Prolog provides a standard set of predicates. These predicates are listed in Table A-1.

Table A-1: Standard String Predicates

str_len	determines or tests the length of a string
str_char	converts between string and char data
str_int	converts between string and integer data
str_real	converts between string and real data
upper_lower	converts a string into upper or lower case
concat	concatenates two strings into one string
char_int	converts between a character and the ASCII code for that character
frontstr	converts a string into two separate strings
frontchar	removes the first character in a string
fronttoken	divides a string into a list of tokens and the remaining string

If you have experience in other computer programming languages, you might think you know how these commands work. However, Turbo Prolog is no ordinary language. In most languages, if you use a variable that has no value assigned you get a predictable outcome. In some languages like BASIC, variables are assumed to have a value – whether assigned or not. In most others, like Pascal, unassigned variables cause an error message. In Turbo Prolog, if a variable is unknown (free) backtracking occurs. In other words, Turbo Prolog is driven to find matches. This can affect the flow of satisfaction drastically. In discussing string predicates, your Turbo Prolog User's Guide refers to flow patterns.

What this means is that the status of the variables in a built-in predicate affects the way the predicates work. Below is a discussion of each standard string-handling predicate. For each the command is shown, along with the data type of the arguments required and a brief explanation of how each works. Below each predicate is an example of the results of various combinations of bound and free variables. You can try each example by booting Prolog and choosing **R** from the Main Menu line. Even though there is nothing in the Editor Window, Turbo Prolog allows you to type in goals.

For each example, the letter "b" stands for a bound variable and the letter "f" for a free variable.

Determining the Length of a String

The predicate **str_len** deals with the length of a strings. The first argument must be a string and the second an integer representing a string length.

(b,f)   Predicate succeeds by binding the number of characters in the string (first variable) to the second variable.

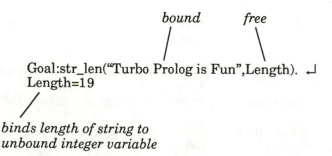

(b,b)   Predicate succeeds if the string has a number of characters equal
          to Length variable.

> Goal:str_len("Turbo Prolog is Fun",19).   ↵
> Yes

> Goal:str_len("Turbo Prolog is Fun",14).   ↵
> No

Converting String Data to Another Type

Sometimes you may want to use a predicate that requires an argument of a certain
data type. You may then need to convert an existing variable to another type.
Turbo Prolog provides five predicates that will convert string data to another type
of data. They are:

str_char	*<——converts data from string type to char type.*
str_int	*<——converts data from string type to integer type.*
str_real	*<——converts data from string type to real type.*
char_int	*<——converts data from character type to integer type.*
upper_lower	*<——converts data between upper and lower case.*

The following is a detailed explanation of each.

Converting a String to a Character

str_char(string,char)

The **str_char** predicate converts a single letter string to a character or tests to
determine if a single letter string is same as the character.

(b,f)   Converts a string to a character. Binds the second argument to the
          single letter string in the first argument.

> Goal:str_char("X",Character).   ↵
> Character=X

(f,b)   Converts a character to a string. Binds the value of the character
          in the second argument to the first argument string variable.

> Goal:str_char(String,"X").   ↵
> String=X

(b,b)   Tests to see if the value of the first argument string is the same as the character in the second argument.

Goal:str_char("C",'C'). ↵
Yes

Goal:str_char("C",'B'). ↵
No

Converting a String to an Integer

str_int(string,integer)

The **str_int** predicate operates on the string and integer domains. It converts a string to an integer, an integer to a string, or tests to determine if the conversion between string and integer or from integer to string is correct.

(b,f)   Converts the string in the first argument to an integer value. The second argument (variable) is bound to the value of the string of the first argument.

Goal:str_int("522",Integer). ↵
Integer=522

(f,b)   Converts an integer value to a string. The first argument (variable) is bound to the value represented by the second argument.

Goal:str_int(String,522). ↵
String=522

(b,b)   Tests to determine if the first argument and second argument represent the same thing.

Goal:str_int("522",522). ↵
Yes

Goal:str_int("522",344). ↵
No

Converting a String to a Real Number

str_real(string,real)

The **str_real** predicate converts data from string to real, from real to string, or tests to determine if both arguments represent the same value. This predicate works exactly the same as the **str_int** predicate.

(b,f)   Converts the string in the first argument to a real number and binds the result to the second.

    Goal:str_real("5.22",Real).   ↵
    Real=5.22

(f,b)   Converts the real value in the second argument to a string and binds the result to the string variable in the first.

    Goal:str_real(String,4.33).   ↵
    String=4.33

(b,b)   Tests to see if both arguments represent the same value. The predicate succeeds if both are bound to the same value.

    Goal:str_real("5.22",5.22).   ↵
    Yes

    Goal:str_real("5.22",4.33).   ↵
    No

Converting a Character to an Integer

char_int(char,integer)

The **char_int** predicate converts a character to its ASCII value, an ASCII value to a character, or tests to determine that both arguments are the same.

(b,f)   Converts the character in the first argument to the integer that represents its ASCII value and binds the result to the second argument.

    Goal:char_int('A',Ascii).   ↵
    Ascii=65

(f,b)   Converts the integer in the second argument to the character that corresponds to its ASCII value and binds the result to the first argument.

> Goal:char_int(Letter,66). ⏎
> Letter=B

(b,b)   Tests to determine if both arguments are bound to the same value. If they are, the predicate succeeds.

> Goal:char_int('A',65.) ⏎
> Yes

> Goal:char_int('A',67). ⏎
> No

Converting from Upper and Lower Case

upper_lower(string,string)

The **upper_lower** predicate provides a way to convert a string from uppercase to lowercase or vice versa. It can also test to see if the first variable is the uppercase equivalent of the second.

(b,f)   Converts the first argument from uppercase to lowercase and binds the result to the second argument.

> Goal:upper_lower("ABC",Lower). ⏎
> Lower=abc

(f,b)   Converts the second argument from lowercase to uppercase and binds the result to the first argument.

> Goal:upper_lower(Upper,"abc"). ⏎
> Upper=ABC

(b,b)   Tests to determine that the first argument is the uppercase equivalent of the second argument. If it is, the predicate succeeds.

> Goal:upper_lower("ABC","abc"). ⏎
> Yes

> Goal:upper_lower("ABC","xyz"). ⏎
> No

Concatenating Two Strings

concat(string,string,string)

The **concat** predicate joins the string in the second argument to the string in the first argument to form a new string. This new string is bound to the variable in the third string. The predicate can also test to see if the value of third string equals the value of the first two. Note that the value of the first two strings must be bound for this predicate to succeed.

(b,b,f) Places the second string at the end of the first string and binds the result into the variable in the third argument.

Goal:concat("ABC","XYZ",Bigstring). ↵
Bigstring="ABCXYZ"

(b,b,b) Determines if the concatenation of the first and second arguments is equivalent to the string in the third argument.

Goal:concat("ABC","XYZ","ABCXYZ"). ↵
Yes

Goal:concat("ABC","XYZ","XYZ"). ↵
No

Converting a String into Two Separate Strings

frontstr(integer,string, st_ring, string)

The **frontstr** predicate converts a string into two separate strings. It requires four arguments. The first is the number of characters of the string to be extracted. The second is the string you want to remove characters from. The characters you want to remove are bound to the third variable. The remaining characters are bound to the fourth argument. Notice that there is only one acceptable flow pattern.

(b,b,f,f) Removes the number of characters in the first argument from the string in the second. Binds the resulting value to the third argument and the remainder of the characters to the fourth.

Goal:frontstr(4,"ABCDEF",Front,Rest). ↵
Front=ABCD
Rest=EF

Removing the First Character of a String

frontchar(string,char,string)

The **frontchar** finds the front character of the first argument string and binds it to the second argument. The remainder of the first string is bound to the third argument. It can also test to see if the first string can be formed by adding the character in the second argument to the string in the third. Here are the many variations.

(b,f,f)   The second argument is bound to the first character of the string of the first argument, and the third argument is bound to the remainder of the string.

        Goal:frontchar("ABC",Character,String).　　⏎
        Character=A
        String=BC

(b,b,f)   To succeed, the character in the second argument must be bound to the same letter as the first character in the string of the first argument. The remainder of the first string is bound to the third argument.

        Goal:frontchar("ABC",'A',String).　⏎
        String=BC

(b,f,b)   To succeed, the string in the third argument must match the first argument minus its first character. The first character of the first string is bound to the second argument.

        Goal:frontchar("ABC",Character,"BC").　⏎
        Character=A

(f,b,b)   Adds the character in the second argument to the string in the third and binds the result to the first.

        Goal:frontchar(String,'A',"BC").　⏎
        String=ABC

(b,b,b)   In order to succeed, the third argument must match the value of the first argument when combined with the second argument. If it does, Turbo Prolog prints **Yes**.

        Goal:frontchar("ABC",'A',"BC").　⏎
        Yes

        Goal:frontchar("ABC",'A',"XY").　⏎
        No

Dividing a String into a Token and a String

fronttoken(string,string,string)

The **fronttoken** predicate makes it possible to extract tokens from a string and to display both the tokens and the remainder of the string. A token in Turbo Prolog is a group of one or more characters that:

> a. constitute a valid Turbo Prolog name,
> b. is a numeric value, either integer or real, or
> c. is a single character other than the space.

For example, given the string "2468hammer", the front token is **2468**. This predicate is useful for parsing sentences.

Fronttoken requires three arguments. The first argument is the string from which the token is to be extracted. The second argument is the token itself, and the third argument is the string remaining after the token has been extracted. All three arguments must be strings.

(b,f,f)   The second argument is bound to the first token in the first string with the remainder of the string bound to the third argument.

> Goal:fronttoken("2468hammer",Token,Rest). ↵
> Token=2468
> Rest=hammer

(b,b,f)   The first and second arguments are bound to a string and token, respectively. If the specified token in the second argument matches the first token of the string, the remainder is bound to the third argument. If not, the predicate fails.

> Goal:fronttoken("2468hammer","2468",Rest). ↵
> Rest=hammer

(b,f,b)   The first token of the first argument is bound to the second argument only if the third argument matches the remaining string of the first argument.

> Goal:fronttoken("2468hammer",Token,"hammer"). ↵
> Token=2468

(b,b,b)   This predicate succeeds if the front string consists of the token bound to the second argument plus the string bound to the third.

> Goal:fronttoken("2468hammer","2468","hammer"). ↵
> True

> Goal:fronttoken("2468hammer,"2468","nails"). ↵
> False

Index

A

Addition, 216-217
    and unbound variable, 217
add_to_kb rule predicate, 439
AI languages, 307
AI programming, 367
AND operation, 131
AND operator, 81
    symbols used for, 82
    using, 83
Anonymous variables, 61-62
    use of, 61-62, 72-76
append_file predicate, 411-413
Appending
    files, 411-413
    lists, 339-349
Arguments
    following a predicate, 240
Arithmetic, 208-233
    exercises, 231-232
    expressions, 209-210
    modulo, 217
    order of operations, 211
    changing, 212
    problems, 232-233
    and semantic net, 213
Arity, 64
Artificial intelligence, 42, 62, 307, 367, 438
ASCII code, 215-216
Asking questions. *See* Goal
asserta(fact) predicate, 424–431
Asserting facts, 423–431
assertz(fact) predicate, 424–431

B

Bachelor rule, 135-142
back predicate, 198
Backslash command, 177-178

Backtracking, 80-129
    and the cut, 366-384
    exercises, 127
    and flow of satisfaction, 85-91
    and memory, 367
    preventing to a previous subgoal, 371
    preventing to another rule, 370
    problems, 128-129
    problems with, 367
    rules of, 84-91
Backup copies, 5
bit predicates, 220-222
Blank line, printing of, 187-188
Booting the computer, 7
Boundary condition, 201, 228, 263-264
Breadth first search, 244, 368

C

Call, 99, 101
Can_borrow_money rule, 373-377
Card catalogs, 244-259
CGA (Color Graphics Adapter), 182
Char, 48
check predicate, 425-437
Clauses
    arity of, 64
    matching goals and clauses, 64-66
    predicates with more than one object, 42
Clauses section, 44-45
clearwindow predicate, 179-180
closefile predicate, 398
Col -, 9
COM1, 391
COM2, 391
Combinatorial explosion, 367
Commands. *See also* specific commands
    choosing, 13
Compile command, 14
Components to a functor
    definition, 236
Compound goals, 75, 80-129
    exercises, 127
    expressing, 83
    problems, 128-129

List
appending one list to another, 307, 339-349
definition, 307
determining members, 307, 314, 332-338
element, 307
finding the last element, 358
finding the nth, 358
printing, 307, 313, 318-331
reversing order of, 307, 316, 349-357
as element, 308-309
empty, 308
head, 310-311
members, 307
notation, 309-311
printing elements of, 307, 318-331
splitting into two, 359
tail, 310-311
List predicates, 312-357
List processing, 306-357. *See also* List
exercises, 359-360
problems, 360-364
Load command, 15, 19-21
Logic, 35-40, 131-133
Logic machine, 35-38
Logical bit predicates. *See* bit predicates
Logical operators, 81-82, 214
LOGO language, 197
Looping, 222-223
counting loop, 226
loop tag, 222-223
procedural, 226

M

makewindow predicate, 172-175
frame_attribute, 174
header_attribute, 174
screen_attribute, 172-173
starting_column, 175
starting_row, 175
window_height, 175
window_number, 172
window_width, 175
Mathematical functions, 218–219. *See also* Arithmetic
Mathematical operators, 82
Menu
creating user-friendly, 193-195
help, 25
pull-down, 14-17
as user interface, 438
Menu driven user interface, 414-418
Message window, 12

mod operation, 218
Mode argument, 182-183
Modulo arithmetic, 218
Monitor
as default output device, 393
colors for, 173
values for monochrome, 172

N

New file command, 15
nl predicate, 176
not predicate, 377
Notation. *See* Programming
Numbers, comparing, 215

O

Objects
order of, 42
simple, 235, 240
openwrite command
arguments of, 397
openwrite predicate, 394-395
Operators, 81-84
Options command, 16
OR operator, 81-82, 131
symbols used for, 82
using, 84

P

Papert, Seymour, 197
Pattern matching, 38
pencolor predicate, 197
pendown predicate, 197
penpos predicate, 197
penup predicate, 197
Predicate form, 39
Predicates. *See also* specific types
and controlling programs, 169-204
create and write to file, 394-395
disk predicates, 433-437
dynamic database, 424
with more than one object, 42
standard, 170-181
string, 467-475
window, 170-180
Predicates section, 45-46
Printer
sending information to, 181
Procedural languages, 132, 170